Language for *All* Our Children

Terry Piper
Saint Mary's University

Merrill, an imprint of
Macmillan Publishing Company
New York

Maxwell Macmillan Canada
Toronto

Maxwell Macmillan International
New York   Oxford   Singapore   Sydney

Editor: Linda James Scharp
Production Editor: Constantina Geldis
Art Coordinator: Peter A. Robison
Artist: Jane Lopez
Text Designer: Jill Bonar
Cover Designer: Robert Vega
Production Buyer: Patricia A. Tonneman
Electronic Text Management: Ben Ko, Marilyn Wilson Phelps

This book was set in New Baskerville by Macmillan Publishing Company and was printed and bound by R. R. Donnelley and Sons. The cover was printed by Phoenix Color Corp.

Macmillan Publishing Company
866 Third Avenue
New York, New York 10022

Macmillan Publishing Company is part of the
Maxwell Communication Group of Companies.

Maxwell Macmillan Canada, Inc.
1200 Eglinton Avenue East, Suite 200
Don Mills, Ontario M3C 3N1

Library of Congress Cataloging-in-Publication Data
Piper, Terry.
   Language for all our children / Terry Piper.
      p. cm.
   Includes bibliographical references and indexes.
   ISBN 0-675-21362-2
   1. Language arts (Elementary) 2. Language acquisition.
3. Linguistics. 4. Children—Language. 5. English language—Study and teaching (Elementary)—Foreign speakers. I. Title.
LB1576.P5785   1993
372.6—dc20   92-9310
                                                     CIP

Printing: 1 2 3 4 5 6 7 8 9   Year: 3 4 5 6 7

Preface

This book is for teachers and for students studying to be teachers. It began when I was asked to teach a course at the University of Calgary entitled "Language in the Elementary School." More specifically, it began as a result of my frustration in finding a text that both met the students' expectations and suited me.

All of the students taking the course had taken methods courses in language and reading (the university's distinction, not mine) and had completed their student teaching. A few were experienced teachers who were doing a postgraduate diploma in teaching, but most were fourth-year elementary education majors in the Faculty of Education.

The course was not meant to be a methods course, but was intended as a reflective look at teaching practice in the area of language. If there was a central question around which the course was organized it was "What do we know about language and learning and how does that inform our teaching practice?"

There were a number of texts on the market from which to choose. The first two times I taught the course, I chose two different ones, but neither was quite right. The problem was that a given book would have either too little about language acquisition and too much about teaching techniques, or too much about language acquisition, and too little about educational practice. Books that made practical sense to teachers tended to concentrate too much on methods and too little on what informs our methods, and they also tended to be light on the subject of language acquisition, *particularly* second language acquisition. On the other hand, those that treated language acquisition adequately tended to treat it *too* adequately, that is, they were written for researchers or graduate students in linguistics.

Perhaps the greatest shortcoming, however, was that very little attention was paid to second language learning and second language learners. I had learned from my reading and research, as well as from my training as a linguist, that second language learning follows a course that bears a striking resemblance to first language learning. I had also learned from my classroom experience that all children, first *and* second language learners alike, benefit from maximally integrated classrooms. The practice, which I saw too often during my own years as a teacher and during my years as a supervisor of student teachers, of segregating the ESL children into a separate classroom (usually next to the furnace room!), restricted their language learning opportunities. Why? Because it cut them off from their peers, who are age-appropriate models, and many of the authentic purposes of communication that they needed to learn.

In the textbooks I considered, the second language learners either were not mentioned or were relegated to a single chapter at or near the back of the book. Yet in the schools in which I had worked, there were always ESL children. I cannot recall a single school I entered during my twenty-three years of teaching that had *no* ESL children. In recent years, some of the schools have had a majority or a very significant minority of ESL children. Not that numbers argue the case more strongly. The language and learning of *every* child is the rightful concern of teachers, and the more teachers know about first and second language acquisition, the better able they will be to plan for effective education for every child who enters their classrooms. That, to keep the tale from growing longer, is how this book came to be. To achieve the balance that I thought was necessary—between theory and practice and between first and second language acquisition—I eventually decided to do it myself. The book is thus organized around the bias that I have outlined and in the belief that language teaching for *all* children is the concern of every teacher.

And so, six years after the search for a textbook began, I have written the book that I could use. I hope that other teachers, teacher educators, and future teachers will find useful my attempt to integrate the theoretical with the practical and, especially, the second language learner with the first.

ACKNOWLEDGMENTS

The support and assistance of many people are necessary for any major writing project. For their contributions to making possible this book, I would like to thank the institutions and the individuals who helped me in so many different ways.

My first debt is to my friend Gail, now deceased, whose diaries of her daughter's language learning gave me the story of Janet. Janet is not the young woman's real name, but I promised her when she was twelve and not wanting notoriety of any kind, that I would not reveal her identity. I will also thank my own sons, Kerry and Christopher, both university students now, for the language data they provided even though, as Chris pointed out, that was not their intent. They were just talking.

The research support I received from the University of British Columbia made possible some of the studies reported in this book. The stories of Michael, Lucy, and Quy would not have been possible had that university not provided the start-up funds for that research project. Allison McCormack, the ESL coordinator for the Prince Rupert, B.C., school district, also deserves special thanks for helping me to conduct the study in Prince Rupert. To my research assistants on that project, Kim Rebane and Chris Grant, who labored for an entire summer doing transcription for that study, I owe a special debt.

Similar funding at the University of Calgary made possible the research that produced all the stories from Mary Kennedy's classes. And, of course, to Mary Kennedy, whom I've often proclaimed to be the best teacher on the planet, I am grateful, not only for her direct contributions to this manuscript but for the insights into children's language and learning that will be with me forever.

The time I spent in Mary's classroom and in analyzing the data I collected there was made possible through a substantial research grant awarded to my co-researcher, David Piper, and me by the Social Sciences and Humanities Research Council of Canada. Special thanks go to my secretary and friend at the University of Calgary, Elaine Heinz, and to the research assistants who helped me there: Joyce Bellous, Christine Laurell, and Ma Qing He (who also served as my Chinese informant). I am also indebted to the Izaak Walton Killam Foundation for the generous research fellowship that freed me from other responsibilities at the University of Calgary to prepare this manuscript.

Saint Mary's University has also supported the final preparation of this manuscript in countless ways, from providing excellent assistance in the university libraries and help when the computer refused to cooperate to supplying the paper for the final few drafts. I owe two other particular debts at Saint Mary's, one to my capable secretary Cheryl Delaney, who protected me from unwanted interruptions, and to Margi Pasquet, who worked tirelessly with me to produce the final manuscript.

I also appreciate the comments and suggestions of the following reviewers: Michael J. Clark, Western Michigan University; Marion Crowhurst, University of British Columbia; Trevor J. Gambell, University of Saskatchewan; Sally Lipa, SUNY Geneseo; Maria J. Meyerson, University of Nevada–Las Vegas; Beverly Otto, Northeastern Illinois University; D. Ray Reutzel, Brigham Young University; Jessie A. Roderick, University of Maryland–College Park; Mary C. Shake, University of Kentucky; Lynn A. Smith, Northern Kentucky University; Marilou Sorensen, University of Utah; John E. Sycamore, Radford University; and Mary Ellen Varble, Eastern Illinois University.

Finally, I must express my gratitude to my husband David for helping me with source materials, for lending me books from his own collection, and, most especially, for his continued patience and support. It is to him that I dedicate this book.

Terry Piper

Contents

PART ONE

The Study of Language

Chapter One

Why Is Language Special?

There is a tendency in schools, as in the colleges and universities that educate teachers, to treat language as a subject like all the others in the curriculum. In most elementary teachers' daybooks, time for language arts is blocked in alongside arithmetic, science, and social studies, and it is what goes on in that period of time which is the concern of most college or university methods courses in language. Admittedly, some attempts have been made to give language wider recognition in courses such as Reading Across the Curriculum or Language Across the Curriculum, but for the most part these types of courses have had little effect on the actual place of language in the school curriculum, and the view persists that language should be treated like any other subject.

But language is special, and what makes it special is that while it *can* be a subject of study, and a fascinating one at that, it is also a prerequisite for the study of all other subjects. Language is the foundation to thinking about and learning math, or science, or social studies, and in this respect it is unique. Language plays a central role in children's learning, tied as it is to the mental processes of perception, comprehension, attention, memory, and that sometimes amorphous activity we call thinking. Moreover, the importance of language is not exaggerated if we claim that children's success in school depends to a very large degree on their facility with the four modes of language—listening, speaking, reading, and writing.

While language is unique in the curriculum because it is needed to study other subjects, the converse is not true; children do not require prior facility with another discipline before they can learn language. For example, children learn basic counting concepts as they learn the language for counting. They do not need to be conversant with theories of mathematics or even know how to count before they learn the language of counting. Like so much of young children's learning, the concepts and the language required to talk about them are learned simultaneously.

When children begin school, they have already begun the lifelong task of acquiring language. This is true in only a very rudimentary sense of the other subjects in the curriculum. More significantly, they have acquired their language without being taught. Children *do* learn a great deal about the world without being formally taught by others, but they are able to do so in large part because they ask questions, they hear people talking, and, eventually, they read about the world in which they live. In other words, they rely on language for their learning.

This cognitive aspect of language is one of many characteristics that earn it a unique place in the elementary school curriculum. Five of these are described here:

1. Language is linked to cognition.
2. Language is natural.
3. Language is culturally bound.
4. Language has structure.
5. Language has many varieties.

Language Is Linked to Cognition

The study or description of human cognition is almost impossible without considering language. They are not the same, of course, and some cognitive development is possible without language, but from the time children begin to acquire language, it affects all aspects of their mental development. Vygotsky would claim, for example, that speech and thought have different roots and develop independently of one another up to a particular point. At this point, thought becomes verbal and language becomes rational (Vygotsky, 1962, p. 44). When children develop rational language, they use it not only to express their needs but also

> to manipulate their perceptions of the world by mentally manipulating language. . . In the process, the perceptions themselves are sorted into categories that are available in the language. Thus, the language to some extent structures the child's developing life-view. (Smith, Goodman, & Meredith, 1976, p. 15)

This is not to say that children cannot think without language but that language becomes the principal means of thought.

Linguistic and cognitive growth occur in tandem and influence each other in complex ways that make them inextricable. Learning, in short, comes to depend on language. We use language to organize our thinking and our actions. We use language to shape our experiences, to store our experiences, and to reshape them when we recall them from memory. We "talk our way through" difficult tasks, we talk aloud to clarify our thinking, and, indeed, to find out what we think. Through language we share and increase our experience and learning. As teachers, we rely on children's language to tell us what order they see in the world and what sense they are making of their experience of living in it.

It is not only oral language that is linked to cognition: "Reading represents one of the most interesting and cognitively complex systems and, as such, has a great deal to teach us about cognition in general" (Dickinson, Wolf, & Stotsky, 1989, p. 231). Although children learn to speak before they learn to read and write, their reading and writing are in a real sense *extensions* of their oral language. They bring their life experiences, shaped first by oral language, to the task of learning to read and write, and so that learning is also cognitively driven. Another sense in which written language is linked with cognition is in children's learning of it. In learning to read and to write, they are active participants. Indeed, research has shown that in learning to read and write, children in grades one and two are capable of assuming responsibility for their own learning. (See Hansen, 1983, for example.) Moreover, theorists are coming to the view that reading and writing, like oral language, are essentially processes of the interactive construction of meaning (Tierney & Pearson, 1984, p. 68).

Once they have learned to read and write, children can use the written language in much the same way as they use oral language—to shape, store, and recall experience. Reading is one of our most important ways of increasing our experience. For avid readers, to paraphrase Frank Zappa, "Some of our best memories never happened."

In Chapters 8 and 9 we examine the role of language in learning, first outside the school as children use language to learn unencumbered by the formal requirements of schooling and then as they encounter the literacy and other somewhat decontextualized language demands of the school.

Language Is Natural

To say that language is natural is not to imply that other subjects in the curriculum are unnatural but rather that children's learning of language is natural in ways that no other human learning is. First, of course, is the fact that language is learned by all children with normal or near-normal mental and physical abilities, and it is learned early in their lives when those abilities are limited in many important ways.

Second is the fact that no active intervention is required. The observation has been made that if parents and teachers were charged with the task of teaching children their native language, they would surely fail. This says a great deal both about the enormity of the task and the magnitude of children's accomplishments, so great in both cases that many theorists have come to believe that children possess innate mechanisms that give them a head start on the task. Cook (1985) observed that to talk of children's "learning" language makes no more sense than to talk of a tulip bulb's learning to become a tulip. Children are born with the biological potential to acquire human language. All that is required for them to do so is a normal human environment.

One of the most interesting issues in language education in the past decades has been whether written language is as natural as oral language. Smith (1984), Goodman (1984), and others argue that it is. Smith contends, for example, that preschool children "know how to learn to read and write because written language presents them with problems similar to those they solve with spoken language" (Smith, 1984, p. 143). Margaret Donaldson (1984), on the other hand, points out that whatever similarities may exist between written and spoken language, the fact remains that most children do not learn to read and write without instruction. Still, research is starting to point to similarities between the way oral language is acquired and the way written language is acquired.

It would appear, then, that acquiring both oral and written language is part of children's nature—so natural, in fact, that many children acquire language despite major physical and mental disabilities or extreme environmental or emotional deprivation. The stories of Helen Keller and of the girl named Genie, who managed to acquire her first language at the age of 13½ after nearly 12 years spent in isolation, speak to the intensity of the human drive to acquire language. Language is so natural that the *failure* to acquire it is what is remarkable.

Even before they come to school, children already know a great deal about reading and writing and even about the nature of literacy itself. (See, for example, Smith, 1984; Goodman, 1984; Bruner, 1984.) As Graves put it:

> Children want to write. They want to write the first day they attend school.
> This is no accident. Before they went to school they marked up walls, pave-

ments, newspapers with crayons, chalk, pens or pencils . . . anything that makes a mark. The child's marks say, 'I am.' (Graves, 1983, p. 1)

In Part II, we will discuss language development in monolingual and bilingual children. We will also meet a child who overcame a major environmental deficit to acquire language. The ideal environment for language growth during the school years is a topic for discussion in Parts III and IV.

Language Is Culturally Bound

The fact that Inuit languages have more words for snow than the English language and the fact that Arabic has more words for camels are often cited as evidence for language being culturally bound in the sense that it is shaped to meet the needs of the speakers who use it. In the place where English originated, as in most of the places where it is now spoken, there is relatively little need to talk in great detail about snow. Our shelters are not built from snow, nor do we drive dog sleds to work. Similarly, we are more likely to cross the Mojave Desert in a Chevrolet or a Jeep than on camels, and we have little need to talk about them except in biology classes or on trips to the zoo. When we do, we muddle along with the words we have, talking about one-hump and two-hump camels or, if we are very sophisticated linguistically, Arabian (or dromedary) and Bactrian camels.

Anyone who has ever studied a second language has discovered that learning a language necessarily involves learning something about the people who speak that language and the society in which they live. Yes, it is possible to learn the verb forms and sentence structures of a language independent of its culture, but that kind of learning constitutes only a very small portion of language learning. Understanding the literature of a language and learning to communicate in a language require some understanding of the people who speak the language and whose lives are reflected in its writing. We will return to this topic in Part II in the chapters on bilingual development and again in Parts III and IV.

We don't have to seek examples in other languages, however, because we can find similar evidence within our own language that language is linked to the beliefs and customs of its speakers. Although a language may have a great many words for talking about a particular subject, only speakers who are interested in or familiar with the subject will know the detailed vocabulary to talk about it. *Grand slam, small slam, no-trump, finesse, trump coup, declarer,* and *dummy* are, for example, terms that have meaning for bridge players but for few others. Other speakers of English will recognize the words, and some will even have alternate definitions for them (a baseball fan will recognize *grand slam* and most people have a good idea of what a *dummy* might be), but the particular meanings of the terms are shared by the community of bridge players because they are necessary to their common communication needs. That is the nature of language; it exists to meet the communicative needs of the speakers who use it and it would be very odd indeed if it were unable to meet those needs.

There is another perspective from which to view language and culture, one that sets it apart from other school subjects, a perspective that is related to language acquisition. As Frank Smith pointed out, children

> . . . Learn that the language we speak identifies us as members of a particular group. Members of different clubs, of different communities, do not speak in the same way. Our own particular language is an emblem of all our cultural ties. (Smith, 1988, p. 6)

Children acquire their first language within their society of language users—the ever-widening social circle that begins with the immediate family. They learn language in order to become a part of that society, and their learning entails a variety of social functions of language. For instance, they learn greetings, leave-takings, apologies, and excuses, and the only way for young children to learn these functions is within the context of their use. They hear people around them greeting and leaving each other and apologizing and making excuses for their behavior, they observe the conditions under which these activities take place and the bodily gestures that accompany the language. Children acquire not only the language of their community but the customs and values as well, and these customs and values vary somewhat among groups who speak the same language.

The evidence is mounting that culture plays an equally important role in the acquisition of literacy. Research by Schieffelin and Cochran-Smith (1984) suggests that children's interest in print emerges from a particular cultural orientation in which literacy is assumed. Children are socialized to be literate. Reporting on their study of nursery school children's early experiences with print, they observed:

> Studies of children's language acquisition and development indicate that, in cultures where adult-child dialogue is characteristic of language learning, children's caregivers initially accept almost any response as the child's part in a conversation. . . These actions provide some insight into the way the nursery school children were acquiring literacy. Adults initially played all

the parts in literacy events, completely producing and comprehending print for the children and behaving as if the children themselves intended for print to be used in particular ways and as if the children themselves were using the print. Little by little . . . the nursery school children took over the various roles in literacy events and needed less and less help from adult intermediaries. (Schieffelin & Cochran-Smith, 1984, p. 8)

Clearly, culture plays a significant role in *all* language learning. We will examine the relationship between language and culture more fully in Part II.

Language Has Structure

Obviously, language is not the only thing in the curriculum or, indeed, in the universe that has structure. The human mind has a strong tendency to impose structure, after all, and language is a product of the human mind. But language structure has always been of special interest, not only to linguists but to average language users. Recently, I was listening to a radio call-in program that had a noted Canadian grammarian as guest. The station's lines were swamped with calls from listeners who wanted to know about the structure of their language. Many were of the (wrong) opinion that they didn't speak correctly and wanted to be told the "right" way, but others merely wanted to ask why some verbs take regular past tense endings and others do not, whether *committee* is singular or plural, and whether it's all right to end a sentence with a preposition. While we may remember high school grammar lessons as tedious and boring, most of us will admit to a certain curiosity about the structural peculiarities of the language we speak.

But language structure is also important from another perspective. It helps us to appreciate the enormity of children's accomplishments in acquiring language. Language is systematic in a myriad of ways. It consists of sounds that can be strung together to make words that can be strung together to make sentences that can, in turn, be strung together to form discourse—not that this is what we necessarily do in normal language production. The point is that no human language allows this "stringing together" to be done randomly. There are laws governing the ways in which elements at every level can be combined. In English, for example, we cannot combine the sounds "m" and "b" in that order unless there is a syllable boundary between them. But Swahili permits this combination (leading more than one Swahili speaker to conclude that the correct syllable division for the English word *hamburger* is *ha/mburger*). Nor in English can we combine words in random order. Try it and note the looks of confusion on the faces of your listeners. Somehow children in the first five years of life must figure out enough about these structures to make sense of what they hear and of what they say.

By the time children come to school, they have mastered much of the structure of their first language and it is the task of the school to extend this understanding to new uses. As teachers, we are likely to underestimate the importance of our task. Because their language accomplishments have thus far been so very impressive, we tend to assume that children know how to understand the highly abstract language of the school when, in fact, they do not. How many children correctly interpret the opening lines of the "Star-Spangled Banner"? How many children have any idea what "pledge" or "allegiance" means or what they are promising when they utter them in the pledge to the American flag? Canadian children are probably equally bewildered by their own national anthem even though the language is slightly more modern. Stories about children's interpretations of the language they hear can be very revealing of the mismatch that frequently occurs between what is said and what children understand.

> A seven-year-old child named Maria came home from Sunday School with a picture she had drawn of a teddy bear with very strange looking eyes. When asked, she told her mother that the Sunday School teacher had asked the class to draw a picture based on a hymn that had been sung that morning. The hymn, Maria told her mother, who really should have known, was "Jesus, the Cross I'd Bear."

> Three brothers, six, eight, and nine years old, were sitting on the floor playing cards. Several times during the play, I heard them say "I'm going to drop one card" or "I'm going to drop two." In every way, the rules of the games they were playing seemed to mirror those of poker. Finally, I asked the name of the game they were playing.
> **Paul:** "Drop poker."
> **Me:** "Is that the same as 'draw poker'?"
> **Paul:** "I don't know that game."
> **Me:** "Why is it called 'drop poker'?"
> **Paul:** (Shrugging) "'Cause you drop the cards you don't want, I guess."

Notice that in the first example, Maria's interpretation is structurally correct and is far more consistent with *her* experience than is the intended meaning. In the second, the children's interpretation is also structurally sound. They have assumed that the "p" which begins poker also ends the previous word. This kind of boundary confusion is perfectly normal in continuous speech for we do not, as we sometimes think we do, pause or leave any "space" between words. This interpretation was accepted by the children since to "drop" cards made as much sense as to "draw" cards, and probably more.

While it is not important for elementary school teachers to know the structure of English in the detail that a linguist does, they should understand the relationship between form and meaning, to what degree and how children have come to master that relationship before starting school, and how to build on their understanding so that it will serve not only their linguistic needs but their other learning needs as well.

One of the ways in which the school extends children's understanding of language structure is in teaching them to read and write. There are similarities between the structure of oral and written discourse, and teachers can capitalize on these in helping children to read and write. But written language shares only some of the structural properties of oral language, and one of the jobs of the school is to teach, or to help children to discover, those new structures. While many children come to school knowing a great deal about the structure of text—they know, for example, how stories are organized—they still have much to learn about creating that structure in their own writing.

We will return to a brief discussion of language structure in Chapter 2 and again in Parts IV and V.

Language Has Many Varieties

No one knows exactly how many different languages currently exist in the world. A hundred years ago, before the loss of many North American Indian languages, there were more, but an estimated four thousand to six thousand different tongues still exist. World migration is increasing, and as it does, so does the number of non-white, non-English-speaking children in North American classrooms. Obviously, no one speaks all the languages of the world and no teacher can be expected to speak all the languages spoken by the children in his or her class. Although knowing more than one language is beneficial in a number of ways, it is not essential that elementary teachers speak more than one. What is important is that they understand that languages can have very different structures from English, that the cultures they reflect and represent may also differ in significant ways, and that the child comes to school equipped with both.

Language variation, however, is not restricted to different languages. A significant amount of variation exists among speakers of a given language. We all know that the Scots sound different from the English who sound different in turn from Australians and Canadians. We know, too, that people from Vermont sound quite unlike people from South Carolina or from Wisconsin. We also know that the differences in the dialects of these groups affect not only the sounds of the language but certain word meanings and sentence structures as well. To the question "Could you fix the leaky faucet?", an Englishman might well reply, "I could do," meaning that he is able to fix it and he might or might not do so, although he might have to have it explained that a *faucet* is a *tap*. In North American English, we find the *do* superfluous, and a linguist would explain that *do* is not required with the modal verb *could*. The variation in the language spoken by the Englishman is an example of a regional dialect. Another type is the ethnic or social dialect.

Within a geographical region, certain groups are sometimes identifiable by the language they speak. We like to pretend that North America is a society without the social classes that are reflected in language in countries such as Great Britain, and certainly there is a less predictable relationship between social groups and language in North America than in the British Isles. Nevertheless, there are marked differences among the dialects spoken, for example, by Francophone children in New Brunswick or northern New Hampshire, by Puerto Rican children in southern Florida, by Mexican children in Texas, and by Sarcee children in Alberta. An important part of teachers' education is that they learn not to accept society's ill-informed judgments about linguistic diversity and, particularly, not to generalize them to judgments about the ability or the potential of the children whose language differs from their own.

In general, dialect differences are neutralized in the written language. In other words, if there is a standard dialect of English, it is probably best represented by the written form. But across languages, there is a great deal of variability in writing systems. The two basic categories are systems that show a clear relationship between sounds and graphic symbols (phonological systems) and systems that do not (nonphonological systems).

Most of the languages of the world that have writing systems employ phonological systems. These include both syllabic and alphabetic systems. The smallest unit in syllabic writing systems is the syllable. Japanese *kana* and Cherokee have syllabic writing systems. The smallest unit in alphabetic systems is the letter, but languages vary in the degree of predictability between the letter and the sound. Spanish, for example, has a very regular correspondence between sound and symbol. But any Spanish speaker would tell us that English does not. Modern nonphonological writing systems are mostly logographic. In these, the graphemes represent words. Chinese and Japanese *kanjii* script are some of the better known languages.

Children who have been born and attended school in non-English-speaking countries may have learned a different language and a different writing system. Even another alphabetic system may be based on a different script (cyrillic or Arabic, for example). If education is to be universally accessible and equally effective for *all* children, then teachers must understand the cultural and linguistic diversity of their students and plan and act accordingly.

We know, for example, that the dialect and language differences that influence children's speech also influence their comprehension of what they hear and read. This is not an insignificant point for teachers, who must keep in mind that such differences reflect, in part, differences in experience and world view that lead, in turn, to interpretations that may differ from those of the teacher or children from the dominant culture. In Part II and again in Parts III and IV, we will return to the subject of the child who speaks a language other than English.

LANGUAGE AND THE CHILD: AN EXAMPLE

The title of this chapter asked the question "Why is language special?" In the previous section, I attempted to answer that question by describing some of the characteristics of language that set it apart from other subjects in the school curriculum. But the question must also be asked and answered from a more personal perspective. Sensible decisions about curriculum and instruction are impossible to make without considering the significance of language in the life of the child. After all, as we saw earlier, language is natural and the child needs neither the school nor the teacher to learn it and to function in it. In this section, we will consider further why language is special in the life of the child.

Lucy

A few years ago when I was conducting research in a kindergarten in a small community on Canada's west coast, I met a young Portuguese-speaking child who taught me a great deal about the role language plays in children's learning. About half the children in the kindergarten arrived in September knowing little or no English. Lucy was one of these children and she caught my attention right away. Every day, she was brought to school and then taken home again either by her mother or by her friend Jenny's mother. In the brief greetings and leave-takings, both girls and their mothers spoke only in Portuguese. I learned from the ESL consultant, who visited the homes of the ESL children, that Lucy's family had been in Canada for only a few months and spoke no English at all. I expected, therefore, that Lucy and Jenny would speak Portuguese at school, at least when talking to each other.

I was wrong. During the first month of school, I never once heard them speaking Portuguese. Actually, I heard Jenny say very little at all, not surprisingly since she knew no English. But Lucy was different. Not knowing English didn't keep her from using it! She chattered away, using the few words she acquired each day in a variety of ways. To an adult native English speaker's ears, Lucy made many mistakes. She didn't bother with past tense endings nor with the third person singular marking on verbs. She had no time for plural suffixes either. She used *teacher* to refer to any adult until she finally sorted out the correct reference, and her few verbs had to do double or triple duty to express the many meanings she intended.

All the time she was busily acquiring English, Lucy "made do" with the language she had at her disposal, but her language grew impressively, with notable changes taking place almost daily. Early in October, Lucy's mother gave birth to a baby boy and on Halloween, I had the following conversation with Lucy about her new brother:

Lucy: He cry. All the time cry.
Me: Who cries?
Lucy: My baby.
Me: Oh, right. Your new brother.
Lucy: Yeah. All the time he cry.
Me: What do you do?
Lucy: I pat him. Hims back. (She pats her own back.)
Me: Does that help?
Lucy: (She nods.) He can't talk.
Me: No, not yet. But he lets you know when he wants something doesn't he?
Lucy: (Doesn't seem to understand.)
Me: Can you tell when he's hungry?
Lucy: (She nods.) Yeah. He cry.

Me: Right. That's his way of talking right now, isn't it?
Lucy: Yeah. I not cry.
Me: No, you know how to talk, don't you? Lucy, how many languages do you speak?
Lucy: (Looks puzzled.)
Me: How many different languages do you know?
Lucy: One!
Me: Which one?
Lucy: Mine!

My last two questions to Lucy were silly ones to ask a five-year-old child simply because answering them required that she think about language as an object apart from herself. Gradually children acquire what we call **metalinguistic awareness**, which is the ability to think about language as language. Much of what goes on in classrooms demands metalinguistic thinking, but a five-year-old just beginning kindergarten is limited in the capacity to think in this way. Lucy's answer makes it clear that using language is much higher on her agenda than talking about it. Even if she had spoken seven languages in addition to English and Portuguese, her answer would likely have been the same. To her, language was part of her thinking, part of her, something that could not be objectified and counted.

Lucy's answer also provided a clue as to why she never spoke Portuguese in school. One of the things children learn very early is to shift registers in different situations. In other words, they learn quickly that the language of the playground may have to be modified for the classroom and yet again for the home. Children make these adjustments in register quite easily, and that seems to be precisely what Lucy was doing as she shifted from Portuguese in the home to English at school. The languages were no more different to Lucy than the two registers of English used by a native English-speaking child moving from "Hey, Sam, gimme the ball" at recess to "Would you please pass the potatoes?" at dinner time.

The brief dialogue with Lucy points again to the naturalness of language acquisition. It also tells us a great deal about the child's role in the process. On the face of it, Lucy's accomplishment may not seem too impressive. In the dialogue, she utters only 31 words and only 17 different words. These 17 words did not constitute the whole of her vocabulary, of course, but we would grossly underestimate her learning even if we were to consider *all* the words she knew. A closer look at the dialogue indicates that we can learn five facts about what Lucy knows about English and about using English:

1. Lucy's utterances were unique.
2. Lucy understood the language spoken to her.
3. Lucy's language was situationally appropriate and showed cultural awareness.
4. Lucy's pronunciation was clear and accurate.
5. Lucy's second language acquisition strongly resembled first language acquisition.

Lucy's Utterances Were Unique.   Although it is true that Lucy must have previously heard the seventeen different words she used here, it is unlikely that she had ever heard them combined in exactly the same way or in exactly the same situation. She combined the words to create the meaning she wanted to make at that particular time.

If we compare Lucy's sentences to those an adult native speaker of English would use in the same context, we see that Lucy's are different. These forms, such as *hims,* which deviate from standard forms are called developmental forms, and they are noteworthy for several reasons. First of all, the presence of developmental forms makes it clear that for Lucy, making meaning takes precedence over accuracy of form. In this dialogue, as in all her language use, Lucy's intent is not to produce grammatically perfect utterances. As far as she is concerned, although most likely she is not conscious of it, she is constructing her utterances in response to the situation, that is, to communicate with me. This centrality of meaning and communication in children's language acquisition is a topic to which we will return in the second part of this book.

Second, Lucy was not taught such forms and it is unlikely that she ever heard them. She created them based on her observation of other forms in the language. In this case, she had correctly worked out that English nouns and many pronouns require an *-s* ending for the possessive form. She had not yet worked out the details of the pronominal system that would prevent *hims.* Lucy was constructing her own language rules based on the observations she had made. In other words, she was not parroting back fully formed utterances she had heard before. She was creating them anew to meet the communication need before her. To do so, she had to have created her own set of "rules" for using English. She would have continually had to hypothesize about the structure and meaning of the language around her, test her hypotheses to confirm or disconfirm them, and either discard or modify those found faulty. While there is little doubt that hypothesizing is one way in which children come to recreate the full set of linguistic rules that govern a language, there is also little doubt that an hypothesis-testing model is inadequate to explain all the learning they do. In Part II, we will look at hypothesis-testing and some alternative language learning strategies.

In the brief dialogue with Lucy, I did not correct her "hims" nor her "he not cry." This is not unusual behavior for an adult talking with a child. Research tells us that parents and teachers rarely correct children's language unless there is an error in content. Research also tells us that correcting either grammar or pronunciation is a futile effort. Numerous anecdotes attest to children's resistance to such correction, one of the most famous of which, provided by Berko and Brown (1960), came to be known as "the *fis* phenomenon":

> One of us, for instance, spoke to a child who called his inflated plastic fish a fis. In imitation of the child's pronunciation, the observer said: 'This is your fis?' 'No,' said the child, 'my fis.' He continued to reject the adult's imitation until he was told 'That is your fish.' 'Yes,' he said, 'my fis.' (Berko & Brown, 1960, p. 531; quoted in Reich, 1986, p. 58)

If Lucy had referred to her baby brother as her *sister,* then I might have corrected her, but for the same reasons that she did not understand the questions I asked her *about* language, she would not have responded to the correction of the *forms* of language.

One other point should be made about developmental forms. It is tempting to think about the mismatches between children's and adults' language forms as deficits or flaws in children's language. To do so, however, implies a particular view of language learning, one that is inconsistent with much of the evidence we have about children acquiring language. According to this view, the task of children in language acquisition is to mimic adult production, coming progressively closer to adult forms. This view considers the child's system as a lesser variant of the adult's, and in doing so, ignores the systematic integrity of the child's *own* system, obscures the facts about that system, and minimizes the child's accomplishment. The enormity of this accomplishment and the conditions under which it occurs are topics for discussion in Parts II and III.

Lucy Understood the Language Spoken to Her.   In the brief dialogue, I used a total of 68 words, 45 *different* words, and a variety of sentence types. In addition to the statements, I asked Lucy nine questions of three different structural types, five of which required more than *yes* or *no* as a response. Of the four that required a *yes* or *no* response, two were tag questions, meaning that there was a question tagged onto the end of a statement, and I merely required confirmation. The remaining two also required yes/no answers but they also asked for information. Even when Lucy failed to understand the question, it is clear that it was not the structure of the question that was problematic but the meaning. She understood a far greater variety of structures and a greater number of words than she produced or was likely able to produce. This is an important observation about language learning: Children are almost always able to understand more than they are able to produce, but the reverse is never true.

When we consider all that is involved in comprehension, we begin to appreciate what the child has acquired. Lucy had to recognize the incoming sounds as speech, segment the unbroken stream into potentially meaningful units, work out the structure that would give those units meaning, and interpret that within her understanding of my intent within the context of our conversation. The comprehension she exhibited during the brief exchange was in itself an impressive psycholinguistic feat.

Lucy's Language Was Situationally Appropriate and Showed Cultural Awareness.   I said above that Lucy responded appropriately to my questions. Her responses were appropriate not only linguistically in the sense that they took the expected forms given the forms of the question asked, but socially as well. Consider an example. Lucy nodded in response to my question "Does that help?" and introduced a new but related topic into the discourse when she stated "He can't talk." This may seem trivial, but given that she had been in contact with English speakers for only a few weeks and considering the range of inappropriate responses she might have given, it is a noteworthy demonstration of her linguistic competence.

Lucy's Pronunciation Was Clear and Accurate.   Since I did not include the phonetic transcription of Lucy's speech here, the reader cannot judge the quality of her pronunciation. Each session was tape recorded, however, and the recording of this dialogue revealed very little of what we commonly call a "foreign accent." In eight short weeks, Lucy had effectively mastered the sound system of English, a system that is appreciably different from that of her native Portuguese. This accomplishment is partly cognitive, partly linguistic, because there is an underlying system or "grammar" to the sound system as well as to the sentence, but it is also a physiological feat. Of course, Lucy did not begin as an infant would. She had already mastered the sounds of Portuguese. But English has different sounds, requiring different kinds of articulatory control and these she mastered in a very short time.

Lucy's Second Language Acquisition Strongly Resembled First Language Acquisition.   Lucy's language acquisition has been described in much the same way as a child's first language acquisition might be, although Lucy was five years old with a first language already well established. This reflects one of the biases of this book, namely, that the acquisition of a second (or third or fourth) language in young children closely parallels first language acquisition. While there are undeniable differences in the conditions under which the two types of acquisition occur, and while the fact that the second language learner already has a language undoubtedly influences the course of second language acquisition, the similarities for young learners are too striking to ignore. This is a topic to which we will return in Chapters 5 and 6.

THE LANGUAGE LEARNING ENVIRONMENT

One of the likely reasons that first and second language acquisition run parallel courses in young learners is the language learning environment. The distinction between second language learning in an informal versus a structured environment is an important area of discussion in second language acquisition. Tarone (1982), for example, has argued that if a learner acquires language "data" in an informal setting, it is less susceptible to interference from the first language. For young learners, a likely case is that the less contrived the language learning environment, the easier the task of learning. The question arising from the dialogue, then, is what was the environment in which Lucy had begun to acquire her second language?

Lucy's teacher did not believe in structured language lessons for her kindergarten class, even though so many of them had limited English. Rather, she took her cue from observations of children acquiring their first language and provided a rich environment for language to grow. Drawing on her knowledge of cognitive development in young children, she provided concrete materials and experiences for them to think and talk about, but she also allowed them to share their own experiences.

The language in the dialogue, then, was not a result of repetition drills or of vocabulary lessons with flash cards. It was a result of a classroom in which there was much to do and to talk about, in which the teacher nourished the natural functions of language in each child's life. In Part II, we look at the language functions that children use and how they acquire them. In Parts III and IV, we return to the issue of language in the school and examine how some teachers have created healthy environments for language growth. Also in Part III, we will sit in on a grade two class where children from eight different countries talk and learn together.

IF LANGUAGE IS SO NATURAL, WHAT IS THERE TO TEACH?

Throughout the preceding pages, I have argued consistently that one of the things that makes language special is its naturalness. If that is the case, a cynic might ask, then why bother to teach it? Or, to put it another way, what is there to teach? In a way, the cynic is right, but right for the wrong reasons. Certainly, if language teaching is construed as sitting children in rows and drilling language structures and spelling lists into their heads, then we might be better off *not* to teach language at all. But language teaching that builds on children's initial experience of acquiring language, which is sensitive to the demands children place on language and to their use of language as a medium for their other learning, is of utmost importance in the elementary curriculum.

This defense of language may seem unnecessary, but there is at least one educational context in which the question has, in fact, been asked. In Canada, which is officially bilingual, many English-speaking children learn French in elementary school by being immersed totally in the language. Even though the children know no French when they begin kindergarten, the entire elementary curriculum is taught in the French language. People unfamiliar with the highly specialized methods teachers use in French immersion mistakenly assume that children "just pick up" the language by being exposed to it in the classroom. Why, they ask, do ESL children require special attention? Why can't they too "just pick it up"?

The answer is that they *could* if the circumstances were indeed the same; that is, if the same or similar environment were created and the same methods employed—in other words, if they received *English* immersion, then they *would* "just pick it up." But the people who ask this question do not understand the nature of French immersion nor the expense incurred to operate it. They do not understand that immersion teachers are specially trained to teach the language *via* the curriculum and vice versa. They do not understand that the immersion teacher knows the symbiotic relationship between language and learning and is expert at creating an environment conducive to both language learning and learning connected to other school subjects. They do not understand that the anglophone children enrolled in French immersion are almost without exception from the dominant language community and have the security of that status to fall back on; education in French poses absolutely no threat to their native language maintenance.

The differences between immersion and "submersion," or putting ESL children in mainstream classes without making concessions to their linguistic differences, are greater than the similarities between them. This is not to say that the mainstreaming of ESL children cannot be effective. Indeed, many elementary teachers have adopted classroom practices and techniques that are entirely consistent with immersion but integrate the ESL learners with native English speakers in the class. One of these teachers is described in Part IV of this book.

Of course, this question has many other answers, all of which apply not only to children acquiring a second language but to *all* children. Some have been hinted at in this chapter and will be developed throughout the book. The fact that language has a special link to cognition, that it is a medium for other learning, that its written forms may require special attention, and perhaps most importantly the role that it plays in children's identities and in their ability to tell us who they are and where they've been are all reasons why children's continued language growth should be an elementary teacher's first priority. It might be argued, in fact, that language deserves special attention in the elementary curriculum precisely because it is natural. Giving language a prominent place in the curriculum permits educators to exploit the naturalness of language. In other words, since language learning comes more easily to children than any other and language is the foundation for success in other kinds of learning, it makes good sense to ensure that the foundation is sound and strong.

THE REMAINDER OF THE BOOK

This has been the briefest of introductions to the issues surrounding language and language learning. The goals of the book are very straightforward—to understand more about how the children we meet in our classrooms acquire language before they come to us and to understand how to build on that early acquisition to create an educational environment in which every child has an equal opportunity to succeed.

The first part of the book is an overview of language and the issues surrounding it. Reflecting the spirit of the book's title, Part II is about language acquisition, not only in monolingual children but also in children who acquire two languages simultaneously and those who acquire two languages in succession. Part III looks at the relationship between language and learning both outside and inside the school. As educators we tend to equate learning with formal schooling, but we must remember that children have had five years of experience learning in the world before we meet them and we must learn to draw on that experience rather than to fight it.

In the fourth part, we continue our examination of language in the elementary school by examining four influences on language in our schools. Society, parents, and educators all have their views on the role of language in the school, and these views may be incompatible with each other and with those of the individual teacher. As an example, all three groups place a high value on literacy, but society also highly values "standard English" (even though individuals within the society would be hard-pressed to explain exactly what it is and why it so important that everyone speak it). Parents and children, on the other hand, may be less concerned with standard English, and many educators are ambivalent. Teachers should consider those views as they form their own perspective on language teaching and as they begin their planning.

In the final section of the book, we look at some of the ways of reconciling such diverse viewpoints in planning for real language growth. Here we find out how actual teachers have created highly effective language learning environments for children from a variety of language backgrounds. Finally, we bring together some concluding thoughts about children, language, learning, and equality in the refrain of the book's title, *Language for All Our Children*.

Chapter Two

Linguistics and Linguists

Much of Chapter 1 was devoted to making the case that language deserves a special place in the elementary school curriculum, partly because it is a natural attribute of being human. Another indication that it is special is the fact that it is so widely studied. Many people with different interests and purposes find it necessary, enlightening, or just fascinating to study aspects of language structure and language behavior. Some study it formally in all the various branches of linguistics and some of the branches of psychology, sociology, philosophy, anthropology, medicine, and education. Others study it as rhetoric or as literary criticism, and still others study it informally as writers, readers, and thinkers about the intricacies of language.

With all these people studying and thinking about language, you might think there would be little left to learn about it. That is not the case; we still know relatively little about language processes or about individual languages, and no one runs any risk of running out of questions or data to study. The number of perspectives on language study grows steadily as it becomes more and more specialized. Older branches such as philology, the study of comparative historical aspects of language, lose ground to relative newcomers such as discourse analysis, and other disciplines discover the depth of their dependence on language. One of these newcomers is educational linguistics. This is really a type of applied linguistics and as such has been influenced by other subdisciplines, the more theoretical as well as older applied areas.

In this chapter, I want to talk about some of the perspectives from which language is studied, particularly those areas whose insights about language influence us in our teaching practice. I will begin with a description of the parent discipline, linguistics, which will entail an overview of the components of linguistic structure—phonology, morphology, syntax, and semantics. This is followed by a brief description of **pragmatics**, or the study of language use. The work of several of the related disciplines is then described as well as the influence these disciplines have had on education and on the emergent field we call educational linguistics.

Because so many branches of linguistics exist, it is somewhat difficult to describe the parent discipline accurately and fairly. A century ago, linguists were those who spoke many languages, and this view still persists to some degree. Today, however, it is fair to say that linguistics, unadorned by any of the prefixes (psycho-, socio-, etc.), is the study of language structure.

Linguists consider themselves, for the most part, language scientists because their purpose is to study how languages are constructed. They use well-delineated and rigorous methods in their work that may take several forms. Usually, linguists specialize in one of the levels of language description: phonology, or the structure of the sound system; morphology, or how words are put together; or syntax, how sentences are constructed. A few specialize in semantics, the study of the organization and structure of concepts and meaning, or pragmatics, the study of language in communication.

LANGUAGE STRUCTURE

There are many reasons for studying language structure, but the most compelling for teachers is to understand what children accomplish in acquiring that aspect of language. Here we examine five aspects of language structure: phonology, morphology, syntax, semantics, and pragmatics.

Phonology: The Sound System

If we think about the sound system from the perspective of children acquiring language, the question is, quite simply, what has to be learned? Obviously, they have to learn to make the individual sounds—the consonants and vowels of their language, a task for which they prepare throughout the babbling period but is more complicated than it seems. Every speaker a child encounters utters each sound a little differently from every other and a little differently in some words than others.

Children must figure out which sounds are distinctive and which are not; in other words, how much variation can be ignored. They must also learn to combine sounds in syllables and words, once more a task that is more difficult than it seems. Consider, for example, the difficulty children have in producing consonant clusters such as the *pl-* in *play* or the *tr-* in *tree.* Finally, they must learn the stress and intonation patterns of their language, another language skill for which they have been preparing since the crib.

Minimal Pairs and Phonemes.   English has many pairs of words that differ from each other by only one sound. These are called *minimal pairs,* and they tell us which sounds are distinctive. For example, we know from the following list of words that the consonants /p, b, g/ are distinctive because substituting one for the other changes the word meaning. For the same reason, we know that the two vowels /I, a/ are distinctive sounds.[1]

pill	pall
bill	ball
gill	gall

On the other hand, each consonant and vowel sound has several possible and permissible pronunciations. We articulate the /g/ in *gill,* for example, just a little differently from the same sound in *gall.* In the first, the tongue touches the roof of the mouth near hard palate, while in the second, the tongue touches the roof of the mouth further back, near the soft palate or velum. Substituting the /g/ sound in *gill* for the one in *gall* will result in a distorted pronunciation that will sound strange to the native speaker, but it will not change the meaning.

For every distinctive sound in the language, there are many permissible articulations, but all articulations of each are distinct from all articulations of any other. These distinctive sounds of a language are called **phonemes;** linguists indicate them with slashes (/ /), and every language has a different set. Phonemes can be classified into two broad categories, **consonants** and **vowels**. There is also a third and smaller category of sounds that resemble both consonants and vowels, called **semivowels**.

Individual phonemes are described according to how the airstream is modified to produce them. During speech, as air moves from the lungs

---

[1]It is not my purpose here to teach the phonetic alphabet, those symbols used by linguists to represent sounds. Where those sounds correspond to the English alphabet, I have used them between slashes (/ /); otherwise, I refer to the alphabetic equivalent. The sound linguists would represent as /n/ (or a "hooked" ŋ) is thus referred to as -*ng.*

through the mouth or nose, it is modified in a number of ways to produce different sounds. In the articulation of consonants, the airstream is either partially or totally blocked in the mouth. In the production of vowels, the air from the lungs is not blocked at all, and semivowels are produced with only very slight interference.

In producing **consonants**, the airstream coming from the lungs is obstructed to some degree, and this obstruction may occur anywhere in the oral cavity. One other alteration to the airstream is made by the vocal folds in the larynx. If the folds vibrate, as they do with the articulation of /z/ and /m/, for example, the sound is voiced. If they do not, as in /s/ and /f/, the sound is voiceless. The consonants of English can be distinguished from one another, then, on the basis of three modifications to the air stream—place in the oral cavity where the air is impeded, the manner in which it is impeded, and voicing.

Vowels are very different from consonants. To begin with, they are all voiced and are highly resonant because the airstream is not impeded in any way. The particular quality of each vowel is achieved by changing the shape of the resonator, that is, the oral cavity. Vowel quality depends on which part of the tongue is raised—front, central, or back—and on how far the tongue is raised—high, mid, or low. High front vowels are those in which the front part of the tongue is raised almost to the roof of the mouth, as in the vowel sounds in *cheap* and *chip*. To distinguish these two vowels, another feature is required. This feature refers to the amount of muscular tension in the vocal tract, principally the lower jaw. Vowels that are produced with a relatively greater degree of movement and with greater tension are called **tense vowels** and those produced with less movement and less tension are called **lax vowels**. This is a particularly salient distinction for elementary teachers because it corresponds roughly to the categories long vowel and short vowel used in phonics. The short (or lax) vowels are produced with comparatively little movement or tension and include the vowels in *bit, blood, put, bat, bought,* and *father.*[2] **Long vowels** are those produced with greater movement and muscular tension and include the vowels in *beep, brood, bake,* and *boat*. Also in the category of long vowels are the **diphthongs** in *boy, bite,* and *bout*. Diphthongs are treated like single vowels, but they are really two vowel sounds produced with one gliding into the other. Because they are produced with a gliding motion of the tongue, diphthongs are tense.

Semivowels are produced with only very slight interference of the airstream in the oral tract. These sounds are, in fact, more like vowels in

---

[2]These last two vowel sounds will be identical for some speakers of English.

their articulation, but in English they function like consonants. They include the initial sounds in *wax* and *yaks*.

Syllables.   The consonants, vowels, and semivowels are not the only units of the sound system. Another important one is the **syllable**, a unit that people intuitively recognize. There are even writing systems based on syllables. English syllables are, however, rather difficult to define formally or even to identify consistently. Does *chocolate,* for example, have two syllables or three? The answer depends on at least two variables—the dialect the individual speaks and how carefully he or she pronounces the word.

English has a number of different kinds of syllables. A syllable can be composed of a single vowel and no consonants (*Oh!*—remember, we are talking about sound, not writing), or a vowel with one or more consonants on either side. (*Car, scar,* and *scars* are all single syllable words.) English permits up to three consonants before the vowel (e.g., *strip*) and up to four following the vowel (*texts*—pronounced "teksts").

Phonological Processes.   The task of learning the individual sounds and the syllable structure of a language is a complex one, and it is made more so by the fact that the actual pronunciation of speech sounds varies under different conditions. For example, we may pronounce a vowel one way when it is stressed and another when it is not. Consider the following pairs of words:

definite (defUHnUHt)	finite
cylinder (cylUHnder)	cylindrical
conventional (cUHnventionUHl)	convene
grammar (grammUHr)	grammatical
Sabbath (SabbUHth)	sabbatical

When we compare each pair of words, we can see that the actual pronunciation we give a vowel depends on whether the vowel is stressed, which depends, in part, on the prefixes or suffixes that are present. The process by which a vowel sound becomes neutralized to schwa when it loses its stress is called **vowel reduction**.

A similar process occurs with certain words when they change their part of speech. Consider these pairs of words:

receive (v.)	reception (n.)
conceive (v.)	conception (n.)

cleave (v.) cleft (adj.)

bereave (v) bereft (adj.)

Notice that in each pair, the same syllable is stressed, but when an additional morpheme is added, in the second column, the quality of the vowel changes. This process is called **vowel alternation** and is very common in English. We see it in the conjugation of certain irregular, or strong, verbs:

leave	left	left	break	broke	broken
lose	lost	lost	sink	sank	sunk
ring	rang	rung	sing	sang	sung
write	wrote	written	bite	bit	bitten

Consonant sounds are also reduced in various ways in continuous speech. In the sentence,

Alma and Fred will have the dog groomed next week

unless the speaker is articulating very precisely, the final /t/ in *next*, normally pronounced "nekst" in citation form, will be left out. A similar process occurs in the pronunciation of *dog groomed*. Here, because the final consonant of *dog* is the same as the first consonant of *groomed*, speakers will often reduce the two sounds to a single /g/. This is one of several types of **assimilation**, or the changing of one speech sound to become more like another sound in its immediate environment. If the speaker is from parts of Britain or New England, he or she may also introduce an /r/ sound between *Alma* and *and* (producing something akin to "almarand"). This is a kind of **dissimilation**, the opposite of assimilation, and apparently occurs to break up two similar or identical sounds.

The Sound System and Writing. When writing becomes part of children's language awareness, the sound system may seem even more confusing because the sound-symbol correspondence is only sometimes predictable. One of the seeming irregularities is related to that strange phenomenon known as the "silent letter." The silent letter is primarily a reading rather than a writing concept. In other words, the issue of the silent letter first arises when we are decoding printed text into sound units, and it might be tempting to try to rid the language of such culprits. It is fairly easy to demonstrate, however, that many letters which are silent in one form of a word make plenty of noise in another. Consider the following pairs:

sign	signature
autumn	autumnal
column	columnar
bomb	bombard

The pronunciation of the words in the second column would suggest that were we to change the English writing system to make it strictly funetik, we might well complicate it instead, since the relationship between such pairs of words would be far less obvious.

Stress and Intonation.   Another important aspect of the English sound system is the **prosody**, or the stress and intonation patterns of the language. *Stress* refers to the force with which a syllable is articulated. When stress serves to distinguish the otherwise identical inVALid from INvalid, for example, it is said to be distinctive. It is also predictable to a certain degree in that there are very general rules that tell us which syllable of a word to stress. For example, for two-syllable words that end in two consonants (words such as *deduct, resent, result, adapt,* and *report*), stress usually falls on the second syllable. In contrast, two-syllable words that end in a single consonant (such as *exit, cancel, festive*) are stressed on the first syllable. The rule is, however, more complicated than that. Consider, for example, *erase, refrain, align,* and *remove.* Stress on these words is on the second syllable despite their single final consonant. This is because the vowel is tense (or long).

Unfortunately, this "rule" for assigning stress to two-syllable words is complicated further by the existence of many noun-verb pairs in English that are identical but for their stress. Unlike the example of inVALid/INvalid given above, these pairs are related in meaning. They include words such as:

Noun	**Verb**
PERfume	perFUME
TORment	torMENT
CONvict	conVICT
REcord	reCORD
SUBject	subJECT

The rules for assigning stress to words in English are complex and they have many exceptions. It is unlikely, however, that children learning the language have to be concerned with learning the rules. The pronunciation of the word includes its stress placement, and it is likely that this is part of what we call **lexical learning**. In other words, the matter of learning individual words is *not* a matter of learning a rule that will apply widely (as is learning to pluralize, for example), but of simply learning the phonetic configuration which identifies that word as unique from all others. Stress is part of that configuration and presents no particular problem to children. Not, that is, until the child begins to read. When faced with the task of matching up the words on the printed page with the words stored in their memories, children are introduced to the systematicity of stress. Similarly, in trying to "sound out" an unfamiliar word, children begin to come to terms with stress assignment rules.

Intonation refers to the pattern of stress and rising and falling pitch that occurs in connected speech. Intonation can also be used for special purposes such as emphasis. Consider, for example, the different meanings that result from the shift of stress in the following sentence:

WHAT are you doing here? (It looks pretty strange to me!)

What ARE you doing here? (You should be somewhere else!)

What are YOU doing here? (I was expecting Arnold.)

What are you DOING here? (Whatever it is, you shouldn't be doing it!)

What are you doing HERE? (Instead of Bagdad!)

This use of stress is called **contrastive stress**, and it is used to give emphasis to a particular part of the sentence. Another intonation feature that conveys meaning is **pitch**. Rising pitch is normally used at the end of a question and is also used to signal uncertainty or doubt in statements or single-word utterances.

The Sounds of Other Languages.   The sound systems of the world's languages vary greatly. Some have a large number of distinct sounds while others have very few. Some Polynesian languages, for example, have as few as 11 or 12 segments, including both consonants and vowels. There is a language, !Xu, in the Khoisan family, on the other hand, with 141 different segments, 24 of which are vowels.

Another way in which sound varies is in the particular consonants and vowels that occur. Most languages have between 5 and 7 vowels, a fact that may surprise English speakers since English and many of its relatives have from 10 to 15. Some languages distinguish nasal vowels (resonance in both the oral and the nasal cavity) from oral vowels. In general, however, the consonants give learners more difficulty.

Speakers of other languages sometimes complain that English has especially troublesome consonants. Certainly English has some relatively rare consonants, including the *th-* sounds. Speakers of German, French, and a host of other languages experience difficulty with these sounds, which are also difficult for very young children just gaining control of their articulators. On the other hand, most English speakers would find the clicks in Zulu difficult, although they are quite capable of making very similar sounds when starting horses or clucking disapproval.

The sound systems of different languages can be distinguished in ways other than the individual sounds. In more than half the languages of the world, the meaning of a word can be changed simply by changing the pitch at which it is articulated. These languages are called **tone languages**, and there are a number of possible tones and combinations of tones ranging from two to six. In Mandarin, which has four tones, the word *mai* can mean either "to buy" or "to sell," depending on the tone.[3] *Mai*, meaning to buy, is articulated with falling-rising tone while *mai*, meaning to sell, is articulated with falling tone. In general, speakers of tone languages have less difficulty learning non-tone languages than speakers of non-tone languages have learning tone languages.

Syllable structures also vary from language to language, and these pose certain problems for second language learners. In Mandarin, for example, syllables normally consist of a consonant followed by a vowel. The only consonants permitted at the end of a syllable are nasals. When Mandarin speakers learn English, they frequently "drop" or fail to produce the consonants at the ends of words such as *cat, dog,* and *rob* but produce words such as *can, sing,* and *rum* correctly. These errors occur as a result of their applying the syllable structure rules of their language to English.

The job of learning the sound system is a formidable one for both non-native and native learners. Learners must acquire motor control of the articulators as well as all the cognitive aspects of phonology. Neither children nor second language learners learn the sound system in isolation. They learn it as part of the process of learning words and larger communication units. One of the central of these is the morpheme.

[3]Special thanks to my Mandarin informant Qing He Ma for this and other examples from his language used throughout this book.

Morphology: The Structure of Words

If we were to ask people who have not studied language structure what the smallest meaning-carrying unit is, most would probably say that it is the word. The word is, after all, the smallest unit that can stand alone in speech or in writing. But it is not the smallest unit of meaning. That is the **morpheme**. Some morphemes happen to be words, but others are smaller and, in English, are either prefixed or suffixed to other morphemes to form words.

Kinds of Morphemes and Word-formation Processes.   One of the earliest language learning tasks children face is to learn the **lexical morphemes** because these carry the burden of meaning in the language. Many of these morphemes may stand alone as words. *Ball, dog, shirt, sun,* and *know* are all free lexical morphemes; although they may have various other morphemes affixed to them (to form, for example, *baseball, dogs, shirtless, sunny,* and *knowledge*), they are words in their own right. Not all meaning-carrying morphemes can stand alone. **Bound morphemes** include morphemes such as *bio-* (meaning 'life'), *phot-* (meaning 'light'), and *anti-* (meaning 'against') and have lexical meaning but must be attached to another morpheme.

There is a great deal more to word structure, however, than the lexical morphemes. When children learn that a *dusty road* is a road layered with dust, they have learned a **derivational morpheme**. The addition of the morpheme {-y} to words such as *dust, rust, might, trust,* and *dirt* to form *dusty, rusty, mighty, trusty,* and *dirty* is highly productive in the sense that it is widely used in English to change nouns to adjectives. Unfortunately for the learner, the "rule" is not quite so straightforward. The same /-y/ sound, for example, turns the adjective *full* into the adverb *fully.* The {-er} that turns the verbs *teach, write, play,* and *sing* into *teacher, writer, player,* and *singer* takes a different form in *actor* and still another in *lawyer.* It also sounds just like the morpheme that turns *cold* and *bold* to *colder* and *bolder.* This latter morpheme, however, is an **inflectional morpheme**.

Learning the grammatical inflections is an important aspect of morphological learning. When they learn a new noun, children do not have to be taught the plural form. Assuming that the word takes a regular plural ending, they can figure out the correct form because they already know how nouns are pluralized in English. Nor do they have to wonder about the past tense of a new verb; knowledge of the inflectional system tells them exactly how it is formed. There are irregular plural forms, such as *women* and *children*, and irregular past tense forms such as *bought* and *rode.*

But learning the regular inflections gives children a head start on the business of word learning.

Other Word-formation Processes.   Another important aspect of what children learn about English morphology is how words combine to form **compounds**. At first blush, the process seems simple enough. *Milk* and *man* combine to form *milkman*, the man who brings the milk (ignoring for the moment that the person may be a woman). Except to the native speaker, however, this relationship may not be at all obvious. A *snowman* is *not* a man who brings snow but a man who is made of snow. We would not be too pleased, either, if the garbage man were to deliver garbage nor if he were made of garbage. A doorman, on the other hand, does not deliver nor remove doors; neither is he made of them. Words in English combine in myriad ways to form new words, but the meanings of combined forms are not nearly as predictable as we might assume.

English, in fact, abounds with words that don't always mean what they should! An **idiom** is an expression whose meaning cannot be worked out from its individual parts, and the learning of idiomatic expressions is a major challenge for both children and non-native learners. "Hit the road" is a good example. Knowing every possible meaning of each component of the phrase is of little value in making sense of the expression. Similarly, if a child has just learned about roots in the garden, for example, what is he or she likely to make of the expression "root for the home team"? Cartoonists often draw their material from the misunderstandings that arise in children's minds because of their imperfect command of idioms (Figure 2.1).

Syntax: The Structure of Sentences

Most native speakers consider the basic unit of expression to be the sentence, despite the fact that many of them frequently do not speak in complete sentences. They think they do, and they recognize the sentence as the means by which they make themselves understood. The study of how morphemes combine to form sentences is called **syntax**.

What Children Must Learn.   To understand and produce sentences they have never heard before, children must acquire a great deal of knowledge about how sentences are formed. If that language is English, they must acquire two kinds: They must know the linear order of morphemes in sentences and they must know something about the hierarchical structure of sentences.

Figure 2.1
RUBES by Leigh Rubin. (By permission of Leigh Rubin and Creators Syndicate.)

Rubes   By Leigh Rubin

Budget cuts and neglect took their toll. Things
at the observatory definitely weren't looking up.

Linear order is an obvious aspect of sentence organization in English. Rearranging the words in an English sentence can have amusing, confusing, or even disastrous results. There is, after all, a significant difference in meaning between "Baby eats goldfish" and "Goldfish eats baby." Less obvious but equally important is **hierarchical structure**, which refers to the ways in which the morphemes in a sentence are organized into coherent groupings or units, which are themselves organized into larger groupings or units. These units are referred to as **constituents** of a sentence. In the sentence "Raymond ate his tuna from a crystal bowl," we can see that there are a number of groups of words that have meaning. We can also see that not all sequences of words make up sentence constituents. For example, most native speakers would agree that "ate his tuna from a crystal bowl" has some meaning of its own and, more significantly, contributes to the meaning of the sentence in a coherent way. Specifically, it tells us what Raymond did; it is the predicate of the sentence.

We can further divide the predicate into constituents. Native speakers would likely agree that the next two major constituents are "ate his tuna" and "from a crystal bowl," even though they might not be able to explain why this is the case. They could even break these two constituents down further if asked.

What is it about these groupings that marks them as constituents? First of all, they do have some meaning of and on their own and could serve as answers to questions. To the question "Who ate his tuna from a crystal bowl?," one might well answer "Raymond." Or to the question "What did Raymond eat his tuna from?," one would not likely respond with the entire sentence but with "a crystal bowl." In contrast, it is difficult to imagine the question to which "tuna from a" might be the answer, although those words appear in that order in the sentence.

A second way in which we know that these are true constituents is that parenthetical expressions can be used between them. We might say, for instance, "Raymond, you might be interested to know, ate his tuna from a crystal bowl" or "Raymond ate his tuna, when he could be bothered to eat at all, from a crystal bowl." Conversely, the sequence "Raymond ate his, you might be interested to know, tuna from a crystal bowl" would be highly unlikely in English. In general, we cannot insert parenthetical comments *within* grammatical constituents.

A third attribute of constituents is that often they can be replaced with a single word. For example, in answer to the question "Who ate his tuna from a crystal bowl?," we could answer with the full sentence or we could answer "Raymond did." In this case, *did* stands in for the entire predicate. Constituents, then, are more than just words or words in sequence. They are meaningful units hierarchically arranged in the sense that a single constituent may be part of a larger constituent, which may in turn be part of a still larger constituent.

Returning to the full sentence, we can see that *bowl* is a constituent of the larger unit "a crystal bowl," which is a constituent of "from a crystal bowl," etc. We could demonstrate this and the other hierarchical relationships in the sentence with brackets:

[[Raymond][[[ate][[[his] [tuna]][[from][[a][crystal][bowl]]]]]]]

This is one way of representing constituent structure, but it does not convey the hierarchical relationship in an easily discernible way. Most linguists today use the tree diagram to show the linear as well as the hierarchical structure of sentence elements. In the tree diagram, each

Figure 2.2
Tree diagram of "Raymond ate his tuna from a crystal bowl."

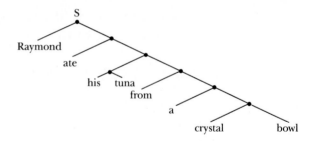

constituent of the sentence forms a branch. The tree diagram of Figure 2.2 conveys exactly the same information as the brackets.

Ambiguity.   Tree diagrams are especially useful for demonstrating the different constituent structures of ambiguous sentences, that is, sentences that share a common expression but have two or more distinct meanings. The sentence "Mad dogs and Englishmen go out in the noonday sun," for example, has two interpretations. In one, both dogs and Englishmen are mad and in the second, only dogs are mad (although both go out in the noonday sun). The tree diagram for each meaning is shown in Figure 2.3.

Sentences that are syntactically ambiguous look the same but have two (or more) different meanings. Just the opposite relationship exists in sentences that are syntactic paraphrases of one another.

Syntactic Paraphrase.   Sentences that are syntactic paraphrases of one another share certain properties: They are comprised of the same main lexical items; they have essentially the same meaning; and other sentences of the same structure can be paraphrased in exactly the same way. Consider, for example, the following sentences:

The teacher speaks the truth.

The truth is spoken by the teacher.

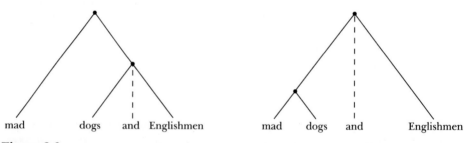

Figure 2.3
Two meanings of "Mad dogs and Englishmen go out in the noonday sun."

What the teacher speaks is the truth.

It is the truth that the teacher speaks.

Each of these sentences has a different form, but they all have the same main lexical items—*teacher, speak,* and *truth.* They all express the meaning that teachers speak truth, and they are all related to each other in such a way that every other sentence with the same structure can be transformed in the same ways:

Cats chase mice.

Mice are chased by cats.

What cats chase are mice.

It is mice that cats chase.

All these sentences have the same basic, or underlying, structure which may be represented as shown in Figure 2.4.

The syntax of English must demonstrate not only the common underlying structure for these kinds of sentences, but it must also demonstrate how that common structure can be transformed in so many ways without changing the core meaning. Ambiguity and paraphrase, then, impose two very different demands on a syntactic description. Ambiguity requires that the syntax account for the fact that two superficially identical sentences may have very different constituent structures while paraphrase

Figure 2.4
Deep structure for four syntactic paraphrases.

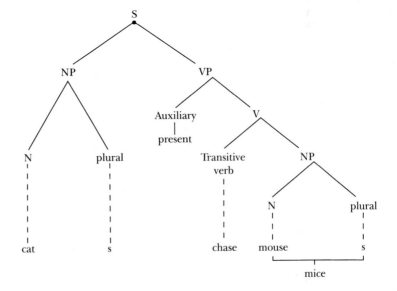

requires the syntax to account for the fact that a number of superficially different sentences may have a common constituent structure. But the demands do not stop there.

Other Syntactic Regularities.   Certain sentences are related to each other in systematic ways, but involve changes in meaning. Questions and negatives are good examples of these kinds of sentences. The systematic relationship between affirmative declarative sentences and various kinds of questions is easy to see:

1.   Uncle Harry wrote the book in prison.
2.   Did Uncle Harry write the book in prison?
3.   Who wrote the book in prison?
4.   What did Uncle Harry write in prison?
5.   Where did Uncle Harry write the book?

Certain regularities can be seen among all four questions. The question word is always at the front of the sentence, whether the question requires a yes/no answer, as in sentence 2, or specific information, as in sentences 3, 4, and 5. Note that in sentence 2 the past tense of *do* has been inserted at the beginning of the sentence because English word order does not permit us to move the main verb to the front of the sentence unless it is a form of *be* or *have*. Likewise, in sentences 4 and 5, *did* has been added just after the question word. This addition is not required in sentence 3 because the question word replaces the subject noun phrase (Uncle Harry) and the verb *wrote* is already at the beginning of the sentence and does not have to be moved. The same regular pattern occurs throughout the language.

The relationship between affirmative sentences and negatives is systematic in a similar way. The following sets of sentences demonstrate the regularity:

6.   The jury acquitted Uncle Harry on appeal.
7.   The jury didn't acquit Uncle Harry on appeal.
8.   Uncle Harry's books sold well.
9.   Uncle Harry's books didn't sell well.
10.   Aunt Maud is angry with Uncle Harry.
11.   Aunt Maud isn't angry with Uncle Harry.

12. Uncle Harry has many original ideas.

13. Uncle Harry hasn't many original ideas.

14. Uncle Harry doesn't have many original ideas.

Once again, a form of *do* is required to "support" the negative in sentences without *be* and is sometimes required in sentences with *have*. We can see, then, that both questions and negatives are related to affirmative statements in a regular and predictable way. These kinds of systematicity must also be reflected in a description of English sentences. This might be accomplished in a number of ways, but the most efficient is through a two-level system of grammar such as the one proposed by Noam Chomsky (1965) and refined by linguists and teachers over the past 25 years.

Transformational-Generative Grammar (TG).   One of Chomsky's major goals in conceiving his bilevel grammar was to account for sentences that appeared to have the same structure but in fact had different underlying meanings. He used the sentences "John is eager to please" and "John is easy to please" to demonstrate that sentences that may appear to be structurally identical have, in fact, radically different constituent structures. His aim was to provide a way of analyzing sentence structure which accounted for these divergent underlying structures. One level of structure was intended as a way of representing the meaning, the underlying structure of the sentence. This he called the **generative component**, or **base component**.

The base component consists of a set of phrase structure rules intended as general statements about how the most basic or core sentence patterns of a particular language are constructed. They consist of statements such as "A sentence consists of a noun phrase and a verb phrase" and "A noun phrase consists of an optional article and a noun which may be singular or plural." Linguists use a notational system that simplifies the writing of phrase structure rules, and would represent these two as:

$$S \longrightarrow NP + VP$$
$$NP \longrightarrow (Det) + N + (Plural)$$

Using this notational convention, parentheses ( ) indicate elements that may occur in some constituents but not others. The phrase structure rules serve as directions for constructing the trees we saw earlier, more properly called **phrase markers.** The structure that results from applying the phrase structure rules is called a **deep structure**.

An example is useful in understanding how the second level of the grammar operates. Consider two of the syntactic paraphrases from an earlier example:

Cats chase mice.

Mice are chased by cats.

Because they are syntactic paraphrases, they have the same deep structure, the one shown in Figure 2.4. The surface structure of the first sentence will look essentially the same as its deep structure, but in order to show the surface structure of the second sentence, a number of changes must occur. Briefly, the changes are:

1. Reverse the order of the subject and object noun phrases
2. Add *by*
3. Add a form of the verb *to be*
4. Add the past participle ending to the main verb.[4]

The transformational component of the grammar makes these alterations to the deep structure, resulting in the tree diagram of Figure 2.5. Remember that this is not a tree diagram showing deep structure, but a diagram showing the structure of the sentence after it has been transformed into a passive sentence.

Transformational rules add, delete, and move sentence elements, but although they may result in slight meaning changes, they do not change the core meaning of the sentence. The structure that results from applying all relevant transformational rules is called the **surface structure**.

Recursion.   The ultimate objective in writing a syntactic description of any language is to account for all possible sentences in the language. This is no minor undertaking because any number of noun phrases can be strung together to form compound subjects:

Raymond chased the weasel.

Raymond and Alice chased the weasel.

Raymond, Alice, and Harriet chased the weasel., etc.

[4]Note that the ending on *chase* is a past participle and not a past tense inflection by substituting the verb *eat*, yielding "The mice were eat**en** by the cat."

Figure 2.5
Tree diagram illustrating
passive construction.

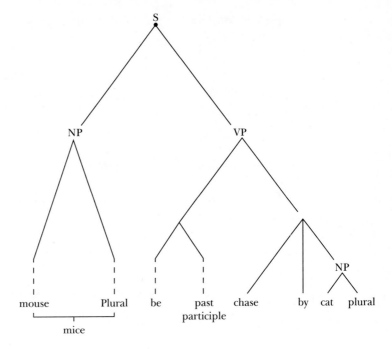

We can also string verb phrases together to form compound predicates:

Raymond chased the weasel and caught the squirrel.
Raymond chased the weasel, caught the squirrel, and lay down to sleep in the sun.

We can also conjoin complete sentences:

Raymond ate his tuna and Alice ate the squid.
Raymond ate his tuna and Alice ate the squid, but Harriet stayed on her diet.

In theory, using conjunctions such as *and, or,* and *but,* subjects, predicates, and complete sentences could be conjoined indefinitely. In this way, the number of possible sentences in English would be infinite. But conjunction is only one way of creating new sentences. Another way is to embed one sentence within another, and English has several ways of doing this. Consider the following sentences:

The man sleeps on the park bench.
The man is my uncle.

Assuming that the man in each sentence refers to the same person, we can combine these two sentences by embedding one within the other:

The man who sleeps on the park bench is my uncle.

We could embed still another sentence:

The man who sleeps on the park bench, which the city painted last year, is my uncle.

And another:

The man who sleeps on the park bench, which the city painted last year, is my uncle whom my mother disowned.

There are other ways of embedding sentences within sentences. In fact, English has an entire class of verbs that take sentences as their objects. Verbs such as *know, believe, imagine, deny,* and *claim* take sentences, frequently beginning with *that* as objects. For example, in the following sentences, the object of the verb is a complete sentence—"he lied to the Senate" in the first and "the Senator lied to everyone" in the second.

The Senator denies that he lied to the Senate.
Sheila claimed that the Senator lied to everyone.

The fact that English sentences can be embedded within other sentences is another reason why the number of possible sentences is infinite. This being the case, we can easily see that an adequate syntactic description of English must include some mechanism for recursion. Otherwise, we would have to generate an infinite number of rules to account for an infinite number of sentences.

A complete syntax of English is beyond the scope of this book. The purpose here has been to introduce the notions of linearity, hierarchical structure, sentence constituents, ambiguity, syntactic paraphrase, and recursion as well as to give a broad indication of the types of rules linguists use to represent the role each plays in English sentences.

Morphemes, Sentences, and Other Languages.   One of the principal ways in which languages differ is in their rules for combining morphemes into words. In English, we are able to combine a number of morphemes in a single word, and these morphemes may impart either grammatical or lexical meaning. The word *dialogues,* for example, consists of three morphemes—{dia-} meaning 'two,' {logue} meaning 'to speak,' and {-s}, indicating that the noun is plural. Some languages are far more ambitious in the number of morphemes that can be combined in a single word. In the Inuit language, for example, the word *angyaghllangyugtuq* consists of five separate morphemes and means 'he' (-tuq-) 'wants' (-yug-) 'to acquire' (-ng-) 'a big' (-ghlla-) 'boat' (angya-) (Crystal, 1987, p. 90). Inuit is referred to as an **agglutinating language**, meaning that words are made up of long sequences of morphemes with each expressing a particular grammatical function or meaning.

Mandarin, to illustrate another extreme, is an isolating language, meaning that there are no endings on words, and word order is used to show the relationships among words in a sentence. The sentence "We sold the horses to the teacher" would be rendered in Mandarin: wo men ba ma mai gei lao shi le:

wo	first person pronoun
men	plural
ba	object indicator
ma	horse
mai	sell
gei	benefactive case marker
lao	venerated
shi	master
le	past tense marker

Between the two extremes are the *inflecting* or *synthetic* languages such as Greek, Latin, and Arabic. In these languages, grammatical relationships are expressed by changing the structure of words. As the name suggests, this is most often accomplished by using inflectional endings. The Latin word *amo* conveys, literally, 'I love,' but also that the verb is in the present tense, is active, and is indicative.

English is somewhat difficult to classify. Because it has been influenced by a number of other languages over the centuries, it shares some of the characteristics of agglutinating, inflecting, and isolating languages. It is agglutinating in the sense that it can build words out of several morphemes (such as *nonreturnable, humanitarianism,* and *cytoarchitectonically*). It is inflecting in the sense that some grammatical relationships are expressed with word endings (plural, past tense, present progressive, etc.), and it resembles isolating languages because the basis of its grammar is word order.

Whichever language a child learns to speak, that learning depends to a large degree on the ability to understand and to produce novel sentences. Language would be very boring to use and difficult to learn if we had to rely on a memorized store of sentences for communication. The ability to generate a new utterance at will and to understand whatever utterances are heard lies at the heart of language acquisition and use. No amount of learning about sentence structure will be sufficient, however, to the task of making and understanding meaning.

Semantics: The Structure of Meaning

Semantics refers broadly to the study of meaning. Of course, the study of any aspect of language is impossible without considering meaning, but in linguistics, semantics is concerned with word meanings, with meaning that results from combining words in various ways, and with how language represents real-world meaning. The study of semantics is particularly fascinating, then, because in talking about semantics we are talking about how people represent reality, which is defined by individual and cultural experience—meaning categories of a language are specific to that language and the culture it represents. It sometimes comes as a shock to a monolingual person to discover that speakers of other languages may not share the same reality. As an example, speakers of English have relatively few words for the fluid that chemists identify as H_2O. If it happens to be falling from the sky, we call it rain, but otherwise we make do with *water* whether it is in a bathtub, an ocean, or a glass with ice. The Japanese language, in contrast, differentiates between hot water (*oyu*) and cold water (*mizu*), and it is impossible to talk of water without specifying which is intended. Clearly this distinction has, or had at some time, particular significance for Japanese speakers.

Colors offer especially rich distinctions among languages, in large part because they offer direct evidence of differences in perception. English has the distinction between red and pink, pink being the color red to which sufficient white has been added to change the English speaker's perception of the color. Blue, however, is blue whether it be navy, sky, powder, or baby. In Russian, the exact opposite holds true. Blue and light blue are expressed by two distinct words, as different as *red* and *pink*, but for the Russian speaker, adding white to red results only in light red.

While to a large degree word meanings are culturally agreed on, subtle differences exist in the meanings words hold for individual speakers of a language. These differences are largely a function of experience. An English-German bilingual once explained to me that the English word *lap* had little meaning for her beyond the dictionary definition (the front of a sitting person, from waist to knees). The German equivalent, *schoss*, on the other hand included memories of being held and cuddled by her German grandmother. She also explained that her reading of the Biblical "bosom of God" had only literal meaning for her, but the German translation, which replaced *bosom* with *schoss*, conveyed a very special message.[5]

These cultural and individual variables have contributed to the frustration that linguists have experienced in trying to formalize semantics in the same way as they have formalized phonology, morphology, and syntax. But there are other reasons why semantics resists precise formalization. Chief among these is that meaning resides in so many places—in words, in sentences, and in larger discourse units. Nevertheless, some linguists have attempted to describe the structure of meaning independently. Working under the assumption that semantics and syntax are distinct language components that can be described independently of one another, they have developed models that are called *interpretive*. Other linguists believe that the distinction between syntax and semantics is artificial, and that a description of the two language components must be integrated. Their work has led to *generative* theories and to *case grammar*. Both these theories hold that syntax is determined by semantics and that it is impossible to consider syntactic structures independent of meaning. While their arguments are compelling, they are beyond the scope of this text.[6]

A certain amount of meaning in a language is semantic in the sense that it resides in the language—in words and sentences—somewhat independent of particular speakers and hearers in particular contexts. Another aspect of meaning is communicative meaning, which resides in social situations and in the relationship between particular speakers and hearers. The study of this communicative meaning is commonly called pragmatics.

[5]My thanks to Gisela Rohde for sharing this example.
[6]For a concise description of semantics and semantic theories, see Gleason (1989); Hayes, Ornstein, & Gage (1987); and Godby, Wallace, & Jolley (1982).

Pragmatics

Pragmatics refers to the use of language for real communication in real time and encompasses almost any linguistic aspect of human society. Although they are less well formalized, rules or conventions have been developed that govern language use in a variety of situations. These range from the conventions for interpreting syntactic paraphrase to gender issues to the use of language for manipulating thought. Unlike other levels of language description, pragmatics cannot be discussed independent of human language users.

In the section on syntax, we saw that when sentences are related to one another in systematic ways, they are called **syntactic paraphrases**. But in actual language use, they are seldom true paraphrases at all. Bolinger (1980, p. 29) points out that English has conventions for arranging sentence elements to signal meaning. These are not grammar rules but usage conventions, and they include, for instance, the following "rule":

> . . . When a modifier goes before a noun, it characterizes the noun, says something about the way the noun 'really is'. When it follows, the 'really is' quality is neutralized. *The corner house* is the house that belongs on the corner; *the house on the corner* could be one in the process of being moved, perhaps parked there overnight. *The people ready were picked up* refers to a temporary state of readiness; *The ready people were picked up* sounds strange because it implies that 'being ready' is something you have with you as part of your nature, not just a temporary condition. Sometimes the same adjective can be used both ways: the only handy tool and the only tool handy. (Bolinger, 1980, p. 29)

Bolinger lists a total of four such conventions that account for the meaning differences conveyed by minor variations in word order, but there are many others. Certainly it is possible to get by in English without any conscious awareness of these conventions, but to become effective speakers and writers, we do learn and follow these subtle rules even though they are rarely taught.

Yet another aspect of learning the pragmatics of language is learning how to manipulate the language for specific purposes. English abounds in opportunities for doing so. It has been pointed out repeatedly that there are many more pejorative words in the language for females and for describing females than for males, and we all know that there are plenty for minority groups as well. But sexism is embodied even in the "neutral" words. To borrow another example from Bolinger:

> If a woman driver makes a bad maneuver, a man may be heard to say *What does that woman think she's doing!* with *woman* lengthened and pronounced with a rise-fall-rise intonation—which makes it an expression of disregard. A similar use of *man* would be taken as an emphatic way of expressing the emotion of the whole sentence, not as a reflection of the man's sex. (Bolinger, 1980, p. 93)

Even if parents were to manage to free children from exposure to sexist language in the home (an unlikely prospect given the fact that a significant degree of sexist bias is inherent in the language), they would encounter it as soon as they started school. The stories and books they read emphasize sex roles and the language uses masculine pronouns and other male terms with far greater frequency than female terms. As Bolinger observes:

> . . . when adults write for one another, they refer to young people as *children*, almost as often as they call them *boys* and *girls*. When writing books and stories for children, however, adults use the gender words *boy* and *girl* twice as often as the neutral words *child* and *children*. . . . (Bolinger, 1980, p. 93)

Bolinger goes on to cite studies showing that in schoolbooks, the ratio of use of *he/him* to *she/her* was almost four to one (Graham, 1975; cited in Bolinger) and that the same disproportion occurs in the 200 million achievement tests commonly given in U.S. schools (Tittle, 1973; cited in Bolinger). While the feminist revolution may have had some impact on the language of books, it takes only a cursory look at the books on the shelves of any elementary school to see that the bias has by no means been eliminated.

A more subtle form of manipulation comes in the language of commercial advertising. Bolinger's delightful example, "We reduced the size because we didn't want to increase the price" (1980, p. 58) is an example of the kind of doublespeak to which we are exposed daily. Because they are to some degree innocent believers in the voices of authority, children are more prone to commercial manipulation than are adults, though, obviously the target of Bolinger's example was the adult population.

Because most language manipulation has a negative impact on society, it might seem best not to learn it or to learn about it. It is hard to justify, for example, the language of sexism and racism. On the other hand, not all manipulation is negative, and more importantly, if language users do not learn to recognize the ways in which language can be used to influence thought, beliefs, and behavior, they have little protection against being manipulated themselves.

Finally, children learn very early the fallacy of the playground taunt "Sticks and stones may break my bones but words will never hurt me." Part of their lifetime language learning is not only to realize but to take responsibility for the fact that words do indeed wound—to learn, in other words, the paradox that oral language is at once ephemeral and permanent. Words find their targets and inflict their wounds, and while the wounds may heal, the act that inflicted them cannot be undone.

LINGUISTS

Theoretical Linguists

Linguists who write formal descriptions of linguistic structures such as those described in this chapter are **descriptive** and **theoretical linguists**. Both have provided invaluable insights into the structure of language, thereby contributing to our understanding of children's language acquisition, our understanding of how they comprehend the language they hear and read, and our view of the language they write. They have also contributed directly to language teaching practice. Traditional phonics instruction is based not only on the observation that there is some degree of correspondence between sound and symbol but on basic concepts from phonemics as well. Phonics rules are problematic, since the sounds of English do not correspond perfectly to its spelling, and a phonics-based approach to teaching reading violates the language-teaching principles of some teachers. But whatever we may believe about the place of phonics instruction in the teaching of reading, we cannot deny the contribution made by descriptive linguists to the writing of modern phonics rules.

Theoretical linguists also concern themselves with philosophical issues such as the essence of language, the relationship between language and formal logic, and the existence and nature of true universals in language (as opposed to universals in human cognition). While their field of enquiry might seem further removed from teaching practice than others within the parent discipline, we must not undervalue the contribution of these theoreticians.

Noam Chomsky (1975), for instance, taught us that language and language behavior were rule-governed and that we could learn a great deal about children's understanding of the rules by observing the language they produced. Although Chomsky was both a descriptive and theoretical linguist, and at times an historian as well, he was arguably the first of the true psycholinguists. He taught us to view child learners as actively instructing themselves in language, a task at which they were so successful, he argued, because they were innately endowed with brain mechanisms directed specifically to language learning. In the three decades since he articulated this position, there have been many persuasive arguments against Chomsky's innatist stance, but the observation that children are active participants in their own learning remains unchallenged.

While all linguists are concerned to some degree with language description and with theories about language, some have a more specialized interest within linguistics. Often that interest has direct relevance for language education.

Historical Linguists

Those who consider themselves to be **historical linguists** trace changes in linguistic structure over time and help us to understand some of the modern-day peculiarities of our language. The rather strange past tense of *go*, for example, makes sense when we understand that *went* is the past tense of *wend*, a verb with a meaning similar to *go* and which has been lost from common usage. By looking at English from an historical perspective, linguists can also explain why certain words that rhymed in Shakespeare or Swift no longer rhyme today:

> O, let him not debase your thoughts,
> Or name him but to tell his faults
> > (Directions for Making a Birth-Day Song)

When Swift wrote these lines in 1729, *thought* and *fault* were a perfect rhyme (there was no /l/ in *fault* in those days; it was "introduced erroneously by classically trained putterers" (Pyles & Algeo, 1970, p. 92).

The kinds of questions that historical linguists try to answer in their research may seem to have little direct relevance for language teaching in the elementary school. Issues such as which sounds might have existed in a language before it was written down, for example, are far removed from the life of a seven-year-old child. But we also have historical linguistics to thank for much of what we now understand about English spelling.[7] What seems at times a chaotic and sometimes random system makes a great deal more sense when we understand, for example, that much of current spelling represents the sounds of English as it sounded at a time several

---

[7]See Pyles and Algeo (1970, chap. 3) for a clear, concise, and entertaining perspective on English spelling.

hundred years ago, and that pronunciation has changed while the spelling has remained the same. While few teachers would choose to tell their seven-year-olds such facts (although it would likely do no harm and might even interest them), the teacher who understands that when we take historical change into account, English is much more regular and predictable than it first seems is less likely to treat it as a puzzle with no solution.

Psycholinguists

Psycholinguists are interested in language and the mind. Historical, descriptive, and theoretical linguists can all base their work on printed language data, the product. Although some speaker may have produced those data at some point, the speaker is not of particular interest. **Psycholinguists**, in contrast, concern themselves with the three processes that comprise human language behavior—language acquisition, comprehension, and production. During the past quarter century, research in psycholinguistics has begun to increase our understanding of how these processes work. Since acquisition, comprehension, and production are central concerns to teachers, it is not surprising that this branch of linguistics has a significant impact on language teaching practices.

An obvious contribution of psycholinguistics, and one familiar to most teachers, is to our understanding of the reading process. Recognizing that reading involves an interaction between reader and text was a major change from earlier beliefs about the nature of reading and methods of teaching reading, which concentrated on the identification of sounds and words. Even this practice, ironically, had a psycholinguistic basis because it required the reader to make the mental connection between the printed symbol and the language sound, but it was a far cry from the kind of active cognitive processing assumed by educators such as Frank Smith when he wrote about reading instruction: "Discover what a child (who is trying to read) is trying to do, and help him do it" (Smith, 1983).

My own experience as a teacher, as a linguist, and as an educator of teachers has led me to the view that the effective elementary teacher is a practicing psycholinguist. This is not to say that she regularly conducts controlled studies and publishes the results in scholarly journals. But let's consider some of her concerns. As she tells and reads stories to the children in her class, she is mindful of making herself understood. She is, in other words, concerned with **oral language comprehension**. She is concerned about language comprehension of another type when, in teaching children to read, she thinks about how fluent readers get meaning from text. When she wonders about why Sarah still substitutes a /w/ for some of her /l/ and /r/ sounds, she is posing a question about both language *perception* and *production*. When she observes that one of her Chinese learners seems to have difficulty with the same sounds that trouble Sarah, she is really asking whether the Chinese sound system is interfering with English or whether that child is exhibiting the same developmental forms as Sarah. Also, she must always be concerned with the relationship between her pupils' language development and their general cognitive growth, a question that goes to the heart of current psycholinguistics. In fact, all these questions with which the elementary teacher routinely deals are asked by psycholinguistic researchers as well. It is to be expected, then, that psycholinguistics is the branch of linguistics that does most to inform our teaching practice.

Since psychology is a science of the mind, it would be reasonable to expect that psycholinguists would include in their domain of study the relationship between language and brain functions. There was a time, in fact, when some psycholinguists did venture into brain study, but the major work in this area is now done by neurolinguists.

Neurolinguists

The major interests of **neurolinguists** are how the structure of the brain influences language learning, in what areas of the brain language is stored, and how damage to the brain affects language learning, production, and comprehension. Most people are fascinated by the subject of the human brain. Science magazines and journals aimed at the educated public publish many articles on brain structure and functioning and these always find wide public appeal.

There are two major types of neurological research that have some potential for informing educational practice in language. One has to do with brain maturation and addresses the question of how the parameters of brain maturation contribute to our understanding of language acquisition in monolingual and bilingual persons (Whitaker, Bub, & Leventer, 1981, p. 59). The other has to do with neurological bimodality and addresses two different questions. The first is, broadly, how the two hemispheres of the brain contribute to the learning of either a first or a subsequent language. The second is how teaching methods might best be constructed to correspond with what is known about right hemisphere and left hemisphere functioning. Danesi (1988a), for example, has made the claim that the failure of many second language teaching methods is due to their unimodality, or appeal to only one side of the brain. He stresses the importance of developing bimodal approaches or methods, but recognizes at the same time that in order to do so, we must be very clear about what kinds of techniques would be appropriate for which hemisphere.

We must remember, though, that neurolinguistic research is still in its infancy. Kinsbourne summarized the state of the field when he wrote in 1981:

> In language acquisition, matters also appear to be simpler than believed. . . Second and subsequent languages are acquired much as is the first, making allowance only for known differences in cognitive strategies at different stages in the life span. The same brain territories are involved in all language acquisition. The aging of the brain during childhood does not diminish ability to learn the vocabulary, syntax, or pronunciation of a second language, and no period of the life span is critical to such acquisition. The well-documented greater plasticity of the immature than the mature brain relates to the ability to compensate for structural loss of brain tissue; it has not been shown to affect the functioning of the brain while it is intact. (Kinsbourne, 1981, p. 56)

These generalizations about the real state of our knowledge are largely true today. Even though the statements are very broad and do not lend themselves to application, they do speak to general approaches to language education, approaches that seem all the more valid for their congruence with the observations of many practicing teachers. For example, the statement that, allowing for the different kinds of cognitive strategies that older learners use, second and subsequent languages are acquired in much the same way as the first is consistent with what many good elementary teachers already do: They shun formal language instruction for their young second language learners in favor of providing a language-rich environment with many opportunities for natural language use.

It would be a mistake, however, to assume that neurolinguistic research is of no interest to teachers. Understanding how the brain functions during language learning and use is potentially of vital significance. But *potentially* is the key word. The field is relatively new and we have barely begun even to understand how to study the questions we want answered much less to find the answers.

Sociolinguists

Sociolinguists study language in relation to social factors. These include age, sex, ethnic origin, social class, and educational level among others, factors that educators have traditionally taken into account for a variety of educational purposes. Sociolinguists might study some of the same general issues as psycholinguists or neurolinguists, but they would do so from a different perspective. All three, for example, might be interested in bilingualism. A psycholinguist might ask how bilinguals process their two languages, what cognitive strategies are involved, or whether they are the same for the two languages. A neurolinguist might ask whether or not the bilingual's two languages are stored in the same area of the brain or whether or not damage to the brain affects both languages in a similar manner. A sociolinguist would likely be more concerned with the community of language users and might study the factors that influence the language a bilingual chooses to use in a bilingual or multilingual community.

Another area of overlap between sociolinguists and psycholinguists is **discourse analysis**. While the psycholinguist may be interested in "discovering the intellectual processes we use in understanding [spoken or written] narratives" (Hatch, 1983, p. 3), the sociolinguist is likely to be more interested in studying how the speech situation (for example, a party or a visit to the dentist) influences speech events (for example, a conversation). There is, in fact, an entire domain of research known as **unequal power discourse**, which studies speech events during trials, doctor-patient interviews, and in classrooms (Hatch, 1983, pp. 150–151).

Broadly speaking, sociolinguists study how members of a community interact. Not surprisingly, many have chosen to study the community of the classroom. Schieffelin and Cochran-Smith (1984), Anderson and Stokes (1984), and Jacob (1984), for example, have studied how the society of the classroom contributes to literacy in children. But it is up to educators and not to sociolinguists to determine just what shape the influence will take. It is the purpose of sociolinguistic research to describe the interaction that occurs in classrooms. It is the job of educators to evaluate those descriptions and to implement changes where they think appropriate.

The study of language varieties within a community also falls within the domain of sociolinguistics. These varieties may be different languages, as they are in the bilingual communities in Texas, California, Ontario, and many other regions of North America, or they may be varieties of a single language, in which case they are usually called **dialects**. Dialect is another issue in which sociolinguistics and educators share an interest. Educators tend to talk about dialect in terms of "linguistically different" children, implying that there are few of these children. This implication is not borne out by the statistics available in the United States and Canada: In Vancouver, British Columbia, where the dominant language is English, half the students in the public school system have another language as their first language. The last U.S. census found more than eight million homes where English was not the first language spoken. If we add black children in the United States or native Indian children in Canada who speak a nonstandard dialect of English, we have a potentially huge population of "linguistically different" children.

The appropriate application of the research findings in all these areas—linguistics, psycholinguistics, neurolinguistics, and sociolinguistics—is the task of educators, but it is also the task of yet another branch of linguistics.

Applied Linguists

Applied linguists take information from other disciplines—the various branches of linguistics, psychology, sociology, and medicine—and use it in various ways. There are two kinds of applied linguist. One applies the principles and theories of linguistics to second and foreign language learning and teaching. The second studies the role of language in practical problems such as lexicography, translation, and speech pathology. We can see in both, but especially in the former, certain areas of common interest between applied linguistics and language teaching. The contribution of applied linguistics is, in fact, highly tangible, concerned as it is with such things as syllabus design. A word of caution is in order, however: The bias of most applied linguists of this bent is toward English as a foreign language and toward the adult learner. The child in the mainstream, dominant-language classroom is not usually their concern.

Educational Linguists

As the name suggests, **educational linguists** concern themselves with those aspects of language research that might find some application in education. Like applied linguistics, educational linguistics draws on information gleaned from psycholinguistics, neurolinguistics, and sociolinguistics for use in answering practical questions, particularly related to matters of teaching and learning.

I said at the beginning of this chapter that educational linguistics is a relatively new branch of linguistics. It would have been slightly more accurate to say that the label "educational linguistics" is relatively new. Writing from the perspective of the United States, Bernard Spolsky published his *Educational Linguistics* in 1978 and Michael Stubbs, writing from the British point of view, published his book of the same title in 1986. Apart from these and a scattered number of journal articles, little else has been published that makes use of this label. When we compare the huge number of books written and the number of journals devoted to each of the disciplines discussed above, it becomes clear that the label is not widely used. But the labeling is not terribly important. Frank Smith, Yetta Goodman, and Kenneth Goodman could well be considered educational linguists for their work linking psycholinguistics and reading; Donald Murray, Janet Emig, and Donald Graves are educational linguists for their significant contribution to our understanding of writing processes. What is important is not what they are labeled, but what contribution they and other educational linguists make to language education.

The aim of educational linguistics, or indeed of any kind of applied linguistics, is not to tell teachers how to teach language. How to teach, and to a large degree *what* to teach, remain the prerogative of teachers and teachers of teachers who study children, classroom interactions, approaches, methods, and techniques of instruction in the classroom environment. Rather, the aim of educational linguistics is to provide the language teacher with the latest theories and the findings of quality research, which serves to inform educational practice. In a sense, then, the educational linguist is an applied psycholinguist, applied sociolinguist, applied neurolinguist, etc. But because there are so many areas to be taken into account, the educational linguist may choose not to conduct original research, although it is certainly possible to do so, but may interpret the scholarship of other areas for use in education. That is no easy job because it requires sufficient expertise in the different branches of linguistics to be able to evaluate and interpret the various studies intelligently and sufficient expertise in education to be able to suggest reasonable, appropriate applications. For our purposes, the issue is what kind of insights we can hope to gain from educational linguistics—or whatever we call it—and how we translate them into practice.

CONCLUSION

As teachers, our responsibility is to assure that the education we provide for all the children who find their ways to our classes be the best we are capable of. We are fortunate in having many experts we can call on, and since our particular concern here is language, many of those experts are the linguists with all the prefixes that denote their specialized interests. In this chapter, we have seen how some of these specialists have contributed and will continue to contribute to educational practice. We have also seen that the potential for misapplication is very great and must be guarded against.

We have not touched on a great many topics, topics such as models of language appropriate for the elementary school, the place of language in the school curriculum, and paradigms for research in educational linguistics. Important as these topics may be, they are best addressed in a book devoted entirely to educational linguistics. My purpose here was only to present an overview of the common areas of interest between certain branches of linguistics and language education. I would like to suggest, finally, that because teachers are in touch daily with children, with schools, and thus with the applications of linguistic theories and research, the collaboration that should occur between linguists and educators should be bidirectional. Teachers have traditionally listened to and learned from linguists, but it is time for linguists to enlist the aid, support, and direction of teachers in the collection and interpretation of their findings. This is true collaboration and our quickest path to discovering insights that will have a meaningful impact on our teaching of children.

PART TWO

Language Acquisition

Chapter Three

Language Acquisition: Theoretical Perspective

The question being asked here is "How do children accomplish what they accomplish in language acquisition?" The true answer is simple: We don't know. The reason we don't know, however, is not because no one has tried to find out. Indeed, research into children's language acquisition has engaged the minds of scholars for much of human history. In the twentieth century alone, we find an immense volume of data. Ronjat, a French linguist, studied and published reports of the bilingual development of his son in 1913, and other major contributors in the first half of the century included Leopold (1939, 1947, 1948, 1949a, 1949b), Jakobson (1941, 1968), and Velten (1943).

Even more data have been collected in the second half of the century, particularly in the last thirty years. Raw data, however, are of interest only to the researchers themselves. To make sense to practitioners, to be useful, especially to educators trying to understand and plan for children's continued language learning, acquisition data must be viewed through the lens of a general theory. The relationship between research and theory is actually very straightforward. The data provide the materials from which a theory can be constructed and against which it can be tested. A coherent theory must account for all the facts of language acquisition found in the mass of data, but as we saw in the last chapter, these facts come from a complex of behaviors encompassed by human language. They come from phonology, morphology, syntax, semantics, and pragmatics, and thus it is not surprising that the task of constructing a general, comprehensive theory of language acquisition is a formidable one.

The task is complicated further by the fact that much of the data, gathered by different researchers under different conditions, seem contradictory. As an example, to understand how language develops in children, we must look at longitudinal data, that is, data gathered on the same children acquiring language over an extended period of time. Much child language data, however, are collected in cross-sectional studies, or studies of large numbers of children at different stages in their language development. These latter designs are not necessarily invalid, and in fact are often important, but they may yield different results from longitudinal data. Since a theory of language acquisition must account for *both* development and language behavior at any point in that development, we must work with both kinds of data. The task is complicated, though, by the incongruities among the findings resulting from the various research designs. To date, then, no one theory can do what a theory should do, namely, "organize the facts from these varied sources, generate testable and verifiable hypotheses, and provide an explanation of the acquisition process" (Gleason, 1989, p. 167).[1]

Nevertheless, research into language acquisition continues, and researchers continue to speculate about the nature of the underlying processes. In doing so, they work within or through particular theoretical approaches. These approaches both guide their inquiry and help them to interpret their results. A number of competing theories of child language acquisition exist, and linguists and educators categorize them in various ways—as behaviorist, linguistic, cognitive, or interactionist, for example. The difficulty with such categorizations is that too frequently theories do not fit neatly into the assigned category. As an example, information processing, which is essentially a cognitive theory, relies on imitation, a notion usually associated with the behaviorists and one that also recognizes the role played by adults in the child's environment, the cornerstone of social interaction theory. This is true, in part, because no theory is ever conceived independently of the theories that preceded it. In any theory that has gained any kind of academic respectability, there is almost always some idea that can be salvaged and carried over to the next theory, even one with a radically different outlook. It would be very unusual, then, to find a theory of language acquisition that bore no resemblance at all to its predecessors. Despite the nonexclusiveness of the categories, they are useful for distinguishing *broadly* between theories. In this chapter we will

---

[1]For a concise description of what a theory of language *should* do, see the final chapter of Peter A. Reich's *Language Development* (Reich, 1989).

examine behaviorist, linguistic (or nativist), cognitive stage, information processing, and social interaction theories of language acquisition.

At a very basic level, the first two types of theory are differentiated by beliefs about the uniqueness of language learning. Behaviorist theories hold that there is nothing unique about language learning, that *all* human behavior, including language, has its basis in physical processes and can only be studied in terms of those processes. Linguistic theories, on the other hand, hold that language develops from structures and processes that are unique to language and are present in the brain at birth. Cognitive theories, and information theory is a particular type of cognitive theory, share with behaviorism the belief that language learning is not fundamentally different from other human learning. Interactionist theories, in contrast, assume that the course of language development is influenced by a myriad of factors—physical, linguistic, and social—and that these factors interact with one another, modify one another, and may produce different effects in different children. Both cognitive and interactionist approaches are generally less extreme than either behaviorist or linguistic theories.

In the next several pages, we will examine specific tenets of these four categories of theory. As we do so, we must keep in mind that no theory is as yet wholly satisfactory in accounting for everything we know from research and observation about children's language acquisition.

BEHAVIORIST THEORIES

What Behaviorists Believe

Behaviorism is well-rooted in North American psychological and linguistic traditions, but with regard to language acquisition, there were two major contributors. Leonard Bloomfield, in his book *Language* (1933) attempted to account for children's acquisition of early word meaning in behavioristic terms. He hypothesized five steps in the process as shown in Figure 3.1.

1.   Based on their innate capacity to vocalize, children make speech-like sounds. After repeatedly uttering a sound, they develop the "habit" of that sound.

2.   An older speaker utters a sound that resembles one of the child's sounds. When the child hears the sound, he/she utters the closest matching sound in the repertoire. This is the beginning of imitation.

Figure 3.1
Bloomfield's five steps in the acquisition of word meaning. (Adapted from *Language*, 1933, pp. 29–31.)

1. Based on their innate capacity to vocalize, children make speech-like sounds. After repeatedly uttering a sound, they develop the "habit" of that sound.

2. An older speaker utters a sound that resembles one of the child's sounds. When the child hears the sound, he/she utters the closest matching sound in the repertoire. This is the beginning of imitation.

3. The older speaker uses the word in the presence of the real object, for example, *ma* for *mama*. Mama's presence becomes a stimulus for saying *ma*.

4. The habit of saying *ma* gives rise to new habits. If, for instance, the child is accustomed to seeing her mother at bedtime, and then one night she fails to appear, the child will say *ma* anyway. Assuming that the child is asking for her mother, the older speaker reinforces the behavior by responding. The child has thus begun to use the word when the stimulus is not present.

5. The child's speech improves as good attempts are reinforced and poor attempts lost through nonreinforcement or confusion.

3.   The older speaker uses the word in the presence of the real object, for example, *ma* for *mama*. Mama's presence becomes a stimulus for saying *ma*.

4.   The habit of saying *ma* gives rise to new habits. If, for instance, the child is accustomed to seeing her mother at bedtime, and then one night she fails to appear, the child will say *ma* anyway. Assuming that the child is asking for her mother, the older speaker reinforces the behavior by responding. The child has thus begun to use the word when the stimulus is not present.

5.   The child's speech improves as good attempts are reinforced and poor attempts lost through nonreinforcement or confusion.

The other major attempt to explain language acquisition through behaviorism was made by B. F. Skinner (1957). Skinner proposed an elaborate scheme of stimulus, reinforcement, and association, and attempted to account for the acquisition of syntax as well as word meaning.

Behaviorist theories focus on observable, measurable aspects of human language behavior. Anything that is not observable is "mentalistic," and mentalistic explanations of language behavior are to be avoided in favor of processes that can be observed and measured. This is not to say that behaviorists eschew anything unobservable, for they readily acknowledge that language behavior has a physiological basis in the brain. What they reject outright is any claim that mental structures correspond to linguistic structures.

Behaviorism assumes two basic processes of learning—classical and operant conditioning.[2] In language learning, classical conditioning is believed to account for receptive learning. For example, it would be assumed to work as follows: An infant sees the family dog everyday and gradually comes to associate the word *dog* or the dog's name, say "Charlie," with the appearance of the dog. If the dog is not in the room and someone says "dog" or "Charlie" the child may look around, expecting to see the animal. Eventually, when the child wants to play with the dog, he or she will say "dog" or "Charlie." The dog itself is the unconditioned stimulus that provokes certain responses in the child, and the words *dog* and *Charlie* become conditioned stimuli that evoke essentially the same responses in the child as the living dog.

While classical conditioning is supposed to account for how children come to understand language, another set of principles is required to account for their productive learning—those of operant conditioning. In behaviorist psychology, operant conditioning is concerned with changes in voluntary, nonreflexive behavior that result from environmental consequences of that behavior, specifically reward and punishment. Behaviors that are rewarded are repeated while those that are punished are extinguished. In the case of early language, behavior would refer to the attempts to produce words, and those attempts that are rewarded are repeated and thus learned and those that are punished are abandoned. The assumption seems to be that those attempts that closely approximate the adult form will be rewarded, and those that do not will be punished. As the child grows more proficient, the adult modifies the practice of reinforcement, rewarding only those attempts that conform to the adult standard. Behaviorists believe that both classical and operant conditioning continue to control learning into adulthood, but they are insufficient to account for the fast rate of language learning that occurs in the early childhood years.

The speed with which children acquire language suggests strongly that they do not learn every word and combination of words by going

---

[2]For a complete description of how both classical and operant conditioning are believed to function in language learning, see Bohannon and Warren-Leubecker's chapter in Gleason (1989).

through the laborious processes described above. There simply has to be a faster route to mature behavior, and that route, according to behaviorists, is imitation. Imitation may be an exact replica of the modeled behavior or it may be an imperfect approximation; it may follow the modeled behavior immediately or it may follow a considerable delay. The concept can even be extended, as it has been by Whitehurst and Vasta (1975), to the acquisition of grammatical frames. They argue that children may reproduce grammatical structures they have heard but substituting their own words appropriate to their particular situation. Thus a child who has heard "Give me the teddy bear," may produce "Give me the cookie," or even, presumably, "Give her the book." It is assumed that successful imitation is followed by reinforcement, and thus the incentive to imitate is maintained.

Behaviorists contend, in summary, that infants begin as producers of random verbalizations. They become meaningful communicators through the simultaneous processes of classical conditioning, operant conditioning, and imitation—processes applied by others in their environment. Or, in David Ingram's words, "To explain language acquisition for the behaviorist, then, is to determine the set of environmental conditions that lead the child to identify and associate events with internal states" (1989, p. 18).

This view of children as *objects* rather than *agents* in their own language learning is at odds with the views of other theorists who consider children to be active participants in, even directors of, their own learning. Before considering their views, however, let us look briefly at some of the arguments against the behaviorist position.

The Case Against Behaviorism

As psychologists and linguists have gathered more and more data on children acquiring language, they have found many aspects of acquisition that behaviorism is at a loss to explain. The case against behaviorism is a strong one, based as it is both on research findings and on reason. The case has six basic components or arguments:

1. Evidence of regression
2. Existence of novel forms
3. Absence or null effect of reinforcement
4. Early acquisition of abstract words
5. Uniformity of language acquisition in humans
6. Uniqueness of human language.

Evidence of Regression.   Evidence of regression in language acquisition comes mainly from phonology and is of two types. The first occurs when a child apparently loses the ability to pronounce correctly a word that was previously correct. In her study of the acquisition of phonology, Lise Menn (1971) reported that the child Daniel's pronunciation of two words actually deteriorated. Where initially he had pronounced "down" as [dãwn] and "stone" as [dõn], he subsequently began to pronounce "down" as [nãwn] and "stone" as [nõn]. These changes occurred at a time when he was acquiring other nasal consonants in words such as "beans," which he pronounced as [mĩnz] and "dance," which he pronounced as [nǽns].

The second type of regression involves the child's apparent inability to articulate a familiar sound in a new word. In other words, the learned sound may remain correct in known words but be deleted or substituted in new words. Menn used the example of Daniel's pronunciation of *hello* and *hi,* both early words and both pronounced with the initial consonant intact. As he learned other words beginning with the same sound, however, he pronounced them without the initial consonant. It would take considerable contortion of behaviorist theory to account for either type of regression, yet parents and others who have observed young children closely know that regression is a common occurrence in their language learning.

Existence of Novel Forms.   The fact that children are able to produce novel forms of language, combinations of words and pronunciations they have never heard before, is another piece of evidence against behaviorism. It is true that the principles of imitation and analogy can account for some novel production, but they cannot be stretched to cover all instances. Consider, for example,

1. Mikey gots no toys. [Mikey has no toys.]
2. Want other one spoon, Daddy. [I want the other spoon, Daddy.]
3. Me wants him all gone. [I want him to leave.]

These utterances are problematic for behaviorism on two grounds. First, children cannot imitate what, in all likelihood, they have not heard before. Second, it is difficult to imagine that any adult ever provided reinforcement for these forms. But then, this is the crux of another central difficulty with behaviorism, the fact that parents provide little feedback in matters of form.

Absence or Null Effect of Reinforcement.   The absence of reinforcement constitutes a major empirically justified argument against behaviorism. Brown (1973; quoted in McLaughlin, 1978, p. 22) found that the basis for a parent's acceptance or rejection of a child's utterance is rarely structural. In response to the child who uttered "Mikey gots no toys," her mother responded "That's not true, dear. Mikey has a clown, and a truck and lots of other toys." She responded to the truth value of the statement and not to its grammaticality.

The second utterance was cited by Martin Braine; the entire dialogue went as follows:

Child: Want other one spoon, Daddy.
Father: You mean, you want the other spoon.
C: Yes, I want other one spoon, please Daddy.
F: Can you say 'the other spoon'?
C: Other . . . one . . . spoon.
F: Say 'other.'
C: Other.
F: 'Spoon.'
C: Spoon.
F: 'Other . . . spoon.'
C: Other . . . spoon. Now give me other one spoon. (Braine 1971a, pp. 160–161; quoted in McLaughlin, 1978, p. 24).

This example points to yet another dilemma in a theory that relies so heavily on reinforcement—that children do not attend to negative feedback about their linguistic forms. Even if parents try to turn children's attention to form and even if they succeed to some degree in getting them to mimic the correct form, children ignore the parent's "teaching" when left to their own devices. Furthermore, few parents try to interfere with infant pronunciations, being charmed instead by the "baby talk," or perhaps understanding the futility of correction. Those who try usually find themselves frustrated as did the researchers who reported the "fis phenomenon" described in Chapter 1.

Actually, even more compelling evidence against the role of reinforcement in language learning is documented. Katherine Nelson (1973; quoted in Reich, 1986, p. 321) conducted a study that compared language development in children whose mothers engaged in selective reinforcement with children at the one-word stage and mothers who did not. She found that the children whose mothers practiced reinforcement developed more slowly than the children whose mothers rarely or never practiced reinforcement of form. If language learning is dependent on reinforcement, and reinforcement does not occur, then learning cannot occur.

But learning does occur in the absence of reinforcement. Therefore, if positive reinforcement of grammatical forms actually impedes language development, then we have even more reason to question the theory.

Acquisition of Abstract Words.   Another piece of evidence against behaviorism comes from children's learning of words with abstract meanings. Children's learning of their first words may be accounted for via a behaviorist notion of conditioning, as indicated in the example of the dog's name, Charlie, above. This explanation is not altogether untenable for concrete words such as *dog, milk, bottle, juice, mama, daddy, water,* and so on. It is far less tenable for words such as *more, big,* and *little,* which do not have concrete referents. Yet these words, and other abstract words, are acquired early, indicating that a more sophisticated explanation is required. So far the argument against behaviorism has been based in research and observation of children's actual language learning. The last two pieces of evidence concern language in the human species.

Uniformity of Language Acquisition in Humans.   A highly compelling argument against behaviorism is the uniformity with which children around the world learn language. Not only do almost all children acquire language, but there is evidence that they do so in a manner that is remarkably consistent. Both Brown (1973) and Slobin (1979) have reported that at the two-word stage children across many different languages exhibit remarkably similar language learning behavior. They express essentially the same kinds of meaning and intent in highly similar utterances. Parents of young children know that they learn very early to say "no" as in ("no nap" or "no go") and to ask for more ("more juice" or "more cookie").

This uniformity of intent and language has important implications for behaviorism. Specifically, it would be reasonable to expect that if the behaviorists were correct and language were merely a result of environmental shaping of an organism with an innate capacity for general learning, then there would be a great deal of variation among language learners. Given such variability in societies and individuals, it would be reasonable to expect that some children would never acquire language at all. Yet this is not the case. Because nearly all children on the planet learn language and because there is so much uniformity in the way they do so, we must again question the assumptions on which the behaviorist model is built.

Uniqueness of Human Language.   The final argument against behaviorism is also related to language and the human species and goes like this:

If language learning were simply a matter of conditioning and imitation as described earlier, then it would be expected that animals other than humans could learn language. Before we can sensibly address the question of animal language, we need some clear definition of language. Otherwise, we do not know whether the waggle dance of bees and the courting calls of jackdaws qualify as language. Clearly each is a communicative system of some sort, but does either constitute language?

Human language, most researchers argue, has characteristics not found in any other form of animal communication. Although they have produced several different lists of attributes that mark human language, most researchers would probably agree that language has three essential attributes: First, it is **productive**, meaning that speakers can understand and produce utterances they have never heard before and they can also create new utterances by recombining elements they already know. Second, language has the capacity to represent ideas, objects, and events with symbols. This property is termed **semanticity**. Third, true language has the capacity of **displacement**, meaning that it can be used to create messages that are not tied to the immediate environment. Bees and jackdaws both fall short of establishing these criteria.

Bees use the waggle dance to tell other bees the direction and approximate distance to the flowers filled with nectar. The information is contained in the movements of the bees' dance. A westward movement tells the other bees to move west, a "round dance" consisting of alternating circles to the left and right indicates that the source of nectar is near, and tail-wagging tells them that it is further away. Dancing bees don't lie about the direction or distance to the flowers. Neither do they comment on the quality of the nectar or hazardous flying conditions, nor introduce any other topic of conversation into the dance. Their message is iconic (it looks like what it is conveying) and it is always located within the context of nectar-gathering, and thus fails on criteria of productivity and displacement.

Jackdaws, relatives of the crow, have courting (or mating) calls, calls used when they fly away, and warning calls that they use before attacking any creature carrying a dangling black object. Like the dance of the bees, this communication system has meaning to its users and thus might be considered to have semanticity. But also like the dance of the bees, it is very strictly bound to the context of the present. It thus fails the criteria of displacement and productivity.

Bees and jackdaws are not the only animals with communication systems. Whales, dolphins, sticklebacks (a small fish), gibbons, and meadowlarks have also been found to possess intricate ways of communicating. But none meets the three basic criteria that define human language. It might be argued, however, that it is unfair to compare communication systems of animals that are such a great evolutionary distance from humans. Perhaps it is fairer to consider only the linguistic abilities of the other primates, and it is certainly easy to do so because a number of attempts have been made to study primate language.

Earlier in this century, there were attempts to teach chimpanzees to talk. These early attempts failed because chimpanzees do not have a vocal apparatus that compares with the human apparatus. Later researchers abandoned the notion of speech and concentrated on the symbolic nature of language, sign language in the case of Washoe, Moja, Pili (Gardner & Gardner, 1975), and Nim Chimpsky (Terrace, 1980), and a form of written language involving plastic tokens in the case of Sarah (Premack & Premack, 1983).

Results of these studies have shown chimpanzees to have a very limited capacity for symbolic representation. There does seem to be some evidence, although not overwhelming at this point, that chimpanzees can be taught to communicate, and that the system they use for doing so has some degree of semanticity. There is serious doubt, however, about the chimps' capacity for productivity and displacement. Studying videotapes of Nim Chimpsky, Terrace (1980) found that most of the chimp's signing was prompted by his teacher, that is, he did not initiate conversation and that Nim's utterances mostly consisted of elements in his teacher's prior utterances. This brings to mind the story of the horse who could do arithmetic problems; it was found that the trainer was unconsciously signaling the correct number of pawing movements.

Perhaps the most concise way of distinguishing between human language and animal communication is by invoking Vygotsky's notions of *signs* and *tools,* or internalized representations and physical objects for dealing with the external world. As Pflaum writes:

> Primates have the ability to signal (to warn of danger, for example), and they use tools. (Van Lawick-Goodall [1971] described chimps' use of narrow sticks to get ants to eat.) Their inability to integrate tools into signs and to generate signs for new situations marks the difference between them and humans and explains their inability to acquire language naturally. (Pflaum, 1986, p. 10)

The linguistic accomplishments of nonhuman primates have so far failed to mount any serious challenge to the position that language is uniquely human. Research currently being carried out with pygmy chimpanzees from the rain forests of Zaire may produce different and more convincing results, since these rare chimps are considered to be more social and more intelligent than the larger common chimpanzees that have been the subjects of prior investigations. For now, it is safe to say that humans alone have language. This argument is viewed by some as evidence for linguistic, or nativist, theories.

LINGUISTIC NATIVISM

What Nativists Believe

As might be expected, the bias of linguistic approaches is toward language structure and the child's ability to learn it. Nativists begin with two assumptions: that there is structure in language which exists independent of language use and that children are endowed with a "dedicated" ability to acquire that structure. They assume, in other words, that language learning differs from all other human learning.

This specialized ability is attributed to an innate capacity for language learning. This dedicated capacity, which Chomsky (1965) called the **language acquisition device (LAD)**, is what prepares the child to make sense of language, to discover the structure and the meaning-making potential of language. How the LAD is actually constructed is the subject of heated debate among linguists. Some argue that it consists essentially of a set of linguistic universals, such things as the existence and possible functions of word order, word classes, and the existence and function of sentences. These universals serve to constrain the possible hypotheses children make about the structure of the language they hear. They also compensate for the "poverty of the stimulus," a phrase that refers to the Chomskyan claim that the language to which children are exposed is limited in both quality and quantity. It provides, in other words, a database that is much too impoverished to allow for children to work out complex linguistic rules.

Others contend that the LAD simply endows children with a set of "general procedures for discovering how language is to be learned" (Crystal, 1987, p. 234). Although this is a weaker interpretation of what a language acquisition device might be, it should be noted that the general procedures are *not* general cognitive procedures for making sense of the world but procedures dedicated to the task of making sense of language. Proponents of linguistically based theories of language acquisition would not deny the importance of the environment in language learning, but they would minimize its impact. Rather than seeing the environment as shaping a child's language development, they view its function largely as one of activating the innate, physiologically based system.

Linguistically based theories hold a certain appeal. Clearly the learning of structure is an important part of language learning, and the speed with which the child learns so much complex grammar is impressive enough to warrant our consideration of an innate device. Moreover, the job of explaining language acquisition is made easier if theorists can assume that certain parts of the learning mechanism are innate. But what is the evidence?

Essentially there are two types. One is research evidence on children's learning of structural rules and the other relies on the argument that humans must possess innate linguistic capabilities. A number of studies strongly indicate that children learn grammatical rules. Slobin (1971) asserts, for example, that the basic organization of language emerges from the time children begin putting two words together. At this stage and very clearly by the time they begin to produce sentences longer than two words, children use principles of hierarchical structure to form their utterances. Moreover, early awareness of syntactic rules has been documented not only in children learning English but also in children learning a number of different languages (see, for example, Braine, 1963, 1976).

Many researchers have focused on the phenomenon of **overgeneralization** (or overregularization) as evidence for rule learning. When children who have previously produced forms such as "made" and "went" suddenly begin to produce "maked" and "goed" (which they are unlikely to have heard before), researchers take it as evidence that they are in the process of learning the regular past tense rule. They have overgeneralized the application of their newly acquired rule to irregular (and previously learned) as well as regular verbs. The phenomenon of overgeneralization has been observed in children acquiring a great many different languages including Spanish, Japanese, Hebrew, Russian, Finnish, Turkish, and English.

Children's knowledge of rules has been studied not only in natural observations of children but in laboratory studies as well. One of the best known of these was devised by Jean Berko (1958) to investigate children's knowledge of plurals and other grammatical morphemes. She showed children pictures of creatures and objects that she gave nonsense labels and asked children to produce alternate forms. For example, she showed a picture of a fat, birdlike creature and gave the following prompt: *This is a wug. Now there is another one. There are two of them. There are two* _____. This procedure has undergone adaptation and been replicated many times. Although investigators have sometimes disagreed on the precise nature of the rules children acquired, most are in agreement that the evidence strongly indicates that children's language is rule-governed.

The second type of argument in support of innatist theories is biological, and there are a number of observations that support the view that children are born with special biological "equipment" which, when triggered, results in language acquisition. For example, a number of studies have shown that very young infants have the ability to perceive relatively fine acoustic distinctions in speech sounds and to respond differently to speech and nonspeech sounds. The fact that they can do so at such a young age argues for an innate predisposition to language learning.

The similarity of the course of early language development in children both within a culture and from different languages and cultures argues for biological innateness. A number of researchers have studied the order in which children acquire the grammatical morphemes of English and have found remarkable consistency. Cazden (1968), Brown (1973), and deVilliers and deVilliers (1973), in their *morpheme acquisition (MAO)* studies established that English-speaking children acquire fourteen grammatical morphemes (ten inflections, two articles, and two prepositions) in a highly similar order. Although there are many studies of children's morphological development in other languages,[3] none is directly comparable with the MAO studies and thus we cannot yet confirm the finding from English. It does seem to be the case, however, that "morphology in all languages appears to be acquired in similar ways and at similar stages of development" (Tager-Flusberg, 1989, p. 149).

There also seems to be remarkable consistency in the order in which children acquire larger syntactic structures. There is evidence, for example, that children acquire *wh*-questions (those beginning with *what, where, who, when, how,* and *why*) in a particular order (Wootten et al., 1979; cited in Tager-Flusberg, 1989). Slobin (1982) observed that young children from a number of different language backgrounds used subject-object word order regardless of the order used by adult speakers of the same language. This ability might be attributed to some sort of innate predisposition toward language, a component of the LAD which "knows" or "expects" that grammatical classes exist.

On the other hand, it is likely that children produce subject-object structures in response to particular semantic relationships they find in their worlds. At the two- and three-word stage, most of the sentences that children produce have semantic agents as subjects. This fact gives children an advantage in working out more abstract syntactic relationships in

---

[3]For an extensive survey of studies of children's morphological development in languages other than English, see Slobin (1985). For a shorter description, see Ingram (1989, pp. 493–498).

more complex sentences (Tager-Flusberg, 1989, p. 143). The fact that children prefer subject-object order, then, does not necessarily argue for the existence of a language acquisition device; it may be evidence only for a generalized cognitive ability to figure things out, among them the fact that agents act on objects. It is fortuitous for English-speaking children that their language happens to express these relationships in the same syntactic order as they initially expressed them.

A final argument for linguistic nativism takes the form of evidence for a biological "critical period" during which language must be acquired if it is to be acquired fully. The notion of critical period comes from the study of behavior among goslings, rats, sparrows, and other nonhuman animals. Specifically, there seem to be certain periods during development during which a certain stimulus has to be present if young animals are to develop normal behavior. One case that is somewhat analogous to the human is that of the white-crowned sparrow. Reich (1986) relates Marler's (1970) observation that this bird learns its own song if and only if it hears the song during a critical period of its development. It does not acquire its song if raised in isolation nor does it acquire the song of other birds even if exposed during the critical period. Apparently, the fact that it does not acquire the songs of other birds cannot be attributed to its inability to produce other songs since it can acquire any of a number of different dialects present among members of the species. Marler argues that these birds appear to be born with a "template" that rejects all but their own song, an argument seemingly analogous to Chomsky's case for humans (Marler, 1977; cited in Reich, 1986, p. 291).

The case for a critical period related to language was first made by Wilder Penfield (Penfield & Roberts, 1959) who based his argument on observations that brain-damaged children have better recovery potential than adults with similar damage. The argument for a critical period was further advanced by Eric Lenneberg (1967) who asserted that all that is required for a child to acquire language between the ages of two and puberty is adequate exposure to language. He also relied on the experiences of brain-damaged children and adults, arguing that if adults experienced injury to the left hemisphere, believed to be the dominant hemisphere for language processing, and failed to recover within a few months, they would never recover fully. Children, on the other hand, were capable of a complete recovery of language functions if the left hemisphere damage occurred when they were very young. Based largely on Basser's (1962) survey of the literature on hemispherectomies, Lenneberg went on to conclude that children experienced no speech disorders following surgery (except where aphasia had occurred before the operation) while adults experienced a variety of language disorders and were unable to recover language function fully.

Later, Krashen (1973) reexamined Basser's data and found that all the children who had their left hemispheres removed were under five years of age at the time of the operation. This fact suggested that if Lenneberg and Penfield were right about a critical period, that it must occur before the age of five and not nine, as Penfield suggested, or thirteen, as Lenneberg suggested. Yet it is the case that a great deal of language learning occurs after age five (and, indeed, some occurs after age thirteen), and so it would seem that a critical period for language acquisition might be critical only for the "triggering" of language acquisition. That is, a weakened version of the critical period hypothesis would claim that if language acquisition is to occur it must begin during a critical period.

But what if it does not? The case of Genie suggests that language learning *can* occur even when it is begun much later than the age of five. In Los Angeles in 1970, a girl of 13 years, 9 months, was discovered after having been kept in physical and social isolation from the age of 20 months. Genie had been kept in a small, closed room where she was physically punished for making any noise and was never spoken to. Her father and brother sometimes made barking noises at her, and her mother was forbidden all but minimal contact at feeding time. There was neither radio nor television in the house. Not surprisingly, Genie's condition was such when she was found that she required hospitalization and she remained in the hospital for almost a year until she was placed with a foster family.

Medical examinations conducted during that time found no evidence of neurological disease or brain damage although functionally the girl was severely retarded (McLaughlin, 1984, p. 51). She seemed to be healthy apart from suffering the devastating effects of complete social isolation. Having been denied exposure to language from the age of 20 months, Genie seemed to be an ideal test case for the critical period hypothesis. Needless to say, linguists were very interested in Genie and her language development has been carefully charted. While she has acquired a great deal of proficiency in English, analysis of her development has revealed a number of abnormalities. The gap between her ability to produce and comprehend speech was found to be wider than normal, she had difficulty in acquiring certain syntactic skills, and her overall rate of development was abnormally slow (Curtiss, 1977). If Genie had acquired no language, her case would have provided very strong evidence for Lenneberg's version of the critical period hypothesis. But despite the fact that she had a difficult time of it, she did acquire a great deal of language, particularly vocabulary, and she did so after the age of puberty. It would seem, then, that her accomplishment offers no clear evidence either for or against the critical period hypothesis.

Genie is not the only child to grow up in social isolation. Crystal lists 48 such children either reared in the wild by animals or in isolation from human contact. Most of the reports of these children are sparse and only a few contain any information about the children's language ability. According to Crystal, what information exists is clear: "none could speak at all, and most had no comprehension of speech. Most attempts to teach them to speak failed" (Crystal, 1987, p. 289). The difficulty in considering these children as evidence in favor of a critical period is the confounding factor of profound social deprivation. In other words, in accounting for these children's failure to acquire language, it is impossible to separate the effects of growing up isolated from normal human society from possible biological effects.

On the matter of a critical period for language acquisition, then, the jury is still out. The evidence is controversial and the conclusions tentative. It does seem that a first language is harder to learn after puberty than before, but since no one would be acquiring a first language at this age except in abnormal circumstances, the import of this fact is dubious. As we shall find later, however, a great deal of second language learning is accomplished by adults. It may be the case that language learning that occurs after puberty requires a different kind of cognitive activity than early language learning. It is impossible to tell, given our present state of knowledge, whether this difference is biologically or environmentally determined or both. The critical period question will undoubtedly remain an important one for researchers in neurology and linguistics for decades to come.

The Case Against Linguistic Nativism

Appealing as nativism might be in comparison to behaviorism, there are arguments against it. Here we will consider five:

1. Occam's Razor
2. Critical period
3. Transformational-generative grammar
4. Negative linguistic evidence
5. Environment.

Occam's Razor.   One argument against linguistically based acquisition theories, and one which lends some credence to behaviorism, is a philosophical one based on a principle of science known as Occam's Razor. Occam was a twelfth century philosopher who articulated what is essentially a simplicity criterion for evaluating theories. Specifically, the principle was that entities should not be multiplied beyond necessity. Applied to language acquisition theories, the principle would lead us to select a general learning theory over a language-specific learning theory, that is, one which accorded language learning special status. It would, then, be "incumbent upon Chomsky and other advocates of special learning principles for language to argue that language is a special case" (Reich, 1986, p. 284). As Reich points out, advocates of this position often depend on this kind of philosophical argument and put little stock in research evidence, especially if it is not consistent with their views (Reich, 1985, p. 291).

Critical Period.   A second argument against nativism concerns the critical period. A cornerstone of linguistic theories of acquisition is the speed of acquisition argument, which assumes that because children learn so much complex language structure in such a short time, they must have a biological advantage. We have already seen, however, that the notion of a critical period for language acquisition remains highly controversial. Certainly there is no known neurological basis for such a claim.

Transformational-Generative Grammars.   A more damaging argument against linguistic theories has to do with the nature of the grammars written by Chomskyan linguists of the 1960s and 1970s. Transformational-generative (TG) grammar, which was considered revolutionary at the time, was the backbone of nativist theories. There is no doubt that TG grammars were impressive in their ability to account for the regularities and the variety of English sentences. But to do so, they were necessarily complex and abstract, consisting, for example, of abstract categories far removed from the surface forms and meanings of real sentences uttered by real speakers in real time (Bohannon & Warren-Leubecker, 1989, p. 197). Language acquisition researchers were troubled by the fact that such grammars were so far removed from the experience of the child acquiring language. If linguistic rules were to be psychologically real, that is, to represent somehow speakers' knowledge of their language, they argued, the rules had to be learnable. The further the formulation of the rule was from the reality of the sentence or what native speakers would perceive as the reality of the sentence, the harder it would be to explain how the child could come to know the rule. As Bohannon and Warren-Leubecker point out, the complexity and abstractness of grammars "becomes an especially damaging flaw in the traditional linguistic approach" as evidence mounts "that the major part of language acquisition involves semantic, not just syntactic, processes . . . " (Bohannon & Warren-Leubecker, 1989, p. 197).[4]

Negative Linguistic Evidence. Perhaps even more damaging to nativist theories than the complexity and abstractness of the grammars to be acquired is the issue of negative evidence. Central to the nativist approach is the belief that children are not generally provided with negative linguistic evidence and that when they are, they tend to ignore it. This being the case, they must have an innate mechanism by which to discover the rules. Otherwise, the "poverty of the stimulus" with regard to positive and negative information about structure would make it impossible for them to learn the rules of language. If, however, children received information about the acceptability of language structure, then the nativist's arguments about learnability would begin to crumble. In fact, a number of studies have suggested that children *do* receive such information.

While parents and other caregivers do not negatively reinforce, in the behaviorist sense, utterances that do not conform to adult structure, there is evidence that they react differently to poorly formed and well-formed utterances. Several studies have been reported that suggest parents do not ignore the grammatical errors of their young children. They may not correct the error overtly, but they repeat sentences with errors less frequently than they repeat well-formed ones (Hirsh-Pasek, Treiman, & Schneiderman, 1984). When they do repeat poorly formed sentences, they usually rephrase them. Parents are more likely to expand their children's ungrammatical sentences and to question children when their previous utterance contains a grammatical error than when it is error-free (Demetras, Post, & Snow, 1986; Penner, 1987). Moreover, Bohannon and Stanowicz (1988) report that "children are more likely to imitate expansions and recasts than any other utterances" (cited in Bohannon & Warren-Leubecker, 1989, p. 198).

It would seem, then, that adults do provide negative information about language structure and that children respond to it. While a great deal more research must be done before we can speak with any clarity on the role of negative information in language acquisition, it certainly cannot be ruled out as a contributing factor. This being the case, one of the foundations of linguistic theories of acquisition is weakened.

[4]For a concise yet thorough discussion of this issue, see the chapter by Bohannon and Warren-Leubecker in Gleason (1989). For an in-depth treatment, see Derwing (1973) and Pinker (1984).

Environment. A final argument in the case against nativism concerns environment. For fairly obvious reasons, nativists have never considered environment, beyond some very basic level of exposure to human interaction, to play a central role in language acquisition. Yet teachers know that environment plays a major role in children's language development during the school years. Later, we will meet a child, Michael, who was not brought up in social isolation but whose language exposure was so limited that he had not at age five acquired very much language. Other research tells us that children whose only exposure to language is television acquire little speech (Bohannon & Warren-Leubecker, 1989, p. 199).

COGNITIVE THEORIES

Cognitive theories of language consider language acquisition as part of children's more general cognitive development. Many kinds of cognitive theory exist, but two are of particular interest to understanding language acquisition. The first includes theories that postulate stages of cognitive development which have parallels in linguistic achievement. The second are based on information processing theory and postulate no particular innate mechanism. In the following pages, we will look at Piaget's theory of cognitive development and, very briefly, at the theories of Luria and Bruner.

Piaget's Cognitive Theory

Piaget's is not a theory of language acquisition but a theory of cognition, which holds that language is an aspect of general cognitive development. It shares certain beliefs with both behaviorism and nativism but differs fundamentally from both. Piagetian theory shares with behaviorism the view that language learning is accomplished in much the same way as all human learning, but the two differ dramatically on how that learning is accomplished. Here Piagetian theory resembles nativism because it relies on the notion of innate structures that function globally in the development of thought. The difference between Chomskyan nativism and Piagetian nativism is obvious: Chomsky postulates an innate device dedicated to language learning, while Piaget believes in an interdependence of language and cognition, that language development has its foundation in the more fundamental development in cognition.

Piaget, however, does not view language as central to cognitive development but rather "as an outside agent." As the child "comes to understand language, he has to assimilate and then accommodate the lingual signs to his thought structures, but if he is to find his own meaning, the symbolic structuring must come first and not be confused by adult language structures" (Smith, Goodman, & Meredith, 1976, p. 133). In other words, according to Piaget, conceptualization precedes language. This is not to say that language does not play an important role in development. Language is a key element in children's social interaction with adults and other children, and this interaction is crucial in order for children to move away from the egocentric point of view.

Support for the Piagetian view of language development would consist of evidence showing links between cognitive development and language structures. Crystal uses the example of the comparative. Before children can express a sentence such as "This car is bigger than that," they must first have the conceptual ability to judge the relative sizes of two objects (Crystal, 1987, p. 234). There is research evidence to support the view that early language correlates with certain kinds of conceptual development. For example, a concept that children acquire early, during the sensori-motor stage, is object permanence. At about the same time, they also acquire the "disappearance" words such as "allgone" (Bohannon & Warren-Leubecker, 1989, p. 200). On the other hand, it would seem that the concept of object permanence should be in place before the emergence of the first words that frequently label those objects, but this does not seem to be the case.[5] What does seem to be the case is that the first words appear once children understand that other people may act as agents for actions (Bates, 1976).

Researchers have also demonstrated correlations between later linguistic and nonlinguistic development. One of the issues they addressed is the relationship between certain inflectional morphemes and the concepts they express, for example, plurality or past time. Children would be highly unlikely to acquire and use the past tense form, for example, before they had acquired the basic concept of object permanence—past tense is used largely to talk about things that are not currently in the immediate environment. And they do not do so, according to work done by Slobin (1979) and by Block and Kessel (1980). Following this reasoning, it is not surprising that children generally acquire the plural and the progressive marker, *-ing*, before morphemes such as the past tense marker or the third person singular marker. These are attached to nouns and verbs; objects and their movements are highly significant in young children's lives, and particularly to their achievement of the concept of object permanence.

[5]For details, see Bates, Benigni, Bretherton, Camaioni, & Volterra (1979), Corrigan (1978), and Bates & Snyder (1985).

Language acquisition, then, as seen from the Piagetian perspective, is not distinct from other human cognitive activity but runs a parallel course with and at the same time depends on maturation of the child's cognitive system.

Luria and Bruner

Of course, other cognitively based views of language acquisition exist that, like Piaget's, are particularly concerned with developmental sequences, or stages. Among them are Luria's (Luria & Yudovich, 1971) and Bruner's (1983, 1984, 1986). The principal difference between Luria and Piaget is fundamental:

> Piaget believes that language, while not completely peripheral to cognitive development, is secondary in importance to 'learning through operations.' Luria, on the other hand, is saying that development in thinking is achieved through the use of language to structure and control behavior. (Stringer, Bruce, & Oates, 1973, p. 93)

Bruner has taken neither view but has offered something of a compromise by suggesting "that in the course of evolution, man has developed three important skills of representation: enactive, iconic and symbolic" (Stringer, Bruce, and Oates, 1973, p. 93). Enactive representation is the representation of behavior in motor terms, for example, the ability to roller skate. Iconic representation is representation through images, for example, the use of a mental picture to guide our activity, and symbolic representation occurs when images become symbols. According to Bruner, these are cognitive tools that develop successively but also overlap to some degree. Moreover, individuals may vary in their use of these tools, depending on a variety of factors including their age, education, and cultural environment.

Information Processing

Not all cognitive theories of language acquisition are stage based. Another approach, which is gaining widespread credibility, especially among psychologists, is the information processing approach. Psychologists and psycholinguists use the term **information processing** to refer to the processes humans use to identify and understand meanings in spoken and written communication as well as the processes by which they store, organize, and retrieve those meanings (Richards, Platt, & Weber, 1985, p. 140). Although interest in this area has traditionally been directed toward understanding the processes involved in comprehension of both written and spoken meaning, the paradigm has recently gained favor as one for investigating and understanding language acquisition. The connection between the comprehension strategies of mature speakers and the acquisition strategies of infants may not be immediately obvious. Certainly making such connections requires that we view children as being similar to adults in important ways. Whether or not they are, a growing number of researchers are trying to understand language learning by beginning with a model of the adult language user's system and then working backward to discover how it might have been created (Gleitman & Wanner, 1982).

Information processing models of language acquisition are highly technical and beyond the scope of this chapter. Briefly, however, they are based on the principles of parallel distributed processing (PDP) and presuppose no innate structures other than a "processor" or learning mechanism. PDP refers to the brain's ability to process a multitude of stimuli simultaneously rather than sequentially but the processing is not mere stimulus-response association. One model of information processing, the competition model (Bates & MacWhinney, 1987), assumes that a number of language forms may compete as stimuli to represent a particular meaning. For instance, both *went* and *goed* would be possible representatives of the meaning of the verb *go* in the past tense. Children eventually learn *went* because they hear it more frequently; it matches the adult form. Children thus learn the language they hear. The correct forms are the ones they hear most often and thus "win" in the competition between adult and immature forms. This model of acquisition requires the child to have no innate mechanism in order to learn to process language.

At the time of writing, insufficient research on language acquisition from the information processing perspective has been performed to evaluate this assumption and, indeed, the theory itself. It would seem, however, that the strength of this theory lies partly in the strong bond it postulates between children's cognitive development and the language environment in which they learn. It differs from nativist linguistic and Piagetian cognitive theories in that it assumes no innate mechanisms but shares with the latter the assumption that language learning is part of more general cognitive development. The difficulty with this theory is its assumption that children are qualitatively similar to adults when it comes to language processing.

The Case Against Cognitive Theories

Cognitive theories are appealing for a number of reasons. One reason is that because they do not postulate a unique status for language acquisition within cognitive development, neither do they violate the simplicity criterion known as Occam's Razor, as described earlier in this chapter. They also appeal to teachers who have observed strong correlations between children's language development and other cognitive and academic growth.

Unfortunately, it is this notion of correlation that identifies a central piece of evidence in the case against Piaget. To be more precise, establishing a correlation between any particular language behavior and an aspect of nonlinguistic development does not mean that either caused or even contributed to the other. Necessarily a number of developmental milestones occur at about the same time as others. The loss of baby teeth, for example, is predictable but probably not related to concurrent language behavior (with the possible exception of trouble with sibilants). On the other hand, if researchers were able to isolate particular cognitive accomplishments that *always* preceded particular language achievements and, further, that the language behavior failed to appear *unless* the nonlinguistic behavior appeared first, then they would be able to make a better case for a cognitive acquisition theory. So far, they have been unable to do so. Additional damage to cognitive language theory comes from the work of researchers who have found that children with Turner's syndrome score poorly on tests of cognitive ability yet appear to have normal language ability (Curtiss, 1977, 1981; Curtiss & Yamada, 1978; Curtiss, Yamada, & Fromkin, 1979). If it is the case that cognitive and language skills are indeed separable, then the cognitive language theorists will have to reconsider their position on their interdependence. To be fair, however, we cannot dismiss cognitive language theory so easily because "the broad assertion that cognitive development determines language development remains virtually untested at this time" (Bohannon & Warren-Leubecker, 1989, p. 202).

SOCIAL INTERACTION THEORY

What Social Interactionists Believe

Social interaction theory shares certain beliefs with behaviorist, nativist, and cognitive theories. With behaviorism, it shares the notion that environment plays a central role in the growth of language. With nativism, it shares the view that language behavior and, thus, learning are unique from other behavior and learning. With cognitive theories, it agrees that language learning is a complex accomplishment involving the child's active cognitive participation. Social interaction theory assumes that a child's acquisition of language is influenced by the interaction of a number of factors that are physical, linguistic, and social in nature. Because children differ in physical and cognitive abilities as well as in the social environment in which they live, this interaction may produce different effects in different children.

A great many researchers advocate the role of the environment in language acquisition. One of them was Vygotsky, a Soviet psychologist who died in 1934. While his work might rightly be considered above in the section on cognitive theories of language acquisition, I have placed it in this section because of the emphasis he placed on the role played by interaction with the environment, and particularly with older children and adults:

> Language is a major stimulant for conceptual growth, and conceptual growth is also dependent on interaction with objects in the environment. Moreover, adults (and older children) have a role in stimulating language growth through a variety of means. (Pflaum, 1986, p. 11)

This stimulation, he believed, should occur within the **zone of proximal development,** which Vygotsky defined as the distance between a child's actual level of development and the level at which she could function with adult assistance. This emphasis on the role of the adult, whether parent, teacher, or friend, in the child's conceptual and linguistic development sets Vygotsky apart from Piaget and puts him in line with current theorists who emphasize the mother's (or other caregiver's) contribution to the child's language learning.

In the past two decades, interest has grown in the part this input plays in the child's linguistic accomplishments, and one of the central findings has been that mothers' talk to their children is by no means as impoverished as nativist linguistic theory assumed it to be. Despite the fact that some parents talk to their children differently from the way they talk to other adults, research has shown that the adaptations they make facilitate rather than hinder language learning. Even baby talk, that unusual vocal behavior that characterizes some adult's speech with infants, seems to help. Field and colleagues (1982) hypothesize that children learn to control their vocal apparatus by watching their mothers making the exaggerated speech sounds of baby talk. Other researchers postulate that the talk and play that occurs between parents and young children forms the basis for later patterns of taking turns in conversations (Stern, Beebe, Jaffe, and Bennet, 1977).

The question of primary interest in language acquisition theory is how children acquire the ability to express their intentions or meanings in language. Interactionists believe that they do so through a process of negotiation with their mothers or principal caregivers. This negotiation occurs partly as a result of mothers treating children's speech, even if it is babbling, as meaningful and intentional. Gradually, as mothers persist in trying to make sense of children's speech, they also begin to negotiate meaning and intent with their children. It is easy to demonstrate how such negotiation takes place. For example, Christopher, age 11 months, is sitting on the living room floor, barefoot, playing with his older brother Kerry (2;0)[6] and their mother.

Chris: Want du!
Mum: You want your shoes?
Chris: (He looks puzzled.) Du. Du.
Mum: (She looks around for something else he might be asking for and holds up a stuffed bear.) You want Gurgles?
Chris: No. Want du.
Mum: (To her other son.) Do you know what Chris wants?
Kerry: He want this. (He holds up the wooden car he is playing with.)
Chris: (Showing no interest in the car.) Du peez. (At this point, he gets up and starts toward the kitchen.)
Mum: Oh, you want juice!
Chris: Yeah. Du.

Here, Chris's mother does not give up easily on understanding him. There is evidence that mothers of even younger children behave in a similar manner and may, in fact, "teach" the child language in what Golinkoff (1983) has called "conversational bouts." Certainly they actively teach children the social routines of greetings, leave-takings, and politeness. Whether they engage in any other active teaching and whether it does anything to facilitate language acquisition are questions yet to be answered, although we do know how little effect the teaching of structure usually has.

Halliday (1975) saw language acquisition as being heavily reliant on communicative interaction. Taking a functional view, he believed that the

---

[6]This is a convention used by linguists in reporting children's ages in years and months. Thus, 2;0 is two years exactly and 3;2 is three years two months.

language structures necessary for realizing the various language functions are learned, along with the functions themselves, through learning to communicate. Obviously, the child does not do this alone.

It seems, however, that environment may play a different kind of role in children's learning of grammar. Specifically, if we assume that children figure out which forms are grammatical from being consistently exposed to correct forms, then the language that children hear plays a significant role in the acquisition process. Parents play an important role in matching the language input to the appropriate level of cognitive and language development of their children. Speech to the very young is much simpler than it is to older children. For example, sentences spoken to young children are shorter and not as varied in structure as those presented to older children. It is probably not the case that adults consciously make such adjustments to their speech; what is more likely is that in their attempts to communicate with children, they unconsciously match their language to the appropriate cognitive and linguistic level for the child.

There is another way in which parents or other caregivers probably contribute to children's language acquisition, and that is by talking with them about and focusing their attention on things that are in the immediate environment. One of the central tasks in learning language is to match language with meaning, a task that parents may facilitate by focusing their talk on whatever is holding the child's attention. If the child is chasing the family cat, the cat is what they all talk about. The child thus comes to understand what the word *cat* means.

It may also be the case, as Bohannon and Warren-Leubecker (1989, p. 190) point out, that the same process may lead children to notice the difference between their own expressions and the more mature ones of the older speakers around them. We saw earlier that parents are more likely to expand and extend their children's imperfectly formed utterances. When an expanded, correct utterance immediately follows an immature one, children may just notice the difference and, gradually, make changes to approximate the adult form more closely. It may be, then, that imitation *does* play a role in language acquisition, but social interactionists would see this role as qualitatively different and as less central to overall language development than would behaviorists.

One of the interesting and compelling aspects of social interaction approaches is that they come down on neither side of the nature/nurture controversy. On the one hand, social interactionists admit to the likelihood that children possess an innate predisposition to learn language. On the other, they believe that while environment alone cannot account for the acquisition process, it serves as more than a trigger for acquisition. It serves, instead, to provide a rich source of data from which children form and test hypotheses about language structures. The relationship between language acquisition and social interaction is symbiotic: Social interaction provides essential experience with language and language affords children opportunities for expanding their social interactions.

The Case Against Social Interaction Theories

As intuitively reasonable as the social interaction approaches may seem, particularly to teachers, they are by no means widely accepted. There are several kinds of counter evidence, three of which are worth noting here:

1. Caretaker speech
2. How adjustments facilitate learning
3. Universality.

Caretaker Speech.   The first argument against social interaction challenges the role of caretaker speech. Some researchers claim that although caretaker speech may be simplified in comparison with speech to adults, it is by no means simple. In other words, the caretaker speech may be different and to some degree simpler, but it retains a great deal of linguistic complexity. Others point out that researchers have failed to show correlations between the simplified input language and the parallel forms that subsequently appear in the child's speech. Bohannon and Warren-Leubecker report studies (for example, Hoff-Ginsburg, 1986; Newport, 1976) showing "the complexity of maternal speech addressed to the children to be unrelated to the children's language gains" (1989, p. 207).

How Adjustments Facilitate Learning.   The second argument goes like this. Social interaction theory assumes that caretakers adjust their speech to provide input that is both comprehensible and useful to children in making and testing hypotheses about language structure. Even given that this is true (and as we noted, it is not by any means universally accepted that it is), it remains for theorists to specify just how such adaptations facilitate language acquisition. They have yet to do so.

Universality.   Perhaps the most persuasive counter argument concerns universality. As Susanna Pflaum (1986) has pointed out, if the dialogue between parent and child is the "critical mechanism" for language learning, then such dialogues would be found in the language learning of all children everywhere. A number of researchers have demonstrated that this is not the case. Heath (1983, 1986), Schieffelin and Ochs (1983), and others have described very different adult-child exchanges in different cultural groups. In one community studied by Heath, for example, it appears that baby talk does not exist and if children wish to participate in the talk of the group, they have to interrupt to do so. In Chipewyan communities, parents do not expect their children to speak until sometime around the age of five (Scollon and Scollon, 1981). Nevertheless, these children and children in all cultural groups learn language.

We must remember in considering the case against social interaction that because it is a relatively new theory, many of its explanations for acquisition phenomena have not been subjected to empirical verification. But this also means that the argument against social interaction theory is speculative as well.

WHAT THEORY HAS TO SAY ABOUT LANGUAGE LEARNING AND ENVIRONMENT

The different theories discussed in this chapter present different views on the contribution the child's environment makes to language acquisition. With the exception of the strict nativists, most agree that some kind of interaction is necessary, but disagree about the degree or kind of interaction that children need to acquire language. Research has not yet resolved the issue, and I would suggest three reasons why this is the case. The first, and most obvious, is that research is never neutral. The hypotheses with which investigators begin, the observations they make, and the methods they use are all biased by their theoretical perspectives. Research cannot be neutral. In a real sense, theory serves as the lens which we point and through which we see research data. It would be expected, then, that research findings would be somewhat contradictory.

The second reason is methodological. Our tools for evaluating social interaction and its impact on language acquisition still need refining. Because they have not been extensively used yet and because their use has been mostly confined to studies of children in the majority culture in North America, they are still relatively clumsy and largely untested.

The third reason is that we still have too few studies of interaction patterns in other languages and cultures—studies of the calibre of those conducted by Shirley Brice Heath, for example. Only when we understand how a variety of peoples interact with their children can we begin to understand how that interaction influences language acquisition.

Still, we must hold onto the fact that no research to date has suggested that interaction plays no role. Even Heath's finding, cited earlier that baby talk does not exist in some communities should not be taken to mean that *no* social interaction occurs. It means only that parent-child interaction as we know it in the dominant white culture does not exist in those particular communities, and yet the children learn language. It also suggests that we need to look further to try to understand social interaction patterns in other cultures before we can really assess the role they play in language acquisition.

CONCLUSION

In this chapter, we have traced the course of language development from infancy through the preschool and early school years. We have seen how children grow from infants with amazing powers of linguistic perception but little productive ability, to school-aged children capable of producing complex sentences and sophisticated meanings. We have also examined several different theories of how they did so. None of these theories stands alone either in the position it takes—we have seen how certain beliefs are shared by different theories—nor in its ability to "tell" us how children acquire language—we have seen that there are cases to be made against each one. Indeed, if anyone could tell us with any certainty how children do accomplish what they do in language learning, we would not need this lengthy description of theory because we would have entered into the realm of fact.

Teachers and students of language are sometimes uncomfortable with theory; because they have to deal with the reality of applying theory, they prefer hard truths. Unfortunately, the hard truth is hard to come by in this field, and so for the time being we must settle for something less. Yet, we are not working entirely in the dark. We have the benefit of an abundance of quality data about children learning language and we have the privilege and the ability to consider those data and the theories they either support or refute within our own observations and experiences as teachers of young children.

My own bias, based on my experience as a teacher, linguist, and researcher, is toward the social interactive view of language, and this despite the fact that, as one of our newer theories, it is probably the least tested. Nevertheless, its assumptions and explanations are consistent with the most effective elementary school teaching, and unless it is rejected or drastically modified, it is a theory through which we can usefully view children's language growth in the school years.

Necessary as it is, theory is not sufficient for understanding language acquisition. We cannot hope to understand the phenomenon of language without witnessing children in the process of acquiring it. In the next chapter, we have the opportunity to put flesh on the skeleton of theory as we witness Janet's language development. We will see firsthand that environment plays a significant role in her language learning and in her early literacy development.

Chapter Four

Janet and Millions of Others: The Course of Monolingual Development

Language development takes a lifetime, but by the time they are school-aged, most children are already fledgling members of their language community. Since language learning neither begins nor ends with the school years, it is important that we take a global view of the path it takes from infancy onward. We do so in this chapter by tracking the language growth of a child named Janet. We meet her at birth and trace the growth of her language through her infancy and preschool years, and her school years right into her teens.

Janet's story is in most ways a typical one of monolingual development, and I use it as a framework in which to describe the course of normal language acquisition. The organization of this chapter is for the most part chronological. Each section covers a particular period of time—usually six months to one year, and is introduced by a general overview of the course of language development during that time. This broad sketch is followed by a description of Janet and her language learning during the same period. This, in turn, is followed by a more detailed description and discussion of the course of language acquisition in most children of the same age.

INFANCY

At one time language acquisition was thought to begin when the infant uttered her first words. The question "Is she talking yet?" or "Has she learned to talk?" could be answered affirmatively only if that momentous first word had been heard. In recent years, however, we have come to realize that the first years of a baby's life are not idle ones by any means. Much of the infant's behavior during this period makes the acquisition of language possible. It is a period during which we observe behavior that might be considered precursory to true language development.

The Precursors to Language

Children before the age of approximately one year are not yet able to produce language as we traditionally think of it—as words or utterances with intentional meaning. They do, however, demonstrate a great deal of sensitivity to and awareness of language. We see behavior in that first year that is obviously foundational to later language growth. This is not true linguistic behavior but "precursory" behavior. Paradoxically, it differs in kind from true language yet is probably essential for the growth of true language.

There are two important differences between precursory linguistic behavior and true language. Although children during their first year perceive and produce sounds, learn about events, objects, and relationships and interact with others in their environments, they do not use the conventions of language in doing so. For example, infant behavior seems to be related to observable events, while in the second year the "conventional mapping relation" that occurs "is not directly observable" even though it uses observable events (Bloom & Lahey, 1978, p. 71).

The second crucial difference between the first and second year of life has to do with intent. Before the age of approximately one year, the infant "reflects feelings and states more that it intends a representation of affect and changes in affect." In the second year, in contrast, the child begins to communicate intentionally (Bloom & Lahey, 1978, p. 71). We refer, therefore, to Janet's language learning in the first year as precursory, not to underestimate its importance, for it was vital, but to emphasize the difference between this and later learning.

Janet As an Infant

From the time Janet was born in Dover, New Hampshire, in January 1972, I have documented her language acquisition fairly regularly. Most of the observations that follow are based on notes and transcripts of my own interaction with her and on her mother's diaries, kept in detail until Janet was seven years old and sporadically until she was fourteen.

Janet's only sibling, her brother Matthew, was 21 months old when she was born. Their father was a research physicist and their mother a lecturer in the English department at a nearby university. Janet arrived three weeks before her expected date of arrival, on her mother's twenty-sixth birthday. She weighed exactly six pounds, and her mother's diary entries during her first six months tell of a fairly untroubled infant. Janet cried when hungry, and seemed to be hungry every four hours around the clock, but otherwise slept well. She was alert and a real "charmer" with big blue eyes and a winning smile. She was a responsive child, particularly to her mother and to the antics of her older brother. The family spoke only English and that was the only language Janet was exposed to until the age of 18 months when she had an occasional Spanish-speaking babysitter.

When she was only a few weeks old, Janet seemed to respond to her mother's voice. Her mother's diary notes that Janet would usually stop crying when her mother made soothing noises. By two months, Janet would stop gurgling or crying and appear to be listening when her brother was in the room and talking.

Janet demonstrated the abilities that all normal babies have in her responses to her mother's voice. At only a few days old, most infants respond to human voices, and by the time they are two to four months old, they respond to different tones of voice. Research has shown, too, that babies as young as one month are able not only to discriminate between speech and nonspeech sounds but to discriminate between speech sounds as similar as /p/ and /b/ (Eimas, Siqueland, Jusczyk, & Vigorito, 1971). This early perceptual sensitivity to the sounds of language makes it possible for them to learn the relevant phonological distinctions needed to understand and to form intentional utterances as they get older.

But it is not at all clear just how this early perceptual ability is related to their later learning, since children appear to lose their ability to make certain discriminations. Research has shown, for example, that while infants of one to four months are able to distinguish between voiced and voiceless pairs of consonants (for example, [p] and [b]), two-year-old children find it one of the most difficult distinctions to make in discrimination experiments (Shvachkin, 1973; Garnica, 1973; Graham & House, 1971).

At about the same time as they are manifesting these perceptual abilities, infants begin to vocalize. This was the case with Janet. During the first two months, most of the sounds she produced were cries, but she did sometimes gurgle and seem to "coo" or "shriek" with delight when something pleased her. From the time she was about six weeks old until the age of three months, her cooing and shrieking behavior increased. Her mother also noted that Janet's cries became differentiated during this period, that is, her cry when she was wet or hungry differed from the late afternoon "fussy" cry, which her mother attributed to fatigue or frustration.

We know from numerous studies that the vocalizations of infants younger than six months or so are likely to be cooing sounds. In fact, spectrographic analysis has shown them to be quite unlike human speech sounds (Titone & Danesi, 1985, pp. 64–65). Nevertheless, cooing plays an important role in later development of speech by serving as a rehearsal of the tongue movements that are necessary for the production of speech.

Even Janet's crying behavior provides important insight into her language development. If her mother was right about the different cries she produced, then we have evidence of precursory language use—purposefully using language for different functions. Just as the older child may use a single word, with variations in intonation, to serve a variety of needs, so apparently did the infant Janet use her cries. The difference, of course, is in intent. The older child clearly intends to signal different meanings, but there is no evidence to suggest such intent on the part of the infant.

One of the more interesting questions about Janet's language acquisition at this age, and one that arose in the previous chapter, is the role played by those around her. Specifically, what effect did Janet's mother[1] and her younger brother have on her early phonological development? This is never an easy question to answer. Her mother's diary and my own research notes from Janet's first year mention a number of occasions on which Janet was heard to imitate her brother. He would make a request, for example, and Janet would "sing" the intonation pattern of his utterance. Later, when she began to produce words, she would often mimic a single word from one of Matthew's utterances. In one instance, he said, "Want to watch Big Bird," and Janet promptly piped up "Buh" (bird).

Babbling

At around five months, Janet began to babble. At first, her babbling sounded to the adults around her like random noises, some of them English-like, but others quite foreign. She seemed particularly fond of glottal sounds during the first month or so, and she combined them most imaginatively. By the time she was six months old, she was producing a

[1]Throughout this chapter, I refer repeatedly to the interaction between Janet and her mother and only rarely mention her father. In doing so, I do not intend to imply that her father was not influential to her language development, for clearly he was. It's just that because Janet's mother was the diarist and principal caregiver, more of her interactions with Janet were recorded.

great many labial sounds, particularly /b/ and /m/ in utterances such as *babababa* or *mumumum*. Gradually, both the rhythms and the speech sounds she produced became more "English-like." This similarity between the sounds the infant makes in babbling and the sounds of the language around her appears to be universal babbling behavior.

During these early months, children may be highly inventive in their production and combination of speech sounds, and they seem to be busily learning the intonation of their language as well as training their articulators for producing the individual segments.

What, then, did Janet's babbling contribute to her learning of the system of her language? Ingram (1976) would say that she had completed the first of six stages of development that run parallel to cognitive stages of development, as described by Piaget (1962). Ingram views phonological development not as beginning with the first word and ending at around age six, as many linguists have traditionally done, but as beginning at birth, and ending at around age 16—extending, in other words, most of the way through the school years.

The first stage is what we have seen thus far in Janet—producing the various sounds of her language (and many others besides) and imitating the intonation contour of the language around her. She was also making a great many unobservable perceptual distinctions. As she became more practiced at babbling, her phonology also improved. There is also evidence that her babbling became differentiated at around eight months. Janet's mother notes in her diary that Janet sometimes seemed to be singing and just playing with sounds. This behavior occurred when she was lying in her crib, either at nap time or on waking in the morning. At other times, especially when she was sitting on the floor playing with her toys, Janet's stress and intonation would sound more "purposeful, almost as if she were giving orders sometimes" (Diaries). Apparently such behavior is not uncommon.

Menn (1976, 1989) has pointed out that such behavior is common in the later stages of babbling when children typically demonstrate two different types. In the first, *sound play*, children appear to be vocalizing for its own sake, presumably for the sheer pleasure of making and listening to the sounds. There seems to be little connection between the sounds they produce in sound play and intentional communication. In *conversational babble*, on the other hand, children really sound like they are talking even though the listener would be hard pressed to identify any of the words. As they engage in conversational babble, children use eye contact, gestures, and the intonation contours of normal speech—all the elements of conversation except meaningful words. "Conversational babble can clearly convey requests for aid, rejection of food or toys, desire to direct attention to ongoing events" (Menn, 1976; cited in Menn, 1989, p. 73). Even in this early stage of development, then, we find not only the precursors to language structure but also the foreshadowing of meaningful language used for different purposes.

In discussing precursory language behavior, we have focused on the infant's awareness of the sound system. Obviously in babies who do not yet produce words, or who produce only a few single-word utterances, it is difficult to speculate about their awareness of syntax. Many researchers believe, however, that infants do exhibit precursory syntactic awareness. Bloom (1973) reports observing a 16-month-old child early in the two-word stage of speech. This child used an interpretable word, /widə/, in combination with other common words in the child's vocabulary. The unusual word always occurred in the second position, and it only occurred with certain of the child's words such *Mama, dada, more,* and *no,* but not with other frequently used words. The child's utterances also indicated her awareness of the stress patterns in English. Bloom interpreted the child's behavior as evidence "that she had learned something about word order—with /widə/, which was consistently in second position, and with the few words that appeared with /widə/, which were always in first position" (Bloom, 1973; cited in Bloom & Lahey, 1978, p. 91).

The child Bloom observed, however, was 16 months old and arguably past the precursory period and into the stage of true language development. Evidence for syntactic awareness in children of around one year or younger is sketchy, but several researchers have made the claim that infants use intonational changes to signal the differences in meaning that will later be signalled by word order. Von Raffler Engel (1973) claimed, for example, "that her son used humming with 'sentence intonation' before he used words, using rising pitch for requests" (cited in Sachs, 1989, p. 45). Nakazina (1962) reported that infants of eight months imitated adult pitch contours, an observation that is consistent with those made by Janet's mother (above). Nevertheless, it is difficult to claim with any degree of certainty that such behavior is evidence of early syntactic awareness. It does, however, indicate a strong sensitivity to *language,* and whether it is sensitivity to phonology or syntax seems hardly to matter.

Before her first birthday, Janet had begun to show signs of moving from precursory language to true language acquisition. As mentioned earlier, the two main differences between precursory and later language acquisition have to do with the use of conventions and intent. Researchers have identified a number of behaviors that they believe indicate communicative intent. They include the increased use of eye contact during gesturing or vocalizing, the emergence of consistent sound patterns in vocalizations, appearing to wait for a response after vocalizing or gesturing, and persisting in attempts to communicate (Bates, 1979; Bruner, 1973; Harding & Golinkoff, 1979; Scoville, 1983; all cited in Sachs, 1989, p. 47).

Janet exhibited some of these characteristics. A month before her first birthday, she was sitting on her mother's lap while her mother read to her. They had just finished reading *Cat in the Hat* and her mother started to put the book down. "No," insisted Janet, trying to retrieve the book. When she failed, she looked directly into her mother's eyes and said again: "No!" In this simple exchange is evidence that Janet was becoming as a true language user—she knew what she wanted and she communicated it effectively.

Transition: First Words

By the time Janet was eight months old, she was producing long strings of babbling, with intonation patterns that sounded very much like English conversation. When she began to produce her first words, a few days before her first birthday, she produced them not as part of her stream of babble but independently. That is, she continued to babble, particularly at night or nap time when she was alone in her crib, but she also began to produce the occasional word in isolation.

After the "No!" which Janet produced in the example above, and which she used a great deal for the next two years, the first word that Janet's mother believed to be intentional was *weo*. Janet was sitting on the floor watching her older brother play with his cars and trucks. He rolled a large yellow dump truck toward her and Janet giggled and shouted *Weo! Weo*, or 'wheel,' which was also her brother's word for wheels, cars, or anything with wheels. She also encountered the word in the title of a favorite book, *Bears on Wheels*. A single word but it marked the beginning of a period of rapid and very impressive language learning.

THE PRESCHOOL YEARS

Sometime after their first birthday, most children begin to combine their growing inventory of single words into two-word utterances. This is the point at which most people think language learning truly begins. While we have seen that this is not the case, it is certainly true that the rate at which children learn language is quite impressive from this point onward. By the time they begin school, most children are producing well-formed, simple and complex sentences expressing a variety of meanings and fulfilling a number of communicative functions.

Overview of Development

As children grow from infants to school-age, their worlds expand to include people other than family and frequent visitors and places other than their own homes. Their linguistic and communicative needs grow as well. This is the period in which children acquire near-adult phonology and the complex rules that permit them to express the meanings they want to express in the increasingly varied situations in which they find themselves. They go from babies who point and produce a single, sometimes unintelligible "word" to children able to produce sentences such as "Shelly no gots bear like mine to play with" (Janet 5;2). While not quite perfectly formed, the sentence clearly and correctly expresses a number of propositions. More importantly, it is not grounded in the "here and now." Neither her friend Shelly nor the bear was present; Janet was simply reporting to her mother about her visit to her friend's house.

The preschool years encompass a wide spectrum of language development. Because children vary so greatly in the ages at which they achieve certain linguistic milestones, researchers commonly describe stages of language development independent of age. A common way of doing so is by mean length of utterance (MLU), or the average number of morphemes a child produces in an utterance. This is the approach taken by Brown (1973) and by a number of researchers, and certainly it makes comparison easier among children.[2] One of the children in Brown's study (1973, p. 55), for example, reached an MLU of 2.8 at 22 months while another reached it at 35 months. It was thus easier and more useful to discuss language development in terms of MLU rather than age. During the preschool years, then, Brown identified five stages of language development, from an MLU of 1.75 to an MLU of 4.0.

Other researchers, however, break down the preschool years differently. Ingram (1976) identifies three distinct subperiods of development that occur during the preschool years. The first corresponds with the latter part of the period, which Piaget calls the *sensori-motor* period. Linguistically, the child enters the period of one-word utterances and acquires a vocabulary of approximately 50 words. The second subperiod, lasting from approximately 1;6 to 4;6, he calls the period of *preconceptual thought*. This marks children's earliest symbolic behavior and results in their "pretend play"—an alphabet block becomes a table, a house, or even a car, for example. Language at this point is grounded in the here and now of the immediate environment but it is a period of rapid growth

---

[2]Because I am describing the development of only one child, I will use the convention of reporting age rather than MLU.

"during which the child progresses from putting two words together to the point around 3;6 to 4;0 when most simple sentences are well formed by adult standards" (Ingram, 1976, p. 13). This is also an important period for phonological growth for it is during this time of expanding vocabulary that children face the first real need for a phonological system.

The third subperiod begins at around age four and continues to age six or seven. This is the period during which children begin to come to grips with reality and "to abandon the dominant use of symbolic play. Rather than modify reality through play, the child begins to use play to express reality" (Ingram, 1976, p. 13). Children begin to enter into social games during this period although they may still not understand that there are arbitrary conventions that govern these games. Any parent who has tried to explain the rules of taking turns in tag to a five-year-old who doesn't want to be "it" will understand very well the limitations on the child's ability to comprehend abstract rules.

In language, more complex sentence structures appear during this period. Verb complements ("Gurgles thinks that's silly!") appear along with a few relative clause structures ("Shelly want the doll that's mine!"), but the chief way of combining propositions is conjunction. Thus, conjoined sentences such as "Shelly want the bear and she took it home and I want it back" account for most of the longer sentences children produce during this period. In the pages that follow, I have assumed Ingram's divisions and terminology, but for the sake of clarity, I have presented the time periods in shorter segments.

Janet from 1;0 to 1;6

Within a few weeks of uttering her first word, *weo,* Janet added to her vocabulary *baba* ('bottle'), *mumum* ('mummy'), *gaga* ('Gurgles', the name of her stuffed bear), and *du* ('juice'). Interestingly, with the exception of *weo* and *du,* these words were of the reduplicated form common in the babbling of children between six months and one year of age.

First words have long interested researchers, who have recorded and categorized them in a number of languages. Although there is variation between cultures and, indeed, between children in the same culture, it seems to be universally true that children's first words identify or label those objects or people in their immediate environments that are particularly salient to them. Broadly, these include family members or frequent visitors, food, actions, body parts, clothes, animals, toys, vehicles such as cars or trucks, and locations. Assigning children's early words to such categories requires, of course, that the researcher, or in the case of Janet, her mother the diarist, make judgments about the meanings and functions these words serve. These judgments are susceptible to bias in the sense that the adults' preconceptions about what the child intends may influence their reporting. For this reason, it is important to have as much contextual information as possible about the conditions under which these early words are produced.

Very rapidly after her first birthday, the number of words in Janet's vocabulary increased dramatically. By the time Janet was 16 months old, her mother had recorded a total of 24 different words. Table 4.1 shows the words, a phonetic transcription, a "gloss" or meaning, and in some instances a brief note about the situation in which the word was uttered.

A number of ways exist for classifying Janet's first two dozen words. Applying adult categories, we would call most of them nouns, or labels for things in Janet's immediate environment. But there were also action words (*stop* and *go*), adjectives (*more* and *dirty*) and the negative. From her mother's diary and my own incomplete observational notes made at the time, it would seem that Janet's early words were used largely in the presence of the named object, that is, she used *gaga* when pointing to her bear and not in its absence. Even *go* was used in what seemed to be an observational sense, that is, when she saw her father with his coat on preparing to leave, she said *go*. There was no indication that she was asking to go with him. The other action word, however, she used in an attempt to direct her brother's behavior, ordering Matthew to stop tugging on her blanket on one occasion. Similarly, *more* was used to demand more of almost anything she wanted, initially cookies.

These first 24 words also reveal a great deal about Janet's developing phonology. We see a number of instances of reduplication (discussed below). We also see instances of homophony, or two different words that sound the same, such as *du* for 'shoe' and 'juice.' This homophony results from the child's simplification of the adult system. In this case, Janet substituted [d], which she was able to produce, for both [s] and [ǰ], which she was still unable to produce. Such substitutions typified Janet's speech at this stage and are, in fact, very typical of children at this and the next stage of development.

Ingram points out, however, that development during this period differs in significant ways from later development. During the early part of this period, for example, the child uses words with shifting reference. A "bow-wow may refer to a dog one day, a horse another, or even a clock the next . . ." (Ingram, 1976, p. 12). We see this to be true of Janet in her use of *pie, cat, bubble,* and *window,* each expressing a number of meanings.

Table 4.1
First words

weo	/wio/	'wheel'	Car, truck, bus or anything with wheels
baba	/baba/	'bottle'	Bottle, milk, or glass
gaga	/gaga/	'Gurgles'	Janet's stuffed bear
mumum	/məməm/	'Mummy'	Used only for her mother
du	/du/	'juice'	Juice of any kind, coffee, any liquid other than milk
du	/du/	'Matthew'	Janet's brother
no	/no/	'no'	
dada	/daedae/	'Daddy'	Used for her father or adult male friends of the family
buh	/bə/	'bird'	Big Bird
da	/dae/	'cat'/'dog'	From *Cat in the Hat*, also used for neighbor's dog and to indicate other Dr. Seuss books
mo	/mo/	'more'	Used also to indicate that she didn't want an action to stop
do	/do/	'go'	
bop/ba	/bap/ba/	'stop'	Used only with Matthew
dee	/di/	'street'	"Sesame Street"
bubba	/bəbə/	'bubbles'/'water'	Bubbles for her bath; water, ginger ale, soap
wimu	/wimu/	'window'/'door'	
du	/du/	'shoe'	
by	/bai/	'pie'/'cake'/'pudding'	
da	/dae/	'Janet'	
guh	/gə/	'duck'	
guh	/gə/	'cup'	
dye	/dai/	'diaper'	
didi	/didi/	'dirty'	Used for soiled or wet diapers and mud on boots
kuku	/kuku/	'cookie'	

In comparison with the next stage of development, the child's sound system at this time is relatively primitive, consisting of a limited inventory of individual sounds and of syllable types. Although a great deal of variability exists among English-speaking children, their early consonants tend to be alveolar and labial stops, particularly [b]. Ferguson and Garnica (1975) have pointed out that [w] is also one of the earliest sounds acquired. Children at this stage of development may have as few as two vowels or as many as six, but [i] (the vowel sound in *feet*) and [a] (the sound in *tot*) are among the most frequent.

In Janet's speech of this period, we find rather extensive vowel development with five vowels and a diphthong. Her consonants included both labial stops as well as [w] and [m]. In addition to the alveolar stop [d], she also produced the voiced velar stop [g] and the alveolar nasal [n], but only in the word *no*. In *window*, she substituted [m], suggesting that [n] was not yet fully established.

Although she did produce some CVC syllables, in her versions of *street* and *mummy*, and one V syllable in *wheel*, she overwhelmingly preferred CV syllables at this stage. Ingram reports that this is the preferred syllable configuration for the first 50 words or so, but VC may be found as well. His child Jennika used a great many VC syllables, while Janet and the children studied by Menn and by Velten rarely did so. We see in Janet's speech another process that is characteristic of children in this stage. When she produced words of more than one syllable, she did so by duplicating the first syllable. Reduplication is a common phonological process in children under two years of age although not all children use the process and others use it to varying degrees.

There are two other aspects of phonological development that are noteworthy at this stage. Ferguson and Farwell (1975) observed that children sometimes appear to regress in their phonological development. That is, their first approximations of new words may be closer to the adult target form than their later attempts. Leopold observed in his daughter Hildegard's successive attempts to pronounce the word *pretty* that her attempt at ten months was better formed than her attempts at 1;3 and even 1;10 (cited in Ingram, 1976, p. 21). Piper (1984a, 1984b, 1984c) reports a similar phenomenon in five-year-old children acquiring English as a second language. The explanation for this occurrence appears to be that at first the child is imitating and does not yet have a productive phonological system of her own. Later, as she attempts to come to terms with the *systematicity* of sound, she uses a number of regular processes to simplify the adult system and thus her pronunciation appears to deteriorate.

We see in Janet's speech at this point only one exemplar of this process, and that is in her pronunciation of *stop*. She first produced [bap] and then a few days later deleted the final consonant to produce [ba]. Admittedly, this is slim evidence for regression, and Ingram notes that it is not well documented in the research literature, but it is one that raises important questions about how the child creates an early phonological system.

A second noteworthy aspect of children's phonology at this stage concerns their selection of words. Ferguson and Farwell provide evidence that suggests that children select words that fall within their current phonological capabilities and avoid those that do not. One of the children they studied acquired words beginning with [b] but no words beginning with [p]. Leopold's Hildegard exhibited apparent "avoidance" of the same sound, and although Smith (1973) does not mention it, his account of his son's phonology from age two shows only three words beginning with [p] at the earliest stage, but a great many more beginning with [b]. It would appear that many children consider sound patterns in choosing the words they acquire, or at least produce.

In describing and discussing the first subperiod in the preschool years, we have focused on the phonological system. This is true because at this stage it is the most "visible" of the child's language systems. This is not to say that the child has no incipient syntax, but only that it is not yet apparent to the observer. In the next six months, however, as Janet began to combine words, we are able to make interesting observations about her syntactic as well as her phonological development.

Janet from 1;6 to 2:0

The onset of this subperiod is marked by a rapid increase in vocabulary and by the child's combining of words into early sentences. According to her mother's diary, Janet added a new word or two each week and at 1;6 uttered her first two-word sentence, "No nap." Table 4.2 shows excerpts from her mother's diary when Janet was 1;10. Here we find both an expanded vocabulary and evidence of two-word sentences.

From this sample we can see that Janet had added *go, there, doggie, cold, nap,* and *kitty.* The diary recorded that she had also produced the words listed in Table 4.3. These new words brought her observed productive vocabulary at age 1;10 to 38 words.

Syntax and Semantic Relations.   Once children begin to combine words, we can attempt to describe and try to understand the rules governing their syntax. Researchers have shown a great deal of interest in the meanings conveyed by children in their two-word utterances. An obvious question is the degree of universality in these early expressions. In other words, when they first begin to combine words, do children produce the

Table 4.2
Janet's sentences at 1;10

1.	Weo go	[wio do]	'Wheel go'	(she is rolling a toy car)
2.	Buh dere	[bə dɛ]	'Bird there'	
3.	Tu no	[tu no]	'Matthew no'	
4.	Dada go	[daedae do]	'Daddy go'	
5.	Dada weo	[daedae wio]	'Daddy wheel'	(car)
6.	Goggie go	[gagi do]	'Doggie go'	
7.	Su kode.	[tu kod]	'Shoe cold'	(Her mother has put a shoe on her that has been on the mud porch)
8.	No nap	[no nae]	'No nap!'	
9.	Tu weo	[tu wio]	'Matthew's wheel'	(car)
10.	Kiki dere	[kiki dɛ]	'Kitty there'	

same types of sentences? The answer seems to be that trends or similarities exist in these early meanings, but there is also a great deal of variation among individual children. Some of the more common meanings include:

An agent performing an action	Katie eat.
An action affecting an object	Kick ball.
An object being given a location	Baby there.
A person or object being described	Katie cold.

(Crystal, 1987, p. 243)

There is, of course, a danger in describing children's utterances in this way since we cannot always be sure what meaning is intended and, therefore, into which categories their words fall. In the utterances above, for

Table 4.3
Janet's new vocabulary at 1;10

hi	[hai]
byebye	[baibai]
up	[ə]
down	[dae]
sock	[dak] / [da]
Oscar	[aka]
crayon	[ge]
book	[bu]

example, there is no evidence that the child is not doing essentially the same thing in both the first and last sentences, namely describing some attribute of Katie. It may be only an adult's imposition of structure on the child's language to assume that a verb is used in one case and an adjective in the other.

Using the categories from Crystal's example, we see that Janet was conveying similar meanings:

> An agent performing an action (4,6)
>
> An action affecting an object (1)
>
> An object being given a location (2,10)
>
> A person or object being described (7)

We also see additional meanings in these sentences. Possession is expressed in sentences 5 and 9 and negative intent in sentences 3 and 8 (see Table 4.2). Janet appeared to be telling Matthew, in the third sentence, not to take her stuffed mouse, and in sentence 8, she was telling her mother that she didn't want to take a nap. Not only was Janet able to create a number of meanings, we see even at this two-word stage clear evidence of early syntactic variety. In 10 utterances consisting of only 12 different words, Janet was effectively using six different sentence structures.

Although the first two-word utterances tend to consist of verb and object (or action and object), very shortly after two-word utterances appear, many children start using two-word noun phrases. The first expansion of the noun phrase usually occurs with the addition of an adjective (*bad doggie*) or a quantifier (*more juice*). After these come, more or less in order, the ordinals (*other spoon*), cardinals (*two bears*), the demonstratives (*this cookie*), possessives (*my hat*), and finally the articles, *a, an,* and *the*. All these may occur as early as age two. By 2;6, children may produce noun phrases with two modifiers before the noun (*this old hat*) and by 3;0, their noun phrases may have three or even four prenominal modifiers.

Phonology.   With the addition of new words, we also find changes in Janet's phonology. She had added to her inventory of sounds two consonants. One was [t], which she now used instead of [d] in 'Matthew' and the other was the [h] in 'hi.' She also used a new vowel [ɛ] in 'there.' Although she still showed an overwhelming preference for the CV syllable, she did produce the occasional CVC syllable, in 'sock' and 'cold.' But notice that in 'sock' the CVC syllable alternated with the CV syllable, suggesting that she hadn't fully "settled" on the CVC form. Indeed, we find a few weeks later that she had chosen [da] as her pronunciation. We also see that she still uses reduplication as a strategy for producing words of two syllables.

Janet from 2;0 to 3.0

Sometime around the second birthday, many children begin to produce sentences of three or four words. Obviously, once they begin to produce utterances of this length, the syntax needed to describe their combinations of words becomes more complicated. Questions and commands appear along with the statements that typified the two-word stage. Although children at this stage may be "telegraphic" in their tendency to omit grammatical morphemes such as the verb *to be* and the conjunctions, this tendency has largely disappeared by the time they are three years old.

Syntax. Two months before her second birthday, Janet produced her first three-word sentence, and by the time she was 2;0, they appeared regularly enough in her speech that her MLU was approximately 2.2. Considering that she still produced a number of single-word utterances, this MLU showed rapid development. When Janet was 2;6, her mother's diary included the list of sentences shown in Table 4.4.

Table 4.4 is not a complete list of Janet's three-word sentences at this age; it consists of those sentences for which phonetic or near-phonetic transcriptions were available. These were representative, however, of all

Table 4.4
Janet's sentences at 2;6

1.	Janet eat cookie.	[da͜e i kuku]	2;3
2.	Matthew eat cookie.	[tu i kuku]	2;3
3.	Matthew cookie there.	[tu kuku dɛ]	2;4
4.	Mummy see kitty.	[mə mi si kiki]	2;4
5.	Daddy go wheel (car).	[da͜eda͜e go wio]	2;5
6.	Matthew face dirty.	[tu ses dədi]	2;5
7.	Daddy big wheel.	[da͜eda͜e bɪk wio]	2;6
8.	See big wheel.	[si bɪk wio]	2;6
9.	Want Matthew gum.	[wa tu kəm]	2;6
10.	Mummy no go.	[məmi no go]	2;6
11.	See doggie there.	[si dagi dɛ]	2;6
12.	Daddy chase Matthew.	[da͜eda͜e ses tu]	2;6

the semantic relations recorded between 2;0 and 2;6. The meanings expressed in these items included:

Agent action object (1, 2, 4, 5, 12)
Possessor possession locative (3)*
Possessor possession attribute (6, 7)
Action entity attribute (8)
Action entity locative (11)
Action object attribute (9)*
Negative agent action (10)*

Most of these relationships are typical of those found in children beginning to form three-word sentences. Except for those marked with an asterisk (*), all were identified by Brown (1973) as prevalent in the speech of children at this stage. It is possible when children get to the three-word stage to begin to view their sentences as having hierarchical structure. The sentence "Daddy chase Matthew," for example, would traditionally be viewed as having two major constituents with *chase* and *Matthew* forming the VP constituent. That is the adult's way of parsing the sentence, but what is the evidence that it is the child's, that the action is more closely bonded to the object than it is to the agent? One kind of evidence, identified in the research literature by Braine (1971b) comes from "build up" or the child's own expansions:

Eat cookie. . . . Janet eat cookie.

Unfortunately, this is an isolated instance in Janet's language and we do not know whether it is a common hierarchical structure. Another type of evidence could be sought in her two-word sentences. If it were the case that action and object were more closely bonded in her three-word utterances, it would likely also be the case that these were the predominant relationships in her two-word utterances. Returning to her two-word utterances, we find both agent-action and action-object bonding. This is consistent with research evidence showing that some children form stronger action-object bonds and others stronger agent-action bonds.

Another important dimension of syntactic development was apparent in Janet's speech at this age, and that was her use of pronouns. Although there are no pronouns in the language data reproduced in Table 4.4, Janet did begin to use pronouns during this year. Most children use *it, this,* and *that* before the personal pronouns, and Janet was no exception, using these pronouns before she was two years old. The personal pronouns, specifically *he, she, him* (sometimes *hims*), *I,* and *me* all appeared with some regularity in her speech by the time she was 2;8. Young children's learning of the first-person pronouns is an especially impressive feat. As Perera (1984) points out, children hear themselves addressed as *you* yet must learn to address themselves as *I* or *me.* Parents don't always provide that much help, either, using names rather than pronouns in sentences such as "Mummy will put Lindsey to bed" (p. 104).

Grammatical Morphemes.   Before the age of about 2;6, Janet's speech was characterized by the absence of grammatical "frills." At about this time, however, she began to produce two grammatical inflections: The progressive form, *-ing* and the possessive inflection on nouns appeared on certain words. These first appeared, as shown in Table 4.5, in two-word sentences, but note that the number of *morphemes* in each utterance remains three.

The period during which children acquire the inflectional morphemes has been of considerable interest to researchers. Brown (1973) charted the order in which the three children in his study acquired 14 grammatical morphemes. A number of other researchers have followed his procedures in both longitudinal and cross-sectional studies. This peri-

Table 4.5
Early grammatical morphemes

1.	Matthew playing.	[tu pen]	2;6
2.	Matthew's wheel.	[tus wio]	2;6
3.	Janet's shoe.	[daens su]	2;6
4.	Janet's baby.	[daens bebi]	2;7
5.	Mummy's juice.	[məmis du]	2;7
6.	Shoes there.	[sus dɛ]	2;8
7.	Shoe in bed.	[su In bɛt]	2;8
8.	Gurgles in bed.	[gagas In bɛt]	2;8
9.	See in window.	[si In wIno]	2;9
10.	Got two book.	[ga tu bʊk]	2;9
11.	Doggie got Gurgles.	[dagi ga gagas]	2;10
12.	Matthew's shoe there.	[tuz su dɛ]	2;10
13.	Matthew chasing doggie.	[tu sesIn dagi]	2;10
14.	Sit on bed!	[sItən bɛt]	2;11
15.	Gurgles jumping!	[gagas dəmpIn]	2;11

od, when children are between 1;9 and 2;10 and the MLU is approximately 2.5, finds them typically adding a few prepositions, principally *in* and *on,* an article or two, and perhaps the plural and possessive forms. Other grammatical morphemes follow as the child marks finer syntactic distinctions. These remaining morphemes are acquired during a time when the child is between approximately 2;0 and 4;0 and the mean length of utterance is between 2.0 and 2.5 (Brown, 1973, p. 271).

The procedure that Cazden (1968) initiated and Brown (1973) modified for determining the order of acquisition of grammatical morphemes is a rigorous one, which has not been applied here. Note, however, that the earliest grammatical morphemes to appear in Janet's language were the progressive inflection on the verb and the possessive inflection on the noun. This is consistent with Brown's finding that two of his three subjects acquired the present progressive before any of the other inflectional morphemes. The possessive came higher in the acquisition order for Janet than for Brown's subjects, but she was well within the age range during which they acquired the possessive. Following shortly were the plural, although *shoes* was the only form to appear for some time, and the prepositions *in* and *on.* It is interesting to note that in learning *in* Janet seems to have acquired not one but two prepositions. In sentences eight and nine in Table 4.5, we find her using two very different senses of *in.*

Phonology.   Although certain infantile pronunciations remained, Janet rapidly added to her inventory of sounds. She maintained her earlier pronunciation of *Matthew, cookie,* and *kitty* but improved on her *Mummy* and *doggie.* Notice that the second syllable of *Mummy* is no longer reduplicated and the initial consonant of *doggie* is now a [d]. While she was still unable to produce consonant clusters, such as the *pl-* in playing, we can see in Table 4.5 that she had added the individual sounds [k,s,o] and stabilized her use of [n], using it instead of [m] in *window,* for example. Another kind of instability appeared, however, as she began her acquisition of the possessive. As she added to her inventory of individual sounds, Janet inevitably began to produce a greater variety of syllable shapes. In the language samples in Tables 4.4 and 4.5, CV syllables still dominate, but we also find CVC, VC, and even a CVCC syllable.

Researchers have investigated the order in which children add to their basic inventory of the previous stage, both in naturalistic case studies and in experimental studies. Despite variation among children, certain patterns of development seem to hold true. Vowels, for example, are acquired first and are usually fully in place by the time a child is three. Janet had acquired the full inventory of vowels by 2;3 although she did not always follow adult pronunciations. For example, she maintained her pronunciation of 'kitty' as [kiki] even though the vowel [I] was in her inventory. She also continued to pronounce 'cookie' as [kuku] although she had both [u] and [i] in other words.

Because vowels occur singly in syllables, an acquisition order is relatively easy to establish. For consonants, such an order is more difficult to describe because they may occur in sequences in syllables and in a great many configurations. Moreover, children do not acquire individual sounds but sequences of sounds. As might be expected, children generally acquire single consonants before clusters. Templin studied 480 children ranging in age from three to eight years and found that by the age of four, children have acquired most single consonants with the following exceptions: [t] between vowel sounds (as in *eating*), the *ch-* sound, the *j-* sound between vowels (as in *budgie*), the *th-* sounds, [v] and [z] at the beginning and end of words, the middle consonant in *leisure*, and word-final [l] and [s] (Templin, 1957; cited in Ingram, 1976, pp. 26-27).

By 2;6 Janet had acquired [p,b,t,d,s,k,g,m,n,w] but not in all positions. She still showed a tendency to delete or to devoice word final consonants, producing [ga] for 'got' and [bɪk] for 'big.' She was still missing a number of single consonants, notably [ŋ, c, ǰ, r, l], but she used words with these sounds nevertheless. She did so by substituting sounds she could manage and by simplifying sequences of sounds. Her pronunciation of 'playing' as [pen] illustrates: She substituted [n] for [ŋ] and reduced the initial cluster to a single [p]. This behavior highlights one of the most interesting aspects of phonological development at this stage, namely the appearance and gradual loss of certain regular processes.

At this age, children are not able to produce perfectly formed imitations of adult speech. Rather, they simplify adult sound sequences to ones that they can manage with their immature cognitive and articulatory abilities. Certain universal tendencies seem to govern the ways in which children accomplish this simplification. By studying the relationship between the forms produced by the child and the corresponding forms of the adult speaker, researchers have been able to describe the regular and fairly consistent processes children use in reducing the full range of adult sounds to a smaller and more manageable set. These phonological processes resemble those described in Chapter 2, but these are developmental and get left behind or suppressed as children become more proficient at producing adult forms.

Developmental processes are of three basic types. Children use one type to simplify the structure of syllables. Because English syllables may consist of consonant sequences that are very difficult to pronounce and because young children find CV syllables much easier to pronounce, there is a universal tendency to reduce syllables to the CV type (Stampe, 1979[3]; Grunwell, 1982). For children learning English, this tendency may be realized in a variety of ways.

A two-year-old who produces [du] for 'juice' or [ti] for 'cheese' is simplifying a CVC syllable to a CV syllable by deleting the final consonant. This is a very early process in children's speech and may fail to appear at all in some children. Grunwell (1982) reports that it has usually disappeared by the age of 3;0 or 3;3. Janet was still reducing some syllables to CV at 2;9 ([ga] for 'got'), but the process had disappeared by 3;0.

Not all syllables are reduced to CV, of course, and even when the CVC syllable is mastered, cumbersome consonant clusters remain to be dealt with. Often, children deal with these clusters by deleting one of the sounds in the cluster. For example, if a child produces *top* for 'stop,' he or she is simplifying a CCVC syllable to a CVC syllable by deleting the first sound in the cluster. Such deletions are rarely random. In two-consonant clusters beginning with -*s*, for example, it is usually the /s/ that is deleted; words such as *pot* for 'spot' and *kate* for 'skate' are common in children under the age of three. In two-consonant clusters beginning with a stop and followed by a liquid, it is usually the liquid that is deleted, producing forms such as *bick* for 'brick' and *go* for 'glow.' We see this type of reduction in Janet's pronunciation of 'playing' and her earlier 'crayon' as [ge].

In the early months of language acquisition, children produce mainly one-syllable words but attempt many words of more than one syllable. Sometimes these early attempts involve deleting the unstressed syllable. Most of us have heard children pronounce 'banana' as *nana*, but *ap* for 'apple' is also possible in the very young child (Grunwell, 1982, p. 170). This process is called **weak syllable deletion**. Although this is an early process, we see a remnant of it in Janet's pronunciation of 'Cinderella' as [sIndrɛlə] at 4;0 (see Figure 4.2).

A second phonological process that children use to simplify the adult system does not alter the shape of the syllable but simplifies the sound system in another way. Through **assimilation,** or making one sound more like another, children effectively reduce the total inventory of sounds that they have to produce. Although several types of assimilation are possible in child speech, two are very common.

In the first type, one consonant in a word affects the pronunciation of another. The following examples come from Janet's speech:

---

[3]Stampe's work is in dissertation form and not readily available in university libraries. Ingram (1989, pp. 386–392) has a concise summary of Stampe's important contribution to phonological theory.

Janet's Form	Adult's Form
[gagi]	'doggie'
[kiki]	'kitty'
[ses]	'chase'
[dãɛns]	'Janet's'

In each of these words, the initial consonants become the same as or more similar to the following consonant in the word. Young children have, incidentally, a preference for voicing consonants that precede vowels (Ingram, 1976, p.36), and this is also a kind of assimilation: One way of making a voiceless consonant more like a vowel is to voice it. Janet, for example, pronounced [s] as [d] in 'sock' and [k] as [g] in 'clock.'

A second very common type of assimilation involves the devoicing of stop consonants at the ends of words. This process is assimilatory because by losing its voicing, the consonant becomes more like the silence that follows it. Common examples of this process include:

Janet's Form	Adult's Form	Age
[gək]	'bug'	1;11
[bɛt]	'bed'	2;8
[bIk]	'big'	2;6
[pɛk]	'Peg'	2;2
[baɛt]	'bad'	2;0

The third major type of phonological process by which children simplify the adult sound system is substitution. In assimilation processes, children substitute one sound for another, but the sound they substitute is influenced by another in the immediate environment. With substitution processes, however, they replace one sound with another apparently without reference to surrounding sounds. This is another way in which the total inventory of sounds is temporarily reduced, allowing children to produce simpler sounds, or those which they can better approximate, for more difficult ones.

Substitution, like assimilation and syllable structure processes, is rarely random. Children behave in similar ways in replacing one sound for another. Ingram (1976) reports, for example, that the process of stopping, or replacing fricatives and affricates with stops, is common in both normal children and in those with phonological disabilities. This process accounts for Janet's pronunciation of 'juice' as [du], 'jumping' as [dəmpIn], and 'sock' as [dak]. Notice that the stop is articulated in the same place as the fricative or affricate that it replaces.

Another type of substitution, also very common in the speech of young children, is called *fronting* and is apparently the result of a universal preference for consonants articulated near the front of the mouth. The most common realization of this process is the substitution of an alveolar consonant for a velar one, resulting in pronunciations such as the following:

Child's Form	Adult's Form	Source
bat	'back'	Menn (1989)
tat	'cat'	Menn (1989)
take	'cake'	Hills (1914)

This was a process that Janet appeared to use only rarely and only when she was very young. Her pronunciation of 'go' as [do] at 1;10 was the only reported incident of fronting. That it was not a process she generally favored is shown in Table 4.2. At the same time she was saying [do] for 'go' she was also correctly producing [k] and [g] in 'cold,' 'kitty,' and 'doggie.' Other researchers have noted that although consonant fronting is a well-attested process in the speech of young children, it is also one that does not occur in all children. Smith (1973) conducted a careful, detailed study of his son's phonological development and found virtually no instances of fronting. In children who do exhibit the process, it usually disappears by the age of 2;6; Grunwell (1982) reports that velar consonants are mastered by all normal children by the age of 3;3.

Most of the examples used so far in describing the more common simplification processes children use in mastering the sound system have involved a single process. In real speech, however, children frequently apply a number of phonological processes at once. Ingram (1976) has reported as many as seven processes operating in a single word, and certainly two, three, or four is common. In a child's pronunciation of 'scratch' as *tat*, for example, we can see three processes operating. The initial consonant cluster is reduced to a single consonant, the /k/ sound in that cluster is fronted to a /t/, and the final affricate is replaced by a stop, /t/ (Grunwell, 1982, p. 182). In Janet's pronunciation of her own name as [dæ̃] at 2;3 (see Table 4.4), we see the substitution of an alveolar stop, [d], for [j] as well as weak syllable deletion.

Identifying the processes that link children's pronunciations with the corresponding adult pronunciations depends to a large degree on how well we *hear* children's speech. Of course, just as we "hear" a foreign language through the filter of our own language, we also hear children's speech through the filter of our adult perception. Even trained transcribers must exercise caution in transcribing children's speech. Using machine analysis, Macken and Barton (1980) demonstrated, for example, that some children who appeared to be using voiced stops at the beginnings of words where they should have used voiceless stops were actually attempting to produce the correct form. What this suggests is that children may be further along their path to phonological mastery than they seem to be, given what we hear as their pronunciations. This is a caution we would do well to keep in mind as we view children's language data. We cannot help but view it from our adult bias and, in doing so, we run the real risk of underestimating their accomplishment.

Janet from 3;0 to 4;0

This was a year of impressive progress for Janet in all areas of language acquisition. She continued her learning of the inflectional and grammatical morphemes, and she continued to combine words into sentences which grew in length to seven and eight words. She gained control of the phonology of her language, leaving only a few minor distinctions unmarked. Two transcripts, one taken the day before her third birthday (Figure 4.1) and the other a week or so after her fourth (Figure 4.2), provide a good indication of the magnitude of her progress.

Janet was making giant strides forward in pragmatics, syntax, morphemic structure, and phonology. These are apparent in comparing the conversations reported in Figures 4.1 and 4.2.

Pragmatics.   Although there was earlier evidence that Janet was learning the uses of talk along with the conventions, we see even in these brief excerpts evidence that she was becoming far more sophisticated and resourceful in her uses of language. In Figure 4.1 we see her clarifying her question when her mother doesn't understand. She was not yet able to say, "No, that's not what I meant," but she very deftly let her know that she wasn't asking about the next number in the sequence but about the color of the paper liner. In the year between the first and the second conversation, we find Janet becoming increasingly adept at using language for a variety of purposes. She moved from a child who used language largely to report and comment on the present to one who attempted to manipulate her mother and then play with the situation and the language in her opening line of "Cinderjanet." While the child Janet at age three still relied heavily on repetition of her mother's phrases, by age four she was initiating utterances without direct reliance on her mother's words or structures.

Janet is standing on a chair "helping" her mother bake cupcakes for Matthew to take to his kindergarten class.

M: You want to help?

J: Me help?
[mi hɛlp]

M: Yes. You can put these in here. (The paper liners in the tins.)

J: Like this?
[laik dIs]

M: Right. Can you count them?

J: Count. One, two, three . . . what this?
[kaut   wən tu twi   wa dIs]

M: Four?

J: No. This one yellow. This one yellow, too. This one
[no dIs wən yɛwo   dIs wən yɛwo tu   dIs wun]

M: Oh, the color. That one's pink. You know pink.

J: Yeah. Pink. This one pink. Me taste?
[yɛ   piŋk dIs wən pIŋk   mi tes]

M: You want to taste? Just a minute while I get you a spoon . . . There. What do you think? Is it good?

J: (Nodding) Good. Matt?
[gʊd   mæ̃ẽ?]

M: Matt? Oh, yes, these are for Matt to take to school.

J: Me too!
[mi tu]

M: You want to go to school?

J: (Laughing).   No. I want this one. (Points to cupcake.)
[no ai wan dIs wən]

M: Oh, you want a cupcake. Well, when they're baked, you can have one. Okay?

J: Okay. This one.
[okei   dIs wən]

Figure 4.1
Janet at 3;0

Syntax and Semantic Relations.   Janet's syntactic development was no less remarkable. By the time they are three, most children take or have taken a giant grammatical leap forward as they begin to produce sentences with more than one clause. These clauses are still largely conjunctive, that is, linked by *and*, and may run on and on. Janet was nearly a

Janet and Matthew have been begging to stay up to watch a television special. Matthew has conceded the battle but Janet continues to argue with her mother while getting dressed for bed.

M: Which gown do you want?

J: Don't want ANY gown!
[dōt wan Ini gawn]

M: Well, that's up to you, but you might get cold.

J: I don't care. (She sits down on her bed and sulks.)
[ai dōt kɛr]

M: I see. Do you care which story I read?

J: Nope. I don't care. I want to watch Charlie Brown.
[nop   ai dōt kɛr   ai wāt tu wač čarli brawn]

M: I'm sorry, it's too late. But you'll be able to see Charlie Brown another time. Don't forget, he's in the comics every Sunday.

J: I want to see him NOW!
[ai wāt tu si hIm naw]

M: We've finished talking about Charlie Brown, Janet. Now do you want me to read to you or not?

J: I'll read.
[ail rid]

M: Will you read to me? (Janet nods) What will you read?

J: How about Cinderella?
[haw bawt sIndrɛlə]

M: That's a pretty hard one. Do you think you can read all of it?

J: (Defiantly "reading") There was a mean wicked mother and she had a poor
[ðɛr wəz ə min wIkId məðər aend ši haed ə po:r]

little girl named Cinderjanet.
[lIto gəro nemd sIndərjǎenIt]

Figure 4.2
Janet at 4;0

textbook case when it came to conjunction. Her mother's diary records the following sentence at 3;6:

> Matt want my baby and I said he can't have her and he take Gurgles and I take his book about bears and he hit me.

Children of this age are also capable of producing sentences with subordinate clauses, principally with *because* (*'coz*), sometimes correctly:

> My baby cry coz she want me (Janet, 3;4)

and sometimes not:

> Spike bite me coz it hurt. (Kate, 2;9)

Before they can use constructions such as these correctly, a great deal of grammatical knowledge is required. Similarly, as they begin to produce longer and longer utterances, greater syntactic sophistication will be required to prevent the kind of muddle of tenses experienced by this child of 3;9 reported by Crystal (1987, p. 243):

> If Father Christmas come down the chimney, and he will have presents when he came down, can I stay up to see him?

At age three, Janet's utterances were from two to seven morphemes in length, and she had begun to produce negatives, declaratives, and questions. It is usual for children to begin to produce different types of sentences at about the same time as the grammatical morphemes begin to appear. We saw that Janet had begun to produce certain grammatical morphemes at 2;6, and the transcript from 3;0 shows her beginning to use questions and some negatives. We still see, however, evidence of telegraphic speech, typical of infancy or the earliest preschool period. When she said *Matt?* with rising intonation, she was letting the single word carry a very large semantic burden, one which her mother recognized in her subsequent expansion of Janet's question.

By her fourth birthday, Janet's utterances ranged from two to sixteen morphemes in length and most of her sentences were well-formed. Certainly those reproduced in Figure 4.2 were nearly perfect. At the same age and for several months previous, she had been producing a variety of syntactic forms including questions, negatives, negative questions, imperatives, and negative imperatives. There is no record of Janet's producing passive constructions during this time, although the dialogues in Figure 4.3 recorded when she was 3.5 and 3;6, respectively, show her quite capable of understanding at least some passive constructions.

This is not to say that Janet's syntactic development was complete. She still relied heavily on conjunction for linking related propositions rather than the more complex structure of the relative or reduced relative clause. That is, she typically produced sentences such as "Matt took Gurgles and Gurgles had a sore ear and I told him not to!" (3;11) and "I saw Daddy's car and it was broken 'coz the wheel was on the ground and now he's going to fix it" (4;0).

Figure 4.3
Understanding of passives

Mother:	What happened here?
Janet:	It broke.
Mother:	All by itself?
Janet:	What?
Mother:	Was the glass broken all by itself?
Janet:	No. I broke it.
Janet:	Your car broken?
Daddy:	Yes, it was hit in the parking lot at work.
Janet:	Who hit it, Daddy?

The semantic relations expressed in Janet's sentences at age three were no longer restricted to the seven simple ones of six months earlier. She was producing well-formed SVO sentences ("I want this one") although she did not yet produce the copula. A moment's reflection explains why this might be the case. With "I want this one," Janet was making her wishes known. Arguably, she could have done so without the first-person pronoun, but the verb, object (one), and even "this" were essential to her specifying, and getting, exactly what she wanted. The copula, *is,* in the sentence "This one yellow" is clearly expendable. It is entirely redundant for expressing the meaning she wished to express. This is to say that children cannot learn *all* of the grammatical conventions of language at once, and so the order in which they *do* acquire them is to a large degree determined by the meaning they wish to make.

Certain observations can be made about Janet's learning of the grammatical morphemes. We saw earlier evidence that she had acquired or was well on her way to acquiring the progressive, the possessive, and the prepositions *on* and *in.* Before the age of three, she had added the plural form and certain irregular past forms such as *broke, saw, ate,* and *took.* Sometime around age three she had added the demonstrative article, *this* (see Figure 4.1) but still produced sentences without the copula ("What this?"). In the next year, however, Janet added the contractible auxiliary ("I'll read"), the contractible negative ("Don't want any"), other prepositions including *about, with, under, over,* and *beside,* as well as the copula in both the present and past tenses. She even made a stab at a complex sequence of tenses reminiscent of the example from Crystal above:

When Daddy would come home if Matthew is not home from school is it—
(at this point, she gave up and started again)

When Daddy would come home and Matthew wouldn't come home, can I go with him to feed the horses? (4;2)

If we were to examine this excerpt for its errors or deviations from the "correct" adult form, we would do Janet a grave disservice. Even though neither sentence is perfect when compared with the adult model, both represent tremendous syntactic growth. In this short excerpt, we find Janet using auxiliary verbs, complement structures ("go with him to feed the horses") and making an attempt to express conditional relationships. She has come a long way from the child who only 18 months earlier was producing mainly two-word sentences.

Vocabulary.   Children at this age are also busily acquiring a great many new words, and in the process sometimes get a bit muddled:

Exasperated Mother: Will you PLEASE behave?
Christopher (age 3): I AM being hayve!

Children of three are estimated to have a vocabulary of between 800 and 1200 words and by the time they are four, that total will have risen to between 1500 and 1900 words (Crystal, 1987, p. 232). Assuming the lower end of each estimate, this means that children learn approximately two new words every day during this year. Parents of three and four year olds will not be surprised by these estimates. If language use contributes to language learning, as it undoubtedly does, then most children have plenty of opportunity to learn. German researchers have reported that children of 3;6 produce nearly 38,000 words during a 12-hour day (Crystal, 1987, p. 244).

Phonology.   Janet's phonological development at age four was mostly complete. Only a few individual sounds gave her any difficulty. She sometimes substituted [d] for the interdental sound in *this* or *there* but at other times produced it correctly, indicating that she had not yet fully gained control of the interdental. She also substituted [w] for [l] at times, but her mother's diary notes that she usually did this when she was playing with her dolls and was, perhaps, engaging in baby talk. We see in Figure 4.2 her pronunciation of *little* as [lIto] and *girl* as [gəro]. This substitution of a vowel, usually [u] or [o], for a consonant, usually [l] or [r], is called **vocalization**, a process that is common among younger children, but it is not known how frequently it occurs in children of four. This is true in part because the process results in a sound that is not greatly deviant, and most adults do not notice it (Grunwell, 1982, p. 171). The fact that Janet's vocalization appeared to be restricted to certain words, for example, *girl,* *little,* and *wheel* and did not influence *I'll* or *call* suggests that it was attached to certain lexical items that she had learned early and were likely in the process of being lost. By the time she reached her fifth birthday all traces of this process had been lost.

By the age of four, Janet could produce most sequences of consonants and, thus, most syllable shapes. She would still occasionally omit or substitute a consonant in a three-consonant cluster such as *spring,* which she produced sometimes as [spwiŋ] and other times as [spiŋ] at 3;11. She also pronounced *scream* as [skwim] until just before her fourth birthday.

Janet from 4;0 to 6;0

These last two years in the preschool period are marked by major language growth, particularly in syntax and vocabulary.

Syntax. By the age of four and for the next year to two years, children gradually solve some of the more complex grammatical puzzles of their language. At this stage, certain kinds of overgeneralizations appear as they work out the details of their rules-in-process:

> Heidi gots too many.
>
> Kate didn't went.
>
> Mummy wented to gets Daddy.

That children of this age are capable of actively working on the rules is evidenced by Janet at 4;4 trying to tell her mother that Spook, the family cat, had not eaten her food in Figure 4.4. The overgeneralizations in *gived* and *gaved* provide evidence that she was working on the regular past tense form. Her two self-corrections suggest that she was intentionally doing so. Her "corrections" show that her past tense and third-person singular rules are still in progress, that is, that she hasn't yet worked

Figure 4.4
Evidence of rules in progress

Janet:	Spook doesn't like this food.
Mother:	How do you know?
Janet:	Well, you gived—gaved it to her last night and she doesn't ate—no, she didn't ate it.
Mother:	Oh, well I guess you're right. What should we do?
Janet:	Give her some different food that she likes.

out the exclusiveness of the past tense and third-person singular inflections. This "sorting out of grammatical errors is a particular feature of 4-year-old speech" (Crystal, 1987, p. 243) and Janet's mother's diary abounds with examples of such grammatical struggles. Sometimes during the sorting out process, children revert to word order, which is typical of an earlier age. Janet, for example, was heard at 4;4 to ask "Where goes Daddy's car?" But at the same time, she was producing syntactically sophisticated sentences such as the last one in Figure 4.4 in which she used an imperative and a well-formed relative clause.

Relative clause formation begins during the preschool years, chiefly as a way of specifying information about the sentential object. Janet's sentence in which she tells her mother what kind of food to feed the cat is a good example. In three separate studies, Menyuk (1971), Limber (1973), and Bloom et al. (1980) found that preschool-aged children never use relative clauses to provide additional information about the subject noun (as in "The dog that bit me is in the garden"). This is a construction that develops during the school years. But the researchers also found that the number of relative clauses actually produced by the children they studied was very small. This was also true of Janet, and the reason may be that children tend to avoid the relative construction because it *is* difficult.

Another syntactic structure that begins to develop during this time is the passive, a construction that is relatively rare in oral speech. It is used mainly to emphasize the object of the sentence by making it the surface subject. In the speech of young children, the passive appears so infrequently that researchers find it impossible to study unless they deliberately try to elicit it in experimental situations (Tager-Flusberg, 1989, p. 153). Such experiments were not performed with Janet, and there was only one recorded instance of her producing a passive construction. At 4;9, she ran into the house to tell her mother that "Spook almost got hit by a car!" In this sentence, the agent was specified, but in general, young children produce more truncated passives, or sentences without agents, than full passives, or sentences with passives (Horgan, 1978).[4]

We saw that Janet's preferred syntactic device for expressing longer utterances had been conjunction for some time. This preference continued between ages four and five when she continued to use *and* to link a variety of propositions. Table 4.6 shows examples of the conjoined sentences she used during this period.

As Table 4.6 shows, the conjunction *and* can be used to express a number of different relationships between the two clauses. Researchers

---

[4]For a concise review of the literature on passive formation in preschoolers, see Helen Tager-Flusberg's chapter in Gleason (1989).

Table 4.6
Examples of Janet's use of
conjunctive *and*

1.	I sawed Big Bird and he was talking to Cookie.	4;1
2.	Mummy made cookies and I helped.	3;11
3.	Matt come home from school and then we wented.	4;4
4.	Daddy fixed his car and now it will go.	4;6
5.	Spook didn't sleep with me and I'm mad at her.	4;7
6.	Grammy was here and now she's not.	4;5

have identified at least four relationships marked by *and* in the speech of young children. They have also found that there is a largely invariant order in which they are acquired (Bloom et al., 1980; cited in Tager-Flusberg, 1989, p. 156). The earliest relationship expressed is simply additive. Sentences one and two in Table 4.6 illustrate this kind of relationship. The second *and* that children use expresses a relation of time between the two elements in sentences such as "Daddy gave me a dime and then I went to the store." The third sentence in Table 4.6 is an example of this relationship. The fourth sentence may be an example of the same relationship or it may be an example of the next one to develop, causality. The fifth sentence more clearly expresses a cause-effect relationship and the sixth could be simply temporal or it could be an example of a contrasting or adversative relationship, the final one to appear. Tager-Flusberg gives the example of "Cause I was tired and now I'm not tired" (1989, p. 156), but Janet's intent was less clear.

Vocabulary.   If Janet was typical of children her age,[5] and there is no reason to suppose otherwise, her vocabulary during this year grew from approximately 1500 words to over 2000 (Crystal, 1987, p. 232). Her words also became more complex during this year as she learned most of the remaining grammatical inflections and some of the derivational ones as well.

Phonology.   By this time, children have acquired a reasonably effective sound system, although they will continue to refine it for a number of years. From 4;0 to 6;0, they continue to lose the simplification processes described earlier, and as they do so, their pronunciation becomes more adult-like. As they learn to cope with longer words, which result in part

[5]Some readers of this chapter have suggested that because of her parents' educational and professional status, Janet was hardly typical. We have seen, nevertheless, that her language development ran a parallel course to other children reported in the research literature, and so she cannot be considered *atypical* either.

from their increasing sophistication with inflectional and derivational morphemes, they will demonstrate that their language is still "under construction." Numerous examples of children's difficulty with longer words show them to be relying on the same simplification processes. At 4;7, Janet announced to her friends that her mother worked at the "unibersity" and that her father was a "searching fizzlist." Certain words continue to be problematic for most children until they begin school or even after. Ingram (1976) reports creative pronunciations of *thermometer* and *vegetables* for children up to 5;11 (p. 45). Janet's pronunciation of *vegetables* as [vɛjə̆boz] at 4;0 and [vɛjə̆bl̩z] at 5;1 are both typical. There is no evidence that she had any difficulty with *thermometer*, either because she did not talk about thermometers much or, as the daughter of a "searching fizzlist," she had no trouble with the word *thermometer*.

THE SCHOOL YEARS

By the time children reach school, they are adept language users. They understand the functions and uses of language and have mastered most of its syntactic structures. They have acquired most of its individual sounds as well as most of its intonational features. Their learning of the sound system during the next several years will be of the finer distinctions marked by intonation and stress—irony, for example—and the sound-symbol correspondence necessary for reading. They already have a substantial vocabulary, but for the next several years, they will continue to add to its size.

Pragmatics

As they grow older, children's social circles widen, placing greater demands on their language. Even in these days of daycare, nursery schools, and preschools, going to school presents new demands on children's language and new opportunities for learning. When Janet, who did not go to preschool, went to kindergarten, she hurried home every day for the first few weeks with a "Did you know?" question. She excitedly reported all the routines of the kindergarten, not realizing that what was new to her was known to the others in her family. She added the vocabulary of the school, words such as *recess, tardy, show-and-tell,* etc. She gradually learned the rules of usage associated with the social structure of the school. Janet observed after her first encounter with the school principal, "She's sort of the boss and we have to be VERY quiet when she comes in."

Learning the roles of the principal, vice-principal, one's teacher, other teachers, janitors, secretaries, older children, and all the people who populate the school also means learning the register of speech appropriate to each as well as the subjects one might talk with them about. Children who do not already know learn very quickly that there are severe penalties attached to breaking the sociolinguistic rules. To her credit, Janet did not make the mistake of a little non-English-speaking girl in her class by answering the teacher's "Would you please be quiet now?" with "No, thank you. I don't want to." Over the next several years, and to some degree for the rest of their lives, children will continue to learn the social rules governing language use.

To become competent language users, children must also learn the rules for initiating and maintaining conversation. They must learn, for instance, that they will likely get off on the wrong foot if they try "That wart on your nose sure is ugly" as an opening gambit. These kinds of rules, if broken, can result in more severe communicative and social breakdowns than broken phonological, morphological, or syntactic rules.

The school years are also the years during which children learn the subtle differences conveyed by syntactic paraphrases or "equivalents." They learn that "The invasion was ordered by the president" imparts a slightly different message than does "The president ordered the invasion" and that there are reasons why governments might choose the truncated form, "The invasion was ordered," over either of the other versions. They learn that they can paraphrase "The cat is black" by saying "The black cat," but if they name the cat, the syntactic rule changes. Thus, "Spook is black" is all right, but "black Spook" sounds child-like. These are pragmatic rules that border on the syntactic, which brings us to the next major area of accomplishment.

Syntax

We have seen that by the time children begin school, they have mastered the basic syntactic structures of English. A great deal still needs to be learned, however, and over the next several years, they will learn more complex structures and the less frequent structures that serve specific functions in the language, such as the passive and cleft sentence.[6] Although it is possible to consider this learning from a number of perspectives, here we will concentrate on two broad areas of syntactic change:

[6]For an excellent review of children's acquisition of syntax during the school years, see Perera (1984), Chapter 3.

the global clause structure of sentences and development within their two major constituents, the noun phrase and verb phrase.

Clause structure refers to the patterns that children use in constructing their sentences—subject-verb-object, subject-verb-object-complement, etc. Research has shown that although children are able to understand and to produce a wide range of clause patterns by age six, they typically produce only a few. The predominant ones are transitive SVO sentences either with or without a sentence adverbial. They also produce a number of intransitive sentences, with and without adverbs, but other structures, such as sentences with two objects ("Matthew gave Spook the food" or "Grammy gave that book to me"), are less common.

Adverbs play an important role in young children's clause structure, and the use of adverbs has been widely studied. The kinds of adverbs children use appear to be established by age six and remain unchanged throughout the elementary school years. The proportion of adverbs denoting place, time, manner, and cause or condition is largely predictable from the order in which they were acquired—place and time first at about 2;6 followed closely by manner adverbials and those expressing cause or condition later. What does change from the age of 6 until the age of 14 or so, is the number and placement of adverbs children use. According to Strickland (1962; reported in Perera, 1984, pp. 94–95), children not only use more adverbials as they grow older, they are more likely to "include an adverbial within the verb phrase, e.g., *have been always trying*," behavior that is rare among six year olds (Perera, 1984, p. 94). While there were only sporadic entries in her mother's diary after Janet began school, an earlier entry shows her constructing a sentence of just this form. This and other samples of Janet's adverbial constructions appear in Figure 4.5.

Perera mentions one final interesting change in clause structure during the school years. The structure is the recapitulatory pronouns, in

Figure 4.5
Adverbials in Janet's speech

Grammy doesn't come always on Sunday.	5;2
Daddy won't go with me never!	4;4
Kick the ball over here!	4;6
Matthew and Daddy will come later?	5;8
Bears on Wheels isn't anywhere!	3;10
I did looked everywhere.	4;4

which the noun phrase is repeated when the grammar doesn't require it (in sentences such as "These students with five classes they shouldn't work"). It appears less frequently in children's language as they grow older. Cotton (1978) found that children between 7;9 and 9;9 use this construction in speech (it is far less common in writing) but use it less with age (Perera, 1984, pp. 96–97). There are a few recorded instances of Janet's using this construction:

Spook she threw up on the floor.	5;4
Matthew and Daddy they left me here.	5;6
That mean boy outside he hit Spook.	5;10
Mummy and me we went to see Grammy.	6;0

The changing structure of the noun phrase is another indicator of syntactic development. Researchers generally believe that the use of complex subject noun phrases is a mark of linguistic maturity. Loban pointed to the fact that the most capable of the twelve-year-old children in his study produced eight times as many expanded noun phrases in subject position as did the less capable (Loban, 1963; cited in Perera, 1984, p. 100). Complex noun phrases, such as "The little dog with the bow on its collar" are more commonly found in writing than in speech, both in children and adults. This fact suggests that complexity in the noun phrase *may* result from some aspect of schooling, either literacy or overt teaching practice, such as sentence combining.

Another interesting aspect of noun phrase development is the acquisition of articles. As most non-native learners of English will attest, the rules governing the use of English articles are complicated, and native speakers do not work out all the rules until age eight or even later. Rules such as the one requiring *an* before a word beginning with a vowel and the plural agreement rule for *this* and *these*, for example, may not be perfectly learned even by age 12. Janet appeared to have worked out both rules before age 12, but at age 7;5, she produced the following sentences:

Matt said that he wanted a apple.

This ones are almost dead.

Another common error that children of school age make and continue to make until age 8 or, more rarely, 10 or 12, is to use an article denoting definite reference, that is, *the,* for something that is unspecified for the listener. Normally, for the article *the* to be used, the noun following it must have been previously introduced into the conversation or be clearly known to both speaker and listener. Hence, to say "The house was painted white" implies that both speaker and hearer know *which* house is under discussion. Children learn gradually during the school years that the use of *the* is restricted in this way. They also learn that the same restriction applies to *this, these,* and *those,* although colloquially, *this* is coming to be used as an indefinite determiner, as in "I was on the bus and I saw this man looking at me" (Janet 14;5). In this sentence, it is not at all clear that Janet had committed a reference error. It is more likely that she was using the language of her peer group, which permits the use of *this* with a non-specified noun.

Verb phrase expansion in English refers mainly to the use of auxiliary verbs. Children master certain auxiliary verbs early. *Is, can, will,* and *could* are acquired early (by about 2;6) largely in negatives and questions. Major (1974; cited in Perera, 1984, p. 110) demonstrated that by the age of 5, most children have acquired *can, could, will, would,* and *should,* but many will not acquire *shall, may, might,* and *ought to* until age 8 or later. By 7;5, Janet appeared to have acquired all the modal auxiliaries, but at 6;9, she produced the following:

> Mrs. Baker should might bring it to school.
>
> Matt will might let me ride his bike.

Other kinds of difficulties with the modals persist well into the teenage years in some children. Conditionals and the hypothetical past presented particular problems for Janet:

> If it would rain, the rain will get in under the tarp. (11;5)
>
> Uncle Jack can't had left early or he'd be here by now. (11;0)

In fact, many native speakers fail to master the modals fully. Sports figures and other celebrities whose careers and fame depend on something other than their facility with language might well produce a sentence such as this one: "If I would have known in advance, I wouldn't have come."

Morphophonology

This is the period during which children add the few remaining sounds to their phonetic inventories so that by age 7, or 8 at the latest, they can reproduce the full range of English sounds. If words such as *thermometer* and *vegetables* still give them difficulty, it is because they have not mastered the production of all sounds in all environments. Much of phonological development during the early school years, however, occurs as a result of or in conjunction with morphological growth. For example, children begin to learn the rules governing the sounds of the plural, past tense, and other inflectional and derivational morphemes that are phonologically governed.

Although this learning continues well into the teens, children between four and seven make major gains. They master two of the three plural forms (the syllabic form that follows words ending in sibilants is learned a little later) and at least the same two forms of the possessive morpheme. Interestingly, children at this stage are better at producing the correct possessive form of *boss* than they are at producing the plural, although they sound exactly the same. Obviously, children are learning something more than phonetic patterns.

When children reach the age 6 or 7, a stage of rapid morphophonemic growth begins. This period lasts for five to seven years and it is during this stage that children acquire many of the derivational morphemes. We saw in Chapter 2 that there are regular sound changes that occur with the addition of certain derivational morphemes. For example, when we add {-ity} to *divine* to produce *divinity*, the pronunciation of the vowel in the root word changes. Vowel alternation is one of the many morphophonemic processes that children learn during this stage, and it is one that Moskowitz (1973) studied in children between 5 and 12 years old. Specifically, her study asked whether children have knowledge of the rules governing vowel alternation and at what age they are acquired. Using a method that required her subjects to add the suffix *-ity* to nonsense forms, she found that 5-year-olds have no knowledge of the vowel alternation rule. She also found evidence that the 7- to 12-year-olds knew the rule, and that information about the rule is attained gradually.

Another kind of morphophonemic information that is acquired during this stage is how stress is used to differentiate compound nouns from noun phrases in pairs such as *BLACKboard* (compound noun) and *black BOARD* (noun phrase). In a study to test their ability to discriminate between such pairs, Atkinson-King (1973) showed children from kindergarten to grade six paired pictures of blackboards and boards painted black, red socks and members of the Boston baseball team, etc. She found that the youngest children could detect a difference but could not correctly signal the difference in any consistent way (cited in Menn, 1989) even though they could accurately imitate each pair. Atkinson-King found that children develop their knowledge of this morphophonemic stress rule gradually from grade one to grade six.

By age 7, then, children have not yet completed their acquisition of phonology; they gradually learn more complex morphophonemic rules until age 12 or so. At around this age, they move into the final stage of phonological development. Ingram (1976) identifies this as the **spelling stage**. It is at this time that children master (or come close to mastering) the spelling of English, a process that has begun much earlier. Ingram links this stage with Piaget's period of formal operations (roughly 12 to 16 years) and with the stage at which the child

> becomes capable of making intuitive reflections on . . . language. . . Decisions of grammaticality can be made. In phonology, the child can also begin to decide what is a possible sound change and what is not. This probably also has an effect on spelling, which develops markedly during this period. (Ingram, 1976, p. 14)

Vocabulary

As they acquire the ability to understand and to use derivational morphemes, children's vocabularies show a dramatic improvement. Estimates of the vocabulary of an average school-aged child vary from approximately 2500 different words (Crystal, 1987, p. 232) to as many as 8000 (Gleason, 1989, p. 4). This variation is caused not only by a wide range of vocabulary size in children this age, but by disagreement among researchers on what should be counted as a different word, or type. Does one, for example, count only root or base words or does one count all plurals, possessives, past tenses, etc., as separate words? Whatever the true figure, it is clear that children understand several times more words than they produce (Crystal, 1987, p. 232). The size of both receptive and productive vocabulary will increase dramatically over the next several years in large part as a result of learning to read.

Literacy

Literacy is, of course, the dominant language learning task children face after the age of five or six. In a real sense, learning to read and write is like learning another language since it involves learning another symbolic system. It is made easier, of course, by the existence of oral language. If children had not learned oral language, the task of learning to read and write would be a great deal more difficult than it is.

Janet learned to read at some point before she began grade one. From the time she was born, she was surrounded by books, magazines, and newspapers. Her parents read to her long before they had any hope that she understood the words. We saw Janet at age four pretending to read *Cinderella*. Sometime in the next two years, the pretend reading gave way to real reading. Janet's mother tells the story of Matthew having to learn a short poem for the Christmas play at school. He brought the poem, which he had printed onto lined paper, home with him to study it. She went into the family room to find Matthew reciting the poem and Janet following the written page. "No, Matt, it doesn't say that," Janet said when Matthew made an error. "It says 'the snows LAY deep and white,' not WERE deep and white." Janet's mother checked the script and found that Janet was right. Janet was one month short of her fifth birthday; Matthew was not quite seven.

It is not unusual for children to learn to read by mere exposure, nor is it usual. The majority of children need some teaching, but some, like Janet, who know the purposes of reading and who have been exposed to a great deal of print, simply learn on their own. Torrey (1973), Ferreiro and Teberosky (1982), and Bissex (1984) report studies of children who apparently learned to read without instruction. Some had the advantage of "Sesame Street" and "The Electric Company," as did Janet, but others did not. What they all did have in common was the view that learning to read presented a challenge that they wanted to meet and being questioners. As Pflaum reports, it seems to be a characteristic of early readers that they *"ask very specific questions* and . . . receive specific answers to those questions" (1986, p. 65).

We come then to the importance of social interaction. Clearly an important factor in children's learning to speak, social interaction might be thought of as less important for learning literacy. Reading and writing, unlike speaking, are, after all, activities that can be carried out in isolation from others. But apparently, *learning* to read and write are facilitated by social interaction.

CONCLUSION

In this chapter, we have seen a sketch of Janet's language development from the time she was born until she reached her teenaged years. While a full description of her language growth at each stage was beyond the scope of this chapter, even the brief examples have served to mark significant milestones in her acquisition of the pragmatics, syntax, morphology, and phonology of her native language.

We saw Janet grow from an infant whose precursory behavior was essential to the development of real language to a school-aged child already established as a lifetime member of her language community. Throughout the chapter, Janet's story has served as a springboard for more general discussion of the course of normal language acquisition. In the chapter that follows, we will see that this course is very similar for other kinds of language learning as well.

Chapter Five

The Second Time Around: Acquiring Two or More Languages

In being monolingual, Janet, the child we met in Chapter 4, is a member of the North American majority. Contrary to popular belief, however, she is in the minority in the world population. Crystal (1987, p. 360) claims that although government policies give the impression that multilingualism is unusual, the fact is that most of the world's population learns and functions in two, three, or more languages. People learn their languages for a variety of reasons and under a variety of conditions, but the fact that they do so suggests that there cannot be anything especially difficult about learning an additional language. Yet, in North America, we seem to find "foreign" language teaching, and even English as a second language, particularly challenging, and anyone who claims to be bilingual a trifle exotic.

However, no clear agreement exists about what it means to be bilingual. Some authors use the term to refer to people with *any* proficiency, even if it is only a few words, in a second language. Others insist that native-like control of both languages is necessary. But, in fact, McLaughlin is correct when he says, "Bilingualism is best described in terms of degree" (1984, p. 9). For our purposes, we will adopt Haugen's useful definition, also used by McLaughlin: "the ability to produce complete and meaningful utterances in the other language" (Haugen, 1956; cited in McLaughlin, 1984, p. 8) This definition does not assume balance; it is not uncommon even for young children to be more fluent in one language or to reserve one language for use in certain situations. It only assumes that children are able to communicate easily in either language at a level appropriate to their age.

In this chapter, we take a look at childhood bilingualism and the issues surrounding it. We begin by marking a very basic distinction between children who acquire two languages more or less simultaneously in the home environment and those who learn their second language in school. Next we examine the issues that an adequate theory of second language acquisition must address.

Because the focus of this book is children's language learning, we will concentrate on the conditions affecting their second language learning, although in the description of the issues affecting theory, there will be some discussion of adult learning.[1] A critical factor in assessing these conditions is the age at which the child begins acquiring a second language, because most other conditions will be influenced by that one. An important distinction in childhood second language acquisition is between acquiring languages simultaneously and sequentially (McLaughlin, 1984; Vihman & McLaughlin, 1982), although it is not always a clear-cut distinction. It is not easy to assign an arbitrary age at which the acquisition of two languages ceases to be simultaneous and becomes sequential. Are children who begin to learn another language at age two or even age three *adding* a language to an established first language? Or are they acquiring two languages at the same time? McLaughlin arbitrarily sets the cutoff at age three, after which children are assumed to be adding a second language to a fairly well-established first. Certainly the child has a good head start in the one language by that time.

We saw in the last chapter, however, that a significant amount of first language growth occurs between age three and the end of the preschool years. More importantly, there is a major difference between the conditions or environment for second language acquisition that occurs in the home and in the school. The former has been termed natural language learning and the latter formal language learning. While recognizing the sometimes useful distinction between simultaneous and successive bilingualism, I have chosen instead to mark the distinction between home bilingualism and school bilingualism. The former refers to simultaneous bilingualism from infancy and any other second language learning that begins before schooling, even in daycare or preschool. The latter refers to

---

[1] I use the terms *acquisition* and *learning* interchangeably, although I am well aware that some theorists, particularly Stephen Krashen, mark a distinction between the two. That distinction rests, however, on other distinctions within his Monitor Model, a model of second language acquisition that is untested and possibly untestable. See Krashen (1977a, 1977b, 1978, 1981, 1982, 1985) as well as McLaughlin (1987), Gregg (1984), and Spolsky (1985) for a fuller description of the model and significant objections to it.

those cases in which children begin to learn a second language when they begin school or at any time during the school years.

HOME BILINGUALISM

When we speak of children who acquire two languages at the same time, it is not really accurate to speak of either as a "second" language. What these children are really doing is acquiring two first languages even though one of the two may eventually dominate. This would be the case, for example, for a child whose French-speaking mother and English-speaking father spoke only their own language with the child. Doubtless, there are a number of these children in North America. What may be more common, though, is the child whose parents speak the same language but who learns another language from a grandparent, nanny, or babysitter, if not perhaps from birth, from a very young age.

Studies of preschool children acquiring two languages (Ronjat, 1913; Leopold, 1939, 1947, 1949a, 1949b; Totten, 1960) strongly indicate that they are able to do so in much the same way as they learn different registers of the same language. Ronjat's detailed study of his son, Louis, learning his mother's language, German, and his father's language, French, indicates that the child learned German and French vocabulary, phonology, and syntax simultaneously and without confusion. According to Ronjat's observations, the child could produce the phonemes of both languages correctly by 3;5 (McLaughlin, 1984, p. 75). As we saw in the previous chapter, this is well within the normal range for a monolingual child, and Ronjat's son was bilingual.

Ronjat reported following his friend Maurice Grammont's advice to keep the languages strictly separated: "each language must be embodied in a different person" (cited in McLaughlin, 1984, p. 75). With his daughter Hildegard, Werner Leopold followed the same advice, speaking to her only in German and her mother speaking to her only in English. Although her learning in both languages was impressive, Hildegard never achieved the balance achieved by Louis Ronjat. This was likely because the family lived in an English-speaking environment and visited Germany only twice in her first five years. So while German was the language in which she communicated with her father, it apparently had little utility outside the home. Some mixing of Hildegard's two languages occurred, most obvious in her early vocabulary development where she seemed for a time to adopt

the strategy of giving things one name only. However, once she realized that there were two languages in her environment, this competition ceased and she managed to use the appropriate words in both languages (although the increasing predominance of English complicated this task). (McLaughlin, 1984, p. 80)

In general, however, Leopold found no evidence that bilingualism in any way influenced the development of either language.

Another study from early in this century is useful for comparison with Ronjat's and Leopold's. Madorah Smith reported in 1935 on the learning of English and Chinese by eight children from the same family. The parents were American missionaries, and all their children were born in China. The parents spoke both Chinese and English to the children, who apparently confused the two languages until about age three. Their preference was for their parents' native English, but they sometimes used Chinese even when playing alone together. Unlike the Ronjats and the Leopolds, the parents of the children in Smith's study mixed the languages, each parent speaking Chinese at times and English at others.

A more recent study of early bilingualism in a family where the parents mixed the two languages was reported by Tabouret-Keller (1962). The little girl's mother was raised in a poor rural area and spoke both her native German and the French she had learned in school. The child's father was a mine worker who had learned both German and French as a child. According to Tabouret-Keller's account, both parents mixed the two languages in speaking with the child, using French about twice as often as German. Not surprisingly, the child had a larger French than German vocabulary by the time she was two years old by a margin of about three to one. She also mixed German and French words in about 60% of her sentences. While mixing would be expected under the circumstances described, the amount of language mixing done by this child exceeded what would be predicted given the proportion of French she heard. But then, of course, the parents were not the only influence on their child's language growth. The family lived in an area where German was spoken and this was the language of the child's playmates.

Numerous other studies report the mixing of a child's two languages (Ruke-Dravina, 1965, 1967; Zareba, 1953; Totten, 1960; Engel, 1965) or three languages in the case of a trilingual environment (Murrell, 1966). One of these studies was particularly interesting for the conclusions it reached about the nature of language structure. Engel's son, who was learning both English and Italian, produced a number of hybrid words, usually English words with Italian endings, and experienced some semantic confusion between the two languages. The sound systems, however, were entirely distinct, leading Engel to conclude that the phonological system is somehow separate from the semantic and morphological systems.

Engel's conclusion received further support from a study of a bilingual child reported by Oksaar (1970). Estonian was the language the child spoke with his parents and Swedish the language he used with his playmates. The sound systems of the two languages are similar, and it is usually the case that children have more difficulty keeping similar systems distinct.[2] Even though the child was in constant contact with a Swedish-speaking playmate, Oksaar found no evidence that Swedish influenced her son's Estonian pronunciation. There was, however, evidence of mixing in his morphology and syntax. Like Engel's child, this child tended to add endings from one language to words of the other. In contrast, Itoh and Hatch, studying the language development of a Japanese-speaking child learning English from 2;6, found an early confusion especially in the sound system. Specifically, they found that the Japanese sound system influenced his English pronunciation (Itoh & Hatch, 1978, pp. 80–83).

It seems to be the case that learning the sound system may be a different sort of task from other aspects of language learning. Analyzing the language development of a three-year-old Spanish-speaking child acquiring English, Hernandez "found that the influence of the new sound system was initially pre-eminent, suggesting that acquisition of the sound system is especially important for a child of this age learning a second language" (McLaughlin, 1978, p. 104). Hernandez also reported the more general observation that Spanish-speaking children attempting to speak English often resorted to using Spanish words and grammar with English pronunciation.

If children tend to keep the sound systems of their two languages separate, what about the other systems? While some children appear not to confuse or mix their two languages, early mixing seems to be much more typical. Crystal identifies three stages of development in early childhood bilingualism:

1. Children build a vocabulary of words from both languages that only rarely are translation equivalents of each other.

2. When they begin to combine words in two- and three-word sentences, words from both languages are used within the same sentence. But the amount of mixing declines rapidly.

3. As the vocabulary grows larger in each language, children begin to learn translation equivalents, for example, *chat* and *cat* or *friend* and *amigo* (adapted from Crystal, 1987, p. 363).

[2]Kellerman (1979, 1984) has explored the notion of interference within the linguistic concept of "markedness," arguing that the greater the perceived distance between the first and second languages, the less likely the learner is to employ a strategy of transfer (interference) in learning the second language.

Crystal cites these stages as evidence that acquiring a single language and acquiring two languages are different processes. On the face of it, this is obviously true. But if we think about the processes from a broader perspective, they don't seem quite so disparate. Both bilingual and monolingual children initially acquire a single label for common objects or actions and only rarely have synonyms in their early vocabularies. When they begin to combine words into sentences, bilingual children use the words they have. Assuming that they attempt to express the same semantic relations as monolingual children, and there is no evidence to the contrary, then they must necessarily mix their two languages. Otherwise, given the nature of their vocabularies, they would be limited in what they could express. As their vocabularies expand, monolingual children *and* bilingual children add synonyms. So while a case can be made for different behavior in bilingual and monolingual children, the different behavior may not signal different acquisition processes.

In addition to the ones cited here, a number of other studies of early bilingualism have been conducted,[3] most of them case studies and thus inconsistent in their objectives, observations, and purpose. Even with such inconsistency, however, it seems that certain conditions facilitate the acquisition of two languages. In general, it seems to be the case that Grammont's advice to his friend Ronjat was sound. Young children experience less confusion between their two languages if those two languages are kept distinct. They seem to have little trouble learning the separate languages of their two parents, or the language of their parents and the language of their peers or other caregiver. The distinction, however, need not be embodied in people. Ruke-Dravina (1967) observed situational specificity in which children playing with the same playmates used their parents' language, Swedish, when playing in the home and Latvian, the playmates' language, when playing outside. The studies also agree that balanced bilingualism is rare, that sooner or later one language dominates, and that once a particular language becomes predominant, it is difficult for the child to switch back to the other language. There may even be a period during which the child refuses to use either language, a silent period until some degree of balance is attained (Engel, 1966; Leopold, 1949b).

What is abundantly clear is that children who grow up bilingual or multilingual are neither linguistically nor educationally at risk. There is no evidence whatsoever that acquiring more than one language is detrimental. As Crystal writes of bilinguals, "By the time these children arrive in school, the vast majority have reached the same stage of linguistic

[3]See, for example, McLaughlin (1978, 1984, 1985) and Slobin (1985).

development as have their monolingual peers" (Crystal, 1987, p. 363) *and* they have an additional language.

SCHOOL BILINGUALISM

Setting and age of the learner are not the only differences between home and school bilingualism. To put it another way, it is not the location of the school that exerts the influence on second language acquisition, but the kind of language that occurs in school. A number of researchers and educators have observed that the language used in schools is significantly different from the language used outside classrooms. Margaret Donaldson (1978) characterizes the difference in terms of children's thinking. They are quite capable thinkers before they begin school, but their thinking tends to be "directed outwards on to the real, meaningful, shifting, distracting world." Success in school, however, requires them to learn "to turn language and thought in upon themselves," to direct their own thought processes in a thoughtful manner. Linguistically, this means that children must be able not only to talk but to choose what they will say, "not just to interpret but to weigh possible interpretations." In short, they "must become capable of manipulating symbols" (Donaldson, 1978, pp. 87–88). Children must learn these new thinking and language skills in contact with the language of the school, the formal, abstract language that is largely decontextualized, logical, and expository. The informal language they have learned at home is, in contrast, context-bound, sequential, and intuitive.

The task is made easier when children have been previously exposed to the literary functions of language by being around people who read and by having books read to them. Still, a great many children find the language demands of the school very difficult to meet. When the language of the school is also a second language for the child, the problem is compounded. In this situation, children from literate homes, children who know about books and the language of books, have a better chance of success, unless, of course, the language of the school can be better suited to match the experience of the children. As we shall see, in school second language programs, this seldom happens.

The majority of children in North America achieve whatever degree of bilingualism they possess in school. Whether they are adding the dominant language (usually English) to their home language or adding a minority or "foreign" language, children may encounter any one of a number of different formal language programs. These include immersion, bilingual, FLES (foreign languages in the elementary school), and submersion.

Immersion

One of the most promising of the second language programs in elementary schools is immersion, and the most comprehensive research literature comes from the Canadian experiment in bilingualism, French immersion. Swain (1976) listed 114 such research reports, and dozens more have appeared each year.

Throughout Quebec in the 1960s, the protection of the French language became a sensitive political issue. It became apparent to anglophone parents that their children's future in Quebec would be brighter if they spoke both their native English and the language of the majority of the population of Quebec, French. Thus began what has since become a national movement in bilingual education, the government-supported French immersion programs. The identifying characteristic of immersion is the exclusive use of the second language in school. Teachers must be bilingual because the children will initially speak only in English. Teachers, however, will respond in French and gradually children start to use French themselves. For the first few years, all instruction in all subjects is in French. For children who begin immersion in kindergarten, English is usually introduced in grade three (or in grade four in some programs) and the amount of English gradually increased until the proportion is approximately 60% English and 40% French.

The children in the first immersion classes are in or have completed university at this writing. As might be expected, they have been rather extensively studied. The results are, on the whole, positive. Not only do children acquire a better level of competence in French than those in more traditional language classes, they also tend to have more favorable attitudes toward French-Canadians. But the research does not indicate that immersion is a panacea. Although their language proficiency is impressive, children from immersion classes are a long way from native proficiency, partly because they have extensive academic or "school" competence but less social language proficiency in French. One very important finding on which nearly all studies agree, however, is that the children's proficiency in English is not at all adversely affected by their acquisition of French in immersion programs. Although they may lag slightly behind their peers in grade two or three, by grade five or six, they catch up.

Since the original immersion programs began, there have been other experiments with variations—**early partial, delayed, late,** and **double**

immersion among them. Early partial immersion begins either in kindergarten or grade one with the day divided between the child's first and second language. Initial evaluations of English-speaking children in French
partial immersion have shown that their English language skills are no
better than peers in total immersion and that their French skills are worse
(although better than children in FLES programs) (Genesee, 1983; Swain
& Lapkin, 1982; Barik & Swain, 1974, 1975).

Even though early immersion has been largely successful, there is a
heavy attrition rate, suggesting that it is not for every child. Moreover,

> Clinical studies indicate that there may be a subgroup of children for whom
> early programs are not suitable. These children could be termed develop-
> mentally immature in the sense that their cognitive and linguistic skills are
> not developed adequately to meet the demands of a bilingual academic
> environment. (Wiss, 1989, p. 518)

Rather than have their children face the possible stigma of withdrawing
from immersion, and worrying that their children's education may suffer
if they begin French immersion too young, some parents prefer to delay
French until later. **Delayed immersion** is essentially the same as early
total immersion except that it begins in grade three or four. **Late immersion** is yet another alternative for some children. It begins in grade six or
later and lasts for one or two years. Results of evaluation studies of late
immersion indicate that the students suffer no harmful effects to their
native language, do very well in French, and develop positive attitudes
toward French-speaking people. They do not, however, do as well in
French as children of the same age who have had either early or delayed
immersion (Barik, Swain, & Guadino, 1976; Connors, Menard, & Singh,
1978; Swain, 1974).

Success in immersion led some educators to experiment with **double
immersion**. Taking the view that if immersion in one language works,
some schools are trying immersion in two languages. A study conducted
in Montreal of English-speaking children immersed in both French and
Hebrew showed promising results in both languages without detriment to
English (Genesee & Lambert, 1983; Genesee, Tucker, & Lambert, 1976;
cited in Reich, 1986, p. 222).

FLES

Perhaps the most familiar bilingual opportunity in North American
schools is that of taking at least one "foreign" language in school. These

courses, unlike immersion and bilingual programs, do not attempt to teach other curricular subjects *in* the foreign language. Rather, language is treated as a subject in its own right. Typically, both the amount and the kind of exposure to the new language is limited in comparison to immersion. The time devoted to the foreign language might be as little as 20 minutes three times per week or as much as 50 minutes per day. During that time, teaching is likely to focus more on the language itself than on content or meaning.

McLaughlin (1985) reported that early FLES programs were not dramatically successful. Although there was greater acceptance of foreign language classes beginning in the elementary school, children did not learn the languages quickly and easily when taught for only one hour per day. One study did report that students who began learning a second language in elementary school generally performed better than children who began in high school (Vocolo, 1967), but most evaluations reported that children lost interest by grades five or six and motivation became a major problem (Page, 1966).

Recent FLES programs have been less ambitious in their goals, focusing on oral skills and cultural awareness. Full communicative competence in the target language is not expected, and both parents and students are told so from the beginning. The most common languages taught in current FLES programs are Spanish, French, and German (McLaughlin, 1985, p. 86).

These studies are strongly at odds with the immersion studies, and the reason probably lies in the teaching method. Until relatively recently, and even now in some schools, the preferred teaching method for FLES classes was essentially a behaviorist approach. As they grew older, the children tired of pattern drills and structure manipulation. Since these constituted the children's only exposure to the language, their learning declined. Immersion, in contrast, never used such methods and focused instead on the subject matter being taught rather than the structure of the language. More recent FLES programs have employed different methods with more positive results, but the language proficiency level achieved is still far less than that in immersion programs.

Immersion and FLES programs are intended as a means for children who speak the dominant language to learn a second language. Educationally, they are important, but they are not critical to the life of the child in the way that language programs for minority speakers are. There are hundreds of thousands of children in both the United States and Canada who speak a minority language at home and then face schooling in English. The next two types of programs attempt to meet their needs.

Bilingual Programs

Language programs intended to maintain the child's native language within an English-speaking environment or to ease the transition between the language of the home and the language of the school are commonly called bilingual programs. The introduction of English in school and the widespread use of English in the community may cause children to lose much of their native language proficiency, unless there is a concerted effort to maintain it. **Maintenance bilingualism** is intended to protect the native language while introducing English as the language of the school. Such programs are not popular in the United States, where the belief in the "melting pot" has led in some states to English-only movements. But in Canada, which has adopted an official policy of multiculturalism, bilingual maintenance programs operate in a number of languages including German, Ukrainian, Hebrew, French, Spanish, Italian, and Cree.

A second type of bilingual program is termed **transitional**. In this type of program, the child's home language is used in the early years of schooling and the dominant language introduced later. Transitional programs are widely used. In India, for example, where more than 200 languages are spoken, at least 80 are used in schools, mostly in the first four years, after which students are switched to one of the major languages (Khubchandani, 1978; cited in Reich, 1986, p. 224). Canada also has a number of transitional programs in place for Chinese, Ukrainian, German, Hebrew, Italian, and some aboriginal languages. The U.S. government as well as some state governments sponsor programs for as many as 58 different languages (Tucker & Gray, 1980).

Surprisingly, very few evaluations of transitional bilingual programs have been published. The ones that have been, including one done in Mexico and one in the Philippines, addressed program effectiveness from the perspective of proficiency in the *second* language. Not surprisingly, they revealed that the longer the children spent being educated in English (the second language in both places), the better their English was. In other words, because the only goal of transition programs was greater success in the second language, they failed. Neither the children's native language proficiency nor their attitude toward schooling was considered, and many educators would consider these to be important factors in the overall development and the education of the child.

Submersion

The success of immersion in Canada and in some U.S. communities has led some educators to the erroneous conclusion that the best language teaching program is none at all. In other words, if immersion children can learn the new language in an environment where they are taught all the school subjects in that language, can't minority children do the same with English? In **submersion**, children are placed in classes where all their subjects are taught in the language of the school even though they may not know the language at all. According to Reich, this is the predominant teaching method for minority speakers in Sweden, New Zealand, China, Belgium, Australia, and many other countries (Reich, 1986, p. 223). It is also the method by which many older immigrants learned English in the United States and Canada.

But is it effective? It is a great credit to the learning powers of children that it does work for some. But on the whole, it is neither an effective nor humane way to learn a language. The U.S. Supreme Court recognized the inadequacy of submersion in the landmark *Lau v. Nichols* case, proclaiming that submersion does not provide equal educational opportunity for children who do not speak English.

Although it may not be immediately obvious, there are several important differences between submersion and immersion. There are, in fact, more differences than there are similarities. Table 5.1 summarizes how the two differ in factors pertaining to the children, their teachers, and the programs themselves. We can see that the only real similarity between immersion and submersion is that initially the children are not proficient in the language of instruction. On the other hand, the children in immersion classes are all at the same level of proficiency in the unfamiliar language, while children being submersed in English will most likely have had varying amounts of exposure to the language. Immersion children come from the dominant culture where their language is protected and respected, and when they begin school, they are permitted to speak in their native language for the first few months. Their teacher is bilingual and will understand. In contrast, the submersion children come from minority cultures and there is little if any protection or respect for their languages. When they begin school, they must use English from the first day, and if they do not, their teachers will probably not understand them anyway.

In the immersion classroom, the teacher knows both the children's native language and the language being taught. The submersion teacher will know English and possibly one other language, but the children in the class will rarely all come from the same language background. The

Table 5.1
Differences between submersion and immersion

		Submersion	Immersion
Children	Same level of L1	No	Yes
	L1 "protected"	No	Yes
	Allowed to use L1 initially	No	Yes
	Members of dominant culture	No	Yes
	All speak same L1	Rarely	Yes
Teachers	Understand L1 and L2	Rarely	Yes
	Specially educated in L2 teaching methods	Sometimes	Yes
	Understand children's culture	Sometimes	Yes
Program	Optional	No	Yes
	Specially funded	Sometimes	Yes
	Elitist	No	Yes
	Taught entirely in L2	Yes	First 2 yrs.

immersion teacher has been educated in language acquisition and in methods for teaching children who do not know the language in which she is teaching. The submersion teacher may have had a course in teaching ESL but frequently must rely on her usual teaching practices. Finally, immersion is optional and prestigious. If children or their parents are unhappy with the program or the children's progress, good educational alternatives are available. Immersion is also specially funded and enjoys an elitist reputation in the community. No one can make such claims for submersion.

We have seen that a number of different circumstances exist under which children acquire a second language and that they do so with varying degrees of success. A number of questions are thus raised both for theory and for practice. The practical issues will be addressed in Chapter 6, after we have looked at the particular circumstances in which two children acquired their second language very successfully. In the remainder of this chapter, we will look at how situation, proficiency, and a number of other factors are addressed in theories of second language acquisition.

ISSUES IN SECOND LANGUAGE ACQUISITION THEORY

As complicated as the task of formulating an adequate theory of first language acquisition is, it is simple compared to the task of formulating an adequate theory of second language acquisition. This is true because the number of factors that may vary in second language acquisition is far greater than those in first language acquisition. Spolsky (1985) framed the problem by breaking down into its component parts the central question about second language learning: Who learns how much of what language under what conditions?

Who can be anyone of any age, ability, and intelligence and with any attitude or personality. *Learns* refers to the process itself and raises questions about the different kinds of learning there are, about innateness, about transfer between languages, and about conscious and unconscious learning, etc. *How much of* refers to the amount of language learning that takes place and what aspect of the language is learned (for example, syntax, phonology, semantics, culture). *What language* refers to the target language being learned, and *under what conditions* addresses the kind and amount of exposure to the second language that leads to learning (Spolsky, 1985, pp. 269–270).

Because first and second language acquisition have two essential elements in common, namely, learners and language, it is not surprising that the theories devised to account for them would have at least basic similarities. In general, they do, and some theories of first language acquisition can be applied with little or no modification to second language acquisition. For example, a behavioristic model has only the additional requirement that the "habit" of the first language be eradicated in the learning of the second. Second language acquisition theories, thus, are partly derived from first language acquisition theories, but because of the variability in the factors identified by Spolsky, they are necessarily more complex. In fact, no one theory has yet been put forward that is comprehensive enough to account for all these factors and the interactions among them. Nevertheless, there has been no reluctance to theorize about second language learning. The details of the many theories that have been advanced in recent years are well beyond the scope of this chapter. Table 5.2, however, identifies nine such theories together with the researchers usually credited with proposing them, sources for recent discussion or evaluation, and some indication of their scope.

Under the heading *Scope* in the table are the designations *learner, process, proficiency, language,* and *condition,* which correspond to different aspects of Spolsky's question. *Learner* variables (*who*) are those attributes of learners that influence their success in language acquisition. These include, among others, age of the learner, cognitive style, and sociopsychological attitudes toward speakers of the target language. *Process (learns)* is concerned with the internal systems devised by the learner or the strategies used in learning, understanding and producing the new language. *Proficiency (how much of)* refers to those things that affect the amount of learning that takes place and the level of mastery a learner attains. *Language* takes a slightly broader view than Spolsky's and includes features of the target language as well as the nature of the input to the learner. Finally, *conditions* addresses the situational factors, for example,

Table 5.2
Nine theories of second language acquisition

Theory/scope	Origin	Evaluation/discussion
Acculturation Learner Proficiency Conditions	Schumann (1978a, 1978b, 1981a, 1981b, 1982)	McLaughlin (1987) Ellis (1985) Larsen-Freeman (1983) Larsen-Freeman & Long (1991)
Accommodation Learner Conditions Proficiency	Giles et al. (1977) Giles & Byrne (1982)	Ellis (1985)
Behaviorism Conditions Language	Skinner (1957)	McLaughlin (1978, 1984, 1987)
Cognitive Learner Process	McLaughlin et al. (1983); McLeod & McLaughlin (1986); Segalowitz (1986)	McLaughlin (1987)
Discourse Learner Conditions Process	Hatch (1978c, 1978d)	Ellis (1985) Larsen-Freeman (1983)
Interlanguage Process Language Proficiency	Selinker (1972)	McLaughlin (1987) Ellis (1985)
Monitor Model Learner Process Conditions Language	Krashen (1977a, 1977b, 1978, 1981, 1982, 1985)	McLaughlin (1987) Spolsky (1985) Ellis (1985) Larsen-Freeman (1983); Gregg (1984)
Neurofunctional Process Language	Lamendella (1977, 1979)	Larsen-Freeman (1983); Ellis (1985)
Universal Process Grammar Language	Chomsky (1980) Greenberg (1966, 1974); Wode (1981)	McLaughlin (1987) Gass (1984) Ellis (1985

classroom or naturalistic environments, that influence second language learning. The discussion that follows does not examine each theory of second language acquisition, as was done for first language acquisition in Chapter 3. Rather, it examines the different variables, noting where appropriate those theories that address them.

Learner Variables

In second language acquisition, more variation occurs among learners than in first language acquisition. This is true for obvious reasons. Because second language learners are older than first language learners, they will have had a variety of linguistic, learning, and life experiences. While any number of learner factors may influence the course of language development, researchers have identified a number of general factors believed to contribute to individual learner differences. Among these are age, aptitude, cognitive variation, and personality traits.

A vast body of research literature attempts to describe and explain differences that are attributable to the **age of the learner**. The results are mixed, as might be expected, but what has emerged with some clarity are the findings that:

> a) in general, the ability to learn languages does not diminish with age; b) more specifically, young children's superiority as language learners is restricted to their learning of the sound system. (McLaughlin, 1981, pp. 23–32)

Some researchers believe that aptitude, or some kind of specialized language learning ability, plays a central role in language acquisition. The research findings are dubious, however, in part because it is impossible to know with any certainty just what cognitive abilities aptitude comprises. If there is an aptitude factor in second language acquisition, it is obvious that it would primarily affect language learning in the classroom. For most educators, however, the question of aptitude is *in practice* not very important. Children need to and have the right to learn the language of the school whether or not some test judges them capable or not. The educator's major concern is not with measuring aptitude, if indeed such a thing could be done, but with planning a language learning environment that enhances every child's learning opportunities.

Cognitive style refers to the ways in which individuals process information or approach a particular task. Although much of the literature on cognitive style seems to suggest that they are dichotomous, that is, that people tend to possess one trait or its opposite, it is more likely the case that people "show a tendency towards one pole or the other, with their scores on cognitive style tests arranged along a continuum between the poles" (Larsen-Freeman & Long, 1991, p. 192). A number of dimensions are included under the heading cognitive style including:

1. **Types** of learning inherent in cognitive tasks
2. Variation in **strategies** individuals employ
3. Variation in personal **cognitive styles** of learning. (Brown, 1980, p. 80)

Types of Learning.   According to Robert Gagne (1965), people employ eight different types of learning for different tasks ranging from signal learning, involving a classically conditioned response, to problem solving, requiring "the internal events usually referred to as 'thinking'" (Gagne, 1965, pp. 58–59; quoted in Brown, 1980, p. 81). Brown claims that learners use all eight types of learning depending on a number of factors including the aspect of language being learned and the learner's previous experience of language learning. Because language learning is highly complex, it is unlikely that the different levels of learning will proceed independently.

Variation in Strategies.   Part of language learning obviously involves problem solving, and people differ in how they seek solutions. In language learning, we generally distinguish between two broad types of strategies—learning strategies and communication strategies. The former refers to the ways in which learners attempt to work out meanings and structures in language and to store them for later recall. The latter refers to how learners manage to encode and express meaning in order to communicate in a language.[4] Learning strategies include such things as memorization, overgeneralization, and inference, and learners make use of different strategies and different combinations of strategies for different purposes. Moreover, older children and adults probably have better developed processing capabilities to build on as they approach the learning of a new language (McLaughlin, 1981, p. 30).

To communicate in a second language, learners generally rely on essentially the same strategies as they do when learning it. Brown (1980)

[4]Ellis (1985) and others divide learner strategies into three categories: learning, production, and communication strategies. Production strategies refer to the ways in which learners use linguistic knowledge to express meaning. Communication strategies are emergency measures and are used only when production strategies fail.

claims, in fact, that learning and communication represent the input and the output of the same process. Nevertheless, differences exist. Avoidance of a structure or a word whose pronunciation is uncertain is a strategy commonly used in communication but which has no obvious parallel in learning. Similarly, generalization, for example, from a known form to an unknown form, is a productive learning strategy that also occurs in communication, although it is difficult to detect because its use results in a correct form. Overgeneralization, in contrast, is not a successful learning strategy, but is all too apparent in communication since it results in an incorrect form.

Variation in Personal Cognitive Styles.   The third dimension of cognitive style refers to the particular way in which a learner approaches a learning situation. In language learning, learners may vary in the amount of explanation they want or need or in their preference for oral or written presentation. Other dimensions of cognitive style that have been identified include field dependence versus independence, reflectivity versus impulsivity, tolerance versus intolerance of ambiguity, and the tendency to "skeletonize" or to embroider in the recall of cognitive material (Brown, 1980, pp.90–97; Hatch, 1983).

Personality traits are those attitudes, feelings, and emotions that may influence an individual's learning. They are sometimes called the **affective variables** and include the learner's attitude toward the language being learned and its native speakers, motivation for learning the language, and ego factors such as self-esteem, degree of inhibition, and capacity for empathy, among others.

Obviously, a complete theory of second language acquisition must account for learner differences attributable to personality and cognitive factors. For educators, however, the concern is a more practical one. They need to understand how such factors influence second language acquisition in order to have some idea about how to plan instruction for the introverted as well as the extroverted child, the analytic as well as the synthetic thinker.

Situation

Situational variables are those things in the language learner's environment that influence the learning and the use of the new language. In short, they encompass everything the learner sees and hears in the new language, and they are highly significant:

> The quality of the environment is of paramount importance to success in learning a new language. If students are exposed to a list of words and their

translations, together with a few simple readings in the new language, they will perhaps be able to attain some degree of reading skill in language, but listening and speaking skills will remain fallow. (Dulay, Burt, & Krashen, 1982, p. 13)

Another, perhaps more theoretical, reason for trying to understand the role played by situation is to explain the fact that in different situations, individual learners may perform differently in the language they are learning. ESL teachers have long lamented the fact that language forms that seem to cause students no difficulty in class give them all kinds of trouble outside. I had a similar experience with a Chinese graduate student who was taking an oral examination for his master's degree. Throughout the examining period, he answered the questions well but continually confused the personal pronouns, producing sentences such as "English is a difficult language because she is very different from Chinese" and "My mother could speak only one language and he was happy when I learned more languages." I had never heard him make these errors in the two previous years I had known him. The question of why a tense situation causes errors has potential impact on our understanding of the very processes of language learning and production, for clearly an interaction occurs between situation of use and the learner's ability to recall correctly a previously learned form.

Identification of all the environmental factors that potentially influence language learning would be impossible, but researchers have identified four broad categories of factors believed to have a significant impact:

1. The naturalness of the environment
2. The learner's role in communication
3. The availability of concrete referents
4. Target language models (Dulay, Burt, & Krashen, 1982, pp. 13–43)

Naturalness of the Environment. Evidence suggests that learners perform better when they "are exposed to natural language, where the focus is on communication" rather than in "a formal environment, where focus is on the conscious acquisition of linguistic rules or the manipulation of linguistic forms" (Dulay, Burt, & Krashen, 1982, p. 42). Certainly, this conclusion is consistent with many of the studies reviewed earlier in this chapter and with the experiences of the children reported in Chapter 6. Also, some exposure to the formal properties of language may be helpful for adult learners.

Learner's Role in Communication. The quality of language learning is also affected by the types of communication in which the learner is most frequently engaged. Communication exchanges may be classified as one-way, restricted two-way, or full two-way. One-way exchanges occur when the learner listens to or reads the target language but does not respond. Restricted two-way exchanges occur when the learner listens and responds either nonverbally, for example, by nodding, or in a language other than the target language. In full two-way exchanges, the learner responds in the target language.

Some evidence indicates that in the earliest stages of language learning, one-way and restricted two-way exchanges may actually facilitate language acquisition for some learners. A "silent period" lasting until the learner is ready to speak seems to be beneficial in some classroom situations. Gary (1975), studying 50 English-speaking children learning Spanish, found that the children who did not engage in any oral response during the first 14 weeks of the course performed better in listening comprehension than did children in classes where oral responses were required. What was more surprising, perhaps, was her finding that the children who had kept silent did as well in speaking as their peers who had been speaking for 14 weeks (Gary, 1975; cited in Dulay, Burt, & Krashen, 1982, pp. 24–26).

Availability of Concrete Referents. An important aspect of the language learning environment seems to be the availability of visible referents. It is much easier to understand a language in which one has limited proficiency if there is adequate context. I once witnessed Stephen Krashen illustrate this point in a simple counting task. He first stood before us and counted to ten in a language I didn't understand. He could have been giving directions for making a moon landing for all I knew. He then repeated the exercise holding up one finger, then two, etc., as he said the corresponding number. The second time he did so, I was able to remember six of the ten numbers. As a counterexample, most of us could sit and listen to Radio Moscow for hours, days, or even weeks without ever learning six words of Russian. Talking about what is present and observable helps the learner to understand and is thus crucial to acquiring language.

Target Language Models. The fourth type of situational variable has to do with the source, or models, of language the learner encounters. The different people that learners come into contact with influence the language they learn. Learners seem neither to learn nor even attend to all the language to which they are exposed. Research on speaker models indicates that learners apparently prefer some sources over others. Milon

(1975) reported, for example, that when a seven-year-old Japanese-speaking child moved to Hawaii, he learned the Hawaiian Creole English of the children around him rather than the standard English of his teacher. Immersion studies in the United States and Canada have reported similar findings and also speculated that a child's language development is actually hampered when the only models are adults. Children exposed to immersion in kindergarten were found to have some grammatical deficiencies in French even after seven years in the program (Bruck, Lambert, & Tucker, 1975). Remember that there are no native-speaking peers in immersion classes. Children seem to prefer peers as language models over both teachers and parents. There is evidence, too, that they make more use of models who are members of their own social or ethnic group than those who are not (Benton, 1964). This is consistent with the immersion findings: Having no native-speaking peer group, the children served as models for one another and their language reflected the fact that they were non-native speakers. Language itself is, then, an important variable in the acquisition of a second language.

Language

Learners are not solely responsible for their language learning. We saw in our discussion of social interaction theory in Chapter 3 that the attempts caretakers make to focus the child's attention or to focus their own language on what is occupying the child's attention contribute to the child's language learning. In second language acquisition, a great deal of research has gone into understanding the characteristics of the language input that promotes learning (**foreigner talk**) and into the feedback the learner provides and its effect on subsequent input (**discourse studies**).

Studies on language input focus on describing foreigner talk, or the modifications that native speakers make when talking with someone they perceive to have less than native proficiency in their language. A number of common modifications have been identified.[5] For example, native speakers typically choose topics concerned with the present, they check more often to see whether they are being understood, they repeat or paraphrase both their own utterances and the other speaker's, and they give shorter responses. Hatch (1983) has pointed out that ESL teachers commonly speak more slowly and use intonation patterns that help the learner to identify syntactic groupings and boundaries. The conversation

[5]For a clear, concise description of the characteristics of foreigner talk and the role it is believed to play in second language acquisition, see Chapter 9, "Input/Interaction and Language Development," in Hatch (1983).

between Wuxing, a Chinese graduate student, and his teacher in Table 5.3 shows the teacher making several adjustments to her speech to accommodate Wuxing's level of English proficiency, as she perceived it.

Understanding the adjustments native speakers make in talking with non-native speakers contributes significantly to our understanding of input. But it is only one side of the coin. Native speakers do not determine input nor the course of conversation all by themselves. Learners provide feedback and this feedback influences the subsequent input they receive. It makes sense, then, to study the interaction that occurs in conversations between native and non-native speakers. **Discourse studies** examine conversational turn-taking, how topics of conversation are nominated and developed, and how meaning is negotiated. They also examine the differences between interactions that occur between adult speakers and those that occur between an adult and a child.

Hatch (1978b) has identified certain characteristics of adult-child interactions. As she describes them, a typical interaction begins when the child requests the adult's attention. "Mummy, look!" would be a common way of opening the communication channel. The adult normally responds by naming the object that has attracted the child's attention: "Oh yes, a bluebird." At this point, depending on the age of the child and the particular situation, this conversation might be abandoned and another "nominating sequence" begun, or it might be developed. Development usually proceeds with the adult requesting some comment on the established topic. "It's a pretty one, isn't it?" or "Why do you think it's sitting in the apple tree?" would invite the child to elaborate.

These conversational routines seem to help children to learn language, although it must be recalled that children in some other cultures learn language apparently without much overt assistance from adults. If children and non-native speakers learn language with these modifications to input and accommodation in discourse and if they also learn language without them, there must be a variety of processing strategies that are sensitive to variations in input and feedback.

Process

Essentially, second language acquisition theory is concerned with two types of processes. The first type is cognitive processes and consist of the types of learner strategies discussed earlier. The second type is linguistic processes that, according to one view,

Table 5.3
Foreigner talk modifications

Example	Modification
W: I need, uh, the book.	
T: The book? Which book?	*Repetition.* She repeats part of his utterance even though she has understood him.
W: From class. Yellow, I think.	
T: The yellow book from class. Let me see. The book about reading in a second language?	*Repetition* and *expansion.* She expands his fragment into a well-formed sentence.
W: No. Uh. Not about that.	
T: Not about reading in a second language. Was it today or last week?	*Self repetition.* She repeats her own previous utterance.
W: Last week.	
T: Last week. (Removing a book from her shelf.) This one?	*Repetition* and *"here and now."* She repeats her own previous utterance and then offers visual aids.
W: No, about universals.	
T: Oh, language universals? Was it by Hatch? Who wrote it?	*Repetition* and *confirmation check.* She paraphrases to confirm that he has understood her question.
W: I don't know.	
T: Was it this one?	*"Here and now"*
W: No.	
T: Well, have a look. Books about universals are there.	*Short response.* *Repetition.*
W: Yellow.	
T: Yes. But I don't classify them by color. Do you understand "classify"?	*Comprehension check.* She asks overtly whether he understands.
W: Yes. But maybe I, uh, blind to color.	
T: You're colorblind?	*Expansion* and *confirmation check.*
W: Yes, maybe. (Laughing)	

involve universal principles of grammar with which the learner is innately endowed. They provide the learner with a starting point. The task is then to scan the input to discover which rules of the target language are universal and which are specific. (Ellis, 1985, p. 17)

This is, in essence, a nativist, or universal-grammar, perspective on the nature of linguistic processes. Interlanguage theory (Selinker, 1972) takes the notion of process beyond the "starting point," referring to the learner's system at any one point in time and also to the system as it changes over time. This system is believed to be separate from the native language system and to be the product of five cognitive processes:

1. Transfer of some features from the first language
2. Transfer from the teaching process
3. Learning strategies
4. Communication strategies
5. Overgeneralization of linguistic material from the target language

The interlanguage hypothesis applies to adults and to children who acquire their second language after the first is clearly established. Although it speculates about different influences on the system, the hypothesis makes little attempt to explain the learning process. Rather, it provides a useful framework in which to describe certain second language phenomena. Not so with Krashen's Monitor Model.[6]

Krashen's model rests on five hypotheses, all of which relate to second language processing. The first and, in Krashen's view, the foundational hypothesis is called the acquisition-learning hypothesis. It makes the claim that there is a distinction between **acquiring** language in an informal setting where attention is directed entirely to meaning, much as the first language is acquired, and **learning** language in a formal setting such as the classroom where attention is directed to form. Furthermore, this distinction is believed to be independent of the age of the learner or other learner variables. Note that Krashen is not merely stating the obvious, that is, the fact of environmental differences. He claims that the

---

[6]Krashen's Monitor Model is discussed here despite its major flaws for two reasons. First, it has contributed to second language acquisition research and theory simply by being controversial. In their efforts to demonstrate Krashen wrong, scholars have raised and answered important issues in their research. Second, it has had a significant effect on second language teaching. This is true, in part, because certain of his hypotheses, such as the acquisition/learning hypothesis and the notion of comprehensible input, hold such intuitive appeal.

learner actually processes and stores language differently under the two conditions. Acquisition leads to "subconscious" internalization of language structures and rules while learning leads to conscious learning.

Although this distinction holds a certain intuitive appeal, little evidence exists to support it. The further claim that language that is **learned** (as opposed to **acquired**) cannot eventually become subconscious knowledge is not only unsupported but "flies in the face of the evidence" (Spolsky, 1985, p. 271). An even more serious shortcoming of the hypothesis is that while it specifies two distinct sources of input, it fails to elucidate how the processes responsible for acquisition and learning differ from one another.

Perhaps the most important and the most controversial claim made by this hypothesis is the one that relates it to the **monitor hypothesis**. Krashen claims that the role of acquired language is to initiate utterances and control fluency, while learned language is available only as an editor or monitor to "correct" the language output before it is uttered. What this implies is that there is no place for "learned" language in comprehension, and this too flies in the face of experience. Attempts to confirm the existence and use of a monitor in experimental situations have failed, and the hypothesis is further weakened by the doubt cast on the acquisition-learning hypothesis that supports it. Quite simply, if the monitor does not exist, there is no purpose for the acquisition-learning distinction and, conversely, if that distinction is false, then there can be no monitor.

The other three hypotheses, the **natural order hypothesis**, the **input hypothesis**, and the **affective filter hypothesis** falter in similar ways. The natural order hypothesis makes the claim that learners acquire the rules of language in a predictable order. The evidence for the claim comes mostly from studies on the order in which certain grammatical morphemes are learned by non-native speakers (for example, Dulay & Burt, 1974; Porter, 1977). Once again, the evidence cited in support of the hypothesis is dubious. First, there are serious methodological problems with the morpheme acquisition order studies, not the least of which is that some of the studies measured accuracy of use rather than order of acquisition. Second, other research has demonstrated that structures in the learners' first language influence the order and the accuracy with which they acquire the grammatical morphemes of English (McLaughlin, 1984, 1987).

The natural order hypothesis is dependent on the fourth hypothesis, the **input hypothesis**. Assuming, "as Krashen does, that learners progress through 'natural' developmental sequences, we need some mechanism to account for how they go from one point to another" (McLaughlin, 1987, p. 36). Krashen claims that learners proceed from their current level of proficiency (i) to the next level ($i + 1$) by understanding language that is just beyond their current level of proficiency. This is called comprehensible input and has the following characteristics: (1) it is focused on meaning; (2) it is roughly tuned to the learner's level of competence rather than finely tuned, and (3) it is based in the "here and now."

Among other "evidence" that Krashen states for the input hypothesis are the existence of simplified speech, the existence of a silent period and the fact that older learners seem to make faster progress in language learning than do children. None of these is really arguable: It does seem to be the case, as we saw earlier, that a period during which speech is not required facilitates learning for some children, simplified codes play an important role when they are available, and older children and adults learn at a faster rate than younger children. But even if all of this is true, does it constitute evidence for any particular internal process? McLaughlin, Spolsky, and Ellis think not, pointing out the absence of any explanation about *how* the mapping from meaning to structure occurs.

The final hypothesis comprising the Monitor Model is the **affective filter hypothesis**, and that it is widely questioned will come as no surprise to the reader. The affective filter is identified as

> that part of the internal processing system that subconsciously screens incoming language based on what psychologists call "affect": the learner's motives, needs, attitudes, and emotional states. (Dulay, Burt, & Krashen, 1982, p. 46)

The affective filter supposedly reduces the amount of input available for natural learning by limiting what the learner pays attention to, what will be learned, and the speed at which it is learned. In other words, if a learner is extremely nervous or tense, as was the case with the Chinese graduate student described earlier, the filter purportedly keeps the learner from paying attention to certain kinds of language data. Or if the learner harbors resentment toward speakers of the target language, the filter may limit the amount of learning that actually takes place. The learner may cling to a heavy accent, for example. But these are hypothetical instances and as with the earlier hypotheses, the hard evidence for this one does not exist.

Unfortunately, the task of evaluating the affective filter hypothesis is further complicated by vagueness. Krashen and his colleagues have never explained just how the filter screens language intake. It would seem that unless the filter screens randomly, it would have to have available some grammar or grammatical template in order to separate those language items to ignore from those to attend to and admit. That being the case, several questions arise, including two obvious ones: What grammar is available to the beginning learner? How does the affective filter get constructed?

Fortunately, there are other theoretical approaches to processing issues. Cognitive theory takes a broader perspective than universal grammar, the Monitor Model, or even interlanguage, deriving its principles not from linguistic theory but from contemporary research in cognitive psychology. As we have seen, cognitive theories of language acquisition do not accord language a special status. Rather, learning a second language is viewed as learning a complex cognitive skill "because various aspects of the task must be practised and integrated into fluent performance. This requires the automatization of component sub-skills" (McLaughlin, 1987, p. 133). Automatization is one of two central concepts in cognitive theory; the other is restructuring.

To produce a meaningful utterance, a speaker must coordinate information of many kinds from a number of sources while making a simultaneous plan for the structure of the utterance and for its articulation. If all this is to be accomplished in the very short time before the listener loses interest, the speaker must have automatized most of the component tasks. McLaughlin (based on Levelt, 1978) conceives of speaking as an hierarchical task structure in which the first-order goal is to express a particular intention. The second is to decide on a task, and the third to formulate a series of phrases. Finally, the speaker must attend to lower order goals, which include retrieving from memory the necessary words, activating articulatory patterns, utilizing appropriate syntactic rules, and meeting pragmatic conventions. When we consider, further, that *each* of these goals entails a number of subtasks, then we begin to understand the importance of automatization. Automatization occurs as a result of practice, of the repeated "mapping of the same input to the same pattern of activation over many trials" (McLaughlin, 1987, p. 134).

Restructuring refers to the constant reorganization of the internal system to accommodate new material. In second language acquisition, the internal system would be the grammar and lexicon of the target language. A beginning learner of English might, on the basis of limited exposure to English, construct the rule that all past tenses are formed by adding [d]. For *gaze, rhyme, fail,* and many verbs in English, this rule works. But then the learner encounters the past tense of *ring* and *sing*. The internal system must be restructured to accommodate this new information and the new "rule" might be that there are two past tense forms, with verbs rhyming with *ring* requiring a vowel change but no ending and all other verbs requiring [d]. The learner then encounters *bring* and *rust* and has to restructure the system yet again. And so on, and so on.

This particular cognitive theory is essentially human information processing. Although it is not the only cognitive approach to understanding language acquisition, it rests on the central assumption that language is acquired in the same manner as other complex cognitive skills. But this reluctance to accord a special status to language, to treat it as just another cognitive skill, is a position about which some researchers and theorists are highly skeptical.

Hatch (1983), for example, questions the closeness of the bond between cognitive development and language acquisition. She argues that the relationship cannot be causal, that is, language acquisition cannot be dependent on cognitive development, and she cites various kinds of evidence. The first is a study by Yamada (1981) demonstrating that a child with low cognitive development (she was unable to count, although she could recite numbers, unable to give her correct birth date or age consistently, and could not name the days of the week) demonstrated complex syntactic ability (Yamada, 1981; cited in Hatch, 1983, pp. 220–221). Hatch also points out that there is no evidence that the operating principles Slobin (1973) identified for figuring out language (such as "Pay attention to the ends of words" and "Avoid exceptions") are truly **cognitive** strategies. They might well be unique to language. She cites as additional evidence cases of Turner's syndrome children (mentioned in Chapter 3) in which children with severe cognitive problems in visual-spatial tasks have superior language ability and cases of hydrocephalics who have linguistic abilities far in excess of their cognitive abilities.

Yet, to be fair, cognitively based accounts of language acquisition and processing are very young and Hatch's criticism is not addressed specifically to information processing (although, clearly, information processing would have to be accountable to the same evidence). Sufficient research is not yet available to evaluate the theory's worth as an account of second language acquisition.

Proficiency

We come finally to the question of proficiency, or Spolsky's *how much*. Not all second language learners become fully proficient in the new language, and second language acquisition theory will ultimately have to account for the variability in levels of attainment. It is obvious that all of the variables we have discussed so far affect proficiency, and thus it may not seem necessary to address it separately. But two theories pay particular attention to the reasons that learners seem to stop learning. **Acculturation** and

accommodation theory account for different levels of success in terms of social and psychological distance.

The acculturation model (Schumann, 1978a, 1978b, 1978c) is based on the belief that language learning is a central part of adapting to a new culture. Schumann argues that learners' success in acquiring a second language is controlled by their success at acculturating to the target language group. Further, both acculturation and second language acquisition are determined by the social and psychological distance that exist between the learner and the target language culture. Social distance depends on differences between groups in size, ethnic origin, political status, and social status. Psychological distance depends on such individual factors as culture shock, motivation, and language shock. Acculturation theory holds that

> social and psychological distance influence second language acquisition by determining the amount of contact with the target language that the learner experiences, and also the degree to which the learner is open to that input which is available. (Ellis, 1985, p. 252)

Thus, when social and psychological distances are great, the learning situation is poor and the learner makes little progress. Schumann terms the failure to progress beyond beginning stages the **pidginization hypothesis**, referring to the simplified form of language that develops under certain conditions when two language groups come into contact. He maintains that when there is a social chasm between learners and the target language group, and thus a reduced motivation to learn the language, language learning may fossilize.

In his accommodation theory, Giles takes a similar view: that the causes for fossilization are rooted in sociopsychological factors. The major difference between accommodation theory and acculturation theory is that the former is concerned with perceived social distance and the latter with actual distance. Both view motivation as central to determining success in second language acquisition, but they see it as having different roots. Schumann apparently treats the distance phenomena as absolute, while Giles believes the important factor is the perception of social distance. Specifically, Giles claims that what is important is how the learner's social group defines itself in relationship to the target language community (Ellis, 1985, p. 256). Giles claims that language proficiency is governed by a number of key variables:

1. How learners perceive their status in their own ethnic group
2. Whether learners make favorable or unfavorable comparisons between their ethnic group and the target language group

3. How learners perceive the status of the ethnic group within the larger community

4. Whether learners view the ethnic group as culturally or linguistically distinct from the target language group or as linguistically related

5. The degree to which learners identify and perceive themselves as having status with other social categories, such as occupational, religious, or sex. (adapted from Ellis, 1987, p. 256)

Both acculturation and accommodation theory are useful in helping to identify some of the possible reasons for the apparent limitations on second language learning that some people experience. Both are concerned to some degree with learner factors and with situational factors. But neither addresses the learning process itself and does not, therefore, constitute a complete theory of second language acquisition. As Table 5.3 shows, no one theory is complete, although several of them taken together represent a fair account of how it all *might* work. It might even be reasonable to say of them individually, as Ellis does about neurofunctional theory, that "they are perhaps best treated as affording additional understanding about SLA [second language acquisition], rather than an explanation of it" (Ellis, 1985, p. 275).

How the Variables Fit Together

It should be obvious by now that the major factors that influence second language acquisition are neither simple nor are they independent. We have seen that they overlap and that they interact in complex and largely unknown ways. The task of theory is ultimately to weave them together into some coherent explanation of how second language learning takes place. Theory is not yet at that point, but Ellis has provided a clear framework in which to think about the relationship among the different variables. He sees situational, input, and learner factors as influencing learning processes, which, in turn, influence the language produced (Ellis, 1985, p. 276).

In the next chapter, we meet two children who have become bilingual under two different sets of circumstances. In witnessing the success of Quy and Lucy, perhaps we can come to a clearer understanding of what factors exert the greatest influence on second language acquisition in children and just what it is that theory must account for.

Chapter Six

The Course of Bilingual Development: Quy and Lucy

I met Quy (pronounced *key*) and Lucy in the early 1980s when I was doing research in a kindergarten class on the northern coast of British Columbia. After spending only a few weeks in the class, I was so struck by the progress they were making, despite the many differences between them, that I began to study the two children more closely. What intrigued me then was the fact that this Vietnamese boy and Portuguese girl, with such widely different experiences of both life and language, were coping so well with the demands of an English-speaking kindergarten. That they were juxtaposed with Michael, whom we will meet in Chapter 7 and whose second language learning was anything but smooth, made them all the more compelling as subjects of study. I therefore determined to gather as much information as possible on their backgrounds, hoping that by so doing, I could come to understand more about the process of second language acquisition in children.

The account of both Quy's and Lucy's language learning from the time they began kindergarten is based on tape recordings made in their kindergarten class once each week for the first three months of the school year and once every two weeks thereafter. In most sessions, the children wore lavaliere microphones during their regular classroom activities and also spent 15 to 20 minutes in private conversation with their teacher or with the researcher. These recordings are supplemented by the teacher's notes and formal evaluation reports, the latter written four times during the year, and by the observation notes taken by the researcher.

Quy's early language acquisition is based on his mother's recollections, recorded in interviews taken over a two-month period in November
and December of their kindergarten year. Her recollections were assisted
by the diary she had begun to keep when she arrived in Canada. I was
also able to interview two women who worked in the preschool that Quy
attended from age 4;0 to 4;9. The account of Lucy's early language learning is also based on interviews, conducted with the help of a Portuguese
interpreter. These were conducted less frequently but over a four-month
period between mid-September and mid-December.

QUY'S LANGUAGE LEARNING

Quy from Birth to 22 Months

During the 1970s and 1980s, there was a massive exodus of people from
Vietnam. Quy's mother and father were among the earliest to leave, and
the conditions under which they did so were apparently so horrific that
Quy's mother would not discuss them even five years after the fact. Quy
was born in a refugee camp in Malaysia, a few weeks after his mother
reached the camp. His father did not survive the journey. The infant and
his mother remained in the camp for just over a year before being accepted as refugees to Canada. During that year, his mother took English classes offered in the camp, but she was not a beginner, having learned some
English in the job she had held in Vietnam during the war.

Quy's mother reported that she sang and spoke Vietnamese with Quy
as an infant. It never occurred to her that he might learn both languages
from her and so she spoke only Vietnamese, the language he would have
heard all around him in the camp. A month after Quy's first birthday, the
young widow and her child boarded a plane for Vancouver, British
Columbia, to begin their new life in Canada.

They arrived in the pouring rain, and although it was 10° Celsius
(about 50° F) and quite balmy for a Vancouver winter, they were immediately struck by the cold. It was to get worse. A church group in Prince
Rupert, a small coastal community in northern British Columbia, had
agreed to sponsor Quy and his mother. They met the new arrivals, and
after one night in Vancouver, the two representatives from the church,
Quy, and his mother boarded a plane for the journey north.

Quy's mother reported that she was in shock for several months. She
said that she was frightened about what the future would hold for her and
her son, and that she found the weather very inhospitable. But not the
people. She said that she seldom felt lonely, and was grateful for the

English she had learned because it helped her to communicate with "the very kind people who wanted to help Quy and me." Her English improved rapidly, but she still spoke only Vietnamese with Quy. They did not have television, but Quy heard English spoken when members of the church group visited their home and when his mother took him to church.

When Quy was 16 months old, about three months after they arrived in Canada, Quy's mother found a job. She was determined not to rely on the charity of her new friends but to support her son herself. At first, Quy was cared for by another Vietnamese woman, a mother of four who also lived in Prince Rupert. The woman's husband was a fisherman whose income was sporadic, and she welcomed the few dollars that Quy's mother paid her. After about six months, however, there was a severe downturn in the fishing economy of the area, and the woman had to find a job that paid more. Quy's mother then placed Quy in the daycare center run by her church group, and his English language learning began in earnest.

Quy from 1;10 to 3;0

Quy had been exposed to some English before he began to attend the kindergarten, but according to his mother, spoke only Vietnamese. She reported that before he entered the daycare center, he had been very talkative, chattering away in Vietnamese. She also reported that he would frequently respond to the questions friends would ask in English, not by speaking but by nodding or shaking his head as was appropriate. She was unsure, though, just how much English Quy really understood.

Quy's mother worried about how he would adjust to an English environment and Quy's behavior during the first few weeks seemed to vindicate her feelings of anxiety. For the first few days, Quy objected to going to the daycare center. While he was there, he tended to play quietly by himself. But he soon stopped complaining and seemed happy about going. Sometimes, he even seemed reluctant to get out of the church van in which he was driven home.

Quy's second birthday was celebrated at the daycare center, and his mother was able to attend the lunchtime party in his honor. She reported that Quy seemed to be pleased with the party, and especially with the cake and ice cream, but he said nothing during the entire hour she was there, except a few words of greeting in Vietnamese when she arrived. When she asked the attendants at the center, they told her that Quy never talked. He didn't even speak Vietnamese with the other Vietnamese child, a three-year-old girl.

Initially, Quy's mother wasn't worried about his silence, but then she started to notice that he was talking less and less at home. By the time he was 2;3, Quy spoke only when his mother insisted and then only in English even though she spoke only Vietnamese. He refused to speak Vietnamese, and would sometimes respond to his mother's Vietnamese by saying "I don't know," which she understood to mean that he didn't understand. Even though she knew that he did understand her Vietnamese, she reluctantly switched to English, which he would speak.

When Quy was about 2;4, his mother once again visited the daycare center. There she found Quy, not exactly talkative, but responding to his playmates in English. He greeted her in English when she arrived, and the attendants reported that he consistently greeted and responded to them in English although he was still reluctant to initiate conversation. At home, he was still mostly silent and still refused to speak Vietnamese.

It was natural enough for Quy's mother to worry that his refusal to speak Vietnamese would eventually lead to his losing it. Even though she knew that Quy would have to learn English to survive in Canada, she was very reluctant for him to lose this important link with his history. She reported feeling trapped. On the one hand, she desperately wanted to preserve his Vietnamese, but on the other, he refused to talk to her in Vietnamese and she was worried about the effect on her relationship with him of continued silence.

Gradually, she relented and began to speak English with him. She would occasionally try to slip in a few words of Vietnamese, but he contin-ued to insist that he didn't understand that language. Then an event tran-spired which Quy's mother marked as highly significant in Quy's emer-gent bilingualism (and which speaks to the importance of motivation!).

Just before his third birthday, Quy was excited by the prospect of get-ting the tricycle he badly wanted. He was in town with his mother on a Saturday afternoon and they walked past a hardware store that had a bright blue tricycle on display in the window. Quy pointed to it excitedly, saying, "There, that. Mama, I want that, please." Quy's mother did not respond, so he repeated his request: "That tricycle, may I please have it?"

His mother thought for a moment and then responded in Vietnamese that she was sorry but she could not understand him. He looked puzzled and repeated his request in English. She repeated that she did not understand. Quy merely pointed to the tricycle and said "Please." Quy's mother then told him in Vietnamese that she assumed he wanted a tricycle, but that since it was winter, he wouldn't be able to ride it anyway. It was Quy's turn to think. Finally, Quy laughed as though they were shar-ing a great joke and repeated his request for the tricycle and then explained that he could ride it in the basement, all in Vietnamese. In perfect Vietnamese, his mother reported; his first language had not suffered from the addition of English. From then on, Quy spoke whichever language was addressed to him.

When I asked Quy's mother whether Quy ever confused his two languages, she said that he did in only one sense. Sometimes, he would be talking to his mother about something that had happened in daycare and would insert an English word into a Vietnamese sentence. She surmised that he had learned the names of certain objects and actions in daycare and simply did not know the Vietnamese equivalent. She would occasionally interrupt and tell him the Vietnamese word, which he would repeat and usually remember. It was her opinion that his Vietnamese pronunciation was fine, but she felt unable to judge the quality of his English pronunciation, so she could not tell whether Vietnamese influenced the English sound system.

Quy from 3;0 to 4;0

Quy stayed in full-time daycare until he was 4;0. During the year between his third and fourth birthdays, he made a great deal of progress in both his languages. At home, he spoke Vietnamese with his mother, although she reported that sometimes when he began to tell her something in English, she would "forget" and respond in English. At the daycare center, he mostly spoke English. Just before his third birthday, however, two other Vietnamese children joined the daycare group. One, a girl of about the same age as Quy, spoke no English and was very shy. Quy began to speak to her in Vietnamese to which she eventually responded, and the daycare attendants credited Quy with easing her adaptation to the daycare environment. The two children spoke Vietnamese at first, but gradually she began to use English words partly as a result of Quy's teaching. She was observed to ask him in Vietnamese what the English label was for various objects. He would respond in English, and at other times would take the initiative in teaching her English words.

Quy from 4;0 to 4;9

When Quy was 4;0, he entered a preschool where he spent his mornings. His mother had changed jobs and was working only part time outside the home. She was thus able to be at home with him in the afternoons where she worked doing tailoring and alterations. They also acquired a television set. According to Quy's mother, the television set had a significant influence on Quy's language growth. She limited his watching to "Sesame Street" and "The Electric Company" in the daytime and one 30-minute program, which he watched each evening with her. Nevertheless, she noticed a dramatic increase in his vocabulary, particularly in the use of idiomatic expressions of the type that she, as a non-native speaker, did not commonly use.

Quy's mother recalled an incident that occurred one night when Quy was about 4;7 as she was putting him to bed. She had read to him and was preparing to tuck him and a variety of stuffed animals into bed. When she asked him, in Vietnamese, whether he needed to go to the bathroom first. He replied, in English, "No way, Jose!" She asked him, still in Vietnamese, "Who is Jose?" to which he replied, this time in Vietnamese, "I don't know. Maybe he's a man on television."

From about this time on, his mother had difficulty tracking his language development in either language, so great was his speed. She had worried earlier that his Vietnamese would suffer if she were his only contact with the language, but the church group sponsored other Vietnamese immigrants and soon a small community existed within which Quy could hear and speak his first language. When I asked her which language was dominant at the time Quy entered kindergarten at 4;9, his mother replied that they were pretty well balanced, but she knew already that once he started school, English would win out. "But," she added, "in Canada, that is necessary."

By the time he was five years old, then, Quy had acquired basic interpersonal communication skills in two languages. Strictly speaking, perhaps, Quy's accomplishment was different from the **home bilingualism** described in Chapter 5. He did, after all, acquire English largely in the daycare center, which he attended from 1;10 to 4;0 and then in the preschool. On the other hand, his mother was bilingual, and although she was reluctant to do so, responded to his English as well as his Vietnamese. What Quy does have in common with Ronjat's Louis, Leopold's Hildegard, and other children who have learned two languages from an early age was the embodiment of the two languages in separate people or situations. From the time he was 1;4, Quy used his two languages in two distinct environments, home and daycare, and, with the exceptions already noted, kept them separate for the most part. More importantly, however, was the fact that Quy, like Louis Ronjat and Hildegard Leopold, acquired basic interpersonal skills in English. He was different from Lucy, Michael, and many other children in the sense that by the time he faced the task of acquiring the cognitive academic language proficiency demanded in school, he already had the more basic language skills on which to build.

Quy in Kindergarten

I met Quy on his first day in kindergarten. Anticipating a number of children who did not speak English, the kindergarten teacher, Mrs. MacKenna, had asked me to assist her in determining the language proficiency levels of the 16 children in her class. In evaluating the language of a second language learner, teachers normally look at a variety of factors. They consider comprehension of the spoken language, the accuracy of forms in comparison to native speakers of the same age, and fluency. The easiest way to evaluate all three is to talk to the child.

It is relatively easy to get a general indication of how much English a child understands by asking questions, as long as the teacher is careful to ask questions to which the child is likely to know the answers. Otherwise, it is not a test of language comprehension. Asking the child's name or the names of common objects are fairly safe. Some children, however, demonstrate culturally determined behaviors that may be wrongly interpreted. Some Asian children as well as some Native American and Canadian children will refuse to look at the teacher and will respond to questions either in an almost inaudible voice or not at all. This behavior is sometimes interpreted as meaning that the child hasn't understood when in fact the child is only behaving politely within the tradition of his or her culture. Quy had been in Canada and among enough English speakers to have adopted Canadian behaviors in school, and so there was no difficulty in getting him to talk and thus determining that his comprehension was excellent.

Accuracy of form is a little harder to evaluate in children of Quy's age. The difficulty is that, unless they happen to be quite talkative, children may not produce the structures that the teacher or researcher wants to evaluate. They have to be manipulated into producing the structures of interest. Means exist for doing so, as in the Bilingual Syntax Measure (BSM) (Burt, Dulay, & Hernandez-Chavez, 1975), but this measure and others of the same type provide only a few opportunities for a limited number of structures to emerge. So while they may be useful for charting development of a limited set of morphemes over a period of time, they tell us very little about how well the child knows the structures of English. The BSM probably tells us more about comprehension since the child has to answer a series of questions designed to elicit certain structures. In talking with Quy, we learned that most of the inflectional morphemes seemed to be in place, although he did show a tendency to overgeneralize certain morphological patterns as shown in Figure 6.1. When we compare the similar forms that Janet produced at 4;4 (see Figure 4.4), we can see that Quy behaved just as a native speaker of English might. In fact, his behavior was so natural that I hadn't noticed it until I read the transcripts.

Fluency refers to the ease with which a speaker produces the oral language, and it seldom requires a formal test to determine second language learners' fluency. Certainly, Quy clearly had little difficulty expressing himself in English. A recording made of Quy retelling a story to his teacher during the third week in September shows why:

T: Have you read this book, Quy? Do you know the story?
Q: Yes. I know.
T: Will you tell me?
Q: Yep. There was a woman and she was—she didn't have much money. So she lived in a shoe. Great big shoe. She had lots and lots of uh, boys and girls—
T: Children?
Q: Yep. Children. She had lots and lots of them and they all gots hungry. Real hungry. (He hesitates.)
T: Yes? And so what did she do?
Q: I don't know.
T: You don't remember? Why don't you tell me what you THINK happened?
Q: (After thinking for a moment) She wented to the co-op and boughted some turkey!

Fluency also entails a good, but not necessarily perfect, command of the grammar, vocabulary, and pronunciation of a language. Without administering any special tests, Quy's teacher and I could tell that Quy had near-native proficiency in all these areas. His pronunciation was native-like, although he had a slight tendency to devoice word-final consonants. This was apparent mainly in the plural ending on words such as *dogs* and *beds*.

Figure 6.1
Quy's overgeneralizations at 4;10

Tran nots here.
Lucy doesn't gots the glue.
My Mom, she boughted it at the co-op.
Mrs. 'Kenna didn't wanted it.

Since even native speakers have a tendency to a slight devoicing of word-final consonants, Quy's doing so was not a cause for concern.

The only other thing that gave away the fact that English was not his first language was his hesitancy in providing the appropriate labels in English for certain body parts and items of clothing. Apparently, he had first learned the Vietnamese words for these things and had to search a moment longer for the corresponding English word. But he did know them, as we discovered when we administered the Peabody Picture Vocabulary Test (PPVT) (Dunn & Dunn, 1981). The PPVT was administered to all children who entered kindergarten with the exception of those who quite obviously did not know enough English to complete it. Quy's score on the test was 4;6, within normal bounds for his actual age of 4;9.[1]

There were two other Vietnamese children in the class, a girl named Thuy (pronounced *twee*) and a boy named Tran. Thuy's family had insisted that she have an English name for school, and she had decided on "Doreen," although by Christmas she had changed it four times, to Dolly, Linda, Shelly, and Suzie. Just after she had decided to call herself Dolly, I recorded the following conversation between her and Quy:

Q: Thuy, give me the white glue.
T: Not Thuy. Dolly.
Q: Why 'Dolly'?
T: (Speaking in Vietnamese) Because I like it.
Q: (Speaking in Vietnamese) Well, I don't. (Switching to English) I'm going to call you Thuy!

It is interesting to note that Quy switched to English even when he was talking about the girl's Vietnamese name. During the many hours of tape recordings of Quy, he only rarely spoke in Vietnamese, although he often played with the other Vietnamese children. He seemed to be reluctant to repeat the role of language teacher that he had played earlier at the day-care center. He was, however, willing to help out in other ways. An old hand at "school," having spent six months in preschool, Quy sometimes provided rapid Vietnamese explanations of school routines. On one occasion, for example, he explained to Tran that he should wipe the finger paint off his hands with the paper towels kept at the teacher's desk. Although Tran's English was good enough for him to have understood, Quy chose to speak in Vietnamese, as he only rarely did. I wondered as I

[1]In comparison, the scores of the other ESL children in the class were consistently lower. For example, the age-equivalent scores for Thuy and Tran were 3.6 and 3.0, respectively. Lucy had virtually no English and was not given the PPVT until a few weeks later.

read the translation whether he had helped Tran to save face by not exposing his ignorance in front of the other children.

When I asked his mother which language he spoke when he was playing with these same children outside school, she replied that they switched back and forth, depending on what they were playing. In playing a traditional Vietnamese game that they enjoyed, for example, they used Vietnamese. When playing with GI Joe, with a soccer ball, or any of the games they had learned at school, they used English, even though the other two children were far less fluent than Quy.

Quy seemed to be in all respects comfortably bilingual. His English language development continued through kindergarten in much the same vein as the monolingual children in the class. At home, he continued to speak Vietnamese with his mother and usually with the Vietnamese friends who visited them. With his Vietnamese playmates, he switched back and forth between languages as noted earlier. Quy was obviously untroubled by his two languages, and perhaps the most interesting question that arises is the degree to which he was aware of having them.

Other than the few instances of language switching cited earlier, there was only one other incident that seemed to speak to Quy's awareness of his two languages. Once early in the year, the children were counting aloud. Quy, wearing his microphone, was counting along with the other children. They all reached ten, counting in English, and stopped. Quy paused, laughed, and continued in Vietnamese very softly, as if to himself. When I had the tape translated, I learned that he had continued counting to 20 in Vietnamese.

As I discovered in talking to Lucy, little is gained by asking a five-year-old child a question that calls for thinking *about* language. If I were to discover how Quy viewed his two languages, for example, whether he felt them to be distinct languages, then I would have to do so in some indirect way. I devised a number of schemes. Once when we were sitting together looking at a book, I began to point to various things in the pictures and ask Quy if he knew another word for them. I hoped thereby to get him to tell me a Vietnamese word. But Quy wasn't playing:

TP: (Pointing to a bird) Do you know what that's called?
Quy: A bird.
TP: Do you know another word for 'bird'?
Quy: Robin?
TP: No, I don't think that's a robin. Can you think of ANY other word?
Quy: Mmm. Sea gull?

TP: Well, that IS another bird. Do you have a word for 'bird' in Vietnamese?
Quy: (Looking puzzled) Bird. That's a bird.

At that point, Quy turned the page, fed up with my silly game. On another occasion, I enlisted the aid of his mother and asked her to show him pictures for him to label in Vietnamese and then to ask him for the English equivalents. She tried, but had little more success than I did. In desperation, I tried a trick. I explained to Quy the directions for making a Halloween pumpkin from construction paper. Knowing that Tran was far less able in English than Quy, I asked Quy to explain the directions to him. Translation is a highly complex cognitive skill requiring that the child keep in mind the entire message while simultaneously constructing a completely equivalent utterance in the other language. To translate, Quy would have to be aware that the two languages were separate. But instead of translating, he turned to Tran and in greatly simplified and somewhat pidginized English explained exactly what he was to do. I gave up.

Once I abandoned my tricks and turned to the transcripts, I found that even though there was no direct evidence of his being aware of having two languages, Quy did have some language awareness. Just before Christmas when the children were making Christmas decorations, Quy and Thuy were working together at a table. Quy began to sing a song the class had been rehearsing for the school's Christmas pageant. Thuy joined in, singing "Shingle bell, shingle bell, shingle all the way. . . " Quy interrupted her, "No, Thuy. It's not 'shingle.' It's 'jingle.' It starts with j- not sh-." It is interesting to note that Quy did not tell Thuy that "bell" should be plural. The reasons are pure speculation, of course, but it is possible that the phonemic distinction was more salient to him than was the singular/plural distinction. Some support for this reasoning comes from evidence that awareness of the phonetic properties of language is one of children's earliest types of awareness, appearing in some children by the age of three (Dickinson, Wolf, & Stotsky, 1989, p. 229).

Quy also joined eagerly in rhyming games, again showing awareness of the sound of language as it exists apart from meaning. Otherwise, I had only the indirect evidence supplied by his mother of his behavior when he was younger from which to make any judgments about his awareness of his bilingualism. It seemed reasonable to conclude that Quy treated his two languages as two registers of the same language, each to be used pretty much exclusively in particular situations. As we shall see, this seemed to be Lucy's view of her two languages, one of which she began to learn much later than Quy.

LUCY'S LANGUAGE LEARNING

There are a great many children who enter school with little or no English who are not immigrants. Lucy was such a child, having been born in Vancouver, British Columbia. When she was a few months old, the family moved to a northern coastal community where her father owned a large boat and employed a number of fishermen. Lucy's family, her mother, father, a sister 17 months younger, and a baby brother born during her kindergarten year, spoke Portuguese. Neither of her parents knew more than a few words of English, and since they lived and worked within the small Portuguese community, they had little reason to learn it.

Lucy's first extended exposure to English came when she attended a playschool for a few months during the year before she started kindergarten. Her mother reported using the playschool more as a babysitting service and that Lucy attended only occasionally, no more than once a week. The playschool teachers spoke only English as did roughly half the children. The others spoke a number of different languages, including Portuguese, Vietnamese, Chinese, and Italian.

When I first met Lucy in kindergarten, it was obvious that she understood some of what was said to her, but she was essentially a beginner in English. She did not have a sufficient vocabulary in English to reach even the minimum age-equivalent score of 2;6 on the PPVT. The school's ESL consultant (with an interpreter) visited Lucy's family at home and reported that Lucy was a very talkative child who was not at all shy and had a tendency to "boss around" her younger sister. She also reported that Lucy's family appeared to be well educated. There were many shelves of books in their home, and they subscribed to several Portuguese-language newspapers and magazines. While the ESL consultant and interpreter were visiting, Lucy brought out one of her books and started to read aloud. The interpreter was astonished to find that Lucy either had an excellent memory for a book that had been read to her many times or she really could read.

Given this kind of evidence about her use of Portuguese, I should not have been surprised by Lucy's progress in English. But I was. When she began, she could give her name when asked and could point correctly to most body parts and pieces of clothing. At this point there was no accuracy or fluency to measure since she used very little English.

Just five weeks later, all that had changed. The teacher gave her the PPVT, and this time her score indicated that she had the English vocabulary of a monolingual child of 3;6. At this point, it occurred to me that Lucy's previous exposure to English must have had a greater effect than it had seemed to at first. Either that or Lucy was a phenomenal language learner. By the end of October, I was convinced that both explanations must be true. This time, the final time Lucy was given the PPVT, her score was 4;0. She was also given the BSM, and some of her responses to those questions, reproduced in Figure 6.2, demonstrate that her comprehension and accuracy were both excellent.

With one possible exception, Lucy correctly understood all the questions asked. She responded incorrectly to the question "What would have happened to the food if the dog hadn't eaten it?" Her answer showed her to be focusing on the dog in the sentence and not the food. Indeed, the dog figured as the subject of all her responses in this section of the BSM. Besides, the question *is* very difficult, calling for the understanding of two conditionals and a focus on the semantic object (the food) rather than the agent (the dog). Lucy's response would not be unusual in a native English speaker of the same age.

For the most part, Lucy's responses indicated a high level of both accuracy and fluency. Notice that her syntax was, for the most part, excellent. She had a good command of basic sentence structure and deviated significantly from adult forms only by omitting frills—modals and the copula, for example. Her developmental "errors" tended to be morphological—using *them* for *they* and using the uninflected form of the verb in *eat* and *drop*. At first glance, it might seem odd that Lucy had such good control of English syntax at a time when she was still making a great many such errors in morphology. But when we look at what morphology Lucy *does* have, then we begin to understand the principle that guides her learning. She has the plural form; one bird differs from two and one cookie from a dozen. It is a meaningful distinction for her to mark. She has *that* in *'Cause that house fat. That* is a demonstrative; it is used to indicate which object the speaker is talking about. In contrast, the morphology she does not yet have tends to carry less meaning. The modal *would*, for example, does not convey much meaning in the presence of *then* (*Then dog die*) and the copula is almost totally redundant semantically.

It might be argued that the overarching principle governing Lucy's second language learning is to pay attention first to those elements that are the most useful for expressing meaning. This makes sense as a comprehension strategy. When one does not have sufficient control of a language to attend to every lexical and grammatical feature, then one must figure out which ones are the most significant for understanding the message. These would, then, be the earliest items to appear in speech, given that the intent of children's speech is to convey meaning.

Figure 6.2
Lucy's responses to selected questions from the BSM

T: What are these?

L: Birds. [bəds]

T: What is the mommy bird going to do with the worm?

L: Give it to the birds.

T: Why?

L: 'Cause them hungry and crying.

T: Why's he so fat?

L: He eat too much.

T: And why's he so skinny?

L: He eat nothing.

T: What are these things?

L: Houses [hausəs].

T: And these?

L: Noses. [nozəz]

T: Why do you think this man lives in this house?

L: 'Cause that house fat.

T: What's he doing to the floor?

L: Wipin' it 'cause it all wet.

T: What did he do with his shoes?

L: Man wet them. (meaning 'He got them wet.')

T: Why is the dog looking at the king?

L: 'Cause dog hungry.

T: What happened to the king's food?

L: Dog eat it.

T: What would have happened to the food if the dog hadn't eaten it?

L: Then dog die.

T: What happened to the apple?

L: Dog drop it.

Figure 6.3
Lucy's telling of *The Three Little Pigs*

> Well. Three pigs. One pig say he make house with straw. Hims brother pig say 'No good. I make house with mud.' Hims brother pig say 'No good. I make house with brick. Very strong.' Then the wolf come. He say 'I huff and I puff and I blow house down.' And he blow down straw house. Little pig cry and run away. He say 'I huff and I puff and I blow house down.' Then he blow down mud house. Other little pig cry and run away. Then wolf say 'I huff and puff and I blow house down.' He blow and blow and hims face look funny. But house toooo strong. So pig laugh and wolf cry and run away.

The answers she gave to the questions in Figure 6.2 give some indication of Lucy's fluency at this point. Her retelling of a story she had heard a number of times before is an even better indicator. Figure 6.3 reproduces part of a transcript of Lucy telling *The Three Little Pigs* during the first week in November.

One of the more revealing "statistics" of Lucy's story is the fact that she used only 40 different words in telling her story of 122 total words. It was told without major hesitations and entirely without false starts, both indicative of a fluent speaker. She was not yet a native speaker, however, and it might be useful to compare her story with one told by Quy at approximately the same time. His narrative, reproduced in Figure 6.4, differed from Lucy's in significant ways.

Quy's story had many features that Lucy's did not. In the first place, he used more than twice as many different words (89) in his 164-word story.[2] Since he had had far more exposure to English, a larger vocabulary would be expected. Quy's sentences were longer than Lucy's, mostly because of his use of conjunctive *and* and *then*. He also used the conventional ways of beginning and ending fairy tales, which Lucy at this point did not. We know that Lucy had been read to and that she was an emergent reader in Portuguese. The fact that she did not use the standard frame for her story in English most likely reflects her relative lack of experience with English stories. What is more important, though, is the strong sense of story conveyed by both children. It is obvious that neither child had memorized the story being told, although there is some evidence of semantic memory operating in repeated expressions such as "no good,"

[2]An interesting comparison between the two stories is the type-to-token ratio or lexical density. This is calculated by dividing the number of different words by the total number of words and multiplying by 100. This procedure yields a lexical density of 32.78 for Lucy and 54.26 for Quy. By March when she told her version of *The Three Bears*, Lucy's lexical density had risen to 50.36.

Figure 6.4
Quy's telling of *Hansel and Gretel*

Once upon a time there was a boy and a girl. Hansel and Gretel were their names. One day they went for a walk to the woods. Their mother told them not to go to the woods 'cause bad people live there, but they were very bad children and so they went anyway. Then they went way, way back in the woods where it was very dark and scary and they were scared and Gretel says 'I'm hungry,' and Hansel says, 'Me too.' And then they see the witch's house and she came out and she had a big sore on her nose. She said 'Please come into my house.' And they did and so she gave them lots of things to eat—bread and meat and cookies and apples. Then they got sleepy and she put them into her oven to cook them. Then a man heard them crying and he came and he killed the witch and they went home. The end.

"cry and run away," and "I huff and I puff and I blow house down" in Lucy's narrative. It seems likely that both children remembered the stories in episodes, that they had personalized the events in what is called **episodic memory** (Glucksberg & Danks, 1975).

COMPARING LUCY WITH QUY

There is no doubt that Quy was a more fluent speaker than Lucy at this time, but Quy had had much more experience as a second language learner. That Lucy was becoming rapidly fluent was obvious to Lucy's teacher. In class, Lucy was a real chatterbox. From the beginning, she made very full use of what resources she had—in English. In fact, she did not use Portuguese even with her two Portuguese friends in the same class. Jenny, Hilda, and Lucy played together both in and out of school, and most of the time when they were playing in one of their homes, they spoke in Portuguese. At school, however, Lucy always spoke English, at least until mid-January.

Many teachers have observed that ESL children who share a native language will often use that language when they are together and use whatever English they possess when they are talking with teachers or playing with English-speaking playmates. Such children may be following the principle *une personne, une langue* recommended by Grammont (Chapter 5). But there are also children who behave as Lucy did, coming to school with little or no English but learning it very quickly and using it exclusively in the school setting. They are also following a principle: They base their choice of language to use not on the native language of their play-mates but on the situation or setting. That is, *if* they have a choice. Choice implies awareness, and there is little direct evidence that Lucy was aware of having two languages. There is, in fact, at least one suggestion to the contrary.

I was visiting Lucy's classroom a few weeks before Christmas and was sitting at a table with Lucy. She had been identifying some pictures for me as part of an informal vocabulary test, but as usual, she was impatient with the task and eager to talk about something else. On that day, the topic was her baby brother who had been born a few weeks earlier. She told me how tiny he was, that he always seemed to be hungry, and that he woke her up before she was ready to get up—"before wake-up time" as Lucy put it. She also said that he couldn't talk at all. When I asked if she knew why, she replied that she didn't. I asked then how she knew that he was hungry, to which she replied, "Cause he cry." I explained that his cries were his way of talking and promised her that eventually he would be able to talk just as she did.

On an impulse, I asked her "Which language do you think he'll speak?" She didn't appear to understand the question, so I tried again. "How many languages do you speak, Lucy?" Her response this time was prompt and very definite: "One."

"Which one?" I asked, although I really should have known better.

"Mine!" Lucy replied and let me know with her tone that she was not likely to put up with much more of this silliness!

This exchange provided a clue about how Lucy viewed her two lan-guages. She seemed to treat her second language as a second register of *her* language. In other words, for Lucy, English and Portuguese may have been a single language with two registers, one for home and one for school. Many native English-speaking children do, after all, learn quite a different variety of English for use at school. It just happened that in her case one of the registers was Portuguese and the other English.

Under this interpretation, it would not be unusual to find some mix-ing of the two languages, yet none of the transcripts reveals any use of Portuguese at all until late January of the kindergarten year. When Lucy did begin to use her first language at school, however, it was for a specific purpose. It was also clearly apparent that Lucy had begun to mark a dis-tinction between the two languages. After Christmas, a new child had begun kindergarten, another Portuguese speaker named Maria. Maria knew a little English, but it was clear that she did not always understand what was going on around her—clear to Lucy, anyway, who took it upon herself to teach her. Frequently when the teacher gave a direction, Lucy would turn to Maria and provide her the instructions in Portuguese. As noted earlier, translation is a highly complex cognitive skill, and it is unlikely that Lucy could have undertaken it without being conscious of the fact that her two languages were distinct. So whether or not she was aware of the distinction between her two languages earlier, by the end of January she was clearly treating them as separate.

From this point on, it would not have been uncommon to find some mixing of the two languages. If there was any, neither her teacher nor I heard it. Nor was there any evidence that her English language learning was in any way inhibited by her work as an unofficial translator. Lucy continued to make impressive progress with English, evident in the story she told me in early March. She was looking at a picture-only version of *The Three Bears* and, with very little prompting, told the story transcribed in Figure 6.5.

Here we can almost hear the language spilling forth from Lucy. So eager was she to tell her story that she took grammatical "short cuts," which eliminated some of the structural niceties of the language while maintaining the meaning. Sometimes she spoke in short, telegraphic sentences, neglected a past tense ending, or left out entire phrases (*Baby bear, his tiny voice*). But because she demonstrated in the telling of the story that she had full command over highly complex morphological and syntactic structures (*Mom's on the other side going 'Somebody was eatin' my porridge'*), it is safe to assume that her short cuts were just that, or in Chomsky's terms, her performance did not accurately reflect her competence.

Figure 6.5
Lucy's telling of *The Three Bears*

> TP: What do you see in this picture?
>
> L: There's Goldilocks playing with her toys. There's a big bed for papa bear, a middle size bed for mommy bear, and a weeny, weeny, tiny bed for baby bear.
>
> TP: Right. And what is Goldilocks doing?
>
> L: Get in baby's bed. Trying them. Sleep. Now they're trying their porridge. Papa say in his loud voice 'Somebody's eatin' my porridge.' Mom's on the other side going 'Somebody was eatin' my porridge.' Pretty soon there's a tiny voice crying 'somebody's eaten my porridge and it's all gone.' So Papa say in big voice 'Somebody sleep in my bed.' Mommy say in middle size voice 'Somebody sleep in my bed.' Baby bear, his tiny voice, 'Somebody's sleep in my bed and here she is.' She open her eyes an shouted 'Who?' Then she ran home. The end. Do you want me sing a song?

The likelihood that Lucy initially considered her two languages as a single code and the fact that she kept them separate according to the situation of use constitute an argument that Lucy learned her two languages in much the same way as younger children such as Quy and other simultaneously bilingual children, that is, as two first languages. The best counterargument is her age. At 4;9, she clearly had a well-established first language, and so her subsequent language learning had to be successive rather than simultaneous. Yet the speed with which she learned the language and the apparent absence of interference from Portuguese suggest that she approached the learning of English in much the same way as she did Portuguese.

Fortunately, for educators, it does not really matter how we label either child's language learning. What is important is that we understand what motivated their learning and the circumstances, particularly those common to both children, under which they achieved their bilingualism.

THE CONDITIONS FOR SUCCESSFUL SECOND LANGUAGE ACQUISITION

At the very least, Quy and Lucy have taught us that children can become bilingual in both the home and school setting. This is good news, particularly since much of the research reported in Chapter 5 hinted that the ideal condition seemed to be for children to learn their two languages at home. Lucy, in particular, taught us that the school can be a good environment for second language learning *if* the language of the school is meaningful and purposeful and if it is spoken by other children and not just teachers. In daycare and preschool, Quy was not taught English but learned it in order to become a member of his peer group. In the kindergarten class, Lucy was not taught the language either; it was simply there for the learning.

It was not the case that Mrs. MacKenna ignored the needs of her pupils. Rather, aware that many did not speak English, she helped them in a variety of ways. She used more repetition than she normally would, repetition of whole language events such as rereading and retelling certain stories as well as repetition of language units—structures, for example, and the words for common classroom objects and activities. She paired native speakers (or very fluent non-native speakers such as Quy) with non-native speakers for many activities in the kindergarten. She talked to the children about nearly everything—about the toys and other objects they brought to show her, about books, about holidays, about television shows they had seen, about the different boats in the harbor, which was visible from their classroom. She made the classroom such an exciting place to be that children were eager to share their observations and experiences. Those who had little English thus were highly motivated to learn enough English to participate. But even before they had much English to use, they had Mrs. MacKenna to help them out. She was able to negotiate meaning even with beginners, as we see in Figure 6.6. The child, Tung, was a beginner in English who had been in Mrs. MacKenna's class for two weeks when he stood up to tell this story in class.

Although he used only seven words in the entire exchange, Tung managed to convey his message: His family owns an old, wooden cup, which is not used for drinking but is decorative and kept in a safe place. It is a small wonder that the children in this kindergarten learned so much English with so much help and encouragement from their teacher!

There is another parallel between Quy's and Lucy's language learning that may not be immediately obvious but is, I believe, essential to their success. I pointed out earlier that when Quy began kindergarten, he

Mrs. Mac:	What have you got there, Tung?
Tung:	(He holds up a painted wooden cup but doesn't speak.)
Mrs. Mac:	What a pretty cup! Cup. Can all of you see Tung's cup? Isn't it a pretty one? (As the other children look at the cup and comment upon it, Mrs. MacKenna turns to Tung and speaks softly.) Can you say 'cup' Tung?
Tung:	Kuh.
Mrs. Mac:	Right! Where did you get your cup, Tung? Is it your Mummy's cup?
Tung:	Mom kuh.
Mrs. Mac:	(To everyone) This cup belongs to Tung's mother. What do you think she does with it?
Children:	She drinks tea. Maybe put flowers in it. My mommy drink coffee.
Mrs Mac:	Those are good ideas. Tung, what does your mommy do with the cup? Drink tea? (She pantomimes drinking.)
Tung:	(Shaking his head.) No.
Mrs. Mac:	She doesn't drink from the cup?
Tung:	No drink. Old.
Mrs. Mac:	Oh, the cup is old? (Tung nods.) So she keeps it in a safe place to look at. (Tung nods again.)

Figure 6.6
Tung and Mrs. MacKenna telling a story

already had basic interpersonal communication skills in English. Lucy did not, but she *did* have them in Portuguese. Both children might, then, have been able to build the more abstract kind of language of the school, cognitive academic language proficiency, on that base. But they did not have to. The environment Mrs. MacKenna created for the children in her classroom encouraged them to develop their basic interpersonal skills in English first. By not "teaching" English and concentrating instead on communicating with the children, this teacher helped them to "grow" the foundational language on which they would later be able to build the more abstract language of the school.

This approach was especially helpful for the beginning ESL learners such as Lucy. There are two probable reasons why it was so important. The first is that however easy children such as Quy and Lucy might make it seem, second language acquisition might not be as easy as adults think. In reporting their study of a two-and-a-half-year-old Japanese child learning English, Itoh and Hatch pointed out that the affectionate interaction with an adult produced the change in attitude toward learning a second language that contributed to his ultimate success (Itoh & Hatch, 1978, p. 77).

The second reason is that a child's success in acquiring a second language in the school setting seems to be directly related to the **language interdependence hypothesis** (Cummins, 1980). The hypothesis holds that the

> cognitive-academic aspects of a first and second language are thought to be interdependent, and proficiency in a second language in a school setting is predicted to depend largely on previous learning of literacy-related functions of language. (McLaughlin, 1981, p. 28)

As noted earlier, there is a basic difference between the cognitive academic language required in most school situations and the more informal, natural interpersonal language that children learn outside. In second language learning, this means that the language children learn on their own outside school is very different from what is involved in most classroom learning. Mrs. MacKenna's classroom was not "most classrooms," however, in the sense that instead of beginning with the more abstract "literacy-related" functions, she first helped the children to develop their informal language within the classroom. At the same time she prepared them for "school language" by reading them a minimum of two stories each day and by telling stories and talking about stories.

From the studies reviewed in Chapter 5 and from the experiences of Quy and Lucy in Mrs. MacKenna's class, we have begun to uncover some of the prerequisites for success in second language acquisition. We know, in short, that the conditions for success strongly resemble those for success in first language acquisition. The implications for the classroom are obvious and fairly easy to implement. They are based on four simple maxims, outlined in Table 6.1. Put into practice, these rules mandate a classroom that is friendly and accepting of learners' language, in large part, because they are based as much on common sense as they are on research and theory.

1. *Focus on meaning rather than language.* All too often it is the case that the first lesson minority children learn is that what they say is less important than how they say it. This lesson does little to facilitate their learning. We will do well to recall the observation in Chapter 3 that adults facilitate children's language learning when they focus their attention and talk on whatever is occupying the child's attention. Quite simply, the best motivation for a child to learn a new language is the strong desire to talk about something or to someone in that language.

2. *Don't worry about initial language mixing or "interference" from the child's first language.* Such mixing is probably more likely to occur when the focus is on communication for the simple reason that in trying to make themselves understood children may call on whatever linguistic resources they have. Children are less likely to do so when attending to the form of what they say. For this reason, mixing should not be seen as evidence that there is anything amiss in the child's second language learning.

3. *Provide a positive and accepting environment.* No teacher of young children needs to be reminded of the importance of the learning environment. For ESL learners, special care should be taken. Praise and encouragement are more effective than correction. Since young children make little use of correction anyway, it makes sense to replace it with support and reassurance. No doubt, some kinds of support are more effective than others. For instance, the teacher who makes a genuine attempt to negoti-

Table 6.1
Four maxims for helping
ESL children

1. Focus on meaning rather than language.
2. Don't worry about "interference" from the first language.
3. Provide a positive and accepting enviroment.
4. Make sure ESL children have ample opportunity to interact with other children.

ate meaning with children is offering better support than one who idly praises correct pronunciation.

4.   *Make sure that children have ample opportunity to interact with other children.* Playing with children their own age provides second language learners with models of language appropriate to their needs and interests. Other children are better models of age- and situation-appropriate language than are adults. Besides, they provide the incentive for the second language learner to learn their language. Following these four "rules" will not guarantee that every ESL child will become fully fluent in a short time, but they will help to make the task of learning a new language easier and more natural.

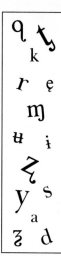

Chapter Seven

Michael's Miracle: Language Disorders in Monolingual and Bilingual Children

COMMUNICATIVE DISORDERS VERSUS COMMUNICATIVE DIFFERENCES

Children such as Quy and Lucy are in a real sense linguistically blessed. By the time they begin school, they have two languages and, as we have seen, there is no reason why their bilingualism should be anything but an asset in the educational process. Unfortunately, not all children are blessed in this way. Some are born with or acquire disorders that inhibit their ability to learn or to function in language. Physical handicaps impair some children's language ability to varying degrees, and others have emotional or learning disorders that make language learning especially challenging. A complete description of the disabilities and disorders that may have an impact on language and learning is beyond the scope of this book; besides, excellent books have been written that are devoted entirely to the topic. Some familiarity with the nature of language disorders is, however, necessary for teachers and anyone else interested in children's language and learning. In this chapter, we will focus on the more common communicative disorders that teachers may encounter.

We begin with an overview of four broad categories of language disorders and conclude the chapter with the story of a child with a somewhat unusual language disorder. Michael is a child with what might be called "induced language delay." His is a type of disorder that affects a small number of bilingual children whose parents are not part of the dominant language and culture. In attempting to understand Michael's language development, we come to an even greater appreciation of the importance of environment. The final section of the chapter will consist of a brief discussion of the problems associated with diagnosing language disorders, particularly in bilingual children.

A discussion of language disorder or handicap can be organized in a number of ways. The two most common classifications are according to apparent cause and according to effect on the language output of the child. The first entails an examination of the language problems encountered by children with particular disorders—hearing impairment, for example, or cognitive disabilities. The second entails an examination of aspects of the language produced—voice quality, for example, or problems with the rate or rhythm of speech. No matter how we structure our discussion, we are really talking about a continuum of dysfunction—from severe disorders resulting in total noncommunication to relatively mild disorders such as hoarseness of voice or an inability to produce sibilants.

Few disorders are linked to a single cause. Although certain disabilities tend to result in certain language dysfunctions, the same problem, or symptom, occurring in two children may have entirely different and unrelated causes. For these reasons, I have chosen to organize the discussion around descriptions of particular language disorders. Before doing so, however, it is important to make an important distinction between communicative disorders and communicative differences.

Communicative disorders result in speech that is so defective that it interferes with one's ability to convey messages clearly and effectively during interactions with community members who speak the same language and dialect (Mattes & Omark, 1984, p. 2).

Children with communicative disorders should receive remedial assistance, but children with communicative differences do not require and, in fact, could be adversely affected by remediation. Communicative differences are variations from the language "norm" of the community that arise out of dialect or language differences. Obviously, where the "norm" of the community is a particular dialect or a particular language, communicative differences are likely to appear in bilingual, bicultural children. We have already seen that the phonology of children's first language may temporarily influence their pronunciation of the second. Indeed, certain pronunciations are expected and almost legendary, such as the l/r confusion experienced by many Oriental learners of English. But we also find language differences among speakers of the same language. There is, or should be, a wide range of acceptability that permits certain of these differences—such as both the British and the American pronunciation of *erudite*. We must not label as "disorder" those things that are merely different, for the latter (1) may be developmental and will change as the child becomes more proficient in the language, or (2) may not need to be changed.

Certainly, dialect should not be confused with disorder. If children demonstrate any speech behavior or language use that others in their peer group or ethnic community also demonstrate, then it is obvious that their language is not "disordered" but different. Theirs is a legitimate means of expression and not in need of remediation. It should, in other words, be left alone. The distinction between disorder and difference may seem obvious, but it is not one that is always made. Bilingual children with an imperfect command of English (which happens to be the language of the school) are too often counted as "functionally handicapped" because their communicative ability is "impaired." That this "impairment" is really only a developmental stage escapes the notice of some educators who send these children to speech or language pathologists for remediation. Of course, bilingual children may have language disorders, but they are no more prevalent in the bilingual than in the monolingual population,[1] and special care must be taken in diagnosing language dysfunction in bilingual children.

FOUR TYPES OF COMMUNICATIVE DISORDER

The most common communicative disorders encountered by teachers relate to:

1. Voice production
2. Fluency
3. Articulation of particular sounds
4. Language processing.

Each type may occur with varying degrees of severity and in both monolingual and bilingual children. We will consider each in turn.

Voice Disorders

Any nontemporary affliction that affects the quality of the voice is considered a *voice disorder.* A condition such as chronic hoarseness that is not

---

[1]According to British estimates in the early 1970s, between 2% and 3% of the total population of children require some sort of speech therapy. These figures include preschool, "ordinary," educationally subnormal in both moderate and severe categories as well as physically handicapped children. There is no reason to expect a different proportion in North American populations.

caused by temporary conditions such as colds or laryngitis, extreme breathiness, or hypernasality *may* be classified as a voice disorder. In severe cases, the pitch, volume, and timbre of the voice may be so distorted that the speaker is unintelligible. In milder cases, the vocal quality may simply be inappropriate to the speaker's age or sex or to the situation, but impede intelligibility only slightly.

Essentially, the two types of vocal disorders are those associated with phonation, or abnormalities in the vibration of the vocal folds, and those associated with resonance, or abnormalities in the modification of the sound as it passes through the vocal tract. Excessive breathiness and hoarseness would be examples of phonation problems, while excessive nasality would be a resonance disorder. There are a number of causes of vocal disorders, but only about one-third of them are anatomical or neurophysiological. Most have other causes such as emotional stress or abuse of the vocal apparatus caused by excessive use of the voice, in singing, speaking, or shouting. Such abuse may result in a temporary physical disorder such as nodules or ulcers on the vocal folds, but treatment other than rest is not usually required.

Teachers need not worry about the accurate diagnosis of a vocal disorder, because competent professionals can do that. Their main concern is in detecting that a vocal disorder might exist, which might not be as straightforward as it sounds. As Mattes and Omark caution, even vocal disorders come with cultural values and biases attached. Cultures vary, for instance, in the degree of breathiness or nasality they consider normal or acceptable in speech. For this reason, educators should exercise some caution in deciding which conditions should be remediated. A sensible guideline is to refer those conditions that result in reduced intelligibility or which are aesthetically displeasing *to others in the child's own culture* (Mattes & Omark, 1984, p. 2). It would not be possible, then, for a teacher who is a member of the dominant culture to determine the effect on members of the child's culture. Whenever possible, bilingual children should be tested for vocal disorders in their first language. Otherwise, it may not be possible to distinguish certain normal vocal behaviors from the first language from those that are indicative of a disorder. In general, classroom teachers need not worry about making an accurate diagnosis of vocal disorder. If there is something unusual about a child's vocal quality that persists and is not apparent in others of the child's peer group, then the child should be referred to a speech or language pathologist or the family physician. A true voice disorder should affect both languages, but since the teacher cannot be sure whether the child is transferring first language vocal habits to English, he or she should make every effort to have an assessment done in the child's native language.

Fluency Disorders

Children with fluency disorders have difficulty speaking rapidly and continuously. They usually speak with an abnormal rate, rhythm, or both. The best known of the fluency disorders is stuttering, but there are others that impede the comprehensibility of speech. One of these is *cluttering,* a less common disorder involving the excessively rapid production of speech. Children with this disorder are "unable to control their speech rate, and as a result introduce distortions of rhythm and articulation into their speech" (Crystal, 1987, p. 278). Unlike stutterers, they also seem largely unaware that their speech is either partly or totally unintelligible to the listener.

There are a great many theories, but at this time no consensus has been reached about the cause of fluency disorders. Physical origins have been suggested as have psychological and neurological ones. Fortunately, treatment programs are in advance of theory; a great many programs and methods exist for the treatment of stuttering, in particular. For the classroom teacher, the most important issue is not the treatment of fluency disorders but referring children who require it.

Children learning their first language frequently experience a temporary fluency dysfunction. The most common symptom is lengthy hesitation and it occurs typically in children around the age of three, although it can affect speakers of any age. Most people, when speaking under pressure, will find themselves pausing as they search for an elusive word or repeating themselves unnecessarily. Care must be taken to distinguish both developmental and temporary stress-induced disfluency from the type that may be a true pathology.

Care must also be taken, as in the diagnosis of voice disorders, to assure that bilingual children are correctly diagnosed. Once again, there is the possibility that what appears to be a dysfunction may be only a difference caused by either the transfer of first language speech and cultural patterns to the new language or by limited proficiency in English. While neither severe stuttering nor cluttering is culturally induced, not all cultures view stuttering as North Americans do. Mattes and Omark report that cultures differ in their views about what should be remediated. North American Cowichans sometimes view stuttering as supernatural, for example, and some other cultures are far more accepting of fluency differences (Mattes & Omark, 1984, p. 4).

A more common diagnostic problem occurs with bilingual children. Children learning English as a second language, for instance, may speak with hesitations, false starts, and frequent repetitions that impede the easy flow of speech. These occur when the child has difficulty in thinking of the appropriate word in English, or perhaps doesn't know it, or when the child is in any way unsure of the language. It would be a mistake to classify these developmental differences as fluency disorders; they will in all likelihood disappear as the child learns more of the language.

Articulation Disorders

Articulation disorders comprise a wide range of problems. At one end of the spectrum are difficulties with the pronunciation of a particular sound that have little impact on intelligibility. Lisping is an example of one of these milder disorders. At the other end are phonological systems that are so severely disordered that speech is totally incomprehensible, sometimes as a result of serious injury to the brain. Children with disorders of this magnitude are easily identified and referred for treatment. The more problematic case for classroom teachers is children whose misarticulations are minor and may not need remediation because they are developmental.

As we saw in Chapter 3, although the phonological system is largely in place by the time a child is school-aged, certain distinctions may still need to be worked out. A few children may still produce [w] for [l], for [r], or for both even after they have begun school. Usually, these three sounds are acquired by the age of four, but occasionally the distinction is not worked out until a year or so later even though speech is normal in all other ways. As Crystal has noted, "many of the pronunciation problems that cause parental concern are due to a general delay in the ability to control movements" (1987, p. 277). Delay is not the same as deviance. If we find that a child's pronunciation is different from that of her peers, then there are two possibilities. If the school-aged child's phonological system appears to be essentially the same as that of a younger normal child, then it is not deviant but simply delayed. It is simply a matter of slower development than is usual. But if there are "patterns of acquisition that never appear in young normal children," then "we can say the child has a *deviant* system" (Ingram, 1976, p. 98). In the case of phonological deviance, the child should be referred for remediation. The speech therapist or language pathologist will be able to distinguish delayed from deviant speech if the teacher is in doubt about the cause of a child's mispronunciation.

Bilingual children may present particular diagnostic problems. Because articulation disorders may be systemic, that is, they may be a result of regular but different phonological processes, there is a possibility that a bilingual child will experience interference between the sound systems of the first and the second languages. This is one reason that some children learning English as their second language pronounce words differently from monolingual English speakers. It has been observed, for example, that French children sometimes substitute [d] or [t] for the *th*-sounds in English.[2] It is thought that this is because French has no *th*-sound. Spanish and many other Romance languages simply have fewer consonant and vowel sounds than English, and thus speakers of these learning English must learn additional sounds. While they are doing so, they may substitute related sounds, either from English or from their own language, for a time. Another type of phonological difference can occur when two languages have the same sound or sounds but produce them slightly differently. Portuguese, for example, has the [p] sound, but it is not aspirated as it is at the beginning of English words. When a Portuguese speaker produces a [p] in the manner of Portuguese, it may sound more like a [b] to an English speaker.

The distribution of sounds in words differs between languages and contributes to some of the articulation problems experienced by non-native speakers. In Mandarin, for example, the only consonants that occur in word-final position are nasals. Chinese children may, thus, leave off final consonants that are not nasal. The important point for the teacher to remember is that in children, these articulation problems are developmental and will be overcome as the child becomes more proficient in the language. While speech therapists use techniques that may be useful with ESL learners whose developmental errors persist, these children should, as a rule, not be referred for therapy.

The question arises, then, of how the classroom teacher knows which pronunciation problems are indicative of an articulation disorder. We return to the criteria discussed above. Bilingual children should be assessed in their native language and referred for therapy only if an articulation disorder is present in that language. If first-language assessment is not possible (if, for example, one cannot find a Cowichan speaker in Boston), then the teacher should proceed under the assumption that there is no articulation disorder. If the child's pronunciation remains heavily distorted over an extended period (more than a year for a child in kindergarten, grade one, or two, or more than two years if the child is older), a speech therapist might be able to do a complete profile of the child's English phonology and make some reasonable guess about the

---

[2]Children of many languages make this substitution, and it may *not* be an interference phenomenon. It may simply be the substitution of the nearest manageable sound for the unmanageable one. The *th*- sound in English is relatively rare in the world's languages, so most second language learners initially make some substitution.

causes of the pronunciation problems. Happily, young children tend to acquire native-like pronunciation fairly easily. Bilingual children may have difficulty with English pronunciation because they have had relatively less exposure and opportunity to practice it, but they are no more prone to articulation disorders than the monolingual population.

Language Disorders

Also known as *language handicap, language disorder* refers to "any systematic deviation in the way people speak, listen, read, write, or sign that interferes with their ability to communicate with their peers" (Crystal, 1987, p. 264). As with voice, fluency, and articulation disorders, language disability covers a wide spectrum of dysfunction and may affect the structure, content, or use of language. The causes are various, but in a large proportion of cases, the origins are clearly physical. Brain damage, which may cause mental or physical disability and have a serious effect on language skills, and deafness are the two principal physical impairments underlying language disorders.

The disorders themselves vary in severity and in the level of language they affect. Language impairments that result from specific brain damage are collectively called **aphasias**. Aphasia refers to the loss of ability to use and understand language and excludes language disorders associated with other physical conditions such as deafness. Although there are a number of different kinds of aphasia, corresponding to the particular area of the brain that is damaged, they can be broadly classified into receptive, expressive, and global aphasias.

Receptive aphasia, also called sensory aphasia and Wernicke's aphasia, results from a lesion to a region in the upper back part of the temporal lobe of the brain called Wernicke's area. People suffering from this type of aphasia typically exhibit no articulation difficulty or disfluency; in fact, their language may be characterized by nearly excessive fluency. What is affected is comprehension, and as a result, their speech may be marked by repeated patterns or formulaic phrases, by unintelligible sequences of words, or odd combinations of words or even phonemes. They may also experience problems in retrieving words from memory (Crystal, 1987, p. 271).

Expressive aphasia is also known as motor aphasia and Broca's aphasia, after the French neurologist who found that damage to the lower back part of the frontal lobe interferes with speaking ability. Patients with expressive aphasia suffer severe impairment to their articulation and fluency. Speech is often very slow and labored, with many hesitations and disturbances in the individual sounds and in the prosodic features of the utterance. Sentences tend to be very short and telegraphic in structure, that is, composed of few words with little attention to the requirements of grammar. In contrast to receptive aphasics, expressive aphasics have little difficulty with comprehension.

In patients with **global aphasia**, the symptoms of expressive and receptive aphasia are combined. They have minimal speech capability and their comprehension is also very limited. Because the prognosis for recovery, or even for significant improvement, is poor, this type of aphasia is sometimes known as "irreversible aphasia syndrome" (Crystal, 1987, p. 271).

The diagnosis and treatment of aphasic children rests beyond the expertise and responsibility of classroom teachers. Most school systems provide specialists to whom children can be referred in the unlikely case that they have not been identified before they reach school age. It would not be unlikely, on the other hand, for teachers to encounter children with some degree of **hearing impairment**, since an estimated 6% to 7% of the population suffers some degree of hearing loss. Again, there are specially trained speech and language pathologists available in most districts to provide advice, but some knowledge of developmental trends in deaf children's language is useful for all teachers.

We saw in earlier chapters that the language environment is essential to language acquisition. Children need to hear language and have opportunities to use it. Hearing impaired children have been deprived, in varying degrees depending on the severity of their hearing loss, of the sensory input of language. Without that input, they will not develop speech:

> Children who are born with hearing impairment that limits their perception of sounds to those exceeding 60 decibels (db), or about the intensity level of a baby's cry, generally will not be able to develop spontaneous oral language that approximates that of normal children. Children born with losses exceeding 90 db are considered deaf and will not develop speech and language skills spontaneously (without educational and therapeutic intervention). (Ratner, 1989, p. 370)

In general, there is a correspondence between the severity of the loss and the degree of language handicap. In other words, when children can hear only a limited range of the sounds produced in normal speech, they will most likely develop speech that is difficult to understand. The greater the degree of deafness, the more distorted the pronunciation, for example. If the hearing loss is only minor, though, children will benefit from most of the language around them. They may not hear whispering or softly spoken language from a distance or outside their line of vision, but in most ways their language will develop more or less normally.

As Ratner points out, an articulatory disability is less influential on children's school success than are disabilities in syntax and semantics, which directly influence their ability to develop proficiency in reading and writing. "Over the years, repeated surveys of the reading abilities of older deaf children and adults suggest that their reading ability may never surpass that of 4th- to 5th-grade hearing children (Hammermeister, 1972; Trybus & Karchmer, 1977)" (cited in Ratner, 1989, pp. 373–374). Other studies point to an incomplete grasp of syntax as the reason underlying the reading problem. Some of the syntactic problems that deaf children have are similar to those experienced by normally developing hearing children. But they also have particular problems with the verb phrase—in particular, modals and other auxiliary verbs as well as infinitives (for example, *To see is to believe*) and gerunds (for example, *Seeing is believing*). Other syntactic structures that cause problems in comprehension include negation, question formation, relativization, and complementation.[3] Deaf children are more likely to produce sentences such as:

> Sheila take the cat no (negation)
> Who the girl take the cat (question formation)
> I saw the girl that the girl took it (relativization)
> Mommy goes to shopping (complementation)

Because language disorders of this severity are caused by a dysfunction in the process underlying the surface production of *any* language, children with more than one language will have all their languages affected. A systemic language disorder of this fourth type cannot affect only one of a bilingual's languages.

LANGUAGE PROBLEMS OF BILINGUAL CHILDREN

When bilingual children were studied earlier in this century, researchers were mainly interested in how bilingualism facilitated or interfered with language development. Many of these studies concluded that monolinguals performed better than bilinguals on measures with one language

---

[3]For a complete description of typical language structures in deaf children, see the work done by Quigley and other researchers (Power & Quigley, 1973; Quigley, Montanelli, & Wilbur, 1976; Quigley, Smith, & Wilbur, 1974; Quigley, Wilbur, & Montanelli, 1974, 1976; Wilbur, Montanelli, & Quigley, 1976).

only. Bilinguals were found to have smaller vocabularies (Saer, 1922; Grabo, 1931; Barke & Parry-Williams, 1938) and to make more grammatical errors (Carrow, 1957; Smith, 1933, 1935; all cited in Abudarham, 1980, p. 236). The flaw in these studies was that most of them considered only one of the bilingual's languages or each language separately. They did not consider the totality of the language system of the bilingual, that is, the full communicative capacity provided by the two languages (Abudarham, 1980, p. 236). Yet researchers all too often reached the conclusion that bilingualism was a disadvantage to the child. As MacNamara wrote, "There is some firmly grounded evidence indicating that the bilinguals have a weaker grasp of language than monoglots" (Macnamara, 1966; cited in Abudarham, 1980, p. 236). More recent research has attempted to correct this flaw by testing bilinguals' proficiency in both their languages.[4] These studies have been useful in affirming the linguistic "normality" of bilinguals, but they have not provided specific measures to be used to diagnose language disorders in bilingual children.

Any language disability that can affect monolingual children can also affect bilinguals. On the other hand, educators have identified certain language problems associated *only* with bilingual children. It has been noted, for example, that children being educated in a second language are usually successful when their native language is the dominant language of the community (Cummins, 1979a). This is the case, for example, with English-speaking children in French immersion programs. In contrast, children whose native language is a minority language fare less well in school. It has also been noted that some children "seem to enjoy cognitive advantages tied to their bilingualism while others do not (Peal & Lambert, 1962; cited in Edelsky et al., 1983) and that older children being educated in a non-native setting are generally more successful than younger ones (Toukomaa & Skutnabb-Kangas, 1977; cited in Edelsky et al., 1983).

To explain these somewhat contradictory observations, Canadian researchers Jim Cummins and Merrill Swain proposed the distinction between cognitive academic language and language used for most interpersonal communication (described in Chapter 6), suggesting that school success is more closely related to children's cognitive academic language proficiency (CALP) than to their proficiency with the language used for social interaction (BICS). Cummins also developed two hypotheses, the **threshold hypothesis** and the **developmental interdependence hypothesis**, which, along with BICS and CALP, were intended to account for the

---

[4]See for example, Fishman, Cooper, & Ma, 1975; Kessler, 1971; Peal & Lambert, 1962; Bever, 1972, as well as the discussion in Chapter 10.

differences in school success among bilingual children. According to the threshold hypothesis, a second language learner must attain "a certain 'threshold' level of proficiency . . . in that language before the learner can benefit from the use of the language as a medium of instruction in school" (Richards, Platt, & Weber, 1985, p. 293). Cummins also asserts that the level of proficiency children attain in the second language "depends upon the level of proficiency the child learner has reached in the first language at the time when extensive exposure begins" (Richards, Platt, & Weber, 1985, p. 293). This is the interdependence hypothesis.

Minority children who come to school without having attained cognitive academic language proficiency in at least one of their languages are supposedly educationally at risk. Children who begin school with neither CALP nor BICS are sometimes labeled as *semilingual*. Although the term is no longer widely used in North America, semilingual is used in Europe, principally in Scandinavia, to refer to bilingual children who have not mastered either of their languages well enough to engage in the cognitive-academic functions needed for success in school (Cummins, 1979a, p. 231).

Researchers such as Carole Edelsky and her colleagues (1983) and Martin-Jones and Romaine (1986) have pointed out, however, that the BICS and CALP distinction, the threshold hypothesis, the interdependence hypothesis, and the assumption of semilingualism are dangerous and wrong. They are dangerous because they essentially constitute a "blame the victim" theory: Bilingual children have trouble in school because of something they did not bring, namely the degree of proficiency in English that the school deems necessary. This view fails to recognize and to take advantage of the totality of the language that these children *do* bring. The two hypotheses and the label semilingual are often wrong because they rely on data from tests and test settings that are inadequate to assess children's language competence.

In general, school personnel test those aspects of language that they know how to test. These include pronunciation and vocabulary, frequently measured by worksheets and standardized tests. These fragments of language are quantified "without regard for their interrelationship with other levels of linguistic organization" (Martin-Jones & Romaine, 1986, p. 29), and in such a way that they tell us more about what children do *not* know than what they do know about language. Based on his own clinical experience in Britain, Abudarham (1980) asserts that standardized tests such as the Peabody Picture Vocabulary Test have "little, if any, diagnostic or prognostic value" with dual-language children (Abudarham, 1989, pp. 231–232) in large part because they reveal deficits in the second language without tapping children's native language resources. The fact that such measures tell us little about what children know about language or what they can do with language does not deter well-intentioned educators from using them nor from reaching conclusions about bilingual children that may be faulty. As Martin-Jones and Romaine point out, most language tests given in schools "are only indirectly related to common sense notions of what it means to be a competent language user" (1986, p. 29). This being the case, it is easy to see the potential for abuse. As the authors point out,

> When notions like 'the ability to extract meaning' become operationalized as scores on, for example, reading tests, a child who fails is then labelled as one who is 'unable to extract meaning'. Similarly, when the 'cognitive aspects' of language are tested in terms of, say, being able to produce synonyms, then the child who can't is branded as 'lacking in the cognitive aspects of language development'. (Martin-Jones & Romaine, 1986, p. 29)

Once educators who make decisions on behalf of bilingual children get it into their heads that such things as mastering complex syntactic structures, providing synonyms on vocabulary lists, and even correct spelling are valid indicators of language proficiency, they cease to question the real nature of language ability and how it might or might not be revealed by such measures. In a real sense, then, the explanation attempted by the BICS and CALP distinction and by the threshold and the interdependence hypotheses constitutes a deficit theory: Bilingual children's lack of success in the majority language and in school is attributed to that which they do not bring to school and not to any deficiency in the school's assessment of such children or in their curriculum for or teaching of bilingual children.

Nevertheless, from time to time a bilingual child will enter school with a particular language disability that is related to decisions made in the home. Such a child has severe and obvious difficulty communicating in either language and, in the past, would have been labeled as semilingual. Today, however, the term has such negative connotations that it has largely been abandoned in North America. Michael is such a child, and the story of his language development is revealing for what it says about the importance of language environment.

MICHAEL'S LANGUAGE DEVELOPMENT

Michael was in the same kindergarten class as Lucy, the child we met in Chapter 6. I first met him when I visited the class in September, about two weeks after the beginning of the school year.[5] He was sitting on the floor with the other children listening as the teacher read *The Three Bears*. He seemed to be engrossed in the activity and watched the teacher intently as he listened. He laughed when the other children laughed but otherwise remained silent. Many of the other children, in contrast, would respond to the teacher's occasional question by calling out answers— "Goldilocks!"—or would comment on the familiar story. During that visit to the classroom, I met with the children individually to try to determine their level of English language proficiency. I sat at a table in the back of the classroom and called the children to me one at a time. When I called Michael's name, he looked up but did not move. Nor did he respond to my request to join me, although when I called his name a second time and motioned to him, he did come to the back of the room.

He sat quietly at the table, following my eyes with his as I talked to him. The only response he made to any of my questions was to give his name when I asked. I tried asking him the names of various objects— shoes, a book, his nose, his shirt, a picture of a bird—but he merely looked at me. I then tried to get him to repeat the names of these same objects. When he appeared not to understand the task, I demonstrated with another child. Michael's repetitions were mostly highly nasalized monosyllables that sounded alike, something like "muh."

At the end of the day, I talked with the kindergarten teacher to try to learn something about Michael's background. Unfortunately, the ESL consultant who usually visited the homes of new pupils had not yet visited Michael's home and the kindergarten teacher knew very little about him. She thought it likely, given his last name, that his family spoke Italian at home but she had not been able to verify this fact. His registration card was only partly complete, and she was able to ascertain only that he was 4;5 and that he had one older sibling who was not in school. She reported that Michael seemed to enjoy coming to school, caused no problems in class, but had not spoken except to say his name when asked. He seemed very attentive and often smiled or laughed at the actions of the other children. Neither the teacher nor I was particularly concerned about his silence; we assumed that he was a beginner in English and we both knew that an extended silent period is quite normal in young second language learners.

[5]The case study of Michael's language learning is also report in Piper (1986a, 1986b).

Michael was absent during my next visit to the class, and it was nearly three weeks later when I saw him again. I could tell by the expression on his face that he remembered me and came immediately to my table when I called him. Once again he watched me closely and he seemed to understand more of what I said. He responded correctly when asked to name pictures of a house, a bear, and a bed from *The Three Bears*. He also responded "I don't know" when I asked him what a picture of a tree was and again when I showed him a picture of a bird and asked what it was. To the other questions he gave no response at all. In all his utterances, his pronunciation remained badly distorted. His teacher had learned nothing more about his background but told me that he was an even-tempered child who seemed to enjoy school, but as a watcher rather than a joiner. He seldom participated in his classmates' activities and waited patiently for crayons or toys to become available. He was still silent, speaking only when he was alone with his teacher and then only repeating the names of objects after her. She could recall no instance of his initiating speech.

Although I visited the class on a number of occasions during the next month, it was not until late November that I learned anything more about Michael. The ESL consultant had visited his home and had met both his father and mother whose native language was indeed Italian. The parents, she reported, spoke very limited English, but the father seemed to understand most of what she explained about the school's kindergarten and ESL programs. She also learned that Michael's grandmother lived with the family and that Michael had a teenaged sister who did not live at home. In short, she was able to learn very little more about Michael.

Michael's teacher, however, had happened to meet his sister and had learned from her more about Michael's background. His sister had been born in Italy and had moved with her family to Canada when she was nine years old, six years before Michael was born. She said that she had found it very difficult to learn English, although it was the impression of the teacher that she spoke fluently and with no foreign accent. She struggled through school, a fact that caused her parents a great deal of anxiety, but eventually completed high school. At that point, when Michael was approximately 2;6, she left home and had only infrequent contact—perhaps once a week—with her younger brother. Before she left and occasionally when she returned to visit the family, she would read aloud to Michael, although infrequently, and sometimes played children's records for him. When the teacher asked her which language she used in communicating with Michael, she gave an answer that was extremely revealing. English, she said, was the only language that her parents permitted to be used with Michael.

Convinced that their daughter's problems in school were a result of her limited English proficiency, his parents had determined that Michael would learn *only* English. Unfortunately, they spoke very little English themselves and his contact with his sister and her English-speaking friends was minimal. According to his sister, Michael understood Italian and spoke a few words, but his parents discouraged conversation in that language and Michael seemed content to listen. They did not read to him in Italian and could not read to him in English, although they did provide a number of English-language children's books and records for him. Michael's teacher found this last observation especially interesting because she had observed that he seemed to be familiar with some of the songs played or sung in class even though he never joined in singing them.

To complicate Michael's learning of English even further, both his parents worked outside the home and he was left in the care of his paternal grandmother who spoke no English at all. She had been instructed not to speak Italian to Michael because the parents were adamant that Michael not learn Italian. Very likely, she did speak some Italian to the child, for it is hard to imagine that she would love and care for him in total silence. But whatever communication occurred between grandmother and grandson was not sufficient for him to acquire a functional first language, at least so far as we were able to determine.

From this time in November until the end of the school year, I took special care to observe and to document Michael's language learning. During that time, I was disheartened on many occasions, convinced that Michael was making no progress at all. He was always attentive in class and in conversation with me, but he rarely spoke except in private conversation with his teacher or with me. At various points in the year, when I compared his language development with that of the other ESL children in the class, I could see that Michael's vocabulary was extremely limited, his sentences short and filled with errors that the other children had either not made or had long since stopped making, and his pronunciation, though improved, still greatly distorted. At the end of the school year, his teacher, the ESL consultant, and I agreed that Michael was not ready to go into grade one in the coming term. His oral language development lagged so far behind that of his peers that it seemed highly unlikely that he would be ready to cope with the demands of literacy in three short months, particularly if he had little practice in English in the summer months. Unfortunately, the ESL consultant had made little headway in convincing Michael's parents to speak and read Italian to him, so it seemed likely that Michael's exposure to any language would be curtailed during the school break.

When the school year ended, then, my assessment of Michael's language learning and my prognosis for future language development were not positive ones. As I began to listen to the tape recordings and read the transcripts from the previous nine months, however, my assessment of his progress changed. At the end of May, Michael's language, when compared with other children in the class, seemed painfully underdeveloped. But as I retraced his growth during the year by listening to the tapes and reading the transcripts, I realized that he had made a great deal of progress. His rate of development and the degree of fluency he had attained by June were well below those of any other child in the class, but when I considered his language on its own merits, I could see growth. His pronunciation, which in the fall had been almost unintelligible, retained some distortion but was intelligible and showed improvement every month. Even at the end of the school year, when he added a new word to his vocabulary, the pronunciation would initially be highly distorted but would soon improve. In other areas of language, Michael showed more impressive growth. His comprehension, accuracy (both in syntax and in choice of words), fluency, and communicative competence all improved dramatically over the school year.

Comprehension

For kindergarten-aged children, comprehension refers only to the understanding of oral language and not written language. It is usually gauged by assessing their verbal and nonverbal responses to the language they hear. Throughout the school year, Michael's teacher had administered the Bilingual Syntax Measure (BSM). The BSM is a test sometimes used to assess English language proficiency in children from about kindergarten through about grade three. It consists of a set of simple, brightly colored pictures and questions designed to elicit certain grammatical structures such as tense markers, plurals, and possessives as well as more complex forms such as the present perfect and conditionals. While this is not a test designed to measure comprehension, it was very clear in early attempts at administering the test to Michael that he did not understand the questions. For example, in January, his response to the question "What is the mommy bird going to do with the worm?" was "Eat it." But the picture makes it abundantly clear that she is going to give it to her baby birds. Thinking that he may have meant that the baby birds were going to eat the worm, I asked him "Who will eat the worm?" to which he replied by pointing to the mother bird. In March, however, and again in June, his responses, "She's give them food" and "Give it to babies," indicated that he had understood the question.

The same pattern appeared in his responses to the question "Why is the dog looking at the king?", the expected answer to which is "Because he's hungry" (the dog, that is). In November, Michael responded "Doggy looking that turkey." In January, he responded "Cause he eat, him eat," which may have indicated correct comprehension and problems with sentence formation. But it was clear in March that he could both understand the question and produce the appropriate response: "Because him hungry."

The evidence from the BSM would not be adequate for assessing Michael's level of comprehension. In Michael's case, however, his difficulty in comprehension was apparent for several months in much of the interaction between Michael and me and between Michael and his teacher. But the same improvement that appeared in his performance on the BSM was also evident in other situations of language use. While it is sometimes difficult to distinguish comprehension errors from production errors—in other words, to know whether a child has not understood what is said or does not know how to respond appropriately—it is certain that no language development would have taken place over the school year unless he had first experienced improved comprehension. Learners' ability to speak a second language nearly always lags behind their understanding of it.

Accuracy

One of the problems in evaluating how much a child's accuracy in using the language has improved is this confounding of accuracy with comprehension. With the BSM, however, this problem is minimized through the use of simple, unambiguous pictures and by the teacher's assuring before beginning the procedure that the child knows the names for the objects and the actions portrayed. In assessing Michael's accuracy in answering the BSM questions, once it was clear that he understood them, it was obvi-

Table 7.1
Selected answers and responses to BSM

Question	Response
What is the mommy bird going to do with the worm?	She's give them food. (March)
Why's he so fat?	Because him eat too lots. (June)
And why's he so skinny?	Because he was eating. (March) Because he's not eating. (June)
Why are their eyes closed?	Because them go bed. (March)
Why do you think she's so happy?	Her like it outside. (June)
Why do you think this man lives in this house?	Because him house is fat. (March)

ous that he responded with semantic accuracy long before he had mastered syntactic accuracy. The excerpts in Table 7.1 illustrate this.

All of Michael's talk with adults and his infrequent spontaneous speech were marked by the same kinds of grammatical errors as his responses to the BSM. What is more interesting, however, is the fact that his grammatical system at any one time seemed to be mostly consistent. It would be surprising if a child acquiring a second language were to manifest a completely stable grammar, especially for an extended period of time. As language learners are exposed to more and more language, they figure out the rules more accurately and their grammars undergo changes. This is the central claim of the interlanguage hypothesis we examined in Chapter 5 and it is certainly true for Michael. We can see an example of his grammar in transition in two of the answers in Table 7.1. He says at one point "Because him eats too lots" and a few minutes later, "Because he's not eating." The third-person subject pronoun is an unstable form for Michael at this time, most likely because he was in the process of modifying his previous grammar, which used "him" and "her" in subject position. This is a process that began earlier and is well under way in June. The following September, I went back to the school to find out whether a number of the observations and predictions I had made about Michael's language growth had been accurate. I found out that when he returned to school in September, he had sorted out the distinction for both the masculine and feminine pronouns.

Fluency

In second language acquisition *fluency* refers to the ability to produce language with relative ease and to communicate ideas effectively. Neither grammatical accuracy nor correct pronunciation is necessarily characteristic of fluent speech unless severe deficiency in either impedes the flow of language. Fluency can be measured in a number of ways, including the number of times a child initiates speech. With Michael, this measure would indicate no fluency at all. In his case, a rough indication was obtained simply by counting and comparing the number of words produced in response to the same set of questions over time. In November, the 21 questions of the BSM elicited 28 words in response, or an average of 1.33 words per response. By January, the number of words jumped to 52, or an average of 2.48, and by June there was an increase to 69 for an average of 3.29. During the school year, then, an appreciable increase in fluency occurred, as indicated by the number of words produced in this highly controlled situation. With a great deal of prompting and the use of a picture book, Michael was able to tell the story of *The Three Bears*:

T: Will you tell me a story Michael? What do you see?
M: The girl leaving in . . . (long pause)
T: What is the girl doing?
M: Leaving in bear bed.
T: What's she doing now?
M: Look in kitchen.
T: And what's she doing here?
M: Her (unintelligible) chair.
T: What did she do to the chair?
M: Wreck chair.
T: Right! And now what's she doing?
M: Sleepin' in bed now.
T: Yes?
M: That's the end.
T: No, not yet. What are these?
M: Those are bear.
T: What are they doing?
M: Them, them, this—the girl eat them.
T: What's this bear doing?
M: Him (unintelligible)
T: What?
M: That girl eat again.
T: What's happening here?
M: That bear-her sleeping on her bed.
T: And now what's the girl doing?
M: (unintelligible) out window.
T: Yes. And what are the bears doing?
M: Lookin' out. (long pause)
T: Is that the end?
M: Yeah.

Michael's telling of the story took a great deal of effort both on his part and that of his teacher, but eventually he more or less got it told. This is not by any means a fluent telling for a child at the end of the kindergarten year, but when we recall that Michael did not speak at all in September, we have to count his hesitant retelling of *The Three Bears* as significant progress. Nevertheless, as a comparison, it is useful to read Lucy's retelling of the same story in Chapter 5 at approximately the same time.

We find much more fluency in Lucy's rendering of the story. Where Michael had to be prompted into speech that came haltingly and in small quantity, the language seemed to pour from Lucy. Her telling also had flawed syntax but once she got involved in her narrative, she told it coherently, using adverbial connectives to maintain continuity.

Other samples of Michael's speech showed the same pattern and rate of growth in fluency—steady but very, very slow. Improved fluency results from improved comprehension and productive ability, but it is also related to a somewhat amorphous aspect of language ability, namely, communicative competence. We have seen that language acquisition has its roots in the child's wish to make meaning, to communicate. As a child's need and desire to communicate grow, language learning takes place. The most important index of language learning, then, is the overall growth in communicative competence.

Communicative Competence

The ability to communicate competently involves more than the ability to form grammatically correct utterances. It refers to the pragmatics of language and thus includes knowing the rules of speaking, how to use and respond to requests, apologies, invitations, thanks, etc, and how to use language appropriately. Communicative competence is difficult to measure, but it is not difficult for a teacher or other observer with extensive opportunity to observe a child to reach a fairly accurate and useful conclusion about the child's level of communicative competence.

In Michael's case, there was little spontaneous speech from which to judge his communicative ability. Over the course of the school year, some growth occurred. In March, the following dialogue was recorded:

I: What are these children doing, Michael?
M: I need big dog.
I: Do you? Why?
M: 'Cause, mm, I leave my mom.
I: You need the dog when you leave your mom?
M: Yeah. Dog, mm, dog go school.
I: The dog would go to school with you?
M: Yeah.

Michael declined to talk about the topic I introduced but used language instead to say something that *he* wanted to say. He was obviously trying to tell me about his wish for a dog and what that dog would do. As brief as it was, the exchange provided some evidence that Michael was increasing his repertoire of language functions.

The fact that he rarely initiated speech is not in itself an indication of poor communicative ability. It does suggest, however, that Michael was using only a limited number of the functions of language. The transcripts revealed a small number of spontaneous utterances, of Michael's using language to express his own meanings. As before, comparison with other second language learners in the class made Michael seem extremely reticent. Late in the year, however, an exchange took place with another child that suggested he was beginning to use language for his own purposes. Three children, Rapinder, Jenny, and Michael, were sitting together at a table during snack time. Jenny had brought a mandarin orange for her snack and Michael clearly craved it.

M: What dat?
J: It's a mandarin. My mommy gived it to me.
R: I got apple.
M: Me too. You want? (offering it to Jenny)
J: No, I want this.
M: Me too. You take. (offering the apple again)
J: No. I want mandarin. (She begins to peel it.)
R: Michael want to trade.
M: Yeah. Want trade.
J: No. I give you one piece. (She continues to peel the mandarin and hands Michael a piece.)
M: Thank you.

It would be presumptuous and likely wrong to label Michael as a semilingual if for no other reason than we had no accurate indication of his proficiency in Italian. Moreover, his English was growing—very slowly, but growing. Nevertheless, Michael was obviously a child at risk in the educational system. Bilingual children with similar but usually less severe language problems do appear in elementary schools from time to time. It may be frustrating for educators who have no appropriate label for them to plan for their education, but it is possible—and without administering sophisticated tests. In Michael's case, no standardized tests were attempted, and the only test administered was the BSM. Even with this test, the results were not used to label, place, or plan instruction for the child. Rather, the teacher relied on information gathered from the parents, on her own experience of other children of the same age, on her direct observation of and conversation with the child, and on her professional common sense in planning language experiences for Michael. In the case of bilingual children, and particularly since language tests are of questionable validity anyway, it is perhaps a blessing that formal diagnostic tests do not exist. There is little doubt that if they did, a great many bilingual children would be wrongly diagnosed as having a language impairment when, in fact, their problems with language were merely developmental.

PRINCIPLES AND GUIDELINES FOR ASSESSING BILINGUAL CHILDREN

Michael's teacher followed a principle that is very basic in assessing the language of bilingual children: *No decision about a language disorder can be made without first assessing the child's entire linguistic repertoire.* In bilingual children, this includes both languages and, in some children, the merger of the two. In Michael's case, it would have been impossible to begin to understand his language problems in school without benefit of the additional information about his situation at home. We saw that Michael suffered from delayed development in his first language, and it was not, therefore, surprising that he had a problem learning English as a second language. But we must also keep in mind the bilingual child who has normal first language development, which brings us to the second principle in assessing language disorders in bilingual children: *If a child does not have a language disorder in the native language, then whatever communicative disorders that may be manifested in the second language cannot be language disorders.*

Once again, we see that assessment in the child's native language is important. But is it possible? Efforts have been made to create language proficiency tests that can be standardized in two languages. In the United States, the *Test of Auditory Comprehension of Language* is standardized on a bilingual population in both English and Spanish. The problem with such a test, however, is that it measures the child's performance in each language independently and does not thus provide any indication of the child's overall language ability. As Abudarham points out, "If a child knows the correct response in the language not being currently tested, he is not credited with a positive score" (1980, p. 239). Abudarham identifies another problem with most language tests used with bilingual learners. Because most language tests assume a developmental sequence, earlier test items are likely to use and test vocabulary appropriate to early childhood and later items will require vocabulary appropriate to older children, etc. For bilingual children who may have acquired their second language after early childhood, these words may be unfamiliar. They may well know *other* words, and they may also know words appropriate to their age at the time of testing, but their test results once again fail to reveal what they do know.

School personnel use tests because they are available, but also because they do not know of alternatives. Yet, if the tests are not providing reliable data, then they must be abandoned. But what is the alternative? We saw already how one teacher gathered information about the language background of one of the children in her class. Of course, not all teachers have access to such information. The following guidelines are intended to help educators in identifying language disorders in bilingual children.

1. Gather all possible information about the child's language background. Without intruding on the family's privacy, try to find out whether the child is a "talker" or is especially reticent, whether he or she has been read to and enjoys books, the parent's attitude toward school. It is also useful to know whether the child has siblings and what languages are spoken by the child's playmates. Enlist a bilingual adult, ideally another teacher, or an older child if necessary.

2. Be careful in how you use the information you gather. Care should be taken not only to ensure the confidentiality of anything you learn about the child and family but also to interpret your "findings" fairly. This latter point is especially important. If you learn, for example, that the child says very little, do not jump to the conclusion that he or she doesn't have adequate knowledge of language. It may be that such behavior is normal within the child's cultural group, which brings us to the next point.

3. Whatever language behavior you observe should be compared to that of other bilingual children with similar cultural and language background. If you find even one who manifests the same or a similar phenomenon, then it is unlikely that you have uncovered a true disorder.

4. Expect second language learners to make grammatical errors. These may resemble errors made by first language learners at an earlier age or they may be unique to second language learners. In acquiring the system of the second language, learners often make generalizations about that system that are only partly true, but these do not constitute evidence of a language disorder. As an example, many Southeast Asians produce the tag "isn't it" in sentences such as "It is a beautiful day, isn't it?", "It is time to go, isn't it?", and "She looks very beautiful, isn't it?" They have obviously made an error in their hypothesis about how tag questions are formed in English, but it is a common error among non-native learners of English. It is not evidence of a language disorder.

5. Under some circumstances, children may lose proficiency in their first language. It is not exposure to the second *per se* that leads to this loss.

Rather, children who lose opportunities to use their first language may lose ground in that language. If, for example, a young Cree-speaking child moves with her family to the city and loses the extended family and Cree community, her Cree language may suffer. Surrounded by English, she no longer has the opportunities to use her own language that she once had. There is also pressure from the school to learn English. If school personnel manage to test her in the Cree language, especially after she has been away from the Cree community for a year or more, they may find that her language seems to be underdeveloped. But the school has failed once again, not only in their assumption of abnormal first language ability but in not measuring the totality of the child's linguistic capability, that in Cree *and* English.

6. Remember that it is normal for some children to use both languages to communicate. Mattes and Omark (1984) differentiate between *linguistic borrowing* and *code switching*. The former occurs when speakers incorporate elements of one language into another, particularly words. An example of borrowing would be the use of a single word from one language in the sentence of another, and is especially common when the speaker does not know the word in the other language. The latter involves switching back and forth between languages but is not limited to individual words. A speaker may begin a sentence in one language and switch to another for a phrase and then back to the original. Both borrowing and code switching are normal phenomena in bilinguals. They represent a legitimate means of communication and should not be taken as evidence of a language disorder.

7. Look for possible cultural and language bias in any test or other instrument used to make decisions about bilingual children. To do this, it will be necessary to implement the following two steps.

8. Learn as much as possible about the traditional and contemporary lifestyles of the cultures that you encounter in your community. Try to understand, for example, the different patterns of human development within different cultures as well as their value systems and beliefs and assumptions about education.

9. Finally, learn to trust your own judgment based on your experience with children of the same age. When there is a doubt about the child's language, adopt a wait-and-see attitude. Many patterns of second language learning are normal and it would be a mistake not to give a child adequate opportunity to learn with a friendly and facilitative classroom environment.

CONCLUSION

Children's need and wish to communicate is so great that they are frequently able to overcome severe handicaps to acquire language. In this chapter, we have looked briefly at some of the more common negative influences on language growth. We have also examined the case of a kindergarten child who was, as his teacher put it, "not quite as bilingual as he should be." The factors that had such a damaging effect on Michael's language serve as yet another reminder to us about the importance of the language environment. Tulips don't grow on rocks and language doesn't grow in the absence of language.

There is a danger that reading about Michael and the apparent causes of his problems will lead educators to the conclusion that bilingualism has the potential for causing severe language disorders. This is not the case, and to think of Michael's case as a warning is to miss the point. That point is, quite simply, that against the odds, and when judged in terms of what he could do with language rather than what he could not do, Michael made impressive gains in learning English.

The chapter concludes with a set of guidelines intended to help those who come into contact with bilingual children to make intelligent decisions about them and to treat them fairly. The guidelines are not intended as a program of intervention but rather as thought-provoking prerequisites to our educational planning.

PART THREE

Language and Learning

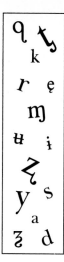

Chapter Eight

Language and Learning Outside School

In making the claim that language is special and in tracing the course of language development, I have perhaps implied that language exists and develops independently of the life of the child. This is not the case. We saw briefly in Chapter 1 that language and cognition develop in tandem. Or, as Alice Yardley puts it:

> . . . there is a close connection between words and thought, and at all stages language development is crucial to thought activity. The two are not identical, but they are interdependent, and the context within which the child acquires language has a permanent influence over the way he learns to think. (Yardley, 1973, p. 13)

Now is the time to talk in greater detail about language and its special relationship to learning. The purpose of this chapter is to attempt to characterize the role language plays in the learning of preschool children so that in Chapter 9 we may compare this early experience with the typical school experience of language and learning. We will begin by looking at the uses to which children put language as they learn it. We will then turn to the relationship between language and cognitive growth in the preschool years, paying close attention to the part language plays in memory, conceptualization, and in the growth of academic skills.

THE FUNCTIONS OF LANGUAGE IN CHILDREN'S LIVES

We saw in earlier chapters that linguists and others interested in language acquisition may study it from a number of vantage points. For teachers, whose interest is in working with children to provide language-rich environments in which their language can continue to flourish, a particularly useful way of thinking about language acquisition is in functional terms. A number of researchers have examined language acquisition and language use from that perspective. Because their purposes and methods differed, each researcher came up with a distinct set of functional categories. We will not consider here all of the functional schemes proposed by researchers,[1] but will concentrate on four, those of Halliday (1975, 1978), Schacter et al. (1974), Tough (1977, 1979), and Shafer, Staab, & Smith (1983).

Four Perspectives on Language Function

One of the first and most influential researchers to use a functional analysis was M. A. K. Halliday, a British linguist who employed the notion of *function* in describing his son Nigel's early language acquisition. He identified seven early functions that accounted for all the uses to which Nigel put the words he was learning. To classify Nigel's early words in this manner, Halliday had to make judgments about what meaning his son intended—what he was trying to accomplish with each utterance. Ingram (1989, p. 171) has pointed out that Halliday provided no operational procedures for researchers to follow in making such judgments, making it difficult for them to apply his method to the analysis of other children's speech in order to discover how universal the functions truly are. Ingram may be right, but he is writing as a linguist with particular goals in studying language acquisition and with rigorous standards for accomplishing them. Parents and teachers, in contrast, are accustomed to making precisely these kinds of judgments about children's intentions. Doubtless they are sometimes wrong, but even then there is opportunity for unraveling intent and recreating the fabric of meaningful discourse. Focused as they are on communicating with children, they find sense in a functional analysis.

The functions Halliday identified included the instrumental, regulatory, personal, interactional, heuristic, imaginative, and informative func-

[1]For a complete account of the different ways of viewing language function in children's language, see the first chapter of Shafer, Staab, & Smith (1983).

tions. All these were present in the child's language before the age of two. Later, he postulated, children make a transition to the more abstract uses of language that characterize adult speech. He therefore added four functional categories to account for the more mature uses to which children put language. These included the interpretive, the logical, the participatory, and the organizing functions (Halliday, 1978).

The functional categories proposed by Schacter et al. (1974) were also based on the analysis of young children's speech. They recorded 6000 utterances made by children playing in nursery schools and then classified them according to how the investigators perceived the intent of each utterance. These researchers identified nine categories: expressive, desire implementing, possession-rights-implementing, ego-enhancing, self-referring-including, joining, collaborative, learning-implementing, and reporting. Notice that while most of these functions demonstrate the highly egocentric nature of preschool children, they also use language for social purposes (the joining and collaborative functions) and for learning (the learning-implementing and reporting functions).

Based on her own work and on the previous work of Halliday, Vygotsky, Luria, Bruner, and others, Joan Tough established her own theory of language functions. According to her analysis of preschool children's language, Tough (1977, 1979) concluded that four functions account for their language use: directive, interpretive, projective, and relational. She went further to describe specific uses that children make of language within each function and also identified specific strategies they use to accomplish each use.[2] Finally, Shafer, Staab, and Smith (1983) adapted Tough's usage categories to a set of five, which they used for their book on developing children's language functions in school. The four different systems are shown in Table 8.1. This shows the four different sets of functional categories proposed by the different researchers together with a description of each category.

The most comprehensive of the functional systems is Halliday's, which postulates seven early functional categories and four later ones. The least inclusive is Tough's with four, but she covers the same language use by developing an elaborate network of uses and strategies for implementing each function. Whichever system we might choose to follow, it is clear that children's capacity to function in language is rich and varied. Although I will refer occasionally to some of the early functions in

---

[2]Tough's is an elaborate but clearly explicated scheme that would be of great value to researchers studying language in preschool children. It may perhaps be too detailed for most teachers to use.

Halliday's system, for the purposes of discussion in this chapter and in Chapter 9, I will use the functional scheme suggested by Shafer, Staab, and Smith (1983), not because it is more comprehensive than the others but because it was created with the stated purpose of helping "teachers to develop various language functions with children in order for them to succeed in school and throughout life" (1983, p. 20).

Table 8.1
Rough equivalents of four functional systems

Description	Halliday	Tough	Schacter et al.	Shafer, Staab, & Smith
Early functions				
Satisfy needs; get things done	Instrumental	Directive	Desire implementing	Social needs
Control behavior of others	Regulatory	Directive	Possession-rights; implementing	Controlling
Tell about self	Personal	Relational	Ego-enhancing	Social needs
Get along with others	Interactional		Joining; collaborative	Social need; projecting
Find out and learn	Heuristic		Learning-implementing	
Pretend, make believe	Imaginative	Projective		
Communicate information to others	Informative		Reporting	Informing
Later functions				
Interpret whole of experience	Interpretive	Interpretive		Forecasting and reasoning; projecting
Express logical relations	Logical	Interpretive		Forecasting and reasoning
Express wishes, feelings, attitudes, judgments	Participatory	Relational	Possession-needs-implementing; self-referring-including	Social needs
Organize discourse	Organizing			Forecasting and reasoning; projecting

Five Functions of Language

We now discuss the five functions of language:

1. Language to assert and maintain social needs
2. Projecting language
3. Language for controlling the self and others
4. Language for informing
5. Language of forecasting and reasoning

Language to Assert and Maintain Social Needs.   This function is comparable to Halliday's *instrumental* function and is one of the earliest to develop. When very young children make a demand ("Want juice!"), they are asserting a need. When they lay claim to a favorite toy ("That mine!"), they are asserting their personal right to have the toy. Shafer, Staab, and Smith identify five subfunctions of this function. In addition to asserting personal rights and needs, they include asserting negative expressions (threatening, arguing, criticizing, and giving negative opinions), asserting positive expressions, requesting an opinion, and incidental expressions ("Oh, no! Gee"!) (Shafer, Staab, & Smith, 1983, p. 41).

The instrumental function appears early in their language because young children are egocentric, and it continues to develop well into the school years. As they approach school age, children's ways of expressing their personal rights and needs will conform more to the socially accepted forms of the adult world. Also, as they grow older, they hear and learn to ask others' opinions, which has the effect of clarifying their personal needs but may also serve to keep the conversation going. Incidental expressions such as "Oh yes?" or "That's right" serve a similar function of moving the discourse along. Children will become increasingly able to voice agreement with other speakers and to compliment others, which contributes significantly to their ability to use language to maintain social relationships.

Projecting Language.   "Projecting is the function of reaching out into other person's experiences or into novel circumstances that we have not actually encountered ourselves" (Shafer, Staab, & Smith, 1983, p. 103). Because they are egocentric, young children's use of projecting language may be somewhat limited until they approach school age. It is difficult for them to assume another person's perspective. Still, there are circumstances which demonstrate that even very young children have the capacity to project themselves into the identities or experiences of others. Much of this occurs within the language function that Halliday calls the *imaginative* function. When children engage in make believe, they are reaching outside their identities into another experience. When they engage in dialogues such as the following, they are using projecting language:

Amy and Martha, both four, are playing house.
M: I'm the mommy and you can be the neighbor.
A: No, I want to be the mommy.
M: I'll let you wear my Mommy's pretty scarf.
A: Okay. But Sally (a doll) is MY baby. She wants to be my baby. Jilly wants to be yours. See, she's nodding her head.

This is clearly an example of projecting language being used in an imaginative context, but it demonstrates Amy's ability to express her own views as if they belonged to the dolls. This is the type of projecting that young children are likely to do. As they become older and less egocentric, they will become increasingly able to use projecting language to project completely outside their own experience. In preschool children, the projecting function includes projecting into the feelings, reactions, and experiences of others, both real and imaginative.

Language for Controlling the Self and Others.   This is the language of getting the job done. It is akin to Halliday's *instrumental* function and to his *regulatory* function. It is the use children make of language when they direct others' actions or their own in expressions such as "Give me that truck" or "Look at this." It is also the language used for requesting directions in utterances such as "What do you want me to do with this cup?" or "Where should we stick the red star?" and for seeking others' attention in commands such as "Watch me!" or "Look at this!" Sometimes this function is directed toward the child's own behavior. A child playing alone, or with other children, might be heard to say "This goes here and now it's done." The comment is not directed to another speaker but serves the purpose of monitoring the child's own activity, much as adults talk themselves through complex or multifaceted tasks. Shafer, Staab, and Smith (1983, p. 65) point out that controlling language may consist either of very explicit statements, such as "Shut the window," or of implicit statements, such as "I think the plant looks dry," which, if spoken with the intent of getting someone to water the plant, is equally controlling in function.

Not only is the controlling function of language used to get things done—a very important function in the lives of young children—it also plays an important role in learning. When it is used to instruct the self or direct others in ways that facilitate understanding, it is helping children to make sense of the world around them and is thus related to Halliday's *heuristic* function, which is a valuable tool for their early learning.

Language for Informing.   Children no doubt hear a great deal of this type of language both before and after they begin school. It is the language for commenting on events past and present ("That's a fat frog; I saw one like it in the park"), for labeling ("That's a bus"), for talking about sequences of events ("You should wait to do that after we put the paint on") and for talking about details ("It's not brown exactly, more like a funny red"). Other subfunctions include the language of comparison ("This blue is better than that one"), the language for making generalizations on the basis of specific events or details ("See the way it's smashed. Someone must have hit it"), and for requesting information ("What do you call this? What color was it before?").

In the very earliest stages of language acquisition, children begin by labeling the objects in their environment—*Mummy, Ginger cat, truck, boat, juice.* Very soon, they expand this function. Any parent of a toddler knows, for example, that requesting information is one of the first types of informing language that children acquire. Children ask questions to sort out the workings of the world, and when parents answer their questions, they are exposing their children to even more informing language. We can see that this function of language serves children in some of the same ways as Halliday's *heuristic* function.

Language of Forecasting and Reasoning.   As we have seen, children put both controlling and informing language to uses that enhance their learning. The principal language function they employ in the business of learning, however, is the language of forecasting and reasoning, the language Halliday identified as *heuristic*. It is the language that expresses their curiosity and allows them to find out about the world. It is used with extreme frequency by toddlers asking "Why can't I?" or "Why does the wheel go 'round?" Subfunctions other than the requesting of information include predicting an event and forecasting or reasoning about causal relationships. Shafer, Staab, and Smith (1983, p. 93) point out that prediction of an event may be based on obvious reasons, either stated or not, or it may have reasons that are neither stated nor immediately apparent. Their example is of a child who looks out the window at a threatening sky and observes "I think it's going to rain." In this case, it is clear that the reason for the statement is the darkness of the sky. Another child, however, might look into a sunny sky and make the same prediction. In this case, there is no obvious reason for the speculation. In the first instance, parents will usually respond by agreeing that the child's prediction is likely. In the second, they will usually try to draw out a reason for the child's gloomy forecast. In questioning the child and offering possible reasons or alternative conclusions, they engage the child in reasoning about an event and provide representative language for doing so.

The forecasting and reasoning function of language provides a window on children's cognitive development. By carefully observing children's use of language to forecast and reason, we gain valuable insights into the growth in their reasoning. The following two dialogues illustrate:

Amy, age four, is in trouble with her twelve-year-old sister Sara.
S: I told you to stay out of my things. Look what you did!
A: No.
S: What do you mean, no? Don't tell me you weren't playing with my nail polish. You got it all over the vanity. Mom's going to kill us both. And it's all your fault.
A: I didn't.
S: Then who did?
A: (Thinking for a minute) Sam was here. I guess he—
S: Oh right. So when did Sam start painting his nails with bright pink polish?
A: I don't know.
S: Well, will you at least help me clean it up.
A: (Relieved) Okay. We won't get in trouble, right?
S: Well, not if we get it all off. Go in the kitchen and get me a whole lot of paper towels.

Six-year-old Danny and his mother are having a "discussion" about his afternoon plans. Danny wants to go to a showing of a children's film at the local library, something he usually does once a week.
D: Why can't I go? James gets to go.
M: I explained already. You can't go because I have to work tonight and I won't be able to pick you up. And Daddy's car is in the shop.
D: Why can't I ride with James?
M: Usually, you can, but today James's mother is dropping him off and then his Dad's picking him up—
D: I can ride with his Dad.

M: Not today because they're not going home afterward. They're going to James's grandmother's house.

D: I can go there, too!

M: No, you can't. You weren't invited this time. But I'm sure James will invite you another time.

We see in the first dialogue that Amy is able to understand her sister's reasoning, helped along by the somewhat perilous situation in which she finds herself, far better than she is able to reason herself. Nevertheless, we see evidence that she is capable of causal reasoning in her "We won't get in trouble, right?," which implies her understanding that if they clean up the mess, they will avoid trouble. We also see her reasoning that because Sam was also in the house, the blame might be laid at his feet, a slightly different type of causal reasoning.

In Danny, we find a child with much better developed reasoning skills. As he makes his case for going to the film, we see an implied justification in his pointing out that James is being allowed to go. We find, too, that he is able to understand his mother's rather complex explanation of the reasons why he cannot go with James. Even though he doesn't accept the argument, he clearly understands it. The two years' difference in the ages of Amy and Danny makes a world of difference in their verbal reasoning abilities.

We have seen in all five functions of language evidence that children's language grows and exists in tandem with cognition. In our discussion of language functions in early childhood, we have considered the relationship from the perspective of language. It is now time to consider the relationship from the perspective of cognitive growth, not independent of language, for that is neither possible nor desirable, but with greater emphasis on cognition than on language.

LANGUAGE AND COGNITIVE GROWTH

Cognition is not a monolithic process. We cannot, therefore, talk about children's cognitive growth as though it consisted of a single process of change. In fact, what we commonly call cognitive development actually involves changes in a number of different capacities including perception, memory, conceptualization, and academic skills. We will not talk at length here about perception because, even though there is little doubt that language plays an important part in human perception, the most interesting aspects of perceptual development occur in the first six months of life, before the onset of language. We will not, therefore, talk here about perceptual development. Rather, we will concern ourselves with the relationship of language to memory and conceptualization and to the child's achievement in academic thinking.

The Role of Language in Memory Development

A simple experiment reported by Carmichael, Hogan, and Walter (1932) demonstrated how inextricably language and memory are linked. In reproducing line drawings they had been asked to remember, subjects in the study routinely distorted them consistent with additional *verbal* information they had received. Language provides not only a means of encoding experience but influences the recall of that experience.

The simple fact of memory development is that as children grow older, their memories improve. But why? What makes this growth possible? Siegler (1991) offers four possible explanations. One is that as children mature, their basic capacity increases. In other words, the physical and physiological mechanisms responsible for memories expand. Another possibility is that children's memory strategies improve; through practice they get better at the procedures involved in storage and retrieval. A third explanation is that as children grow older they learn more about memory and how it works and use this knowledge to manage their own memories. Finally, because older children have greater prior knowledge of the content they need to remember, it is possible that they have a sounder basis on which to remember new material (Siegler, 1991, pp. 173–175).

In fact, all four explanations have some basis in reality, that is, increased capacity, greater sophistication in using strategies, metamemory, and other experiences all contribute to memory development. For our purposes, however, the question is not the degree to which any one explanation contributes to cognitive growth but how language is involved in each.

Basic Capacities.   *Basic capacities* include those frequently used components of memory that form the foundations for cognitive activity. Such processes as recognition, association, storage, and retrieval are prerequisites to all thinking. How language is involved may not be immediately obvious, but if we consider just what constitutes development of some of these processes, the relationship becomes clearer.

Recognition is at the heart of memory; cognitive development could not proceed without it. With regard to language, however, recognition is not an especially interesting phenomenon because the ability is amazingly well developed even in newborns. What role language plays in auditory recognition is unclear. We saw in an earlier chapter that very young infants are capable not only of recognizing human speech sounds but also of recognizing subtle differences between speech sounds. One interesting piece of research does, however, shed light on the nature of the interaction between language and early recognitory behavior.

We saw in Chapter 4 that infants as young as one month are able to discriminate between certain speech sounds such as voiced and voiceless consonants. Infants seem to be able to mark this and certain other speech distinctions no matter what language is being spoken around them. This very early ability would suggest that some innate mechanism is operating. The question that arises is at what point the infant's recognitory ability becomes attuned to a particular language. Two studies, reported by Reich (1986, p. 25), shed some light on this question. Researchers in one study found that infants in the first six months were unable to recognize certain acoustic distinctions that their Spanish-speaking parents recognized (Lasky, Syrdal-Lasky, & Klein, 1975). A second study of children who were seven months old showed that children of Spanish-speaking parents could recognize the Spanish distinction better than children of the same age exposed to the English language (Eilers, Gavin, & Wilson, 1979). It would seem, then, that around seven months is the age at which children begin to recognize the distinctions appropriate to the language around them.

Another aspect of basic memory capacity that is present at birth but increases with age is association. It also changes in character. Infants are capable of associating certain stimuli with certain responses. In one experiment with three-month-old infants, researchers attached a string from their ankles to a mobile. The babies quickly learned that kicking their legs caused the mobile to move. Another study showed that they could remember what they had learned as long as eight days later (Sullivan, Rovee-Collier, & Tynes, 1979; cited in Siegler, 1986). As children get older and acquire language, they are able to make an entirely new set of associations, verbal associations, and their memory and learning capacities thus increase.

Further evidence that language is important in the development of memory is found in the phenomenon of infant amnesia. Adults have very long memories. Most of us can recall events that occurred years ago or recognize people that we knew decades ago. Even young children are very good at recognizing pictures they have seen even though a considerable time has passed. Yet few adults have any memories of infancy. Those who claim to recall an occurrence from early infancy are usually found to be remembering someone else's account of those events. The passage of time alone cannot account for our inability to recall the first months of life. What may account for it is a difference in the way in which infants encode events and the way older children and adults encode events. As Siegler points out:

> Whether people can remember depends critically on the fit between the way in which they earlier encoded the information and the way in which they later attempt to retrieve it. The better able the person is to reconstruct the perspective from which the material was encoded, the more likely that recall will be successful. (Siegler, 1991, p. 178)

This is where language comes in: Older children have language as part of the context of experience and thus language is available as a means of encoding; infants do not have language. It seems probable that the onset of language represents an important device for increasing basic memory capacity. It also provides the child with a valuable memory strategy. We have all had the experience of repeating over and over something that we wanted to remember later. This strategy of rehearsal is one of several that is central to the development of memory.

Memory Strategies.   Those conscious activities that we engage in with the hope of improving our chances of remembering are called *memory strategies*. They occur at some time between the event or experience to be recalled and the act of recalling. Rehearsal is one such strategy and language is crucial to it. Research has established clearly that the strategy of rehearsal plays an important role in memory improvement. Children who verbally rehearse the names of pictures can recall more pictures than children who do not rehearse the names. Without language, of course, they would be unable to do so.

A second strategy involves organization. Children of five and six years old make less use of categories than do children of nine or older. That language plays a central role in our ability to categorize is easily demonstrated by an experiment commonly done in psychology classes. Consider the following list of words:

desk

computer

telephone

bookshelf

cat

bird

dog

hamster

tomato

lettuce

radish

cabbage

If you try to remember the list as a list of unrelated words, you may remember as many as half the items. If, on the other hand, you mentally organize the list into three categories, office equipment, animals, and vegetables, you will do much better. If you go even further and subcategorize the latter two as household pets and salad ingredients, you will do better still. The ability to categorize is closely associated with language; categorization is impossible to do effectively without the verbal labels for classification.

One additional strategy for improving memory deserves mention because it is closely related to linguistic development. Elaboration can be similar to organization in that it involves making connections between items or events, but it differs in that it can occur even when no categorical relations exist between them. Elaborations can be images, such as when a girl trying to remember to buy an umbrella, a bottle of ink, and shampoo forms a mental picture of herself holding the umbrella to protect her clean hair and the bottle of ink she is carrying, or they can be verbal. Mnemonics are common verbal elaborations. Many of us can recall learning the names of the lines of the treble clef (e, g, b, d, f) by using the phrase "Every good boy does fine" and the spaces by spelling *face*. There is evidence that children four years of age can be taught to form verbal elaborations for remembering two terms and use them successfully in recall. Attempts to teach them to form visual images are less successful.

Language is clearly involved, then, in the strategies children employ to store and to retrieve experience. It is also involved in the improvement of metamemory.

Metamemory.   A component of metacognition, *metamemory* refers to the knowledge children have about how memory works. Examples of the use of metamemory are not hard to find. Take the adult who is watching a television drama and reading the newspaper at the same time. She goes back and forth, sampling information from the television screen and the newspaper page in turn. The procedure goes smoothly enough until she discovers she has missed something, say in the television program, and what is happening no longer makes sense. What she will do in such a case is to abandon the paper and pay close attention to the television, hoping to find clues to what she has missed. Usually in television, this strategy works, but it is the decision to employ the strategy that constitutes metamemory. As children grow older, they learn about the limitations and the fallibility of memory, and this knowledge directs them to develop a feeling for what is hard to remember as well as strategies for remembering those things.

At the very heart of metamemory is the act of monitoring, and an experiment conducted by Markman (1979) sheds light on the nature of monitoring growth in young children and on its relationship to language. Children between eight and eleven years were read a short passage on the making of Baked Alaska. In the second sentence of the passage they heard that the ice cream melts in the hot oven. Two sentences later, they heard that the ice cream stays hard and does not melt. Nearly half the subjects in the study failed to identify the contradiction even when they had been warned that the story was problematic. The children who did not notice the disparity seemed to be concentrating on the soundness of each individual statement rather than on the sense they made in total (Markman, 1979; cited in Siegler, 1986, pp. 242–243). Their monitoring of their own understanding differed in kind from that of older children and adults.

But how does monitoring relate to language? From about two years, children are able to correct their own language errors, indicating use of a language monitor that compares their utterances with what they know of language. They apply this monitor to their own pronunciation, vocabulary choices, and grammar. As we also saw in Chapter 4, they monitor what they hear, rejecting adults' infantile pronunciations when they fail to correspond to those stored in memory. Once children begin school, they begin to apply the same kinds of monitoring to their reading, eventually learning to monitor their comprehension of what they are reading and to intervene, much as our television watcher above, when it is found wanting. In general, the ability to monitor one's own comprehension marks an important distinction between good and poor readers. More mature and better readers do frequent comprehension checks and go back and read again if they find their understanding wanting. Ironically, less able readers, who could benefit most from such rereading, seldom do so.

Finally, we come to the place of *content knowledge* in memory development and its relationship to language. The more children know about the world the easier it is to find conceptual "pegs" for new information. Actually, content knowledge influences memory in at least two ways. It affects the amount of information recalled as well as what is recalled.

Take, for example, two women attending a cat show together. Both have seen cats, of course, but one has never been to a cat show before, never owned a cat, and prefers dogs. The second woman has two cats of her own, has always had at least one cat, and has attended many cat shows. The second woman will be able to recall more about what she has seen and different information than the first. While the first woman might report going to a cat show and seeing a lot of cats, some with long hair and some with short, some white, some black, and some striped, the second woman is more likely to recall seeing a prize-winning flame-point Himalayan and a lilac-pointed Siamese and the fact that there were only three Burmese when normally she would expect to see at least a dozen. The content knowledge that the second woman has about cats has provided an organizational framework to facilitate her storage and recall of the information surrounding the cat show.

The availability of background content knowledge sometimes leads to the recall of details that, although plausible, never occurred in fact. In the act of reconstructing a sequence of events surrounding a baseball game, a person knowledgeable about baseball may recall that there were four batters in the third inning and that the first one struck out. In attempting to explain the remainder of the inning, she may report that the second batter was walked and the next two struck out when, in fact, the second and third *both* walked and the fourth hit into a double play. Either sequence of events is plausible, and because she has the framework of the rules of baseball and prior experience watching the game, she constructs a perfectly conceivable but inaccurate account. A person unfamiliar with baseball would not make such a mistake; neither would she recall as much about the game.

The role that language plays in content knowledge is twofold. First, it is the medium through which children acquire much of their knowledge about the world. Second, it facilitates the formation of organizational networks that not only make this knowledge more readily available but make possible the integration of new, related items. We have already seen in our discussion of memory strategies that language plays a central role in categorization. The ability to categorize makes it possible to store and retrieve *more* information, thus improving memory.

Language, Memory, and the Child's Perspective

In the previous section, the questions under discussion were what capacities change in the process of memory development and what is the role of language in those changes. These are adult interpretations of the issues, not child interpretations. Indeed, infants would be quite surprised to learn that at such a tender age they are engaging in such esoteric activities. We may never know just what children's perspective is on any aspect of growth in the very early years, but it is important that we try to understand what actually happens from the child's perspective while these important changes are taking place.

Put another way, the question is: What are children doing while the basic capacities, memory strategies, and metamemory develop and how does the process contribute to that development? Children's auditory discrimination becomes attuned to the native language at around six or seven months of age. It is unlikely that they are conducting acoustic experiments on themselves. Rather, they are engaging with their mothers, fathers, or others in a variety of language activities. A recording of Janet's mother talking to her when she was not quite six months old illustrates the kinds of language experience an infant has:

> And what would our princess like to wear this morning? How about this purple jumpsuit? Do you like purple? Yes. This is definitely purple, isn't it? Okay. You'd rather play with that one. Okay, why not? You play with it and I'll put this yellow one on you instead. That's Daddy's favorite color. Daddy? You like Daddy don't you? Well, he'll really like this outfit, won't he? You sure are happy this morning. What's making you so happy? (She picks up Janet's stuffed mouse named Mealey.) Is Mealey happy, too? Why do you think Mealey's so happy? 'Cause he loves Janet.

In many of these sorts of interactions since birth, Janet has come to realize that the language noises she hears are purposeful and communicative and that they are associated with pleasurable events, particularly the society of other people.

Similarly, what concerns children as they make associations between objects and labels is not the increased memory capacity nor even the enlarged vocabulary that will result. They are consumed, instead, with a lively and eager curiosity. They want to know what the things in their world are called, and when they find out, they rehearse or practice them until they can remember them. Most likely, they don't practice in a conscious effort to remember, but because playing with language in this way is fun. They engage in rhyming word play because it is fun to do and is a way of actively exploring the characteristics of the language they are beginning to learn. That they are also developing verbal elaboration strategies that will increase memory is of no consequence to them. At this very young age—even before the first birthday—children are already taking charge of their own learning.

They are still in charge as their vocabulary grows and they begin to mark meaning distinctions. As they learn that some furry four-legged creatures are cats and others dogs and that certain features distinguish them, children are not aware that they are also developing another memory strategy. They are learning which distinctions matter in their world. Acquiring content knowledge helps them to organize their experience and to retrieve it more easily, but they don't do it for that reason. In organizing their experience, they are trying to discern meaningful order in their worlds. Their curiosity and need to understand the world lead them to work out the distinctions that are relevant to it.

Language, then, is central to the growth of memory, which, in turn, is central to children's cognitive development. From children's perspective, language is the principal means by which they come to understand and to organize their experience, in play and in all sorts of social interaction. The desire to learn and the desire to learn language are rooted in a common ground—children's active attempts to understand, to make sense of the world in which they live.

Role of Language in Conceptual Development

Anyone interested in children's learning must also be interested in conceptual growth and in theories of conceptual development. After all, what we believe about the nature of concepts shapes our beliefs about human learning:

> . . . Different views of the nature of concepts lead to different expectations about the order in which children will learn particular concepts, to different explanations of why some concepts are difficult for them to learn, and to different implications about how children should be taught new concepts. (Siegler, 1986, pp. 260–261)

There is no universal agreement among philosophers, psychologists, and educators as to the definition of *concept* although at a very basic level most would agree that a concept consists of a grouping of objects, events, ideas, people, or attributes that share some similarities. Conceptualization seems to serve two functions in human cognition. First, as we have already seen, categorization, which is at the heart of conceptualization, is important to the development of memory. Second, concepts allow us to take our understanding beyond the bounds of our own experience. As an example, the woman in our earlier example who has never seen a *Blue point* will immediately know something about the animal if she is told that it is a cat and more still, if she has learned anything at all at the cat show, if she is told that it is a Siamese cat.

Psychologists' and Linguists' Views Compared.   Nowhere is the importance of language to cognitive development more obvious than in conceptualization. We have only to compare psychologists' theories of concept formation with theories of semantic development to see the connections. Take, for example, Pease, Gleason, and Pan, writing on the categorical or semantic feature theory of semantic development:

> One explanation of early semantic development is that children acquire categorical concepts and that categories are defined by certain features. For instance, the word *dog* refers to a category of animals with a set of distinguishing features: they are alive and warm-blooded, have four legs, bark, and are covered with hair. According to Eve Clark (1974), when a child learns a new word, it is in the context of a specific situation: the word *dog* may at first be understood to apply only to the child's own dog. Only later comes the understanding that other creatures may also be called dog as long as they share the small set of critical features that uniquely define the category. (Pease, Gleason, & Pan, 1989, p. 105)

Their example of how semantic feature theory might work bears a striking resemblance to Siegler's description of a theory of conceptual development known as defining-features representations:

> Defining-features representations are like the simplest and most straightforward dictionary definitions. They include only the necessary and sufficient features that determine whether an example is or is not an instance of the concept. (Siegler, 1991, p. 213)

These two authors, though writing from different perspectives, are describing the same thing; the first is merely focusing on language as the medium by which concepts are represented. Note, however, that although many linguists and psychologists have written about children representing concepts in terms of defining features, there is by no means universal agreement that very young children are capable of representing concepts in this way. Piaget was one theorist who believed that young children categorize on the basis of themes—a dog and a bone might be put into the same conceptual category because dogs eat bones—and that the nature of conceptual development lies in their learning to conceptualize on the basis of shared characteristics.

An analogous parallel occurs between aspects of probabilistic representations in conceptualization theory and prototypes in language acquisition theory. In conceptualization theory, the probabilistic view holds that some objects may be perceived as better examples of a particular conceptual category than others. People may view Persians as better examples of cats than manxes, apples as better examples of fruits than raisins, and steak as a better example of meat than chopped liver. The reasons why they have these preferences is that they consider the properties required for an object to belong to a certain conceptual category and choose as best the one that has the most. Thus, a Persian might be considered a better example of cat on the basis of its length of hair and length of tail; on the basis of these features, the probability is higher that the Persian is a cat than the manx.

There is an echo of this reasoning in the description of the prototype theory of semantic development:

> Yet another theory suggests that we first acquire concepts that are protypical, or the best examples of the categories we are learning (Rosch & Mervis, 1975). Rosch and her colleagues have shown that we all share the view that some members of a category are much better representatives, or exemplars, than others. A German shepherd is a better dog than a Chihuahua; a robin is a better bird than a chicken. According to prototype theory. . . ., children acquire these core concepts when they acquire meaning and only later come to recognize members of that category that are distant from the prototypes. (Pease, Gleason, & Pan, 1989, p. 105)

There is also a parallel between the nature of children's development as it is seen within an exemplar-based representational view of conceptualization and language growth, which proceeds from lexical to rule learning. Those who believe in exemplar-based representation believe that children store numerous examples of objects and events as they occur in life. When they encounter a new object or event, they compare it to other examples in memory to determine whether the new object or event matches stored examples or the exemplar-based representations they may have created from stored examples. Under this view, development would consist of moving from exemplar-based representations to the learning of rules or regularities. Indeed, research has shown that seven-year-olds learned more effectively under conditions that encouraged them to pay careful attention to particular examples and ten-year-olds learned equally well under this condition and under the condition that promoted rule learning (Kossan, 1981).

Both linguistic and interactionist theories of language acquisition would claim that while children may begin by learning individual words and their meanings and, possibly, that early sentences are learned as wholes, language acquisition cannot progress until the child begins to learn the rules for putting words into sentences. They would cite as evidence the fact that the number of potential sentences that can be understood and produced is infinite and that no one can learn every exemplar sentence in a language.

The similarity between theories of concept formation and those of semantic development is not merely serendipitous. The first words that children acquire and the use to which they put them provide a mirror on the concepts they are acquiring. More likely than not, language influences those concepts. Certainly there is evidence that people "find it easier to make a conceptual distinction if it neatly corresponds to words available in their language" (Crystal, 1987, p. 15). It would follow, then, that children's increasing facility with conceptualization corresponds to their increasing facility with language.

Language and Conceptualization from the Child's Perspective.   In the lives of children, language and the ability to conceptualize provide a means for them to extend their understanding beyond the bounds of their own experience. Although an idea or a concept can be understood without being able to put it into words, it is the very act of putting it into words that clarifies and makes understanding precise.

Attempting to verbalize a "fuzzy" idea serves to crystallize both what we know and what we do not—our understanding and our ignorance. Most of us are aware of the former—Donald Murray has often said that he writes to find out what he knows. The latter notion of revealing ignorance is, perhaps, less familiar. Yet learning involves, in Margaret Donaldson's words, "a simple realization of ignorance" (1978, p. 76). Implicit in the notion of wanting to know is the awareness that we do not. There is no better way of capturing that awareness than to try to put into words an idea or a concept of which we have imperfect understanding. In a real sense, then, children talk their way to understanding. This is true of learning in general and of language learning in particular.

Children begin to talk long before they are masters of the language and it is through talk that they acquire the skills to *become* masters. In their early talk, we find not only evidence that they practice or rehearse the language they are learning, but evidence that they are actively engaged in the figuring out of the system that is language. A dialogue between Shelly, a child of 3;6 and her mother illustrates:

M: It's cold outside. Let's put on your pants.
S: Where?

M: There, on your bed.
S: Pants? No, only pant. One.
M: Oh, I see. No, these are called pants even though there's only one of them.
S: Why?
M: I don't know. Maybe 'cause there are two legs.
S: Oh. Pantlegs.
M: Very good!

In this exchange, we see that Shelly has acquired both the concept and the language to express the plural. But her understanding is not perfect, and so she assumes, quite reasonably, that because *pants* sounds plural, it must be plural. She is initially unaware of her "ignorance," but once her mother explains the error, she readily incorporates the explanation into her vocabulary and to her comprehension of the rules for plural formation. Perhaps the most important idea to be made here is that Shelly does not wait for someone to instruct her in the ways of language; she gets on with the business of learning language at the same time as she learns about the world around her.

Role of Language in the Development of Academic Skills

It may seem out of place to raise this issue in this chapter. After all, most of children's academic thinking surely develops during the school years, and we will be looking at the school years in Chapter 9. Nevertheless, it has been estimated that 33% of a child's academic skills are attained before age six (Yardley, 1973). How language serves to shape children's academic thinking is thus of utmost concern since this is the time during which the foundations for their future success in school are laid. Before they begin formal schooling, children have a great deal of experience in learning. In fact, in some ways, very young children may be at an advantage. As Alice Yardley observed, "The pre-speech child has a distinct advantage in that because he has no words, he is protected from being told what to learn and how to learn it, and how to solve his problems" (1973, p. 16). Wise parents refrain from providing too much help and thus depriving the child of the rewarding experience of finding a solution independently. Whether the problem is putting the shoe on the appropriate foot, fitting a round puzzle piece into its proper space, or figuring out the mechanics of a zipper, the parent who insists on telling the child how to solve the problem, or worse, solving it for him, takes away the experience of learning.

Fortunately, childhood abounds with such opportunities and even children with overhelpful parents will find a great deal to learn and will develop a great many strategies for doing so. Much of this learning is related to the subjects they later encounter in school, because their parents have actively taught them, because they have watched educational television programs such as "Sesame Street" and "The Electric Company," or in some instances, they have found their own resources for learning. Three areas in which they have learned a great deal about how to learn are reading, writing, and arithmetic.

Early Learning of Mathematics.   Most of today's children know how to solve addition problems with sums lower than ten before they enter school. One of the strategies that preschool children use is to choose the larger of the two numbers to be added and count upward from it the number of times indicated by the smaller number. Thus a child adding three and five would begin with five and count up three. Note that the ability to apply this strategy rests in memory and in language. The child has to be able to remember the strategy and then, in essence, rename one as six, two as seven, and three as eight. This is not the only approach children use, however. Sometimes they simply put up their fingers and count on them; other times they simply recall the answer from memory.

Children also use counting strategies to solve subtraction problems, counting either up from the lower number to the higher or down from the higher number the number indicated by the lower. Which of the two strategies they use seems to depend on which requires the fewer "counts." For the problem, 6 - 2, for example, children would likely count backward from six two "counts" since this is easier than counting upward from two to six, which would require four. For our purposes, what is interesting about these early strategies is that they all require the child to count and counting is not possible without language. It is not unwarranted to claim, then, that children's early mathematics ability resides in language.

What kinds of experiences do preschool children have with learning mathematics? During the latter years of the 1980s, there were a number of disturbing reports in the press of "yuppie" parents who transferred their own ambition to their children and enrolled them in high-pressure "academic" preschools or engaged them at a tender age in such questionable educational practices as superlearning. While it may turn out that these early "enrichment" programs did in fact produce children who achieved superior marks in school and were assured of entrance to Harvard or Oxford, we have to wonder about the cost to the child of a lost childhood. Happily, such high-pressure programs are not necessary; the child in the course of a normal childhood develops a natural interest in numbers. From the time the infant notices that the cookies have been eaten and observes "No more" or "All gone," the foundations for numeracy are established. Later, the addition or subtraction of objects within their own worlds of experience—blocks, small wooden people or animals, finger puppets—propel children along the path of counting, which leads eventually to addition and subtraction. Parents need not "teach" basic arithmetic to their children—for example, drill the sums, requiring children to memorize "one plus one is two, two plus two is four," etc. In fact, they may impede the child's own problem-solving skills by doing so. All they need do is to encourage their children's natural curiosity and, possibly, to play counting and rhyming games with their children. By doing so they will be in a real sense laying the foundations on which later success in school mathematics will be based.

Mathematics is not the only academic skill that children begin to acquire before they start school. It is only one of the three *Rs* that our society normally considers to be the rudiments of academic learning. Reading and writing are rudimentary not only as subjects in their own right, but because they are essential to success in almost all subjects children encounter during their twelve or thirteen years of formal schooling. A number of researchers have established clearly that children learn a great deal about both before they get to school.

Early Learning Associated with Reading.   The question we have been asking about the role language plays in early learning is silly when the early learning is of reading and writing. The question is more sensibly put: What is the role of *speech* in children's early reading? Shortly we will see that it does play an important role. But we also need to have a broader understanding of the reading process. To understand the nature of children's early knowledge of and about reading, we could take one of two broad approaches. We could attempt to describe the roughly chronological stages of the reading process, that is, what children typically know and do at a particular age. Or we could break the reading process down into a number of component skills and describe the learning associated with each. For our purposes, it is most revealing to do the latter, focusing in particular on letter perception, phonemic awareness, word identification, and the processes involved in the comprehension of larger prose units. The question before us, then, is what is the nature of children's knowledge of these components of reading before they begin school and how did they come by it?

To begin with, a great many children do learn to read before they begin school. By reading I mean not only word identification of the type they learn on "Sesame Street" but also the ability to recreate meaning from printed text whether that text is a sign in a grocery store, a toy advertisement, or a children's book. My elder son began to identify individual words well before his third birthday. Noticing his interest in the words on "Sesame Street," I placed large-print labels on many of the more common objects in the house but made no further effort to teach him to read. He learned the associations very quickly and by the time he was just past three was sounding out the words in his own books that I had been reading to him for some time. He already knew the stories the books told and had learned from "Sesame Street" that letters had sound equivalents and had put the two kinds of knowledge together, in essence, teaching himself to read. My experience with my son is consistent with what research has to say about early readers: The factors that determine whether a child will learn to read before schooling are the degree of interest the child has in reading and the degree of interest the parents have in reading as demonstrated by their reading to the child, reading for pleasure themselves, and having plenty of reading materials available in the home (Durkin, 1966).

Even children who do not learn to read text before they begin school know a great deal about the process of reading. They have acquired certain abilities that are necessary to reading ability. These cognitive correlates of early reading ability include the perception of letters as being distinct from other kinds of marks, drawings, and squiggles that might be encountered in the world and as being distinct from one another. Marking these kinds of discriminations is a complex perceptual task, requiring children to learn which curved, horizontal, vertical, and diagonal lines are meaningful and which only incidental. Both parents and educators have pondered the question of whether teaching children the names of the letters helps the children learn to read. The research evidence is not clear on the subject. On the one hand, DeHirsch and colleagues (1966) found that children's ability to name letters predicts their reading achievement through grades one, two, and into three. On the other hand, there is no evidence that there is a causal relationship between the two: Children who learn letter names at a young age may do so because they have an interest in words and this same interest makes them better readers. But if interest is such an important factor, and we saw earlier that both the parents' and the child's interest correlate positively and strongly with later reading ability, then it would seem that teaching children the names of letters might be beneficial.

Another cognitive correlate of reading ability that preschool children attain is phonemic awareness. However disparate their views of the reading process, most experts agree that *some* degree of sensitivity to the fact that words consist of individual sounds is important to successful reading. Children learning to read English and other alphabetic languages must understand, at the least, that words consist of letters and those letters represent separate sounds, which may also exist in other words. It is not at all clear, however, that their understanding of phonemic awareness need be much more sophisticated than this. The reason is that the ability to divide a word into its component sounds is the converse ability to the one required in reading, which is to blend the sounds together to form a sequence of sounds that is sufficiently familiar to permit word recognition. It *is* clear, though, that word recognition is essential to the task of learning to read.

What strategies do preschool children develop that enable them to identify words? Word recognition is a necessary prerequisite to reading, and it is a complicated process to describe. To simplify the procedure greatly, children must examine the printed words and then locate the corresponding entry from long-term memory. Whether they use a phonologically based method or a visually based method of retrieval, this aspect of the task is the same. Using a phonologically based method, they will first recode the printed word into a sequence of sounds and search for a corresponding sound sequence. Using visually based retrieval, they will search for a visual match, skipping the *sounding out* stage. Children who are especially adept at phonological retrieval will not need to recode the entire word, and even children who normally adopt a visual procedure may occasionally recode the first letter or two of a word.

Although these two methods of retrieval correspond to two approaches to reading instruction, the phonics-based and the whole-word, there is evidence that without instruction children genuinely differ in the strategy they prefer. The traditionally held belief that children begin by sounding out words and then "graduate" to visual recognition is simply not true for all children. Obviously, many children need to begin with phonological recoding; others recognize the word on the basis of its visual configuration and the context. On confronting the word *stop*, for example, one child may assign a hissing noise to the first letter, a voiceless alveolar stop to the second and so on until a pronunciation is reached that corresponds to one already in memory. Another child may learn the word *stop* by making the association with red hexagonal sign on which it usually appears. To become efficient and fluent readers, all children must eventually abandon phonological recoding as a general strategy although it may be reactivated as a backup strategy when others fail. To illustrate that even proficient readers use a phonological "attack" strategy when confronted with unfamiliar words, we have only to consider our own behavior with unfamiliar words. If we encounter the pseudoword *grane,* for example, and search our memory on the basis of the visual information alone, we will fail. What we do instead is to assign it a pronunciation on the basis of our knowledge of sound-symbol correspondence, and then search for a match. We then conclude that it is a misspelling of *grain,* a mistyped version of *crane,* or simply a nonsense form, depending on the context. A phonological strategy is available in problem situations such as this, but it is too inefficient as a general strategy, and children who rely on it exclusively will never become proficient readers.

To become proficient readers, children must acquire more than letter perception skills, phonemic awareness, and word identification strategies. To become true readers, they must be able to recreate meaning from printed text. Although we use the word *comprehension* to refer to this ability, it is not meant to convey a passive process. On the contrary, reading comprehension is probably one of the most cognitively active and complex activities in which we engage. It is also one of the most important in the lives of young children. To a very large degree, success in reading comprehension will predict children's success in school, but just as important, it will give them the means to develop and pursue new interests for the rest of their lives, to escape boredom, and to acquire a vast amount of information about the world around them and about worlds they may never experience directly. What occurs during the preschool years that serves to shape children's facility to comprehend text?

To answer that question fully is beyond the scope of this book,[3] but it is possible to describe the basic processes involved in comprehension. Notice that in the last sentence, I wrote *comprehension* and not *reading comprehension.* That is because reading comprehension is not an isolated cognitive phenomenon. It involves many of the same processes as listening comprehension. Both listening and reading require us to form and integrate propositions and to draw inferences about what is read or heard and to relate it to what is already known. The fundamental difference between listening and reading comprehension lies in an additional step in reading; the reader must be able to recognize and identify the graphic symbols that represent individual words, which makes possible the identification of propositions.

Perfetti has postulated two broad components of text comprehension. **Local processing** refers to "those processes that construct elemen-

---

[3]For an excellent and complete treatment of the psychological processes involved in reading, see Perfetti's *Reading Ability* (Oxford University Press, 1984). For a more concise explanation, see Chapter 9 of *Children's Thinking,* 2nd ed., by Robert S. Siegler (Prentice-Hall, 1991).

tary meaning units from text over a relatively brief period" (Perfetti, 1984, p. 33). He includes as local processes the identification of words (lexical access) and the building of propositions (proposition assembly). Text modeling refers to the processes the reader uses to combine local processes with

> knowledge about concepts, knowledge about inferences (inference rules), knowledge about the forms of texts, and general knowledge about the everyday world. . . . to form a representation of the text meaning. It is this representation that the reader consults at some later time to recall or to answer questions about what has been read. (Perfetti, 1984, p. 40)

As an example, let us consider how a proficient reader might come to understand the following sentences:

1. Joe and Jen went to a used car lot.
2. They waited for a salesman to appear.
3. After awhile, they began to look around for themselves.
4. They spotted a blue truck sitting in the shadows.
5. Just as they approached the truck, a smiling man appeared.

Using local processes the reader would construct a rudimentary level of meaning. To begin with, the reader would have to have some kind of recognition and retrieval system to match the words on the printed page with the words stored in memory. Also, the reader would have to select the contextually appropriate meaning for words with more than one meaning. *Lot* in the first sentence is a good example. Its position in the sentence as well as the meanings of the words around it will lead the reader to discount the "large number" *lot* in favor of the "plot of land" *lot*. Locating, or encoding, the individual words permits the reader to encode the elementary units of text, propositions. The first sentence in the example has eight:

1. Joe exists
2. Jen exists
3. lot exists
4. cars exist
5. they go to the lot
6. they go at some time in the past

7. cars are located at the lot
8. the cars are used

Ignoring the fact that the eighth proposition probably contains at least one other proposition, these are the basic meaning elements the reader has to encode. Each sentence consists of a number of such propositions and so a text can be said to comprise a set of propositions embedded in a set of sentences. The next step in the local processing of these sentences is to assemble and integrate the propositions for longer term memory. The term *integrate* refers to the combining of "successively occurring propositions with each other" (Perfetti, 1984, p. 38). The eight propositions of the first sentence must be integrated with each other and then with propositions in successive sentences. A number of conventions of writing facilitate the reader's ability to do this. One is the use of pronouns. Notice how *they* in sentences 2 through 5 serves to link these sentences to each other and to the first sentence, which carries the referent, *Joe and Jen.* Another is the use of the definite article. When the truck is first introduced into the text in the fourth sentence, the indefinite *a* is used. When it appears again in the fifth sentence, the use of *the* reminds readers that they already know about the existence of this truck. The definite article is used in a different way in the fourth sentence where we find the truck sitting in "the shadows" even though there has been no previous mention of shadows. In this case, the definite article serves as a signal to the reader's inferencing mechanism. If the reader knows that lots *can* have shadowy places, then the proposition is integrated easily with the others. As Perfetti puts it, ". . . integrative processes depend on linguistic triggers and the accessibility of linking propositions in memory" (1984, p. 40). In very young children, these triggers and links are largely based in their experience of oral language.

We have not yet achieved comprehension of our short text, though. A useful way of demonstrating the nonlocal or long-term comprehension process is to reconsider the five sentences we saw earlier. As I write this paragraph, those sentences no longer appear on my computer monitor— I have typed three or four screens beyond them. I shall now reconstruct them from memory and see what variations occur:

1. Joe and Jen went to a used car lot.
2. They were looking around.
3. They didn't see a salesman present.
4. They saw a blue truck sitting in the shadows.
5. As they approached the truck, a smiling salesman appeared.

In my recall of the passage, I correctly reproduced only the first sentence but I did reconstruct the propositions in the other sentences more or less correctly. Notice that I included a proposition not included in the original, namely that the man who appeared was a salesman. This is an inference that was made possible by my knowledge of the world of car lots. My comprehension of the passage, then, resulted from the three local processes combined with my general knowledge about the everyday world.

It does not sound like a very complicated process, but in fact it is. What has to develop in the young child to make reading comprehension possible? Siegler has suggested that it is a product of five different processes. First, children need to be able to recognize and identify words quickly, with minimal attention to the task and while simultaneously attending to higher level tasks. This is called *automatization of lexical access* and means simply that the child must be able to recognize words without conscious effort. Second, children's short-term memories need to expand so that they can remember longer and longer pieces of text. The ability to remember what they have just read is important because it makes possible the integration of the previous propositions and allows them to draw inferences among them.

The third dimension of development that children must undergo in order to become proficient readers has to do with background knowledge. Specifically, as children learn more about the worlds in which they live and learn to structure that knowledge in some coherent way, they stand a chance of becoming better readers. As an example, children who are familiar with the standard organization of fairy tales can recall new fairy tales more easily than children who have never heard fairy tales. When it comes to reading an unfamiliar fairy tale, the child who knows how they are structured has a head start on comprehension over the child who does not know. This is true of other types of reading as well. The child with experience of how knowledge is organized for a particular reading task will fare better than the one without.

A fourth area in which children must develop if they are to become successful readers is in monitoring their comprehension. Researchers have demonstrated that the better readers within all age groups are the ones who monitor their understanding of the text they are reading and adopt strategies for dealing with any problems they have. These strategies include returning to the source of the problem, correcting words they have identified incorrectly, slowing down, or creating concrete examples for abstract characterizations (Forrest & Walker, 1979; Clay, 1973; Baker & Brown, 1984).

The fifth facet of development that drives reading comprehension is children's increasing ability to adapt their reading strategies to the demands of the particular task. Different types of reading require different types of reading strategy. As adults, most of us can read a novel in a busy airport or even in front of the television set. Most of us probably could not read a chapter from a university-level physics text in the same setting. Moreover, if we *tried* to read the physics text in the same way as the novel, we would probably not understand or remember very much of what we read. This is because our strategies for comprehending different kinds of text depend on our purpose and on the way the material is structured and presented. Different material makes different demands on us as readers. The ability to adjust our reading behavior to those demands is a significant part of our development as readers.

Very similar cognitive processes operate as we listen to oral language and similar kinds of cognitive development must occur to make us proficient listeners. The fact that listening and reading comprehension have so much in common has led parents and educators to raise the obvious question of why so many children fail to become proficient readers. In their quest for an answer, it has also led many of them to concentrate their attention on that aspect of reading comprehension that most notably differs from listening comprehension, namely, lexical access or word identification. Following such reasoning, a reading teacher's thrust would be word attack skills—if the children can identify the words, they can create the meaning. And for some children this *seems* to be the case. Unfortunately, such reasoning ignores a number of other differences between listening and reading. Children, from birth, have been exposed to oral language being used for communicative purposes. No attempt was made to "teach" them to listen, and the internal knowledge structures (the general knowledge about the everyday world necessary to comprehension of oral or written text) were built at the same time as the language was being created. From birth, they have known the structure of talk and the purpose of talk and no one ever expected them to participate without knowing those things. For some children, there is a genuine difference with reading. If they have not had direct experience with reading, they may not know about the forms of text or about the "world" of text, or the kinds of things that are written about. They have general knowledge about the everyday world, but this may not be enough to see them through the reading comprehension process if they are lacking in the other kinds of information needed to construct a "text model." If we think of words as blocks and the task of reading as building a castle from blocks, then the problem is easy to see. Having the blocks is essential, but unless you know what a castle looks like, there is little hope of success in getting it built. No amount of "block identification" activity will help, but some pictures of castles or some kind of building plan for a castle would help a great deal.

Most children *do* become proficient readers, eventually, and the foundation for their success is laid in early childhood. It is a simple fact of human nature that most people like to do those things at which they are good. Children who have learned to love stories from infancy and who have thus developed an avid interest in print will succeed as readers *unless* the educational system somehow manages to negate all the positive influences of those early years. We will see in a later chapter that this is entirely (and unfortunately) possible. For now, we shall turn our attention to the other side of the reading coin, writing.

Early Learning Associated with Writing.   On a number of occasions, Donald Graves has remarked that learning to write should be as easy as learning to read. When we think about their obvious relationship to one another, reading and writing would seem to be essentially mirror images of each other—and perhaps they are. We simply do not know as much about how children learn to write as we do about how they learn to read, although fortunately, researchers are beginning to study young children's writing. They are beginning to find that it makes many of the same demands as speaking, but is in some ways more demanding.

The business of committing to paper a first draft, whether it is a story told by a six-year-old or a term paper written by a university student, requires a complex network of interactive processes. In both cases, the writer faces the demands imposed by unfamiliar topics and by multiple goals as well as the mechanical chore of getting thoughts recorded whether on paper or to computer memory. Both the child drafting the story and the university student drafting the term paper must begin by retrieving information stored in long-term memory, information relevant to the topic at hand. If the idea for the story (or the term paper) is the writer's own, he or she has a slight advantage over the writer who is assigned a story or term paper topic and may have little relevant material stored in long-term memory on which to call. Even when information is stored, the writer may not have it conveniently organized, and may have to pull it from diverse regions of memory. A paragraph from a first-year university exam paper and a story written by a child in grade three illustrate:

> Linguistics is the study of language. It is a popular course at many universities and is useful for people studying to be teachers, daycare workers, social workers, doctors, lawyers and dentists. One branch of linguistics which is widely studied is psycholinguistics. This is quite unlike historical linguistics

which almost nobody studies anymore and would not be useful to daycare workers, social workers, doctors or dentists but might come in handy for very old teachers and lawyers. And historians, of course. People who study linguistics are called linguists. They know a lot about languages but do not know how to speak them.

This student was obviously unprepared for the topic demands of this exam and was forced to pull from his long-term memory every bit of information he could about linguistics. The child who wrote the next passage solved a similar problem in much the same way:

About Deserts

Deserts are hot places wear the wind blose. Not very many peple liv on deserts. Kaktus and tubble weeds grow and maybe some animals but I don't no wich ones. There is a big desert somewear in California and another one in Sehaira, but none in Nova Scotia. TheEnd.

A second demand made on the writer is to formulate goals, or plans, and to keep them in mind long enough to complete the draft. We can see the difficulty with planning in the child's piece on deserts. It is organized in the sense that all the sentences relate to the title, "About Deserts." There is little connection between any of the sentences except that they relate to the title. (Unfortunately, this is true of the university student's paragraph as well!) Apparently, this kind of organization is typical of children in grades two through four (McCutchen & Perfetti, 1982) and demonstrates their difficulty with keeping track of both the point of the topic sentence and the details of other sentences. The result is that their writing sounds more like a list than exposition, narrative, or description.

Finally, the process of drafting makes complex mechanical demands on children. The job of coordinating small fingers to form letters and getting them ordered into words demands so much attention that children may lose track of what they want to say. Research has shown that when children are permitted to dictate their stories rather than write them, they write better quality stories (Bereiter & Scardamalia, 1982). In brief, children's writing ability, where ability consists of being able to tell a story or form a coherent description, is underestimated if we consider only the words they write down. Their sense of story, developed in early childhood, will carry them a long way if they are freed, in at least some writing tasks, from the mechanical demands of writing.

Language and Academic Skills from the Child's Perspective

Adults, not children, categorize some learning as academic and other learning as not. For children, it is all part and parcel of the same thing and it is driven by their natural curiosity in the context of *real felt problems*. Margaret Voss relates a story of her son's early learning about reading that makes this point clearly:

> One summer afternoon just a month before his third birthday, Nathaniel sat at the picnic table in our backyard. He had just enjoyed a treat, a jar of apple blueberry baby food. As I turned the jar to examine the label, wondering if I'd just given my son some added sugar, Nathaniel suddenly proclaimed, 'Make way for applesauce.' Amused and confused, I asked, 'What?' 'Make way for applesauce,' he repeated, pointing to the label. Then he reached out and ran his fingers underneath some words, just as I sometimes do as I read book titles to him. He continued, pointing to and 'reading' one word at a time: 'it say, 'Make . . . way . . . for . . . applesauce.'" (Voss, 1988, p. 272)

Nathaniel had obviously worked out from his previous experience that print says something —Voss reports that she had been reading his current favorite *Make Way for Ducklings* over and over. But he also knew that the print on the label probably related to the contents of the jar, which he also knew. He extrapolated from his prior experience in trying to make sense of a new one. Nathaniel had begun to teach himself to read more than two years before the schools would get their chance.

It is parents and educators, not children, who insist on dividing and packaging learning and that which occurs in school is, broadly speaking, academic. But before they get to school, children have learned a great deal and they have learned a great deal about learning. Several centuries of research have provided no small amount of insight into the nature of children's early learning, but we hardly need review it all to make some commonsense observations about what goes on in children's worlds as they build their world views, which to adults is the basis for their academic learning.

There are six characteristics of children's preschool learning that are of particular importance to teachers of children:

1. Children's learning progresses according to their degree of readiness.
2. Young children are, for the most part, in charge of their own learning.
3. Play has an important role in children's learning.
4. The role of parents in early learning is as facilitators not instructors.

5. Interaction is essential to children's early learning.

6. Learning is embedded in the process of socialization.

Children's Learning Progresses According to Degree of Readiness. The degree of physical, cognitive, emotional, and social maturity children have attained governs what they learn and when. The most obvious example is language itself. It does no good for a mother to coax and coach her month old son to say *Mama* or *Dada*. The child has not yet achieved sufficient motor control over his articulators to produce the sound reliably. He has not the memory capacity to make the correct associations or to reproduce the correct sequence of sounds reliably. Neither will he be able six months later to produce three- or four-word sentences—no matter how much teaching occurs, which brings us to another characteristic of early learning.

Young Children Are in Charge of Learning. This is not to say that children know they are in charge, but simply that they determine, for the most part, what and when they will learn. These decisions are governed, in part, by maturity but also by their natural and robust curiosity about the world around them. My older son, Kerry, could put together wooden jigsaw puzzles with several pieces well before his second birthday. Initially, he was driven to try to put the puzzles together by his desire to see the picture as a whole and, I suspect, by an equally compelling desire to find out if he could do the task. By the time he was three, he had taught himself to read by watching "Sesame Street" and by repeatedly asking me to identify words in his books, on signs, everywhere he saw them. Figuring out the relationship between the sounds of words and their written form was very likely another kind of puzzle that he needed to solve.

My other son, Christopher, had no interest in the puzzles at all, possibly because he had seen his brother playing with them so often and knew too well what they were supposed to look like, but long before his second birthday, he wanted to learn to count. He insisted that I count his fingers, my fingers, his toes, books on his shelf, plates at the table, all sorts of things over and over. He would repeat after me, one-two-three at first and gradually into the tens, twenties, and thirties. This child, incidentally, went on to achieve a near-perfect score on the math SAT some fifteen years later. Chris decided not only what he was going to learn but how he was going to learn it. In this he was not unusual. Children are born with curiosity and the drive to satisfy it is the essence of learning.

Play Is Important in Children's Learning. A great variety of learning occurs as children play. Playing on swings, monkey-bars, on tricycles, wagons, and even on stairs helps them to acquire gross motor skills and bodily coordination. Playing with smaller objects such as the puzzles Kerry loved or pencils, crayons, or small blocks helps them to develop fine motor skills as well as eye-hand coordination. But play is also significant to academic learning. Parents who play games with children to keep them from getting bored are providing more opportunities for learning than they realize. When they play rhyming games, I spy, or read road signs or license plate numbers, or count red cars and white cars, they are providing occasions for children to sharpen their recognition and discrimination powers and providing experiences important to literacy. All children play "pretend" games and benefit from them in at least two ways. First, they are wonderful for the imagination, giving children opportunities to think about the past and to integrate it with the future. Second, fantasy games provide important opportunities for children to use language that is not bounded by the present—they begin, in short, the process of decontextualizing language, of using language that does not refer to real objects in present time.

Role of Parents in Early Learning.   The role of parents in early learning is as facilitators, not instructors. As much as I might be tempted to do so, I cannot take credit for my older son's ability to put together puzzles or the fact that he was a very early reader nor for my younger son's learning to count. I helped, of course, but with both children, my job was to sense their readiness (though they made it fairly obvious) and to provide the help they requested and a number of different materials that would help them to extend their understandings—different kinds and progressively more difficult puzzles for Kerry and an abundance of things to count for Chris.

Perhaps the most important contribution parents make to children's early learning is as partners in daily interaction. Whether the activity is routine, such as washing hands and putting on pajamas, or special, such as decorating a birthday cake or trimming the Christmas tree, the dialogues that occur between parents and children are the means by which children learn. The very first thing they learn, as John Holt points out, is that speech has purpose:

> Children get ready to speak by hearing speech all around them. The important thing about that speech is that the adults, for the most part, are *not* talking in order to give children a model. They are talking to each other because they have things to say. So the first thing the baby intuits, figures out, about the speech of adults, is that it is *serious*. (Holt, 1989, p. 10)

Once children have learned that the talk around them is purposeful, parents begin to play another role in their dialogues with their children. That role is not as teacher so much as it is facilitator. Gordon Wells explains:

> Meaning making in conversation should be a collaborative activity. But where there is a considerable disparity between the participants in their mental models and their linguistic resources, the more mature participants must make adjustments in order to make collaboration possible. (Wells, 1986, p. 89).

Parents, as the more mature participants, make those adjustments that make meaningful dialogue possible. If they are wise, they do so not by appropriating the child's conversation as their own or by interfering with the child's attempts to make meaning but by holding the conversational doors open in an effort to understand the child's intended meaning. Parents' who understand that their own perspective, their own knowledge, cannot be transmitted directly also understand that their role is to guide their children gently as they rebuild the world for themselves.

Interaction Is Essential to Early Learning.   Children are not passive participants in the business of learning, vessels awaiting someone to pour in knowledge. Possessed of a boundless curiosity, they eagerly seek answers, test hypotheses, and reconfirm those hypotheses as they essentially reconstruct the world through their own experiences.

In the simple act of questioning, children find out what they need to know, extend their knowledge, and open themselves to new ideas on which to build. Consider the following exchange between Matthew, age three, and his father:

M: What that?
D: Screwdriver. It's called a screwdriver.
M: What do?
D: Well, I'm using it now to put this thing—see it, it's called a screw—into the wood here so horsie's head won't fall off.
M: Horsie head. What that? (Again asking about the screwdriver)
D: Screwdriver.
M: 'tew . . . (He falters.)
D: Screw - driver.
M: Tew diver.
D: Good.
M: Tew diver. Tew diver. Here? (He points to a screw holding on one of the wooden horse's legs.)

D: Yes. That's a screw. I can use the screwdriver to take the screw out. (He begins to remove the screw.)
M: Tew diver. Out.
D: Right. It takes the screw out, too.
M: (Watches his father loosen the screw.) No!
D: Don't worry. We'll put it back again. (Begins reversing the screw.)
M: Tew diver. In.

It is doubtful that Matthew fully understood his father's explanation, but in this situation, he discovered a new word, a new label for something in his environment. He doesn't have to wait until he has perfect understanding (or pronunciation!) of the word to use it. As he uses it in a variety of contexts, its use will be refined. That refinement will come in dialogues similar to this one, in collaboration with adults. But, of course, in this and other such dialogues, Matthew has learned far more than single words. John Holt points out that word learning may come nearer the end of children's language learning than the beginning. Before they learn words, children learn

> . . . the large idea of communication by speech, that all those noises that come out of people's mouths mean something and can make things happen. Then, from the tones of people's voices and the contexts in which they speak,. . . a very general idea of what they are saying. . . . Then they begin to intuit a rough outline of the grammar—i.e., the structure—of the language. *Finally,* they begin to learn words, and to put those words into their proper slots in the very rough models of grammar which they have invented. (Holt, 1983, p. 93)

There is an important distinction to be marked here concerning what children learn in dialogue with adults. An adult cannot pass along a whole, perfectly formed word meaning or concept to a child. What is passed on is the infrastructure, on which, in continuous interaction with adults and other children, children will build. Sometimes, children show a great deal of creativity in the language constructions they build, creating forms or categories that bear little resemblance to those accepted by the adult community. John Holt relates another story of a child named Jackie, a two year old,

> who had created in his mind a class of objects that we would call 'dry, crumbly things to eat—cookies, crackers, dry toast—to which he had given the name 'Zee.' Neither his father nor his mother knew how he had come to pick that word. . . . Clearly the baby had decided for himself that it was a good name for this class of things. (Holt, 1983, p. 91)

This child had created a category that does not exist in his native language and a word to label it. Such behavior should suggest to us that the role adults play in children's language is not and should not be to teach language. In the dialogue between Matthew and his father, we see an honest, companionable exchange with little if any covert teaching happening. Let's compare it with a dialogue between Barbie, age 2;10, and her mother:

M: Do you want peanut butter or cheese today?

B: Peanut butter.

M: And jelly or —

B: No jelly.

M: You don't want jelly. What do you want?

B: Fuff.

M: Marshmallow fluff?

B: Yep. Fuff.

M: Can you say 'marshmallow'?

B: No.

M: Sure you can. Try. Marsh - mal - low.

B: Mawo.

M: Good. Marsh - mal - low.

B: Fuff.

This dialogue differs from the one between Matthew and his father in one important way: Barbie's mother takes advantage of the opportunity to do a little language teaching. In this instance, she isn't very successful, but we have to wonder whether such thinly disguised attempts to teach language to young children are good, bad, or necessary. Barbie herself shows that they do little good, and John Holt points out that "billions of children learn to speak who have never been spoken to in this way" (Holt, 1983, p. 96). So, we have to consider the strong possibility that surreptitious teaching is a waste of everyone's time. If children do not benefit from it, then we must next decide whether it may do harm. Probably not, but there is at least a slight possibility it does for the simple reason that if children find talk useless or uninteresting, they might not bother with it, and that could be detrimental to their learning it.

What, then, is the role of dialogue with adults in children's language and learning? To answer this, we need to look at the adult's role not as *talker* but as listener. Parents who work very hard at understanding what young children say to them contribute very significantly to their children's learning. Children catch on quickly when people aren't really paying attention, and if they too frequently have the experience of not being able make themselves understood or to get a response to their overtures, they may conclude that there is no point in even trying to make themselves understood. Parents who persist in trying to understand children's attempts to communicate and make sense of the world will foster in their children a positive attitude toward language and learning. Finally, Holt captures the essence of the role of the adult when he says that if children find talk to be honest, companionable, and fun, then they will want to do it and will learn to do it. Talk related to activity, talk about things of significance to children, talk introduced by children—all kinds of *real* talk— inspire children to figure out how to do it.

Learning Is Embedded in Socialization.   Children's lives are not like school curricula. They are not divided up into components and assigned different periods of time—an hour to work on motor development, half an hour for memory development, twenty minutes for hygiene, and an hour and a half for socialization into the family and community. Their learning occurs in an unfragmented whole as part of the process of acquiring full membership in the local society of the family and community. Humans are social animals; they live in groups, and children's early learning is directed toward achieving group membership. They don't learn to say words because it is biologically time to do so or even because language is part of their internal curriculum. They learn language because that is the means through which people connect with one another. From the perspective of children, their preschool years are spent not in learning words, improving their memory, learning concepts, or acquiring the bases for academic learning but in learning to become like the people around them.

CONCLUSION

This chapter has been about the duality between children's language and learning in the preschool years. In the first section, we examined the intertwining of language and learning by viewing learning through the lens of language. In particular, we saw that parents and teachers can gain valuable insights into children's learning by examining the functions to which children put language in their lives. We identified and traced the development of five of these language functions.

   In the second section, the duality was examined from the perspective of cognitive growth. In particular, we looked at the development of memory, conceptualization, and academic thinking and the role language plays in each. Throughout, an attempt was made to understand the relationship between language and learning from the child's point of view.

Out of all these discussions came six characteristics of children's preschool learning.

If they are to understand what happens in school and, in particular, why some children experience difficulty in school, parents and teachers should understand how children learn *before* they get to school. They then have the basis for understanding why the environment of the classroom is so alien to some children. In Chapter 9, we continue to explore the dual relationship between language and learning, taking our investigation into the school years and the environment of the classroom.

Chapter Nine

Language and Learning in School

> When children arrive at school, things begin to change. Now a child is one among many, known by teachers in ways less intimate. A child is no longer known in her entirety; it is as if her life history begins again when she walks through the classroom door. (Kuschner, 1989, p. 45)

In the previous chapter, we examined children's language and learning in the early years before they go to school. At the end of that chapter six characteristics of this early learning were outlined. If we were to condense those characteristics into a single observation, we could do no better than to borrow from Gordon Wells's fine book *The Meaning Makers*:

> In the preschool years, . . . talking and learning go hand in hand. Children talk about the things that interest them and try to increase their understanding; and, for much of the time, their adult conversational partners sustain and support their efforts, seeking, where appropriate, 'to add a pebble to the pile.' What is characteristic of such learning is that it is spontaneous and unplanned and, because it arises out of activities in which one or both of the participants are engaged, it is focused and given meaning by the context in which it occurs. (Wells, 1986, p. 67)

In the chapter these lines introduce, Wells makes direct and systematic comparisons between children's language and learning in the home and in the school. That is the purpose of the present chapter as well, and although I take a very different approach from that taken by Wells, I rely in part on the data he reported and on the insights he gleaned from his famous study in Bristol, England.

THE ATTITUDES OF SOME EDUCATORS

If this were an orderly and logical world, we would assume that those charged with the responsibility for young children's education would begin with two questions: What is the nature of human learning? What is the best way of teaching to facilitate that learning? They should probably ask a third question, as well, about *what* is to be learned, but for the moment let us assume that the answer to that one is known. To refine the questions slightly, they would be asking what *experience* of learning children bring when they begin school and how educators can build on that experience in preparing for the next stage of children's education. In other words, it would make sense if we thought of schooling not as the beginning of education but as the continuation of something that began five or six years earlier and as the next stage in the progression of learning. With regard to language learning, and literacy in particular, we would think of the school years as providing new opportunities for children to acquire more language and more uses for their language, to grow in and with their language.

Some educators might view education exactly in that way, but if so, it has escaped the attention of writers such as Gordon Wells, John Holt, Judy Lindfors, and other researchers and writers in the last two decades. I would claim that it is not the way most teachers of elementary school children think about their jobs. They are part of the hidden "culture" of education that favors the view that education *begins* when children start school.

The first day of school has always been a momentous occasion, one most of us remember even after the passing of several decades. In the past and for some children, the significance of the occasion may have resided in the fact that school marked the beginning of separation from home and parents. But it remains a noteworthy event for children today, many of whom have already spent a number of years in daycare or nursery school first. As David Kuschner says of his daughter, Emily:

> Somehow my daughter knew that there was something special about going to kindergarten, that there was something special about starting school. Even though she had attended a day care center for two years, knew what it was like to move through activity times and learning centers, knew what it was like to have 'school friends' as something different from neighborhood friends, and knew what it was like to have teachers, she had it in her mind

that kindergarten would be different. . . . I don't know when or how she had learned about school, but somehow she knew it would be different. And she was right. (Kuschner, 1989, p. 44)

Schools take responsibility and credit for all manner of "new" learning, chief among which is literacy, even though many children know a great deal about reading and writing when they arrive at school. All in all, we carry on as though learning is what begins when the child first puts a tentative foot inside the classroom door, as though children's minds are blank slates to be written on or soft clay to be molded. But despite the fact that there may be much "writing" and "molding" yet to be done, children arrive at school neither "blank" nor "unformed."

Change the Child

It is just common sense to assume that children whose school experience bears the most resemblance to their home experience will be the most successful. This is an assumption that schools and parents have shared and has been borne out by research. Hence, as Gordon Wells's study and many others have shown, children who have engaged in the "school-like" activities of reading and story-telling are most successful in school. That leaves the children whose homes do not provide this preparation for school at a disadvantage, and programs that have addressed this disadvantage, such as Head Start, have traditionally concentrated on changing the child rather than changing the school. This is a totally unreasonable attitude for a number of reasons. In the first place, such a solution views the child as having a deficit. I find this to be arrogantly objectionable in itself, but even if it were true, from a practical perspective, we probably cannot "undo" the home experience of the child, even if such an action were necessary or defensible. In the second place, it ignores what we have discovered in the past decade about sociocultural bias. As David Dillon writes in an editorial for an issue of *Language Arts* dedicated to home-school relationships,

> . . . there are different kinds of literacies characteristic of different cultural, religious, and especially socioeconomic groups. Being literate according to the norms of one social group does not mean being literate within another social group. (Dillon, 1989, p. 7)

He also points out that research hasn't even begun to address the effect this kind of thinking has on nonmainstream children. Experienced and sensitive teachers can tell us, however, that thinking about education in such a narrow way means that we fail to take advantage of the assets, the experience children already have of the world and of learning. In short, the direction of educational thinking has traditionally been on preparing children for school rather than on preparing schools for children and it has resulted in failure for too many children.

Change the Language

When educators set about to change children, one of the first things they identify as needing change is their language. Sometimes, misinterpretation or misapplication of sociolinguistic theory is to blame. In the 1970s, a British sociolinguist named Basil Bernstein hypothesized the existence of two kinds of oral language. The first, called the elaborated code, was the language used in formal situations (such as school) and was characterized by complex syntactic and stylistic conventions. It was considered to be the language for representing abstract thought, its meaning created by linguistic means alone. The other, called the restricted code, was used in informal situations and was characterized by a simpler stylistic and syntactic range and a restricted vocabulary. It was also thought to rely more heavily on accompanying context (situation and gestures, for example) to make its meaning clear and to be incapable of expressing abstractions. Bernstein's observation that middle class children have access to both codes and that some lower class children may have access only to the restricted code led many educators to take the view that children from lower socioeconomic classes have a language deficit that must be overcome if they are to succeed in school.

The hypothesis has largely been discredited now, due in part to the work of Labov (1982) and Wells (1986). Labov demonstrated that the so-called restricted code is perfectly adequate for expressing abstract concepts. Based on his monumental and impressive longitudinal study of children acquiring language in Bristol, Wells reached what he considered to be his most important finding:

> . . . up to the age of 5, there were no clear differences between the middle- and lower-class groups of children in their rate of development, in the range of meanings expressed, or in the range of functions for which language was used. (Wells, 1986, p. 142)

In describing his findings, Wells disclosed one fact that helps to account for the tenacity of the belief that lower class children come from linguistically deficient homes. He noted that the "half dozen or so most advanced children . . . did tend to come from the better-educated, professional homes" and that "the half dozen or so least advanced children came from homes where the parents were minimally educated and worked, or had worked, in unskilled or semiskilled occupations." But he was quick to point out that for 90% of the 128 children he studied, "there was no clear relationship between family background and level of language development attained" (Wells, 1986, p. 134).

The myth should be put finally and forever to rest. We can proceed in confidence that the language of the children we meet in school has served well the demands placed on it, and there is no evidence that children from one socioeconomic class make more demands on it than children from another. The problem is that the language of the child may differ from the language of the school, and it is the school that refuses to change. I have collected a number of accounts over the years, which taken together constitute evidence that when it comes to children's language, some classrooms are far from being user-friendly. Incredibly, some take what seems to be an openly hostile attitude to children's talk. Children who are most successful in school make the necessary linguistic adaptations—they learn to play along. But not all are successful, and in this chapter, we will learn some of the reasons why.

We will look at the language of schools and in schools. Ideally, anyone interested in finding out about the language experience of children in schools will spend time in schools watching and listening. But this is not possible for everyone and, even when it is, some preparation is necessary to make the observations worthwhile experiences. This kind of background is provided, in part, by the observations of others. Some are anecdotal, the stories told by teachers and children and others who have had experience in classrooms. Others are more formal, reports of studies conducted by researchers interested in children's language growth through the school years.

LANGUAGE IN SCHOOL: THE NEGATIVE SIDE

I must begin this section with a cautionary note. Finding fault is easy, but that is not my purpose. I realize that I run two tangible risks here. The first is that by selecting anecdotes to make my points about the disparity between natural language and school language, I present only the negative when in fact I have never visited a classroom where nothing good occurred. The second is that I present a view that seems to undermine my own belief in teachers and in education. Both are dangerous, so let me attempt to control the damage before it is done.

First, a great deal of good teaching and learning occur even in a poor school situation, and that good may not be apparent in the anecdotes related here. Second, *all* teachers work under conditions that are less than ideal. In recent years, salaries and benefits have improved in some states and provinces, but rarely have they kept up with relative gains in the economy. More importantly, classroom conditions have worsened. The demands on teachers have increased dramatically in the latter half of the twentieth century. As the structure of the family has become more fragile, teachers have had to assume roles and responsibilities that were once the domain of parents. Educating children to the dangers of drugs, protecting them from abusive strangers and family, and generally preparing them for a life that is harder and less friendly than it was a half century ago have left teachers with less time to devote to what were once major goals of schools. Because teachers work under such hardship, we must be *very* careful not to sit in judgment on them, particularly when it is as uninformed as ours is on such scant evidence. That is not my intent and I hope that I need not reiterate my support for and belief in the teachers who take on the responsibility for education but receive so little of the credit for what goes right.

Later in this chapter, we will meet two teachers who provide good, healthy experiences; the anecdotes that follow here are offered as extreme examples of how children should *not* experience language in a classroom.

"No Talking" and Other Unfriendly Signs

In 1983, John Holt wrote, ". . . in almost all schools, hardly anything is done to help children become fluent, precise, and skillful in speech" (p. 123). This allegation, and it is a serious one, was made toward the end of a chapter about how children learn to talk. His point was *not* to cast aspersions on schools, though he would hardly cast them bouquets either, but to identify the fundamental disparity between children's language and learning when they are left to their own devices and what they experience in schools.

A few years ago, a research assistant was observing a kindergarten class in which she recorded the following dialogue, which has been edited only slightly:

Teacher: (Pointing to a dog in a picture in a picture book.) Molly, do you know what this is?
Molly: Yes.

Teacher: What is it?
Molly: A dog.
Teacher: Very good. And what's he playing with?
Molly: A ball.
Teacher: And what color is the ball?
Molly: Red.
Teacher: Right. (Pointing to a girl in the picture.) What is she wearing?
Molly: A skirt and blouse.
Teacher: What else?
Molly: Shoes and socks.
Teacher: That's good Molly. What do you think about this picture?
Molly: It's nice.

At the time the recording was made, Molly was 5;6. She is of normal academic ability and her first language is English. The teacher was not teaching Molly new English words, nor was she reading a story. It is not immediately clear, in fact, just what the teacher was doing. This is, I freely admit, a radical example of bad classroom talk. Yet, for many teachers, this dialogue will be at least vaguely familiar, if not in substance then in character.

Suppose Molly had responded to the teacher as an adult might have if asked the same questions. The following might have transpired:

Teacher: Molly, do you know what this is?
Molly: Of course I do, don't you?
Teacher: What is it?
Molly: A dog. Geez! Any three year old knows that.
Teacher: Very good. And what's he playing with?
Molly: Looks like a dump truck to me. Only kidding. That's a ball.
Teacher: And what color is the ball?
Molly: Color blind, too? Red.
Teacher: Right. (Pointing to a girl in the picture.) What is she wearing?
Molly: How much longer are we going to keep this up? Whadaya think she's wearing, a barrel? She's wearing clothes. Okay, a skirt and a blouse.
Teacher: What else?
Molly: Shoes and socks.
Teacher: That's good. What do you think about this picture?
Molly: I think that girl's mother must be crazy to let her go out to play with the dog in her good clothes. No kid I know wears a skirt to school much less to play in.

But this dialogue is fictitious. Molly did not respond in this way because in the course of a few months in school, being subjected to talk little more purposeful than that in the first dialogue, Molly had internalized many of the characteristics of school talk. She had learned that in school, language is unreal. People, especially teachers, talk about things that no one cares much about. She had learned that school language is decontextualized. Not only do teachers habitually talk about things that aren't there, they seem to avoid opportunities for talking about real things. In the first dialogue, the teacher didn't relate the picture to a story she was reading or make up a story about the picture or provide any real-world context at all for the child. Nor did she encourage Molly to relate the picture to her own life through talk.

Molly had also learned that people, teachers anyway, ask silly questions. Sometimes, they ask questions for which they have already determined the correct answers. Sometimes, they even ask questions that *everybody* knows the answers to and then praise the answers. She had learned that much school talk, devoid as it is of purpose and meaning, is easy. Once she figured out just what game the teacher was playing, it was not difficult to play along.

It is also telling to examine the dialogue from a functional perspective. It doesn't take long. Although superficially, the teacher's questions seem to request information, in fact they do not. She already knows the answers and her questions serve only to instruct—to draw Molly's attention to a picture in which she probably would not be otherwise interested. The true function of her language seems to be to control Molly's behavior, to direct it toward the teacher's unclear but likely pedagogical purpose. Beyond this, it is hard to find any other function. She is even less successful in providing opportunities for Molly to use language in different ways. Molly only responds to the questions she is asked, mechanically giving the expected responses. We cannot even claim that she is using language to inform, because both she and the teacher know that they both already know the answers. The teacher is steering Molly through a match game, checking to see if the child's answers are identical to the expected ones.

It is ironic that when children get into minor "trouble" at school, that trouble is so often "talking." Children learn very soon that although schools purport to value language, they don't much value *talk*, not children's talk anyway. The truth of this observation was driven home to me during a visit to a southern California school a few years ago.

A Canadian teacher, a former student of mine, had been hired to teach ESL in a junior high school, considered by the local Board of Education to be one of the best in the area, a model school in many regards. While I was visiting him, the young teacher took me to visit a number of classrooms, but one stands out in my memory. The room was filled with bright, colorful travel posters of exotic places. A VTR and monitor stood in a prominent place in the front of the room and every piece of furniture, every object in the room was labelled with its name in clear black letters on a white card. What I remember best, though, was the largest sign in the room, placed above the blackboard in letters about nine inches high. In this ESL classroom where the purpose was to foster children's language learning, the sign said "NO TALKING."

We shouldn't assume that there was no talking in that classroom for most assuredly there was. But this brings us to another problem with classroom talk, and a very serious one: The people who would most benefit from honest, purposeful talk are the ones who get the least opportunity to do it. Teachers don't need the practice; children do. But they get little of it in the worst situations and not nearly enough in the best. We don't need research studies or even samples of classroom talk to tell us that this is true. We only have to consider the normal protocol of the classroom. For the most part, it states that children talk only to the teacher and only when requested to do so.

Teachers "Value" Talk

The message on a "No Talking" sign is unambiguous, but sometimes it is less clear. Every time a teacher asks a question to which there is only a single correct answer that she will accept, she is sending the message that a child's talk is important only if it fits her expectations. It is in this sense, then, that teachers "value" talk; they *evaluate* it. When he makes a value judgment about a child's language, as he does when he tries to correct it or change it, a teacher is telling the child that her talk doesn't count. The message is sent in myriad ways. A student teacher recorded the following dialogue, which tells a wonderfully revealing story about children with dialect differences and underscores my point:

> A teacher in a Western Canadian school had a number of minority children in her grade one class. Among these children were represented three different aboriginal languages. One of the children, Bob, was a native speaker of English, but it was a nonstandard dialect since he had learned it on the reservation from his parents and their generation who were not native speakers of English. The teacher was of the misguided opinion that these

children needed ESL and thus, her lessons sometimes had that flavor. One morning a few days after the beginning of school in September, the teacher was "teaching" the names of items of clothing, and the following occurred:

Teacher: (Pointing to her shoes.) What are these called?
Child 1: Shoes.
Teacher: Right. And what do you wear with shoes?
Bob: Socks (pronounced "shocks"). I gots green ones.
Teacher: Those are 'socks' Bobby. Can you say 'socks'?
Bob: Yeah. Shocks. I got shum blue ones too.
Teacher: Some blue what?
Bob: Shocks.
Teacher: No, say 'socks.' Those are 'socks' not shocks.
Bob: Das what I say. Shocks.

By this time Bob, and probably the other children as well, wondered why they were dwelling on such an inane topic. Surely there was no one left in the class who didn't know what socks were. This teacher made several mistakes but chief among them were the assumption that talk in the classroom would serve *her purposes* and that *she alone* was the arbiter of correct pronunciation. This teacher should have counted herself very fortunate if Bob ever ventured to speak again. Why would he? This anecdote, like the earlier ones, is extreme in illustrating its point. But there are thousands of dialogues each day between teachers and students, and many of these are characterized by dishonesty and manipulation.

Dishonest and Manipulative Talk

By dishonesty, I do not mean that teachers tell children lies and by manipulation I do not mean to suggest that teachers consciously manipulate children's behavior to selfish ends. Rather, I mean any kind of classroom talk that is unnatural, that is directed toward pedagogical ends and not toward communication with children. Some see this kind of talk as epidemic in classrooms. As John Holt writes:

> . . . if we think that every time we talk to a child we must teach her something, our talk may become calculated and fake, and may lead the child to think, like so many of today's young people, that all talk is a lie and a cheat. (Holt, 1983, p. 107)

We saw this kind of dishonesty in the dialogue—it could hardly be called conversation—between Molly and her teacher. Such extreme examples aren't necessary, however, to make the point. We have only to consider the false tones that primary teachers sometimes adopt when talking to children or the fact that we plan so much of our talk to lead us down some pedagogical path.

A number of researchers have described this "pedagogical register" or "teacher-talk register." Heath has observed that it uses a higher pitch than other speech registers, and has exaggerated enunciation and intonation patterns (Heath, 1978; cited in Roller, 1989). Cazden has mentioned "the myriad expressions of control; the prevalence of 'testing' questions; the use of boundary markers such as *now, well,* and *okay*" (1987, p. 31). We have all heard this kind of "teacher talk," and if we recognize it, we can be certain that children recognize it as well. They may not make quite the same judgments about it, but with enough exposure, they must surely come to understand that it is different from the registers used when two people are engaged in an honest conversational exchange. The pedagogical "register proclaims not that 'we are talking together,' but that 'I am teaching you'" (Roller, 1989, p. 497).

Teacher talk also reveals itself as dishonest when it is directed toward a pedagogical point and entirely controlled by the teacher. Cathy Roller provides a good example of this kind of talk and of the pedagogical register in use in the following example:

T: The first question I'd like to ask you about today is whether or not you've participated in a science fair or some kind of contest where you had to make something. Think for a minute. How did you feel when you were entering this contest? Give me a low signal when you're ready to tell about your past experience. OK, C1.
C1: When I was in Cub Scouts we had to make a robot out of boards, bottle caps, and (unintelligible). At first I though I was going to win, but when I got to the judging I saw other things that were a lot better than mine.
T: While you were constructing your robot you thought you probably would win. Were you nervous?
C1: No.
T: Not too nervous. Who else has been in a contest like that?
C2: I was in the same thing. I wasn't, I got it done. I knew I wouldn't win anything.
T: Uh, huh.

C2: Turns out I was sick that night so I never got to take it in.

T: You never got to take it in. C3, have you ever entered a contest or something like that? Some other kind of competition maybe, where you're up against other people and they're doing the same kind of thing you're doing? C4?

C4: In fourth grade where we had a Valentine party. We had to make these boxes. When I first made it, I didn't think I was going to win at all because I just got some old things and put it together so.

T: What kind of box was it?

C4: Just a Valentine's box in fourth grade where we used to put our envelopes into.

T: Uh, huh. I can remember doing that in school too. C5? Have you ever entered a competition?

C5: There was a Halloween where you had to color a picture in or draw it. I entered it but I didn't win anything.

T: How did you feel?

C5: I didn't really care.

T: You didn't care whether you won or not. Well, in the story today is a girl named Maria, and she's entering a science fair, so she has to have a pretty elaborate project. How do you think she feels? Just think about it a minute. The importance of the project. C3?

C3: I think she feels really nervous.

T: Nervous. C4, how about you?

C4: She's anxious.

T: OK. Let me get some of these words down. I like these words. Nervous, anxious (writing on board). Anybody else? C1.

C1: Scared.

T: Scared. C5, do you agree with those?

C5: Uh, huh.

T: Is that what you think she probably will be feeling? OK (Roller, 1989, pp. 495–496).

This is an excellent example of talk that scores of teacher educators in the past touted as good teacher talk, as good preparation for the basal story to follow. After all, as Roller pointed out, the "teacher initiated the discussion, directed the turns, and, after each child's response, commented" in her relentless pursuit of her teaching point, which presumably was to relate the children's prior knowledge to the reading they were about to do (Roller, 1989, p. 496). There was a time when some teachers believed this was as it should be. But is it? Admittedly, it is not as bad as the talk that occurred between Molly and her teacher, but we have only to look more closely at the interchange to see that it is highly controlled and manipulative in a number of ways.

First, it was carried out according to the teacher's agenda. She had a purpose and she manipulated the children's talk to that purpose. She initiated the turns, decided when they were completed, and controlled the topics. She conveniently ignored the fact that some of the children's honest responses did *not* lead them in the direction she wanted them led (most of them reported feeling no nervousness or anxiety) because it did not matter; she soon wrested control of the talk back and called on another child who might give a better response.

Second, it was conversationally dishonest. No adult would stay around very long to talk to someone whose only contribution to the conversation was to repeat what was last said and then turn to someone else. The repetitions of the children's responses served no purpose whatever. They did not, for example, elaborate or expand the children's language.

Third, the exchange was dishonest in the sense that although it pretended to draw out children's experiences, it did not do so in any meaningful way. As Roller observed, even though the teacher directed many questions at the children's experience, she also controlled the bounds of the communication. She determined what was appropriate for discussion and made it clear that what was appropriate was what she wanted to hear (Roller, 1989, p. 497).

This excerpt demonstrates another difficulty with classroom talk. Even if it had been characterized by honesty and directness and high interest for the children, it did not provide much opportunity for each child to talk. Instead, the children formed a captive audience, witnesses to the teacher's controlling language. She used language to accomplish her own agenda, ostensibly providing opportunities for children to engage in meaningful talk but in fact setting severe limits on the language they used.

Teacher Talk is Teacher Talking

At home, most children have ample opportunity to talk even if they have to share the time with a number of siblings or members of an extended family. But that changes when they get to school. As Cazden notes, "In the classroom, the group is larger than even the largest families gathered at meals, and so getting a turn to talk is much harder. . ." (1987, p. 31). Children need to talk and, for the most part, teachers do not, yet we can see that teachers do most of the talking. In the excerpt above, we saw a teacher dominating the proceedings, but a closer examination gives us some idea about the impact of that domination on the "air time" accorded individual children. We don't need a sophisticated analysis; we can get a rough indication by comparing the number of words uttered by each speaker. Table 9.1 shows the proportion of talk attributable to the teacher and each child measured in words. We see that even in comparison to the total amount of talk allowed the children, the teacher gets the lion's share with more than 62%. When we consider what this means to each child, the picture grows even darker. At best, C4 generated a total of 59 words for just under 13% of the total talk.

When he directly compared the language of the school with the language of the home, Gordon Wells found that the number of child utterances directed to an adult was nearly three times greater at home than at school and that children initiated conversation nearly three times more often at home than at school. The number of child speaking terms per conversation was greater at home, by a ratio nearly of two to one, but the most telling of the results were these:

1. The proportion of display questions directed by an adult to a child was seven times greater at school than at home. (These are questions that do not request information but provide an opportunity to "display" knowledge, such as "What color is the ball?" asked of Molly by her teacher.)

2. Adults used language to extend children's meaning twice as often at home as at school.

3. By a proportion of two to one, teachers develop their *own* meanings more than parents do when talking to children. (Wells, 1986, pp. 67–94)

Teachers' domination of classroom talk costs dearly. As Wells points out, "conversation is a reciprocal activity: the more one participant dominates, the more the opportunities for the other participant to make his or her own

Table 9.1
Proportion of teacher talk

Participant	Total Words	% of Total
Teacher	288	62.3
C1	48	10.4
C2	33	7.1
C3	6	1.3
C4	59	12.8
C5	28	6.1
Total	462	100

personal contribution are reduced and constrained" (1986, p. 87). It would seem that classrooms are poor places for developing conversational skills.

Not only do teachers control the amount of time children spend in talk, they also control the purposes to which it is directed. The child Molly learned very young that when school talk has purpose, it is usually the *teacher's* purpose. She had recognized the kind of talk John Holt reviled when he wrote:

> . . . The teacher does most of the talking, and now and then asks the children questions, to make sure they have been paying attention and understand. Now and then a bold teacher will start what they call a 'discussion.' What happens then is usually . . . 'answer pulling.' The teacher asks a series of pointed questions, aimed at getting students to give an answer that he has decided beforehand is right. Teachers' manuals are full of this technique— 'Have a discussion, in which you draw out the following points. . . .' This kind of fake, directed conversation is worse than none at all. Small wonder that children soon get bored and disgusted with it. (Holt, 1983, p. 123)

And if they are bored, how can they be expected to learn? Much of the time, they don't. Jon McGill, writing of talk in his history classroom, tells of his efforts to bring his "information-dispensing" talk to life:

> A recent lesson to fourth year CSE[1] pupils involved lengthy outlines of the origins of trade unions. Though I specifically wanted an information giving lesson I also wanted to entertain. Though I conveyed the information using dramatic language, role play and gesture, I was nonetheless left feeling that, in summarizing the lesson, students would see it simply as the teacher having talked—and remain unimpressed by the pyrotechnics which tried to disguise the fact. The next lesson with these pupils demonstrated that they retained little except the drama and the display. What I said was of little impact and during my 'exemplary' lesson, they had said little (McGill, 1988, pp. 78–79).

Claire Staab (1991) reported results of a study that showed that in the grade three and grade six classrooms she studied, 78% of class time was devoted either to the teacher talking or to quiet time. This research showed that although 98.5% of the participating teachers professed to believe that "oral language should be a way to learn all content areas," in practice the oral language tended to be their own (Staab, 1991, p. 44).[2]

---

[1]Certificate of Secondary Education.

[2]Staab also found that women teachers provided "significantly more opportunities for students to speak formally than did male teachers" although no other demographic factor had a significant effect.

Staab also found that her results were essentially the same as those report-ed twenty years ago, suggesting that all the research and writing about the importance of talk in classrooms has had little effect.

Teachers talk and, sometimes, children listen. Even less often, it seems, they learn. The same tale is told in thousands of households each day as children return home from school to be asked the time-honored question "What did you do in school today?"

Parent: What did you do in school today?
Child: Nothing.
Parent: Surely, something happened.
Child: (Thinking about it for a moment.) Nope.
Parent: Nothing at all?
Child: No. The teacher talked a lot. And Mary Beth got in trouble.
Parent: What did the teacher talk about?
Child: I dunno. Stuff.
Parent: What did Mary Beth get into trouble for?
Child: Talking to Peter and me. She was telling us about how her brother broke his foot. You know James? Well he went skiing for the first time ever and. . .

School Talk Is Homogeneous

Talk at home is unstructured and relatively free. Parents do not schedule time for conversation, although they may schedule time for a bedtime story. Conversation happens as the people in the household go about their daily activities. Similarly, most children are exposed to a wide variety of talk—numerous dialects and numerous purposes. Dillon (1980) describes the kinds of language a child encounters in the simple act of getting ready for school in the morning:

> Susan's grandmother, who lives with them, tells Susan that her lunch is in the ice box. Susan is in a hurry as she gets it, and her mother calls after her, 'Susan, close the refrigerator door.' As she stops to do this, Susan hears the morning weather report. It's an interview of a New England resident and sounds something like 'The stawm dumped a lawt of snow heah,' and she wishes her own Midwestern town would get some snow soon. She meets her friends on the way to school and greets them one by one. 'Hey, what's up?' 'Boy, sure is cold!' 'Think it'll snow?' As they approach the school, the chil-dren meet the principal. 'Good morning, Mr. Lawrence,' Susan says. 'How are you today?' He responds and heads for his office as Susan and her friends hurry to class. (Dillon, 1980, pp. 29–30)

In the course of a few minutes, Susan has been exposed to variations caused by language change over time—her grandmother uses *icebox* and her mother *refrigerator*. She hears and has no difficulty understanding the regional dialect on the broadcast news. She switches easily to the subject and vernacular of her peer group and, when she gets to school, to the more formal requirement of greeting the principal. She hurries to class where she will find *some* variation among her classmates, but chances are that the language she encounters there will be somewhat more homogenized than the language of the home.

In the first place, most schools perpetuate a variety of English they call "the standard dialect." Even in schools that have dropped the notion of a standard, preferred, or educated dialect, a high degree of conformity is still present. This is true in part because children hear teachers for the most part whose speech has likely been sanitized as they acquired the education needed to become teachers.

In the second place, there is a sameness to the kinds of things talked about in classrooms. Routines and rules by which classes are conducted and which teachers talk about are essentially the same throughout English-speaking North America. Many language programs are organized to correspond with the scope and sequence charts detailed in the teachers' manuals accompanying basal readers, yielding even more conformity of language and limiting what is talked about.

Third, as we have seen in a number of different examples, school talk seems to be restricted to a very few functions. Staab's (1991) study, while not directly addressing language function, in identifying the fact that teachers did most of the talking provided strong clues about the nature of the talk. Indeed, teachers spent 49% of the total class activity time talking, mostly lecturing, or "instructing," and so we can presume that the most commonly used function was the informing function. They spent an additional 29% of the total time "asking students to work quietly and independently" thus giving a good indication of the other kind of language that dominates classrooms: the language of getting things done, that is, controlling language, or to use Halliday's term, instrumental language. Of the 22% of time left for students to talk, 15% was described as "informal talk" leaving 7% for all the other kinds of talk in which children might engage.

Fourth, and this is perhaps the most frightening and depressing aspect of homogeneity, schools often assume through the language of teachers and the teaching materials they choose that all children have the same background, interests, and experience of language. The individual child, the private person known wholly to her parents becomes the recipient of a preplanned and largely prepackaged school curriculum. Even if they pay lip service to the facts of individual variation among children, schools are only rarely able to respond in ways appropriate for all children. It is a very strong claim, but one that is supported if not directly then at least obliquely by the research evidence,[3] that one of the chief reasons for children failing in school is the fact that schools make this erroneous assumption.

School Talk Intimidates

Perhaps one of the reasons that the first day of school is such a momentous occasion is that the oral culture of childhood has spread the word that school is a pretty frightening place to be. We may wonder from our adult perspective how this can be so given all the efforts we make to create comfortable, safe, learning environments. But from the child's perspective, the temporary feeling of safety may be lost when we challenge his ownership of knowing.

> Although it has been fifteen years since the incident occurred, I remember clearly the day my older son came home from grade one in tears, a grimy worksheet crunched in his fist. When I asked him to show it to me, the cause of his distress poured out. "I got minus," he sobbed, pointing to the mark at the top of the page. (The teacher used a plus, minus, check system to indicate that the work was excellent, deficient, or satisfactory, respectively). 'And I did it right!' he sobbed. I looked at the worksheet. There was a capital letter D at the top and the directions to circle all the items pictured which began with the letter d. Kerry had dutifully circled the first two, a dog and a door, but had stopped at that point. 'I think your teacher expected you to circle ALL the things which start with the d sound. Why did you stop there?' 'Because I knew how to do that.'

At age six, Kerry had assumed that school was for learning to do things he didn't already know how to do. Once he had worked out what he was supposed to do with the worksheet and that he knew how to do it correctly, he abandoned the project and turned his attention to something he didn't know. In this instance, he had turned to a science fiction book borrowed from the school library. He had failed in school because he chose to read instead of circling ducks. His learning at school had come into conflict with his previous experience of learning at home.

[3]Gordon Wells's findings are particularly relevant here as are those of Shirley Brice Heath demonstrating that the progress of nonmainstream children may be hampered "by the difference in the ways in which language is used and questions are posed in homes and schools." (Commins, 1989, p. 29)

> Parents tend to respond to the child's meaning and rejoice in each indication of progress. The role of the teacher is generally different: There is a strong demand for correctness, and teachers tend to view errors as failures rather than partial successes. The responsibility for effective communication and for progress falls upon children. Those who do not succeed may be labeled as being lazy, slow, or even disabled. . . ." (Zutell, 1980, p. 19)

Kerry was in almost continual "trouble" at school that year—for talking, for not finishing his worksheets, and for not participating in his reading group. When I went to school to discuss "his" problems with his teacher, she opened our conference by saying, "I'm very worried about Kerry. He's a bright little boy, but he's having such trouble in reading." Recall that this is the child who had taught himself to read before he was three years old (Chapter 8). At home, he was reading, admittedly with some difficulty, grade five and six level science fiction, but at school he couldn't read. What his teacher was really saying, of course, was that he wasn't doing the activities deemed appropriate during the time allotted to reading. Chances are these had little to do with real reading, for Smith (1975) was likely right in his estimate that in every hour assigned to reading instruction in the elementary classroom, children only spent about four minutes actually reading (cited in Zutell, 1980, p. 19). Staab's (1991) study, though not directed precisely to this question, showed that children in grade three and grade six spent about 15% of their time in activities designated as reading. But more than 40% of this time was taken up by the teacher talking. Children spent 47% of this time in "quiet classroom" activities that surely included reading (although the researcher does not indicate how much of this time was spent in actually reading). Estimating generously that 90% of the quiet time was spent in reading, the figures would translate into approximately 20 minutes per day.

It would seem that Kerry was one of many children Jerome Bruner was talking about when he said that "much of what we do and say in school only makes children feel that they do not know things that, in fact, they knew perfectly well before we began to talk about them" (Holt, 1983, p. 95). When we lead children to mistrust their own knowledge, then we are using language to intimidate.

School Language Is Disembodied

At home, children's language is grounded in the reality of family life. They have parents and sometimes siblings who support in myriad ways their attempts at communication and thus their learning of language.

Learning in the home is characterized by demonstration and performance. Children watch their fathers bake cookies or fix tires and ask questions, as we have seen in earlier chapters. In watching and assisting, they learn various kinds of skills and the language associated with them. When they get to school, however, children are "instructed" in how to do things and then get to "practice" doing them.

The fact that instruction and practice differ from demonstration and performance is easy to establish. Take reading for example. We found out earlier that children who learn to read at home learn by demonstration—they see parents and older siblings getting meaning from print—and by performance—remember "make way for applesauce." At school, rarely do they witness the teacher reading for her own purposes and when they do, no one seriously believes that it is part of the reading "lesson." No, teachers tell students what to do in order to be able to read and then children "do" their reading, except that doing reading is seldom reading. Word attack skills, spelling lessons, handwriting practice, and a myriad of other "language" activities come between the child and the reading. Language is no longer the medium; it has become the instructional message. That we routinely disembody language is implied in John Holt's "lesson" on the teaching of reading:

> What we must do in helping anyone learn to read is to make very clear that writing is an extension of speech, that beyond every written word there is a human voice speaking, and that reading is the way to hear what those voices are saying. (Holt, 1989, p. 31)

What Holt suggests is, essentially, that we embody the language of print. We would do well to consider that advice in all our teaching for it is not only in the teaching of reading that we separate language from reality. Too often, for example, we talk about numbers and their properties rather than demonstrating them with real countable objects and allowing children to do their own manipulations with them.

We can learn a valuable lesson from second-language immersion classes in this regard. When children do not understand the language of instruction and when the teacher is responsible for teaching not only the content but the language as well, she cannot talk about numbers in the abstract. She cannot say, "If I have two oranges and give Peter one. . ." and expect the children to understand what she is saying. And if they do not understand what she is saying, they will not understand the subtraction problem she is presenting. Rather, she must use visuals—she must demonstrate the concept with real oranges and real people in real time.

Immersion teachers routinely rely on concrete objects and on demonstration to make themselves understood. In the process, the children learn not only the content but the language simultaneously because the language of numeracy is embodied in the concepts of numeracy.

LANGUAGE IN SCHOOL: THE POSITIVE SIDE

The last several pages have painted a rather bleak picture of language learning in schools. If I were to end the chapter here, I would leave readers with the impression that schools are language deserts where the only children who flourish are those who are nurtured outside in the oasis of the home. That would be patently unfair. There are fine schools in North America populated with children who are thriving in an environment rich in language and language learning opportunity. Many of these schools have embodied in their curriculum and teaching methods the principles of whole language. In such schools, teachers have taken a critical look at their practice, found it wanting, and in response have embraced a new ideology and its corresponding teaching practices. They have accepted and acted on the truths about language learning that we have learned already—that children learn language best when it is used for real purposes and when teachers refrain from fragmenting it into meaningless pieces of isolated skills.

Whole language has, in fact, become the dominant educational trend of the past decade. When the tenets of whole language are implemented in a sensible manner, it has been a successful approach. Unfortunately, some educational malpractice has also been perpetrated in the name of whole language. Teachers or educational administrators who have not fully understood the concepts supporting whole language practice have sometimes used it as an excuse for a type of pedagogical *laissez-faire,* which has not had the desired effect on children. But where whole language practice has been consonant with its definitions and principles, the result has been beneficial to children's language development in school.

Whole Language Defined

What, then, is whole language? Undoubtedly, there are nearly as many definitions as there are practitioners, but most definitions will encompass certain common beliefs. The definition provided by Froese in his introduction to the text he edited entitled *Whole-Language, Practice and Theory*

(1990), is a representative one: ". . . we define whole-language as a child-centered, literature-based approach to language teaching that immerses students in real communication situations whenever possible" (p. 2). Even in such a short definition can be found the potential for profound change. The approach is *child-centered*; so is the language situation in which most children have been successful language learners. The approach is *literature-based*; children who learn to read are those who are read to, and the stories and books they hear are chosen for their interest and appeal, not for the sequence and scope of vocabulary or language structures. The approach immerses children in **real communication situations**; before school, children learn language by talking to people about real events and objects in familiar environments.

Whole Language in Practice

Definitions are useful as broad indicators of an approach to language teaching and learning, but they provide few insights into what actually happens in practice. How do the lofty goals implicit in the definition get realized in classrooms full of children? To answer the question, we will visit the classrooms of two teachers who claim to be practitioners of whole language and find out how they translate a set of principles into classroom life.[4] We can't stay long in either class, but a even little time will give us some insights into whole language in practice.

Teacher 1, Mary Kennedy, Calgary, Alberta. Mary Kennedy teaches grade two in an urban school in Calgary, Alberta, a city of approximately 750,000 located in the foothills of the Canadian Rocky Mountains. There are 24 children in the class, and only 8 are native speakers of English. Of the remaining 16, 8 are beginners and the other 8 are at various levels of proficiency ranging from low intermediate to advanced. These children come from a variety of linguistic and ethnic backgrounds—Sarcee, Chinese, Vietnamese, Korean, Polish, Spanish, and Thai.

The classroom is a warm and inviting place to spend the day. Colorful labels are stuck almost everywhere, a particular help to the non-native speakers just beginning to learn spoken and written English. There are bright displays of the children's art work, a listening center with dozens of audio tapes and corresponding books. In one large corner of the room is the library where dozens of children's books are arranged for

---

[4]For detailed descriptions of whole language classrooms, see *Portraits of Whole Language Classrooms*, edited by Heidi Mills and Jean Anne Clyde (1990).

easy access and chairs and large floor cushions invite children to linger and read. In a prominent position in the reading area is an oak chair similar to the one that sits behind the teacher's desk (where I've never seen Ms. Kennedy sit). This oak chair has stretched across its back a blue banner with gold letters identifying it as the "Author's Chair." From this chair, children read their finished work to others in the class. For sharing earlier drafts, they work in other parts of the classroom, usually the tables where they write, but for the premiere of the published work, the authors come proudly to the author's chair.

Every morning begins in exactly the same way. For the first 15 minutes or so, Mary reads to the children. She reads a book from the classroom library, one from the school library, or one that she or one of the children has brought from home. The book may be a Big Book, a brightly illustrated book, or even one with few pictures or illustrations. Her main criterion for selection is the children's interest and so she quite naturally lets them choose the books at least part of the time. Whenever she reads to the class, Mary turns on the tape recorder. She does this so that at a later time, children may listen to the story again. All the children enjoy listening to the story at the listening center, but perhaps the most noteworthy benefit is to the non-native speakers. Many of them cannot yet read in English, and often they can be found at the listening center listening to the tape as they follow along in the book, thus closely replicating the experience of being read to by an adult.

After Mary finishes reading the book, the children talk to her about the story. She actively seeks their reactions, and usually refrains from judging their input. The following dialogue is typical:

M. K.: Michael, I noticed that you were laughing a lot during the story. What did you find funny?

Michael: The way they all got stuffed into the mitten! My mitten is too little!

Laura: One time my kitty tried to get in my mitten and she got her head stuck. It was funny the way she tried to get out but couldn't.

M. K.: It would be funny, wouldn't it, to see lots of little animals trying to get into one little mitten?

YanHua: (Holding up a child's glove.) This?

M. K.: That's very like a mitten, YanHua. It's called a 'glove.' (She turns and writes the word on the paper chart beside her.) Glove. Can you say that?

Michael: I've got mittens. I'll show you! (He leaves the group to go to the coat room.)

M. K.: Michael's going to get his mitten to show you, YanHua. While we're waiting, I was wondering if someone else wanted to share how you felt about the story?"
Gi Ping: Me! I like 'quirrel!
M. K.: What did you like about the squirrel?
Gi Ping: Look funny. Not like real 'quirrel.
M. K.: No, you're right. He doesn't look much like a real one, does he? Oh, here's Michael with his mitten. That's a bright color, isn't it?
Michael: My grandma made it for me! See?

The talk here is genuine; it has not been contrived by the teacher to make her point, and it is of interest to all those who take part. It is also allowed to range, as natural conversation frequently does, from topic to topic as attention shifts focus. Notice that it is functionally rich talk. In contrast with some of the examples in Chapter 8, we find here informing talk used genuinely—when Mary asks Michael what he finds funny, for instance, she doesn't already know the answer—as well as talk that helps to foster language for meeting social needs. In this discussion with the children, she is also providing them with opportunities for projecting into the experiences of the animals stuffing themselves into the mitten.

Ms. Kennedy organizes her teaching around themes, and she integrates the entire curriculum into those themes. Science, arithmetic, language arts, social studies, art, and music are all focused on a single theme, be it dinosaurs, rivers, Christmas, winter, or outer space. The children never seem to get bored with this approach; on the contrary, they seem to enjoy the opportunity to concentrate on a particular subject and not to have to experience the frustration of becoming deeply involved with a subject only to have the teacher suddenly pry them away because it's time to do something entirely different. One of the reasons for their high interest level is that they are consulted on the choice of themes. Sometimes Ms. Kennedy offers them a choice from several themes, and at other times the children offer their own suggestions. One year when the children wanted to include "transformers" as one of their themes, the teacher-pupil roles were reversed for a time as the children supplied much of the information and ideas for activities needed to develop the theme fully.

Writing has a central place in the classroom lives of these grade two children. They have each written something about each theme. Some themes, such as Christmas, generate books that may be short "novels" or collections of stories, poems, and drawings. Others generate shorter pieces—whimsical couplets, limericks, or even riddles. The choice of form is left up to the children, but they write every day, sometimes for an hour or more. A good illustration of the sophistication of the written language that the children in this class produced after only a few months is the "book" written by a Vietnamese girl named Doan (pronounced to rhyme with Joanne). Doan had been in Canada for only 18 months when she wrote the three-chapter story reproduced below.

The Little Rabbit Princess Named Lindary

Chapter One

Once in a dark, dark forest there lived a young Princess Rabbit. She was only two months old when her grandpa and grandma died. Her mother, the Queen had eighteen kindly witches and two wicked witches. One day it was Princess Rabbit's birthday. Her friends, Tung the bobcat, Tyson the tiger, Thuy the owl, Que [pronounced Kway] the cat, Quy the dog and Tammy the pig, all went to Lindary's hole house. They played hide and seek, tag and frozen tag. They ate ice cream, carrots, potatoes, tomatoes, bugs and they drank orange juice and also they drank apple juice. They were very polite at the party.

"These friends are very kindly and wild animals," said Lindary's dad the king. Soon her birthday was over. Her friends went home.

Chapter Two

It was 19 years later and her mother the queen and her dad the king died at last. Her mother and father died because they were too old. She lived alone in the hole.

It was Christmas. One frozen winter day she went up the hole to get a small pine tree to fill in the hole house. But she couldn't carry the tree because it was too heavy for her.

So she called to some of her friends Tung bobcat, Tyson the tiger, Thuy the Owl, Que the cat, Quy the dog and Tammy the pig. They tried to carry it. At last they got it in the hole. They celebrated Christmas the other day.

Chapter Three

Soon Lindary was 20 years old. Just then she met a Prince rabbit and Lindary talked to the prince but while she was talking to the prince, the prince replied, "I want to marry you." "So do I" answered the rabbit princess. The next day they got married and they lived happily every after.

The End

Teacher 2, Colleen Maguire, Halifax, N.S.   Ms. Maguire[5] teaches grades three and four in a neighborhood elementary school, which is located within view and easy walking distance of the Bedford Basin. Split grades are not common in this district any longer, but a few remain and Ms. Maguire says that she enjoys teaching the three/four split. She teaches all subjects in the curriculum although an art teacher comes once each week to supplement the activities planned by Ms. Maguire. She does music herself because music is important in her life. She has made it an important part of the children's daily lives as well.

Each morning after the children have arrived and put away their coats, mittens, and boots, they gather around a low table in the back of the room where Ms. Maguire has put cartons of apple juice, orange juice, and milk as well as miniature whole-grain muffins that a local baker makes each day for the school. Most of the children will have had breakfast at home, but for those who haven't, the nutritious food is welcome. For all, it is an opportunity to begin the morning in a friendly and relaxed way. After 15 minutes, the two children who have been designated as helpers for the week put the milk and juice in the refrigerator, put the muffins away to be eaten later, and the other children select their instruments for the morning rhythm band concert.

Ms. Maguire goes to the piano to begin what has quickly become a ritual for the children. The words and music for the day's song are displayed on an overhead projector and, if the song is new to them, the children sit quietly while Ms. Maguire plays and sings the song once. She then plays through the song again, explaining as she goes what each instrument is supposed to do. She is not highly directive in her explanation and often invites the children to participate when and how they see fit. Some children prefer singing to instrumentation and sing along with her.

Ms. Maguire does not introduce a new song every day; sometimes the class will work on one song for a week or more, rehearsing it, changing it, enjoying it until it is ready for "performance" or until they are ready to move on to another song. Performance may be for other classes in the school, for the principal or visitors, or a recording to take home for their families to hear.

Though the day begins musically, it is not spent entirely in song. After the children have put away their instruments, they go to look in their mailboxes and spend the next 20 minutes or so in dealing with the morning mail. The mail is the medium through which Ms. Maguire

[5]This is not Ms. Maguire's real name; she asked that her name be altered and the name of her school omitted for publication. Mary Kennedy is, however, that teacher's real name.

responds to the children's writing. The writing may be in the dialogue journals the children keep with her or pieces at various stages of development that they wish to share with her. Sometimes they simply write her or each other letters. One morning, a third grade girl named Beth was responding to a letter from a fourth grade boy named Lyle. The letters are reproduced, with the permission of Beth, Jody, and Lyle, in Figure 9.1.

Once they have attended to the morning mail, the children gather around Ms. Maguire to plan the day's work. They each make a list of things they want to accomplish, including Ms. Maguire, but the children understand that they do not have to complete every task on the list. Beth made the list shown in Figure 9.2 for November 21, 1990.

There are other, more structured, activities in the children's day. On this day, for example, the children were working on problems related to the distances between the earth and the planet from which the UFO in a story they had read had come. Ms. Maguire worked through one problem with the class and then they referred back to their math logs for assistance in completing the rest. For most children, the math log was a reflective account of the process of mathematics as they experienced it in the classroom. It was a combination of notes about how to reach solutions and editorial comment about the difficulty or the mental processes they used to find them.

Ms. Maguire's class might not seem like a typical whole language class, whatever that might be. Descriptions of whole language classrooms rarely include lengthy accounts of music activities. But Ms. Maguire's class is a whole language classroom in an important sense: Her concern is with the *use* of language and not with the *practice* of language. In songs and in the talk that goes on about songs and performance, children are not just rehearsing for communication; they are communicating. In making their "To Do" lists they are not only using language for a real purpose, but even more importantly, they are to a large extent taking charge of their own learning. In keeping their math logs, they are using language for learning, for monitoring their own experience, and for recalling past solutions to problems.

SIX CHARACTERISTICS OF LEARNING: A COMPARISON

This chapter began with a statement from Gordon Wells that served to crystallize the six characteristics of children's preschool learning from Chapter 8. In the following pages, we saw that many schools are still a long way from reproducing these characteristics. Let us now return indi-

Figure 9.1

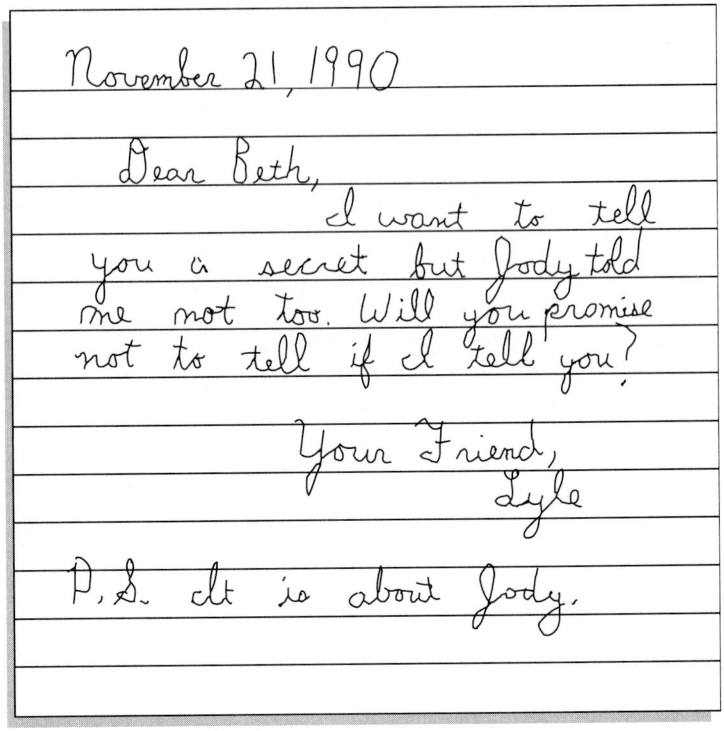

November 21, 1990

Dear Beth,
          I want to tell you a secret but Jody told me not too. Will you promise not to tell if I tell you?

                    Your Friend,
                         Lyle

P.S. It is about Jody.

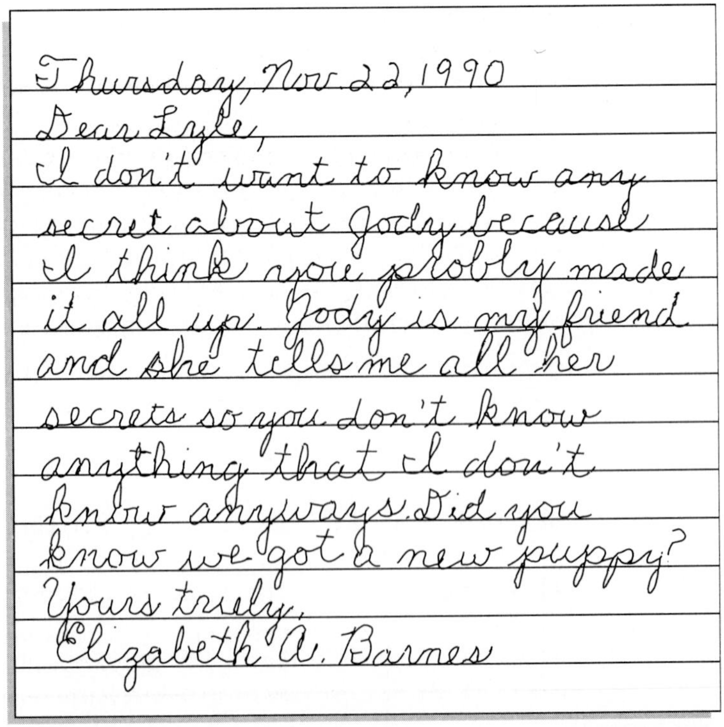

Thursday, Nov. 22, 1990
Dear Lyle,
I don't want to know any secret about Jody because I think you probly made it all up. Jody is my friend and she tells me all her secrets so you don't know anything that I don't know anyways. Did you know we got a new puppy?
Yours truely,
Elizabeth A. Barnes

vidually to those six characteristics to see how each fares under the harsh scrutiny of the classroom lights.

Children's Learning Progresses According to Degree of Readiness.   I am certain that there are schools that can claim this statement as true, but I am equally certain that there are many more that cannot. Some educational practices purport to recognize and provide for individual children's needs. But even some of these are bastardized. A good example is the notion of "reading readiness." This term *should* imply that children learn to read when they are ready to learn. But in practice, it has come to mean that the school has to *do* something to children to get them ready. As John Holt pointed out in *Learning All the Time,* one of the more foolish notions advocated by educators was

> that the way to get children 'ready to read' is to show them a lot of books full of nothing but pictures and ask them a lot of silly questions about them. . . . What children need to get ready for reading is exposure to a lot of print. Not pictures, but print. (Holt, 1989, p. 10)

The simple fact of the matter is that well-intentioned educators find it difficult if not impossible to tailor educational practices in accordance with individual children's readiness to learn. One of the reasons for this difficulty is that most schools are still organized around a common curriculum for each grade, a narrow range of instructional modes, and a limited variety of materials. It is not difficult to understand why schools organize themselves in this way; they are institutions charged with the responsibility of educating large numbers of children within a finite time and budget. That they would attempt to regularize the task in some way is understandable. But the regularization of schools means necessarily that learning cannot proceed according to the child's degree of readiness but must proceed according to some predetermined syllabus.

Figure 9.2
A third-grader's agenda

Beth's Things "TO DO"

1.   Finish picture of UFO

2.   Write poem to go with picture.

3.   Listen to story about space monsters [Ms. Maguire tape records the stories she reads to the children so that they may listen to them later.]

4.   Recess!

5.   Work on math log.

This is not the case in whole language classrooms. The goals of whole language are entirely consistent with the fact that children proceed according to their degree of readiness. Whole language is, after all, child-centered, and it would be impossible to have a child-centered curriculum that sets rigid goals and dictates means for achieving them. The goals of whole language tend instead to be more flexible—to help each child continue to grow in language in the way and the time that best suits him or her. Whole language practitioners recognize that there are many ways for children to achieve those goals and that they will do so according to their own developmental schedule. Comparing whole language practice with this particular characteristic of children's learning results in a close fit, one that can be seen even on a daily basis. For example, it was Beth's decision to put "write a poem" on her "To Do" list, and because it was her idea and she was ready to carry it out, the experience was probably more satisfying for her than it would have been had the assignment been handed down by her teacher.

Young Children Are in Charge of Learning.   If schools are unable to respond to children according to their individual level of readiness to learn, schools will probably not be able to provide environments that permit children to take charge of their own learning. Allowing children to decide what they want to learn and how they want to learn it requires a great deal of faith in children's desire to know and it requires the relinquishing of control, or as John Holt would have said, the *illusion* of control.

First, it is easy to understand why educators would doubt children's ability to take charge of their own learning. Schools take away children's independence as learners and then complain about the results. Holt recognized this phenomenon in a number of his writings. Describing a child's learning when left to his own devices, he wrote of a boy learning to write who was not content to repeat his successes but kept moving on to harder tasks, setting himself increasingly difficult tasks. Generalizing to other children, Holt wrote:

> This is what all children do as they grow up—until they get to school. What all too often happens there is that children, seeing school challenges as threats, which they often are—if you fail to accomplish them, you stand a good risk of being shamed. . .—fall more and more out of the habit of challenging themselves, even outside of school. (Holt, 1989, p. 17)

Second, to permit children to set, meet and evaluate their own challenges, schools—and teachers in particular—must be willing to relinquish absolute control of learning. It is an illusion anyway since it is quite impossible to determine what another human being will or will not learn. We *do* have control of curricula, materials, and the mode of teaching, but we are deluding ourselves very seriously to believe that we can truly control what children learn. So why not give up the illusion and begin to let children, who are not inexperienced at the business of learning and who are the true experts on how they themselves learn, guide their own learning?

This is, of course, exactly what whole language classrooms have done. We saw even in the snapshots of Ms. Kennedy's and Ms. Maguire's classes children taking charge of their own learning—writing their "To Do" lists, reading and writing letters from their mailboxes, keeping in their math logs whatever they thought would help them to remember, deciding what kind of response they want to make to a story they have heard in class, or helping to choose the theme they will study next. An incident that I observed in Ms. Kennedy's class one day illustrates that even practices that might not ordinarily be thought of as consistent with whole language principles may, in fact, in the environment of whole language reveal children to be in charge of their own learning.

One little girl named Jill was highly resistant to invented spelling (spellings that children create for words when they do not know the conventional spellings). She had observed the consistency of the spelling in books and, quite of her own accord, wanted her writing to be "right." Frustrated with her attempts to spell "through"—she had tried *thru, thoug, tough,* and *thrugh*—she finally asked Ms. Kennedy: "Wouldn't it be easier if you just *taught* me how to spell?"

Jill's point is a good one. There is a danger in our zeal to adopt whole language that we will overlook the need of some children to be taught in more traditional ways. That is a danger inherent in any new educational practice—that established methods will be abandoned in favor of newer ones even though, for some children at least, there may be merit in the older methods.

Play Is Important in Children's Learning.   Part of the hidden culture of schooling is the idea that school is serious business. Children such as Emily, mentioned earlier in this chapter, know this to be the case before they get to school. It is one of the things that makes school different from kindergarten. They learn when they get there that recess is not just an opportunity to get a breath of fresh air; it is *the* time for play and represents a distinct break from the hard business of schoolwork. That learning and play might happily coexist is an alien notion to many educators, particularly those who put up "No Talking" signs.

It is hard to imagine how classrooms in which "No Talking" was an important rule of behavior could possibly value play as a medium for learning. How can children play without talking? It is equally hard to imagine how teachers who need to control and manipulate talk to their own purposes could place any educational value on the talk that children do for *their* purposes. In contrast, the tenet of whole language, which emphasizes immersing children in real communication situations, is entirely consistent with this characteristic of children's learning. What could be more natural to a child than play?

Role of Parents in Early Learning.   When we transport this characteristic from the home into the school situation, the obvious parallel is for the teacher to act as facilitator rather than director of learning. Yet in example after example earlier in this chapter, we saw that this was not the case. Many teachers attempt to control learning from the curriculum planning stage right through to the manipulation of children's talk to push them toward a particular teaching objective. We saw the teacher-as-director in Molly's dialogue with her teacher and we saw it again in Jon McGill's history account of the "information-dispensing" talk in his history class.

The model of teacher as instructor is deeply ingrained in our culture. Our entire pedagogical history is of the teacher as the giver of information, the holder and granter of wisdom. To abandon this view of the teacher's role means bucking 2000 years of tradition. Even teachers who want to change may find it very hard to give up the notion of teaching as the dispensing of information. After all, they went to a university for four, five, or six years to learn all that information; surely it's their duty to teach it to someone else. It takes a great act of faith, or as Ms. Kennedy put it, "many years of experience. I don't know why it took me so long to give up the old ways since my better judgment told me years ago that they weren't working anyway." Mary's conversion began before the label "whole language teacher" existed and was completed when she went back to the university for graduate study and learned that her instincts were consonant with a change that was taking place in language education.

Relinquishing control of and thus some of the responsibility for learning to the child is at the heart of whole language thinking. Teachers who create the kinds of environments conducive to learning and to wanting to learn are playing a role that is every bit as important and a great deal more effective than teacher-as-instructional-director.

Interaction Is Essential to Early Learning.   Before they come to school, children learn their language and most other things they know through their interactions with people and the environment. In school, they continue to learn through interactions but the quality of those interactions may not be comparable to those of the home. We saw in many of the earlier anecdotes in this chapter that children's interactions with teachers are often contrived by teachers to reach a particular goal established by teachers. The fact that some teachers believe that all their talk must be directed toward a pedagogical end is evidence that their interaction is suspect. We "heard" in the register adopted by some teachers and in the asking of questions that both teacher and child know not to be real questions a falseness that disclosed the truth of their intent. We heard teachers trying to "teach" language. These behaviors do not constitute true interaction.

In contrast, we saw in the two whole language classrooms a quality of interaction that was similar to the interaction that occurs in children's homes. We saw and heard teachers not attempting to teach language but talking with children honestly, in real voices, and toward purposes that had legitimacy for both teachers and children. When Ms. Maguire wrote letters to the children in her classes and responded to their letters to her, when the children in Ms. Kennedy's class told her what they liked and didn't like about the stories they heard, and when Ms. Kennedy declined to pass judgment on these opinions, we were witness to productive interaction. Because it is partly defined by its emphasis on real communication for real purposes, the whole language approach should always result in quality interaction between teachers and children. Where there is quality interaction, there is more likely to be learning.

Learning Is Embedded in Socialization.   There are doubtless many reasons and many conditions under which humans learn. During our earliest years and, if we are fortunate, throughout our lifetimes, we learn for the sheer pleasure of it, for the delight in knowing something previously unknown. But our learning is also driven by more pragmatic drives—the *need* to have information, knowledge, or skills for a particular purpose. It is also motivated by less obvious drives—to achieve group membership, for example. As we saw in Chapter 8, as children learn language in the home, they are being initiated into the rituals and expectations of family membership. As they venture forth into the world, they become members not only of the family but of the larger community, and a significant part of that community is the school. Through schooling, in fact, children in Western society learn much of what they need to know to become lifelong participants in society.

Language learning, and indeed all learning, during the school years should provide the means for socializing children to the role of community member, of citizen. To some degree, it does. The knowledge they acquire in schools takes many forms. Part of it is factual—the history of the nation in which they live, its system of government, its laws. These facts provide the basis for citizenship just as the facts of mathematics provide the basis for their coping with the worlds of finance and science. What they acquire in school also includes linguistic knowledge that cannot be quantified as a list of facts. I have already suggested earlier in this chapter that the lessons they learn about language may not be the ones we want them to learn. When their talk is not valued, children may well internalize a "rule" to the effect that some people's talk, namely, those in positions of authority, is more important than other people's talk, namely, those not in power. When they witness the use of language to manipulate their own behavior, they learn the power of language to corrupt. When they experience the homogenized talk of the school, children may fail to develop appreciation of the linguistic diversity that does not divide us but helps to identify us as individuals and as distinct groups within the larger English-speaking society. When their talk is channeled and controlled as it so frequently is in school, they risk losing the spontaneity and whimsy that is the stuff of verbal creativity. These are the lessons taught, perhaps unwittingly, but too often and by still too many schools.

But not by all. In some schools, as we saw earlier, language is not scheduled into the school day as a subject to be dissected, analyzed, or memorized. Rather, it is part of the process of children's learning and part of the process of their joining the community of educated people. These rather lofty goals are accomplished by teachers and children who communicate with one another and share responsibility for growth in language and in learning.

CONCLUSION

How do the schools fare in comparison to the home as an environment for language and language learning? The question has two answers: not very well and very favorably. We saw in the first part of this chapter that far too many schools still provide environments that are hostile to language development. When children do succeed in these environments, it is a great tribute to their own determination and to the nurturing environment of their homes. We saw later in the chapter, however, that some schools provide classroom environments in which children's language can thrive and grow. We will have an opportunity to visit other schools and other classrooms that provide healthy language environments for children and to explore in greater detail the attributes of those environments. First, however, we will back away from the child and the school and examine the influence exerted on schools from outside—by society as a whole and by parents in particular.

PART FOUR

Putting it all Together

Chapter Ten

A Broader Perspective on Language in School

In the previous chapters, children's language learning was described as it occurs at home and at school. In attempting to understand what language learning is like for children at home, we necessarily considered the role that parents play. In examining language learning as children experience it in school, we considered the role that teachers play, perhaps implying that they are largely responsible for the quality of children's experience. But it would be erroneous to assume that teachers work autonomously, that they alone make the decisions governing how language is taught in their own classrooms. Certainly they have some latitude, but they are influenced, some might even say governed by those who administer the institutions in which they work (and by *institutions*, I mean not only schools but the entire administrative hierarchy in which schools are embedded), by parents, by other groups within the larger society, and indeed by society itself.

My intent in this chapter is to examine the influences exerted on schools and on language education policy by different communities. The notion of a *community* is a useful one for thinking about the various types of influence exerted on language policy precisely because it permits overlapping membership. As Mary Ashworth observed in her book *Beyond Methodology* (1985), there are at least three different kinds of communities and they exist in differing relationships to language policy. The first, geopolitical communities, "lie within fixed physical boundaries and perform political functions" where *political* refers to a community that has the well-being of its citizens in mind (Ashworth, 1985, p. 33). Geo-political communities consist of nations, states, provinces, counties, municipalities, electoral districts, and school districts. According to Ashworth, however, neighborhoods, including reservations and ghettos, should also be thought of as geo-political communities. Certainly, their "political" nature can be seen in those communities that serve their members by organizing food banks, daycare, or neighborhood watch programs.

The second type of community Ashworth identifies is the common interest community: "Within geo-political and reaching across their boundaries are common interest communities—groups of people who share a common history, experience, language, culture, or political or religious ideology" (Ashworth, 1985, p. 33). Families can be thought of as common interest communities because they share a history, language, culture, some of their experiences, and possibly political and religious ideologies. Spanish speakers in Los Angeles, English speakers in Quebec, or French speakers in Canada are examples of other common interest groups, each bound by a common language and culture.

The third kind of community identified by Ashworth is the professional community. Although she confines her description to those concerned with some aspect of language teaching, professional communities are, more broadly, those linked by professional goals or interests. The National Council of Teachers of English, the International Reading Association, and the International Association of Applied Linguists form large professional communities with language unifying them. Except for large national associations, professional communities are usually close-knit. Members typically know one another and share a commitment to the interest that unites them. In education, professional communities are defined by their dedication to some aspect of quality education for children.

Individuals, of course, typically belong to a number of overlapping communities. An Hispanic teacher in Kansas City belongs to a number of geo-political communities such as neighborhood, school district, municipality, county, and nation. She may also belong to a variety of common interest communities including her family, Spanish speakers in her neighborhood or city, and perhaps a community of Hispanic urban professional women, whether or not this last group officially recognizes itself in any way. As a teacher she is undoubtedly a member of several professional communities—the community of teachers in her school, the local teachers' organization or union, perhaps the PTA, and one or more specialized professional associations. Any one or all of the communities to which she belongs may have an effect on or be affected by language education issues, but despite her membership in all the communities, each community may have a different interest or view language from a different per-spective.

In the pages to follow, we will examine how three communities influ-ence educational practice, particularly language education. One is a com-mon interest community, namely parents. The second is a professional community, the community of educators, and the third is a geo-political community, the broader community who are the beneficiaries of educa-tion. It is important to remember before pursuing our discussion that influence is exerted from both directions—language teaching policy affects communities as surely as communities affect language teaching.

THE COMMUNITY OF PARENTS

> Children will have many teachers in their lives, but only one family. It must be the family who helps to maintain the continuity of the child's educa-tion. . . . Participation of these coeducators in the child's learning program will function best at the level suitable to the teacher and the parent. (Potter, 1989, p. 28)

We can think of parents as forming a community in two senses. In the larger sense, parents of all children share a common interest in their chil-dren's happiness and well-being and are thus a common interest commu-nity. In a narrower sense, however, they are parents of children in French Immersion, parents of children in School A, or parents of children in Mrs. B's class. Pointing out that the community of parents is indeed a diverse one, Snyder (1990) has identified five different subgroups of parents. "Mature parents," she labels as those who are established in their careers and may be older than parents of elementary children have traditionally been. As she puts it:

> Articulate, educated, affluent, competitive amongst themselves and for their children, these parents stress image and achievement as important mea-surements of success . . . desirous of the best, [they] make demands; they shop for schools and for teachers, and compare and compete with others. (Snyder, 1990, p. 219)

The group she calls "activist parents" are characterized by their role as advocates for different causes. Some may be devoted to feminism or envi-ronment or, more worrisome for teachers, may lobby for the removal of certain books from the school curriculum on the basis of their nonconfor-mity with that group's political or religious beliefs. Another subgroup are the parents of special-needs children. According to Snyder, this group is becoming increasingly vocal, and their requests include "special methods and materials in regular classrooms to meet needs of autistic, learning-disabled, visually-impaired, gifted, or other special children" (Snyder, 1990, p. 220). She also includes in this group parents who are functionally illiterate.

The fourth subgroup is the one Snyder calls "available parents." These are the ones who can be counted on to accompany the class on a field trip, to volunteer in the classroom, to bake cookies for bake sales. This group is vitally important to the life and success of the school. The fifth category of parents Snyder identifies are the multilingual, multicultural groups. These are the parents of minority language or race children whose concerns we will examine separately below.

All parents are, in fact, members of a number of different common interest communities, some by virtue of being parents, some by virtue of where they happen to live, and some by virtue of a common belief (in the value of bilingual education, for example). Sometimes these different memberships conflict with one another.

Consider, for example, the case of a family from Francophone Quebec that emigrates to anglophone Alberta. Because the children speak only French, they are put into ESL classes in the school they attend. The parents thus belong *de facto* to the community of "parents of non-English speaking-children." They may, however, have very little else in common with the other parents who are immigrants to Canada. Perhaps both groups share a desire to preserve the heritage language of the children, but they hold that view for different reasons, and they almost certainly have different views about how English should be taught and about the place of their children's heritage language in the school curriculum. Their particular experience of English and English speakers in Canada, the political history of their own province and its history within Canada will have influenced their views in such a way as to make them disparate members of that particular community. Where the immigrant parents may desire immersion English for their children at school and assume responsibility for maintaining the native language at home, the Francophone parents may want official recognition of their children's language by the school, demanding maintenance French or even fully bilingual education. The community in this case may not speak with a single voice in order to represent the beliefs or interests of all its members.

Even though parents may belong simultaneously to a number of communities and although they may not agree with all the values or beliefs of any one, it is still possible to talk in an educational context about the community of parents. For our purposes, the community of parents is assumed to have the following characteristics:

1. They have children of or approaching school age.
2. They care about the educational welfare of their children.
3. They have certain expectations about the outcomes of formal education.
4. They have beliefs abut how those outcomes might best be achieved (although they may or may not be willing to express those beliefs in public).

Parental Participation

There may have been a time once when parents believed that they could leave the education of their children to the school, when they looked to the school to teach their children "the basics" to prepare them for higher education or for the working world. There may have been a time when the school was considered the proper place for children to learn to read, for example, where the school and teachers were "expected to work this magic with children without assistance from the home" (Winter & Rouse, 1990, p. 383). But if there was such a time, it is passing. The 1980s wrought a new and vocal community of parents. Some continued to participate in rather traditional ways, either by membership in the PTA, by working as volunteers in classrooms, by helping teachers to organize field trips, or just by visiting their children's teachers on a regular basis. But others began to seek more active roles and to assume more responsibility for their children's education.

One has only to peruse newspapers and popular magazines of the past decade to know that parents have become increasingly active in seeing that their expectations with regard to their children's education are met. Some parents work in partnership with schools and teachers to provide the best education possible for their children. Others, in what educators undoubtedly see as a cynical practice, make use of one of several companies springing up in the United States that provide parents with the names of school districts in specified metropolitan areas that meet the parents' preferences with regard to school size, class size, counseling services, etc. (Wells, 1991). Others opt out of public education, choosing either private schools for their children or deciding to take responsibility for their children's education at home. An increasing number of parents in North America have chosen this latter route. The *New York Times* (Celis, 1990) reports that "hundreds of thousands" of parents, "dismayed at the troubled state of public education and certain they can do better," reject both public and private schooling in favor of educating their children at home. Children educated at home are still and likely will remain a small minority, however, and what we are concerned with here is the involvement of parents whose children do attend school.

Parents' Views on Education

Parents hold a variety of beliefs about language education. A poll reported in *The Reading Teacher* revealed that many parents of elementary school children have strong views about their role in their children's reading instruction. One question asked parents "to indicate whether or not they had any responsibility for teaching their children to read, and, if so, to indicate the proportion of responsibility they felt belonged to parents versus the amount that should belong to schools" (Rasinski & Fredericks, 1989, p. 262). While every one of the respondents indicated their belief "that parents do bear some responsibility for teaching their children to read," there was disagreement about how this responsibility should be divided. Of the 67 parents responding, 51% felt that the school should assume most of the responsibility and only 13% felt that parents should bear the major burden for teaching their children to read. The remainder indicated that an equal division of responsibility was ideal. "Overall, the division of responsibility question assigned schools an average of 58% of the responsibility for reading instruction with parents holding 42%" (Rasinski & Fredericks, 1989, p. 263). It would seem that a majority of parents in this study share the view of the Missouri parent who stated "A lot of parents just more or less take care of their kids until they go to school. They expect the teachers to teach them. But while our children are at home, we are the teachers at a time when they are learning the most the fastest" (Winter, 1985; quoted in Winter & Rouse, 1990, p. 383).

The fact that most parents believe that the school should assume the responsibility for teaching reading does not mean that they have no ideas about how teachers should do so. Some parents believe that their children should be taught language, and especially reading, in the way that they were taught. The same *Reading Teacher* poll revealed that 36% of the respondents believed the schools do a poor job of teaching reading and an additional 13% were equivocal, saying that reading instruction was "average" or "so so." According to the researchers who conducted the poll,

Frequent recommendations made by parents for improving school reading instruction included the following (in descending order): having (a) more reading in school, (b) smaller reading groups, (c) more intensive skills and phonics instruction, and (d) more activities in which students read aloud. (Rasinski & Fredericks, 1989, p. 262)

While parents responding in this way may not have recognized the bias in their views, it is nonetheless the case that most of the practices they recommend are more closely associated with the years during which *they* were educated than with current educational thinking. The mismatch between what parents believe about language education and what teachers believe is bound to cause frustration on both sides. As one teacher wrote,

In the last few years, my interaction with the parents of my students suggested that the parents' expectations were out of line with the objectives of my class. Some asked me why I didn't teach grammar or diagramming. Others wanted to know why I didn't mark every error on their children's papers. (Davis, 1991, p. 62)

Still, it would be a mistake for teachers not to consider the opinions of all parents, even those they might consider ill informed. Patricia Davis responded to her own frustration by undertaking a project designed to foster parent's participation in their children's writing. She invited parents to write with their children, taking the time to explain in her letter of invitation that the purpose was not to evaluate the parents' writing but merely to share their stories. The experiment was successful in many ways, but as she reports,

Perhaps the most important benefit of the exercise was that during the rest of the year the parents were supportive. They understood why we were writing so frequently, and why not all of the writing was graded. (Davis, 1991, p. 64)

What parents think about schooling is important: "The parents were the child's first teacher and will remain the most important throughout the child's life" (Potter, 1989, p. 28). It can only benefit children to have parents and teachers working cooperatively in trying to make their education a success.

So far, the focus of our discussion about parental influence and involvement in language education has been on reading and writing. That is because most parents assume that their children already know how to speak and that the main job of the school, with regard to language, is to teach them to read and to write. This bias is one that teacher's confront every day and provides a good argument for encouraging parents to take part in their children's education: Parents who understand what the teacher is doing and why are more likely to be supportive of what happens in the classroom.

At the beginning of this section, I made the point that the community of parents is unified by a common interest in their children's educational well-being. I also made the point that they are a diverse group sharing a variety of views, many of which depend on the status of the parents' native language in the community. Minority language parents often have special concerns about their children's education, concerns that might be of less importance or less often articulated by the majority community.

Specific Concerns of Minority Parents

Minority parents constitute a truly diverse community. Sometimes, they will all come from the same ethnic background. This is the case with pocket ethnic communities in some urban centers or in small fishing villages along Canada's coasts where most of the immigrants will be from other fishing economies. But such homogeneity is rare. Usually, the community of minority parents does not share a language, a culture, or a history. Some parents are immigrants, but others were born in North America, sometimes to parents who were also born here. What binds them together is their common interest in their children's educational well-being and by the fact that they and their children speak a language other than English or a dialect of English other than the dominant one of the community. This latter characteristic is unifying in a way that tends to be negative as far as schools are concerned. Being outside the dominant language group, non-English speakers are unified by being collectively viewed as a "social problem" by the dominant language group. As a study conducted by Hurtado and Rodriguez confirmed, schools justify taking the view that a language other than English (in this case Spanish) is "problematic" on two grounds. First, they make the argument that English is required for economic and social mobility, that "to speak Spanish was to be 'UNAMERICAN' and choose to stay within their ethnic group" (Hurtado and Rodriguez, 1989, p. 413). Second, they argue that language use should be divided according to domain—English for the public and Spanish for the private domain—Spanish is acceptable at home but not at school.[1] Minority children thus *begin* their

---

[1] The English-only legislation passed first by California and under consideration in a number of other states is evidence of the vehemence of reactions to language diversity. It is also indicative of the second argument, that there is only one acceptable *public* language and that is English.

schooling already labeled as a social problem for the mere fact of their language. Minority parents have, justifiably, a great many educational concerns. These relate to general **educational practice**, to language policy, and especially, given the "social problem" mentality of schools and society, to **racism**.

Minority parents have found a great deal in educational practice to object to, which is hardly surprising given the monumental challenges their children face. As Commins writes:

> As children mature, they develop a sense of themselves within the context of their language and culture. Students who come from homes where a language other than English is spoken must struggle not only with the difficulties of learning a second language, but also with all of the affective dilemmas posed by becoming acquainted with and pressured to adopt the values and customs of another culture. When linguistically different children leave home and enter school, they are not only entering a new environment, they must also learn to negotiate a new reality. (Commins, 1989, p. 29)

Because they have tended to adopt an assimilationist attitude, schools have been rather slow to assume their share of responsibility for negotiating a mutual reality with minority children. As a result, many minority parents have become more vocal in recent years in rejecting the European bias in education and curriculum, demanding that schools not only respect but participate in the teaching of minority culture and history. It is a demand that has been made with some trepidation. A *New York Times* report on the education of American Indian children stated that there are "powerful and seemingly contradictory forces" pulling on these children (Johnson, 1990). On the one hand, there is an effort by educators and parents to instill in them an appreciation of their Indian heritage. On the other, there is pressure to assimilate them into mainstream American culture as a way of ensuring educational and thus work force success. Parents who reasonably insist that schools take some responsibility for helping their children to maintain and to value their cultural heritage and identity are sometimes made to feel that doing so jeopardizes their children's future welfare in the mainstream society in which they will have to survive.

There is little doubt that a great deal of conflict may result when minority children come face to face with the mainstream culture of the school. They learn very quickly what the mainstream does and does not reward, and chances are good that much of it is different from those things their own culture does or does not reward. Parents play an important role not just in helping their children to adjust but in helping teachers to adjust the classroom environment to make it more conducive to their children's learning.

Much of educational practice relates to a stated or unstated **language policy**. In the 1960s and 1970s, teachers struggled with the conflict between the standard English of the school and the dialects spoken by increasingly large minorities. Black English was one of the more common nonstandard dialects on which attention was focused in the United States. Many views were expressed. Some held that it was the responsibility of children to learn the dialect or language of the school, effectively denying the existence of a problem *for the school*. Others completely accepted the principle of children's right to use and to have their own dialects treated with respect. The U.S. Supreme Court, in fact, affirmed in law children's rights to equal educational opportunity, establishing that equal opportunity was *denied* if children could not understand the language of their teachers. In *Lau vs. Nichols*, Chinese parents argued successfully that their children were denied equal access to educational opportunity because they were not given special instruction in English. The defendant, the San Francisco Unified School District, argued that its responsibility extended only to making available the same facilities, textbooks, and curriculum to all children. The Court reasoned that schools do not provide "meaningful education" for children if they do not make particular efforts to eliminate the language barrier.[2] Providing ESL classes is a possible answer for non-English-speaking children; it is *not* an answer for children who speak a nonstandard dialect of English.

A very common response of educators to the question of language rights, however, was the assimilationist argument again: Children have a right to a nonstandard language or dialect *but* must learn the standard language to succeed in school and thus the work place. The argument is suspect on a number of grounds, chief among them the fact that it is circular. For the most part, those people who succeed in school also succeed in the working world, and it is the school that sets the criteria for success. Schools become, in this view, mere protectors of the *status quo* and lose their potential as agents of social change. Increasingly, minority parents have come to fault this argument and, as they have simultaneously begun to emphasize the centrality of their own culture, history, and language in their children's lives, have begun to reject the schools' position. The result has been programs such as those proposed by black educators that concentrate on "the basics." But the *basics* in this case are "a nurturing school environment, parental involvement, and curriculum relevant to black

[2]For a complete account of this case, *Lau vs. Nichols*, 414 U.S. 563, and subsequent legal cases related to this ruling, see Teitelbaum and Hiller (1977).

youngsters' lives . . ." (Wilkerson, 1990, p. 6). If these were what all parents and educators considered to be the basics, then education might not be in a crisis state in the 1990s. Language education for children would especially benefit from such attitudes.

Language policy translates into very specific teaching goals and practices. For parents of minority students, a number of issues arise. The most basic one may be the conflict between the language of the home and the language of the school. It is all too typical of schools to view children's bilingualism as a deficit, not openly, of course, but by concentrating on bilingual children's deficiencies in English rather than the fact that they are in the process of mastering a second language, schools justify their own English-only practices at the cost of minority children's self-esteem. Parents play an important role here, not in supporting the second language at home but in providing the strongest possible language experience in the first language, particularly in reading. A great deal of research supports the view that first language literacy exerts a powerful influence on second language literacy, that what is important is not the *language* of literacy but the fact of it. Cummins and his associates presented compelling data on Japanese school children living in Toronto which showed that their skill in reading English was largely determined by their skill in reading Japanese. Since the writing systems of Japanese and English differ fundamentally, this was a particularly significant finding. Edelsky (1982, 1986) concluded that grade one and two bilingual writers make use of their knowledge about writing in their first language—about strategies for writing description, for example—when writing in their second language. In a study of the writing skills of 38 fourth and fifth graders in a Spanish/English bilingual program, Lanauze and Snow demonstrated that children with excellent first language skills can transfer those skills to the second language, effectively "shortcutting the normal developmental progression in L2" (1989, p. 337). These research findings support Cummins's "interdependence hypothesis," which holds that there is an underlying language proficiency that necessarily originates in the first language but exerts influence on the second as well. To put it more plainly, the best predictor of proficiency in a second language is degree of proficiency in the first (Cummins, 1979a, 1984).

The task of schools and of teachers, then, is to work in partnership with minority parents, not to "instruct" them, but to join them in helping their children to become bilingual and bicultural. Schools and teachers must adopt the attitude that the dominant language is an *additional* one for minority children; it does not replace the first language. They must begin to view the first language or dialect of the child, whatever it may be, as an *asset* the child brings to school, at least as much as they value the fluency a mainstream child occasionally acquires in a foreign language. Only with such changes in attitude can they begin to make the changes that must be made before they can even begin to work in partnership with minority parents.

Another major worry of minority parents is the effect on their children of coming into contact with **racism** in the school setting. Whether racism comes in the obvious but very painful guise of name-calling, whether it is more subtly manifested in books and materials that represent only the dominant culture, or whether it is manifested even more subtly in our snobbish judgments about what constitutes acceptable English, children confront racism, and it is traumatic to them and to their parents. If schools are to free themselves of racism, they will find in parents a valuable resource for identifying it and for finding ways to eliminate it. The impact of society's racism on education is a topic we will consider in greater detail later in this chapter.

Encouraging Parents to Participate

It is perhaps ironic that even though most parents still see the schools as having the principal responsibility for their children's literacy education, educators are keenly aware of the importance of parental participation.

> It is not unusual to hear teachers complain that parents are not accepting their responsibility for their children's education. That complaint and some of its causes have pushed family literacy into the center of today's educational discussions. (Smith, 1991, p. 700)

Both groups are right. Schools and teachers *are* primarily responsible for education, but they cannot do the job alone. They need the support and the participation of parents. An optimal level of parental participation does not just happen; it must be initiated and nurtured by teachers and schools. A partnership program entitled "Parents-as-Teachers," begun several years ago in Missouri, had as its goal "to create new partnerships and shared responsibilities for the development of young children" (Winter & Rouse, 1990, p. 383). This program is an early-childhood program that promotes emergent literacy activities, but the attitudes and some of the practices could easily be transferred to families of school-aged children. Practices such as storybook reading not only facilitate language and literacy but also have a "powerful influence on the social-interactional development of the family" (p. 384). Parent educators encourage such activities by introducing the parents to "developmentally appropriate books" and by modeling how to use the books (p. 384). One of the strengths of the Missouri program is that by encouraging parental participation in preschool education, the organizers set the stage for active involvement during the school years; parents who were accustomed to dealing with the educational system and to talking with others about their children's development will be more comfortable in their dealings with teachers and schools at a later date.

Missouri is not the only state to respond pro-actively to the need for parental involvement. The state of Kentucky established a family literacy project

> to counteract a serious problem with the undereducation of the state's adult population; the belief is that this problem is the result of persistent patterns of school failure within families across generations. (Smith, 1991, p. 700)

Programs such as the ones established in Missouri and Kentucky are significant not only because they encourage parental participation in their children's schooling but because they provide an educational service to the entire family. "There is a sense that supporting family learning will not only help schools but will also bring greater cohesion to American families" (Smith, 1991, p. 700). These family-school cooperative projects also have an impact on parents' beliefs about how education should proceed.

THE LARGER COMMUNITY

Parents are a large constituency of the greater public and, as such, their views provide a good indication of how the public views education. A *good* indication, but not a perfect one. Forces are at work that influence the larger society, and these forces may operate somewhat independently of the parent constituency. There are political and business interests in education, for example, and these may partly reflect and partly be at odds with those of parents and educators.

Business Interests and the Accountability Movement

As evidence that certain groups in society have a major impact on education, we have only to consider two stories that appeared in the *New York Times* in the early 1990s, both showing the impact of business interests on education. One story reported that a retired New Jersey businessman had donated $125,000 U.S. to set up a project to pay grade five children for good grades. According to the report, children would be paid on a scale equal to the grade received and would collect the money only after graduation and only on the condition that they use it to enroll at an approved college or university (Lynwander, 1990). In the second story, the *Times* reported that a New York City schools chancellor proposed a "warranty" on each of the city's high school graduates. The warranty would guarantee employers that graduates of local schools could read, write, and calculate proficiently. Any employer who found otherwise would be permitted to "return the worker" to school for remedial programs, at no cost, for up to one year (Berger, 1991).

Educators who read these and similar stories of the intrusion of business interests into classrooms are justifiably worried, and not because they do not believe in quality education or even in accountability. They worry because they believe that the terms of reference are wrong, that quality control in schools is fundamentally different from quality control in factories. Although both stories raise very serious issues about educational accountability and the erosion of education as a profession, the first story is perhaps less alarming than the second. At least in the first story, the idea came from a businessman, whose primary experience and interest had been with trade. The second idea was put forward by the overseer of a school district, someone whose primary concern is supposed to be the quality of children's lives in the education system. While the interests of children may have been in his mind, they were colored by his perceived needs of the workplace. There is, of course, nothing inherently wrong in striving to educate people to function productively in the world of work; it is a necessity in modern times when few of us have the independent financial means to survive without working. But to make education accountable primarily to the requirements of business reduces it to job training, and our children deserve better.

Alarming as it is, the idea that children's minds can be "under warranty" is entirely consistent with the notion of accountability that swept through North America in the late 1980s and early 1990s. Implicit in the notion is the idea that education should be subject to the same kinds of "quality control" as industry. It is understandable why manufacturers are interested in quality control. If a washing machine manufacturer makes washing machines that regularly break down during the rinse cycle, and if the machines are guaranteed, his profits will be eaten up very quickly if defective washing machines must be replaced continually. Without a guarantee, he cannot expect to sell many washing machines and if they do not work, he cannot afford to guarantee them. He needs to know before the washing machine reaches the market that it will work. He can then afford to warrant that his product will function properly because he knows that he will not have to replace many machines. This is how the manufacturer is "accountable" to the consumer. When business minds turn their attention to education, they tend to think in the same way. Indeed, politicians, possibly because many have been in business, tend to speak in the same terms:

> There are greater, more certain, and more immediate penalties in this country for serving up a single rotten hamburger in a restaurant than for repeatedly furnishing a thousand school-children with a rotten education. (U.S. Education Secretary, William J. Bennet, 1987, quoted in Finn, 1991)

Having been through the process of education, high school graduates are "marketed" as a bundle of skills. If they do not have those skills or fall short of the expectations of the consumer, in this case, business, then they are defective and the manufacturer, in this case, the school, is accountable.

The "Back to Basics" Movement and Its Shortcomings

It would be a mistake, however, to assume that the accountability movement that swept the United States, and to a lesser degree, Canada, in the late 1980s occurred simply because the business world was displeased with the level of education attained by graduates of North American schools. In fact, the cry for accountability, often heard as the "Back to Basics" slogan, was heard on many fronts. In an unprecedented ruling, the Kentucky Supreme Court in 1989 declared the *entire* public school system of that state unconstitutional. The case on which they were ruling was not brought by business interests nor by parents but by 66 mostly rural Kentucky schools whose intent "was to secure equitable and adequate funding for public schools" (Foster, 1991, p. 34). The Court, however, extended their ruling beyond the fiscal matter and ruled that the entire state school system was both deficient and unconstitutional. The effect of the ruling was to make schools accountable for the failure of *any* student. This is a radical departure from traditional definitions of the constitutional right to education. As Jack Foster, Secretary of the Education and Humanities Cabinet for the State of Kentucky, writes:

> Historically *all* children were not expected to master the entire curriculum. Universal education meant universal opportunity, not universal achieve-

ment. Schools were expected to sift and sort out the unmotivated and poor performing students in favor of those with some promise of academic excellence. . . . Kentucky now intends to hold its schools accountable for the failure of all students to learn. (Foster, 1991, pp. 34–35)

To do so, the state had to specify both the skills or subject matter (what needs to be mastered?) and the standard (how good is good enough?). But haven't schools been doing both these things for years? Aren't standardized achievement tests intended to provide educators with an indication of how children in their schools measure up against national norms, that is, all other children writing the tests? That may have been the intent; it has not been the fact. There are two basic reasons.

The first lies in the nature of standardized tests. They are, by definition, norm-referenced. In other words, they measure an individual student's performance in comparison to others at their age or grade level. Under certain conditions, the standardized test might be useful to educators in finding and correcting educational deficiencies. If, for example, children in a certain school consistently score significantly higher than the norm, the school might conclude that it is doing much that is right and pat itself on the back. But to do so makes important assumptions about the test that may not be borne out in fact. When test writers are constructing an achievement test, they seek advice from curriculum experts to establish what students at a particular age or grade level should know about a particular subject. They then construct test items and try them out on various groups of students. Those items that almost all students get correct or almost all get wrong are dropped from the test. Others are dropped as well, including those which are confusing or those on which high-scoring students do no better than low-scoring students. Eventually, the test writers settle on a test that gives results consistent with what they have come to expect in large populations of children—that is, something approaching a bell-shaped curve.

Now, consider what this means if a particular test is developed and given to several million children in a country whose educational system is in crisis. Knowing where a child (or a class or a school) stands in relation to his or her peers on this test is not terribly revealing. In other words, if *all* children or most children are being poorly educated, then the standardized test will not do a great deal to reveal the deficiencies and nothing to correct them. In short, there is no *ideal* against which education is measured; it cannot hope to evaluate itself meaningfully much less to improve.

The second reason is closely related to the first, and that is in what gets measured. Because they are to be objectively scored, questions on standardized tests tend to be those with clearly correct answers—facts. Such tests do not readily lend themselves to the more thought-provoking, open-ended questions, the answers to which might reveal evidence of quality thinking or intellectual reasoning. The educational system that could be accurately judged by standardized tests would be one that concentrated on the teaching of facts and formulas and not on the thinking and reasoning skills that might be of broader use in children's futures. As Wiggins summarizes the problem:

> Here we see where American education has gone so wrong: we have uniformity in testing, but no exemplars; we have standardization of *input*—the items on the test—but no standards for judging the quality of all student *output*—performance on authentic tasks. We have cutoff scores, but no way of ensuring that scores correspond to qualitative distinctions in real-world performance—authentic standards. By over-relying on these audits of performance, our students are just as the Resnicks[3] declared: the most tested but the least examined in the world. (Wiggins, 1991, p. 19)

Surely there is no one who would argue *against* standards in education, no one who believes that the schools should not be accountable to some degree for educational outcomes—but the accountability path may be a perilous one. One of the perils is in determining the standards against which schools are to be measured and another is the degree to which schools can be reasonably held responsible for children's learning when so many of the factors affecting it lie outside their control.

An Example

Suppose a state or province requires that each school demonstrate a steady increase in the number of students who achieve the expected score or "standard" on a particular test. Assume that somehow the governing body has also managed to specify just what students should know and be able to do at various stages in their schooling and to devise appropriate ways to assess their performances. So far, so good. Few would argue against schools knowing what they hope to achieve and having definite plans about how to do so. But given the fact that so much of what influences learning is outside the control of the school and the additional requirement that an increasing percentage of students in every school achieve those outcomes until all children achieve them, is it a feasible expectation? On the surface, yes. Minimal standards are set that are mea-

[3]See Resnick and Resnick (1985).

sured by independent means. Each year, after the results are in, schools then go about revising their curricula, teaching methods, or materials to improve their performance for the next year. But let's think for a moment about what might happen in practice. Suppose you are the principal of a school in an area that has a great many socially and economically disadvantaged children, where the literacy rate of families is low, and where many speak a language other than English. The first year of testing reveals that 50% of the pupils in your school achieve a less than acceptable score on at least one component of the Standards Test. You meet with the teachers, review the curriculum, make a few adjustments, and make sure that they understand that they and the children must do better in the next year. After the second year, the test scores remain unchanged. You review the test results closely and meet with your teachers. They are depressed by the test scores, but assure you that they are doing the best that they can. One of the problems, they say, is that the test makes no allowances for the non-English-speaking children in the school. They are expected to perform at the same standard as the native speakers and their scores are pulling down the school's average. They also say that many of the children are slow to learn to read because they come from homes where there is little or no reading done. What can they do about that?

What do you say? You may be tempted to send the ESL learners to other schools to keep them from "diluting" the results of the school. But this is neither a feasible nor humane solution. Your resources are already strained; you can't afford to hire another teacher. So you rearrange your resources. Perhaps you reduce the librarian's position to half-time or replace him entirely with a number of volunteers or teachers' assistants. You and the teachers in the school know this is bad for *all* the children, but it is unlikely to have an immediate negative impact on the test scores. Then you have to decide where the ESL teacher's skills might best be used. At first, it is tempting to have her work with all the ESL learners, but there are 150 of them in your school, and you know that she can't possibly meet all their needs. How do you decide what is the optimal use of her time? Recalling that the test results led you to take this course of action in the first place, you will very likely place her where she will have a measurable short-term effect. In our hypothetical case (as in Kentucky, incidentally), the "benchmark" grades are three, five, eight, and twelve. Your school has grades one through six, so you decide that the ESL teacher will work with learners in grades three and five, hoping that by next year you can find the resources to provide ESL for children in grade four as well. For the moment, you will simply have to ignore the needs of children in other grades beyond the help you were already providing before the latest set of poor test marks.

But what can you do about the children who seem so unprepared for literacy? If you have the resources, you might propose a project similar to the Missouri intervention study described earlier, but you know that it takes a few years for such programs to show results and you and your teachers are under the gun *now*—not that you have the resources anyway. You recognize that class sizes are too large in kindergarten and grade one and know that smaller class sizes in both years might improve children's chances of learning to read and write well. But you have no money to hire another teacher so you look again at reorganizing the resources you do have. This time, the half-time music teacher will have to go to make room for a half-time kindergarten teacher, and although this is an unfortunate loss, the Standards Test does not cover music concepts or performance. Perhaps the art specialist or the physical education teacher will have to go to make room for another grade one teacher. These are difficult decisions to make, but the school must improve its test scores.

At the end of the third year of testing, a slight improvement is noticeable. This time 55% of the students achieve an acceptable score. Is this a significant enough improvement for you to continue the practices you've already established? You might think so, but the Board of Education does not. They are making you accountable for the school's results and demand that you present a plan of action for raising the school's pass rate by 10% in each of the next four years. Of course, they don't give you any more money, so you have to go back to the teachers. But the teachers rebel. They are doing their very best, they say, and can't be held further responsible for the results on what they claim is a poor test anyway. Several of them quit and leave the profession entirely. Those who stay may well reach another decision at this point. If you want test results, they say, then you have to teach for them. The skills demanded to pass the test will become the curriculum. If this sounds far-fetched, consider the words of Jack Foster, Kentucky's Secretary of Education:

> So long as test results are publicly scrutinized and school 'quality' is measured by them, teachers will teach what these tests expect students to know and be able to do. In the new Kentucky system, we hope instruction will be consciously influenced by the assessment process. . . . In effect, the assessment tasks *become* the new curriculum, so they must be as rich and complex as the learning outcomes they purport to document. (Foster, 1991, p. 36)

Educators may be rightly skeptical about how "rich and complex" any curriculum will be that is based on the assessment process mandated by government, even government advised, as was the case in Kentucky, by a council made up of a broad cross section of the public. Teaching to the test is a route fraught with danger and very likely unsound, but it is almost unavoidable given the kinds of tests that North American students normally write. The kind of "knowledge" that is best judged by such tests is factual, but education, of course, consists of more than a compendium of facts. And standards in education must mean more than providing those facts and strategies for acquiring them. As Wiggins observes:

> High standards are only to be found in completed tasks, products, and performances that *require* such intellectual virtues as craftsmanship, self-criticism, and persistence; when complex tasks are done consistently well, we easily and validly infer that the worker has high standards. By requiring only a circling of an already formed answer to a simplistic question, our tests cannot reveal anything about student intellectual virtues or vices. And worse, such tests may be abetting the very vices we deplore: students learn to quickly go through each test item without lingering too long on any one, and they learn that being right matters a great deal more than whether one can justify a result. (Wiggins, 1991, p. 21)

If we apply Wiggins' reasoning to language teaching and learning, we can see easily the dangers of teaching to the test when the test is the *wrong* kind of test. A number of commonly administered achievement tests require children to read a passage and answer a number of questions about it as a way of measuring their reading comprehension. Experts are very good at compiling questions that go beyond the simple identification of information printed in the passage. They ask "higher level" questions that require children to engage in higher level thinking, to make inferences about what they read, to recognize relationships among facts or to make judgments about matters that might not be overtly stated. But it is very hard in standardized tests to avoid questions with a single correct answer. The danger in teaching to these kinds of tests is that the tests are too simplistic, too limited in their scope. They do not require true intellectual activity and thus teaching to the test, under the assumption that we are teaching for standards, actually undermines those standards.

Working within currently used testing paradigms in the United States, these pitfalls are very hard to avoid. If we consider a reasonable goal of education to be that every child finishing grade twelve be able to read, understand, evaluate, and respond intelligently, orally, and in writing to an editorial in the *New York Times*, then it makes no sense to judge their ability to do so by administering a true-false or multiple choice test on a reading passage even if it happens to be taken from the editorial pages of the *New York Times*. What makes sense is to require students to complete the actual task on which they are to be judged—authentic tasks.

Those who are concerned about the accountability movement are not against improved education. On the contrary, few teachers want anything else. What is worrisome about accountability is the business and production framework in which it is being proposed, justified, and judged and the likelihood that the measures taken to make schools accountable will have an adverse effect on children and on teachers.

THE COMMUNITY OF EDUCATORS

Educators as members of the larger society might be expected to hold at least some of the same views about education. To some degree, they do, but a fundamental difference exists, and that difference lies in the forces that shape their thinking. For the most part, the public view of education is shaped by their memories of what education was "in the good old days," memories that are no doubt idealized, as well as by their perception of the changing needs of an industrialized society. Educators' views, in contrast, cannot help but be shaped by their experience and role as children's advocates. Because they are on the front lines, so to speak, educators are more likely to assign more importance to the abilities and needs of individual children and to understand first hand the direct impact of social change and family instability on children and their schooling.

Educators share many views with the public. Educators agree that standards are needed and, for the most part, that independent absolute exemplars or criteria will best ensure a quality education. Educators, however, worry that some children's needs will be overlooked in the standards race (the ESL children in our hypothetical case, for example), that the standards will be set and regulated by those without the professional qualifications to do so, and that the curriculum will lose its flexibility and the child-centeredness that some teachers have fought hard to attain.

The Accountability Movement and Whole Language

These concerns are paramount in language education. In Chapter 9, we looked at whole language and saw that for many reasons, mostly to do with its kinship with natural language learning, it is considered to be a sound approach to language arts. But is it compatible with the accountability movement? This is not a simple question to answer, although I will ultimately argue that the answer is yes. But first the obvious. Those who carry the standards banner highest, who proclaim accountability loudest, tend to blame whole language and other child-centered approaches for what they consider to be a crisis in education. They equate standards with *basics* and *basics* with reading, writing, and arithmetic taught by "traditional" methods such as phonics for reading, studying of rhetorical models for writing, and rote memorization for arithmetic. No wonder they see much wrong with current educational practice. If, however, as I argued earlier, setting a standard means setting an authentic, real-world criterion against which to judge the effectiveness of schooling, then these "basics" and "traditional" methods are incompatible. Whole language, on the other hand, is entirely compatible precisely because it emphasizes real language use over contrived language "activities." It is not sufficient for the standard to be authentic; the test must provide a valid indication of performance against that standard. Moreover, a long-term view must be taken. For example, if the decision is made that a reasonable standard for writing is that a child finishing grade eight should be able to produce a 250-word, polished expository piece that is competently constructed and essentially error-free, then it is also reasonable to expect that standard spelling be used. It is *not*, however, necessarily reasonable to expect that the task be completed in one hour because this is not an authentic task. Neither is it reasonable to expect that younger children will be able to produce error-free work. For a child in grade one or two, invented spelling is a natural and desirable stage in learning to write, and the child should not be penalized for using it, but for a grade eight student, standard spelling would be expected. This may sound as though it is necessary to have a shifting standard—different criteria for younger children than for older. In fact, this is not exactly the case. As Wiggins rightly observes,

> It makes no sense . . . to talk of different standards and expectations for different groups of students. A standard offers an objective ideal, serving as a worthy and tangible goal for everyone—even if, at this point in time, for whatever reason, some cannot (yet!) reach it. Watch kids play basketball, Nintendo, or the keyboard. They are making measurable progress toward meeting the high standard set by the best performers before them. (Wiggins, 1991, pp. 19–20)

The goal, then, is the same, but the expectation for younger students is less. Wiggins goes on to point out that the British have developed precisely such a system for their national assessment which has student work

> . . . judged on a 10-point scale built from a standard of exit level excellence and used *over the course of the student's career.* Thus, elementary students are expected to produce good work (in the sense of norms for one's age-group), but the best work would likely receive a 3 or 4 out of 10. (Wiggins, 1991, p. 20)

He also points out that there is no stigma attached to receiving low scores because "the point is to give students a realistic sense of where they are in terms of where they ultimately need to be." Some school districts in the United States have already adopted similar schemes. Wiggins cites one in Ohio in which teachers score all language "work across the K-3 grades using the same rubrics and locally devised reading tests that use real books deemed worthy by the faculties of those schools" (Wiggins, 1991, p. 20). Whole language, then, is clearly not in conflict with standards or the assessment of standards as long as both reflect real learning through the use of real materials.

In using the whole language examples in the preceding paragraphs, I have perhaps given the impression that educators agree that whole language is the best approach to language education. They do not. One of the most compelling arguments made against whole language is not against whole language *per se* but against the exclusivity of it. In early 1990, *The Reading Teacher* published two articles relating a discussion on literacy education held by five "renowned educators," including Ira Aaron, Jeanne Chall, Dolores Durkin, Kenneth Goodman, and Dorothy Strickland. In the course of their discussion, the issue of whole language came up a number of times. Dorothy Strickland made the point that there is a kind of exclusionary attitude about it, that one of the problems with whole language is that ". . . there are people who feel that they are the pure whole language people and others are not." She went on to argue for a kind of principled eclecticism, stating that within whole language there are not necessarily "prescribed ways of doing things" when in fact there are a great many options (Aaron et al., 1990, p. 310).

The Nature of Change

The need to view whole language, or indeed any other approach, in this way may result from the tendency among educators to think about and promote change as replacement rather than improvement. Walter MacGinitie claims that educators "never seem to try to improve education; we are forever revolutionizing it" (1991, p. 56). The point he is making is that by focusing on what is new rather than on improving what works, educators run the risk of throwing away established procedures that work simply because they may be superficially at odds with the new doctrine. This happens when new methods or approaches are carried to extremes:

> A recent and familiar example of the extremes to which most educational fads are carried can be seen in the way we broke down reading into innumerable skills. We all know of classrooms where most of the children are quite capable of doing independent reading but where there is little time for it. The children are fully occupied, instead, with a mandatory and seemingly interminable series of exercises and skills tests. (MacGinitie, 1991, p. 56)

Whole language, MacGinitie argues, is susceptible to the same extremism and thus carries a similar educational risk. He writes of the danger: "because whole language is entering the scene in the guise of a replacement, many will interpret whole language as a total rejection of phonics, and the progression of fads will continue" (1991, p. 58). In other words, the total rejection of phonics will eventually cause a reaction that will lead educators again to overemphasize skills instruction.

What MacGinitie is advocating is essentially principled eclecticism, or using what works even if it happens to seem to be incompatible with a currently accepted approach. As reasonable as this may sound, not all educators agree. Kenneth Goodman, in a panel discussion on literacy sponsored by the International Reading Association, warned against eclecticism:

> I want to say a few bad words about eclecticism, because it's comfortable to say teachers should listen to everything and then pick and choose. It's comfortable to say that if there appear to be polar positions, then the truth must lie some place safely in the middle. The middle of the road is a very thin, white line, and it's a dangerous place to try to stand. (Aaron et al., 1990a, p. 310)

That may be, but extremism is equally dangerous. A cursory review of trends in language education in this century allows us to see that educators are prone to extremism. A good example is the *open classroom,* which

> was introduced, widely misinterpreted, and carried to extremes that destroyed both the movement and the values it contained. Many of the schools without walls became schools without substance. Earlier, the curriculum for educating the whole child drifted to extremes that frustrated parents' wishes that their children's education include a core of traditional subjects. (MacGinitie, 1991, p. 56)

We can all think of several others. In ESL, for instance, several come to mind including the Silent Way, Suggestopedia, and the Natural Approach among others. Each was seen as a cure for all the "ills" of the previous method and each was doomed to fail. Why is education prone to such extremism? Is it simply that, frustrated by poor results, teachers choose revolution over smaller changes that might work for some children if applied with persistence? MacGinitie argues that this may be the case: "Revolution—political or educational—may seem necessary when conditions have become insufferably bad." He goes on to observe that "It is undoubtedly more stimulating to participate in a revolution than to do one's job better" (1991, p. 56). But there is another reason. The community of educators consists not just of teachers but of a great many other "educationists" who have a stake in and influence on teaching. Among these are the so-called "experts" who advise or educate teachers and administrators. They write the textbooks, speak at professional gatherings, and teach university or college courses on "how to teach." MacGinitie credits this last group with causing much of the educational extremism, blaming the university system that forces "professors to make a name for themselves by promoting something 'new.'" Their attaining tenure, promotion through the ranks, and status in the academic community "depend on having articles published and on getting grant money. The chance of being published is greatly increased if you write about the latest trend" (MacGinitie, 1991, p. 56).

MacGinitie argues that professors' careers depend to a large extent on the ability to create status for themselves, "to sell a 'new and better' product in order to succeed . . . or at least survive." If their field is education, the product will be a method or approach for teaching. Not all professors are capable of creating a new method, of course, or one that will gain acceptance. Sometimes they have to settle for extending someone else's new idea beyond its original constituency. A good example of this practice is for professors working in second languages to borrow ideas from first language teaching for application in second language teaching. "Whole language in the ESL class" was a predictable topic for articles shortly after whole language began to make inroads into mainstream education.

Of course, the new and better method or approach may not immediately influence teaching in the schools. There may be

> a time lag while the professor indoctrinates a sufficient number of doctoral students to constitute a critical mass of new professors committed to the new method and while the extremes of the current curriculum become sufficiently oppressive to make the field ripe for change. Then the new method, promoted by these new professors, sweeps in and prospers for awhile. (MacGinitie, 1991, p. 56)

The curriculum will grow and develop as each new professor adds details until "the new method in its turns becomes the 'saber-toothed curriculum,' ripe for ridicule and replacement by a *new* new approach" (MacGinitie, 1991, p. 56).

Publishers are there to jump on the bandwagon of the new method, although they can scarcely be blamed for introducing new methods, since it is very risky to introduce anything too new or different to the mass educational market. Once they see that a new idea is gaining acceptance, publishers are quick to adopt it, adding "all the bells and whistles they can sell" (MacGinitie, 1991, p. 57). Like professors, they also try to extend their profits by extending an idea beyond the original market for which it was intended—up or down the grade levels, or from first to second language classes, for example.

Different Perspectives on Whole Language

The debate among language teachers is not only about whether or not to adopt whole language. Among those who profess to believe in whole language, there is a great deal of variability in what they believe, in how they actually teach, and in the class activities in which their pupils engage.

In her forward to *Portraits of Whole Language Classrooms* (Mills & Clyde, 1990), Virginia Woodward acknowledges the misconceptions that surround whole language pedagogy. She quotes the observations of a number of educators to illustrate that the approach is widely interpreted. Four of the remarks made by different educators reveal the spectrum of conceptions about whole language and suggest, as well, the breadth of practice they mandate. The four are:

1. I do whole language; I use Big Books.

2. It seems like whole language is just glorified language experience.

3. We do whole language activities on Fridays.

4. Whole language is what good teachers do naturally. (Mills & Clyde, 1990, p. ix)

Closer examination of these observations, which are selected but not unrepresentative of those held by a great many educators, say much about the assortment of practices that take place in the name of whole language.

I Do Whole Language; I Use Big Books.   Using Big Books is certainly consistent with whole language. They allow what Judith Newman refers to as "shared reading . . ., an important component of a whole language curriculum." She continues:

> The enlarged books allow the teacher to create an intimate atmosphere with a number of children at once. The large book sets a stage for involvement with both the story and the print since the children are all able to see what's on the page as they listen to and watch the teacher read along. It is through such shared reading that children begin to understand how print and meaning are related. (Newman, 1985b, pp. 62–63)

But does using Big Books mean that a teacher is using a whole language curriculum? Or, is it necessary to use Big Books in a whole language curriculum? The answer to both is no. Big Books could be used within a skills-based curriculum that fragmented language into modes (listening, speaking, reading, and writing) and modes into discrete skill areas (writing into printing, handwriting, spelling, sentence construction, paragraph construction, etc.). On the other hand, a whole language approach is quite possible, even with young pupils, without using Big Books. Teachers without the budgets to buy a great many Big Books have managed very well using a number of alternatives. Moreover, whole language is implemented in the higher elementary grades where Big Books would not be appropriate. The important thing is *the shared experience of reading*, which can be accomplished in a number of ways.

It Seems Like Whole Language Is Just Glorified Language Experience.
Again we have a practice that is consonant with a whole language curriculum but does not define it. Language experience may be incorporated into a whole language curriculum because

> Language, whether oral or written, is learned through active 'play' with language, through experimenting with different ways to express ideas, and exploring relationships between the children's language and their knowledge. Language experience stories evolve from the children's interests and activities. . . . Language experience stories are an excellent tool for helping children make sense of written language because they emphasize the importance of the connection between a reader's experiences and written language. (Newman, 1985b, p. 62)

Although it might be argued that language experience is one of the cornerstones of whole language, there is a great deal more to it than language experience. Moreover, language experience activities can be used in ways that are fundamentally incompatible with whole language. For example, I once visited a grade one classroom in which the teacher used language experience, in her words, "to teach reading," and allotted it a set period of time. But once reading instruction time was over, the children turned to their "language" activities, an unrelated lesson on antonyms. Nor did this teacher use Big Books, sustained silent reading, or any of the other practices commonly associated with a whole language curriculum.

We Do Whole Language Activities on Fridays.   We can only wonder what happens the rest of the week. Clearly, this teacher has no understanding of what whole language is and why it works. Perhaps it is better for a teacher to "practice" whole language one day a week than not at all, but it is a little like following a 1000-calorie diet on Monday and eating indiscriminately the rest of the week. Children may enjoy the Friday activities more, and they probably won't do any harm. Neither will they contribute much to their beliefs about and progress in language learning.

Whole Language Is What Good Teachers Do Naturally.   This statement is my favorite, partly because I wish it were true; unfortunately, that is not quite what the educator who made this comment meant. What I wish were true is that all teachers, having given a great deal of time to reading and thinking about language acquisition, would come to realize that language teaching and language learning could and should have much in common, and that they should plan their curricula accordingly. What the person who made the comment implied was that whole language is just common sense, that whatever an effective teacher does is by definition whole language. It would be impossible to identify all the traits that make some people good teachers, but even if we could, we could not make the claim that whatever they did constituted whole language. Doubtless, there are effective teachers who use other methods, and these other methods work because the teachers are so committed and dedicated to the method and to the children they teach. It is also true that what many teachers "do naturally" has more to do with the way they were taught than what they truly believe about children's language learning.

These four observations have served to crystallize the divergence in how educators think about whole language. Collectively, the four remarks indicate misunderstanding about what whole language is. Even among teachers who *do* understand it, however, there are vast differences in the classrooms they inhabit. The description of the diversity is beyond the scope of this book,[4] although we saw in the last chapter brief sketches of whole language in practice and will get glimpses into the approach again in Chapter 11.

[4]For descriptions of whole language in action, see Mills and Clyde (1990) and Froese (1990).

Whole language is not the only teaching practice on which educators fail to agree; it is simply the current one and the one that has received the greatest amount of attention in recent years. It is discussed here because it is also the approach to language curriculum that is most consistent with our best understanding of how language acquisition occurs and the most enlightened theories of language. Since a teaching approach should be informed by both a theory of language and a theory of language learning (Richards and Rodgers, 1986), then whole language merits special consideration in any book on language acquisition that encompasses the school years.

CONCLUSION

We have seen that education is not the province of teachers alone. They work in conjunction with, in response to, and within the confines of a number of different communities. The community of parents, if they choose to do so, may have a direct influence on educational practice at the school or classroom level. Even if they do not choose to become actively involved in schooling, their views and their participation are important because they are the first and most enduring of their children's teachers. Their educational views are influenced by a number of factors, among them their recall of their own educational experience and their perceptions of what is needed educationally in modern society.

The larger community—the public that participates in opinion polls and elections—perhaps exerts the most visible influence on education. They tend to be responsive to the needs of the economy—business and industry—and are largely responsible for the call to standards or accountability movement that swept North America in the 1980s. What has become increasingly clear is that because they influence the politicians who control school funding, they will have to be taken seriously. If their "solutions" are not the ones favored by educators, and if teachers want to avoid having solutions imposed on them, then educators, who themselves hold diverse views and who are sometimes prone to extremism, will have to be prepared to offer viable alternatives. To do so, every teacher will have to have a clear understanding of what outcomes are desirable and devise flexible plans for achieving them.

With regard to language education, this means that the profession will have to reach a consensus on what constitutes an acceptable standard of literacy for a high school graduate and how to measure it. They will also have to make difficult decisions about what functions of the oral language are important to children's lives as well as the role the school will play in helping to achieve them. They will have to plan curricula that are consistent with their best knowledge about language acquisition and that will simultaneously allow children to work toward the standards that have been set, and will allow all children to work toward a common standard without sacrificing the possibility that now exists in child-centered curricula for meeting the individual needs of each child. The challenge is a colossal one, but as we shall see in the next two chapters, it is one that schools and teachers have begun to make.

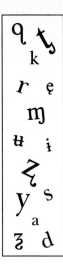

Chapter Eleven

Reconciliation

In earlier chapters we explored the nature of language acquisition in early childhood and throughout the school years in both monolingual and bilingual children. We looked at the differences between children's experiences of language learning in the home and in the school. Our purpose in doing so was not to propose or defend a particular teaching method but to try to gain insights that will help teachers to reach rational and effective decisions about children's language education. In Chapter 10, we discovered that teachers must take into account not only the facts of language acquisition and children's experiences in and out of school, but also the views of certain communities outside the school that have a stake in education in general and language education in particular.

NINE PRINCIPLES FOR RECONCILING DIVERSE VIEWS

At this point, it might seem that the task of the teacher simply cannot be done. There are just too many masters to please—the researchers and theorists who tell us how language is learned (even though they seem rarely to agree among themselves), the parents of the children in school who may have their own ideas about their children's learning, the larger community, which consists of a variety of interest groups, including those of business and industry, and other educators who influence teachers' attitudes about language teaching as well as what goes on in the classroom. Indeed, the job is a monumentally difficult one and one to which few people are well suited. But it can be done. The purpose of this chapter is to extract and synthesize from the previous chapters not a teaching method nor even a formula for finding one, for these are things that all teachers must do for themselves, but a set of principles that is intended to assist teachers in reconciling the disparate views as they attempt to please the different masters.

There are nine of these principles, as shown in Table 11.1. The first six address the issue of reconciling theory and practice, specifically what we know about language acquisition in the home and school and how that should inform our teaching. The second three are concerned with how to deal with the divergent views of the other communities who are stakeholders in language education policy.

About Language Acquisition

Principle 1: There Are Many Right Ways to Teach.   We saw in Chapters 3 and 5 that a number of competing theories exist about how children acquire language, and that no one theory accounts for all the available data nor answers all the questions that parents, researchers, or teachers might ask. Fortunately, we do not have to construct a theory of language learning so the fact that these disparate theories cannot be readily coalesced into a single theory of language learning need not concern us greatly. As teachers, we are more concerned with the facts of language development and how these inform our teaching practice. Since there is no single theory that accounts for all the facts of language acquisition, it is not surprising that there is no single theory of language teaching and that many different ways work.

Table 11.1
Nine principles for reconciling diverse views about language education

1. There are many right ways to teach.
2. Know why you do what you do.
3. Remember that language learning is a whole-to-part enterprise.
4. But don't forget the parts.
5. A second language is an asset some children bring to school.
6. Make sure that the method of evaluation corresponds to what happens in the classroom.
7. Involve parents and the community.
8. Don't be dogmatic.
9. Be professional.

Consistent with our best knowledge about language acquisition, there are a number of ways of planning for children's language development in the school years. Because no single method of teaching *anything* is right for *every* child, it is something of a truism to say that there is no single best way. But let's go further than that. The facts of language acquisition do not dictate any single method; they perhaps prohibit a few—rote learning of vocabulary items out of context, for example—but they permit a wide variety of practice. The important thing is to remember to incorporate the information about language acquisition into all language activities for children. That information includes the five attributes of language set forth in Chapter 1: Language is linked to cognition; language is natural; language is culturally bound; language has structure, and language has many varieties. It also includes the following attributes about language learning that were discussed in later chapters.

Children learn and use language in a social setting. They are most successful in both if they are full participants, that is, if parents and teachers talk *with* rather than *to* them and join with them in reading and writing activities. In Janet, Quy, Lucy, and Michael we saw children learning language in very different circumstances. What was common to all, however, was the fact that they learned language within a setting of real use and with the encouragement of parents and teachers.

Children need to be "taught" very little about language. None of the four children was "taught" English, yet all learned it. What they needed and had was opportunity and the environment in which to learn. This is not to say that the teacher does not play an important role, but only that the role may be more usefully "seen as 'leading from behind' by supporting the language learning capabilities of students indirectly through the activities we offer them" (Newman, 1985a, p. 5). This may be a difficult part for some teachers to play, accustomed as they are to "dispensing" information to children. Certainly the role is a very demanding one, but the demands are "offstage," so to speak, for instance, when the teacher takes the time to get to know as much as she can about all the children in her class by observing them carefully and by meeting with or writing to parents, or when she sits down at the end of the day to make journal entries, recording the insights she or the children may have had into the learning process or notes about one child's progress and another's frustrations. In short, when that teacher takes the time to consider the needs and to plan for each individual child, "teaching" happens in a manner that may not be readily apparent to a casual visitor to the classroom but is extremely important to the pupils' success.

Second language acquisition in children bears a strong resemblance to first language acquisition, and the younger the child, the stronger the resemblance. The story of Lucy's language learning provides authoritative testimony to the truth of this claim. The implication for teachers is that with some adaptation of materials and plans and with some extra time given, teachers can use many of the same methods for teaching ESL learners as native English speakers. This is not to say that the ESL learner should be ignored but only that teachers who base their teaching on children's language needs and on good information about first *and* second language acquisition will usually be effective. While it is always important to consider the needs of individual children, it is not necessary to start from scratch with ESL learners. There are a great many techniques and activities that work well for both native and non-native speakers. This is especially true of kindergarten through grade three.

In planning for the ESL children in their classes, teachers should remember that these children bring an abundance of cultural and linguistic experiences to the task of language learning. They also bring curiosity and the need to learn English they can use immediately. It is necessary but not sufficient to surround ESL children with all kinds of oral and printed language; that language has to be comprehensible. Teachers who remember to use all the resources at their command to get meaning across—other children, pictures, photographs, pantomime, whatever it takes—will give ESL children the kind of input they need to begin to make sense of the new language.

It is especially important to involve ESL learners as early as possible in the same activities being done by the other children in the class. For example, when the others are writing in journals, ESL children can dictate their journal entries using whatever English they have or using the opportunity to learn new words from the teacher to express their meanings, or by drawing or even writing in their native language (a parent or older child can usually help you to translate). Whatever the language activity the class is engaged in, that activity can usually be adapted so that ESL children can take part as well.

Children don't need to practice language; they need to use it. We should remember that in acquiring their first language, children do not need an extended rehearsal period before they are permitted to speak in public. Rather, they get on with the business of communicating from the very beginning. A child's desire to communicate and to participate in the immediate society motivates them to learn language. This single fact should remind us of a great many things we should *not* do in school while simultaneously reminding us of a great many worthwhile activities—reading quality books and engaging in real discussion about them and writing for a real audience, for example.

Even ESL learners need to communicate in their new language from the very beginning. The teachers' task is not to oversee or direct their practice until they are ready to use the language but to find ways in which they *can* communicate successfully from the first day they arrive in class. To do so, children must understand that their language need not be "perfect," which means that teachers should keep in mind two corollaries to this axiom.

First, teachers should be more concerned with fluency than with accuracy. In other words, they should expose second language learners to and encourage them to use as much language as possible with little regard for correctness. Children will work out the "rules" in their own way in their own time, asking for help or otherwise indicating that they are ready to be taught the standard forms. Early or overemphasis on form will send the message to children that how they say something is more important than what they say, and this is not a message that is consonant with an environment conducive to language learning.

Second, language learning, indeed *all learning,* involves risk. In language learning, writing provides a good example. Even proficient writers cannot grow in their craft if they stay within comfortable modes. Journalists need to try short stories, novels, and poems in order to expand their skills and their understanding of their art. Short story writers need to experiment with drama, poetry, and magazine articles. I remember an incident that occurred when I was a student of Donald Murray's at the University of New Hampshire. For several weeks, I had been writing competent expository pieces on a variety of "safe" topics. Even though he had repeatedly encouraged me to try something a little different, I stayed with a formula I knew to be successful because it had worked with countless English teachers before. Finally, in one of our weekly conferences, he wadded up my most recent effort and threw it at me. "You've demonstrated that you can write competent prose. But you're never going to get any better unless you take some risks. I don't like to tell anyone what to write about, but if you can't write something a little riskier next week, don't bother writing anything at all." I took his advice and it was from that point on that I truly began to learn about writing.

It is neither necessary nor desirable to create a risk-free environment. What is important is to permit learners to take chances in order to optimize their learning. It is essential to create conditions that say to children that it is all right to take chances and to make mistakes, that it is more important for everyone, including the teacher, to try than to be "correct."

Principle 2: Know Why You Do What You Do.   One of the major purposes of this book has been to provide teachers a basis on which to make informed decisions about their language teaching practice. We examined in earlier chapters a number of competing theories of language acquisition and concluded that no one is suffient for accounting for the available data on children's language learning. Each theory has its strengths, and clearly there is something that educators can learn from each one. If we learn nothing else from behaviorism, for example, we learn that the environment is very important to language acquisition, that children cannot learn language without being exposed to it. From the nativists, we learn that there is something unique about language learning, that it enjoys special status in human learning. From the cognitivists, we can take the highly significant notion that language learning involves children's active participation. It does not just seep into their heads; children do not learn by "watching" or "listening"; they have to "do" language. From the social interactionists, we draw the conclusion that language acquisition is influenced by a number of factors—physical, linguistic, and socioenvironmental. We may also conclude that because these factors differ among children, the interaction among them may produce different effects in different children. In other words, certain differences exist among children in how they acquire language, in what they acquire, and when. These insights from theory provide some help, but applying the principle articulated here means finding a specific answer each time we ask ourselves why we make a particular curricular decision or choose a language activity.

Admittedly, there may be instances when "because it works" is an acceptable answer to the question of why a teacher does a particular activity. But this answer should only be given after careful reflection about whether the method or activity really works and why. In her introduction to her fine book on whole language, Judith Newman asserts that ". . . the clearer we are concerning our beliefs about language and learning, the sharper our focus on what is happening in front of our eyes." She goes on to articulate the questions that she and the other continually asked themselves as they prepared the book:

1. What do I believe about language and language learning?
2. What do I want this activity to demonstrate about reading, writing, and learning?
3. Why is this a useful activity for some particular student or group of students? (Newman, 1985a, p. 5)

These are questions that teachers should regularly ask themselves as they plan for the children in their classes and as they assess themselves at the end of a day or a week. It is especially important for teachers to have a clear understanding about language acquisition against which to measure their practice. They must also have well-defined ideas about language learning because otherwise it is impossible to evaluate their effectiveness as teachers. As Meredith Hutchings observed about writing in her classroom:

> Only after I have identified my own beliefs about the writing process can I begin to answer the questions: What am I actually demonstrating about the writing process to my learners? (Hutchings, 1986, p. 43)

Having examined and specified their beliefs, if teachers then find that they are habitually planning activities that are incompatible with their beliefs about language and language learning, then they should seriously reconsider their entire approach to teaching. If they cannot state their expectations or objectives or if these are frequently inconsistent with their beliefs about language learning, then they probably should abandon the activity. And surely it goes without saying that if they find that they cannot specify how an activity benefits at least some if not all the children who participate in it, then they should replace that activity with one with demonstrated relevance.

What this principle advocates, in basic terms, is practice informed by research and theory. Those whose teaching is guided by a solid grounding in language acquisition and who regularly ask themselves the three evaluative questions above may make mistakes—for who indeed does not—but they will make fewer. They will also be better able to correct the mistakes they do make, to learn from them and to avoid them as they proceed along the course of learning with the children in their classes.

Principle 3: Remember that Language Learning Is a Whole-to-Part Enterprise.   This principle might have been included within the discussion of the first principle above. But since it is rather more specific and is such a vitally important one, I gave it separate treatment here. It is crucial because its violation in the past has led to some of our worst failures in language education. It would be tempting to blame the linguists for these communal errors in judgment. After all, as we saw in Chapter 2, their analysis of language into its component parts has been crucial to our understanding its complex structure. But they did not dictate practice. It was educators who misapplied linguists' methods and their findings to language teaching. By breaking language down into its component parts and thereby rendering it meaningless, generations of teachers greatly complicated the business of language learning, particularly reading and writing, for countless children. By treating language as something separate from the child that could be "done" in assigned periods of time, the same teachers robbed it of its inherent appeal. By thinking about language analytically rather than synthetically or functionally, they reduced it to a series of exercises in manipulation, memorization, or worse, and many thousands of school children developed reading problems or failed to learn to write clearly. Their problems with literacy eventually resulted in the reactionary movement that has come to be known as the accountability or back to basics movement.

Real language is whole and should stay that way. That does not mean that teachers should never talk about parts of language, how to spell or how to pronounce a particular word, for example. It only means that these activities should take place within a larger language context. A simple example will clarify the distinction. Teacher X spends a half-hour in round-robin reading of a story in a basal reader. She follows that up with a writing exercise in which the children complete worksheets based on the reading. The worksheet has four columns headed by four words from the story. The children's task is to circle all the words in the column that begin with the same letter (or rhyme with or have the same vowel sound as) the word at the top. Because the words at the top also appeared in the story the children read, the worksheet phonics activity might appear to be contextualized within the larger activity of reading the story. But this is nominal context at best and the activity is artificial; the words were isolated from the story and studied for some reason other than the meaning they contribute or the effect they have or the children's reaction to them. In fact, it is hardly relevant at all that they came from the story. The four words do not provide a strong enough connection between the two activities to relate them. The two activities do not support each other in any way.

Teacher Y, on the other hand, takes the same amount of class time in a different way. She begins by initiating a discussion about a field trip she and the children have taken to a chicken hatchery. As they talk, she makes notes on a large flip chart, writing down some of their observations, words that aptly describe something about the trip, or their reactions to what they have seen. Together teacher and students decide that they want to write about the trip and they go off to their writing places to do so. Some children sit at their desks. Some stay near the flip chart in the carpeted reading area. Others prefer the long table at the back of the room. One boy is writing a lengthy entry in his journal. A girl is looking up information about the length of time it takes to hatch an egg in response to a question raised during the discussion. Another girl works on a story about the only red chick hatched in a nest of six, all the rest fuzzy yellow chicks. After she has been working for about twenty minutes, she tells her teacher she would like to read the story aloud. She begins, "Their was a mother chicken named Sandra who layd six big white eggs." Then she interrupts herself: "I know I spelled some words wrong, but I'll fix them later." And later she does. She asks her teacher: "Is that the right 'there'?" "Why do you ask?" responds Teacher Y. "Because I know there's another one like in 'They lost their mittens.' But I can't remember which." Teacher Y then spends a few minutes on *their, there,* and *they're,* offering one or two suggestions for keeping them straight. Before she finishes, three other children are standing nearby listening. One goes away and silently makes a correction; another beams in pride that he has it right in his story.

In this teacher's class, oral language, reading, and writing all support one another and are not fragmented in any way. The children read what they and others have written, and that writing is based on their earlier talk, which was based, in turn, on their mutual experience of visiting the chicken hatchery. All the morning's activities involve the authentic use of language and are related directly and naturally to the children's own experience, in this instance a field trip. There is even a time for the teaching of spelling, but notice that it originates in a question asked by one of the children—a genuine question and not a demonstration question. The teacher has merely taken advantage of a teachable moment, but in doing so has demonstrated the importance of the next principle.

Principle 4: But Don't Forget the Parts.   Attention to the wholeness of language and learning need not and should not mean that the parts are lost. In other words, children must learn the conventions of the language, and doing so may entail for some of them paying attention to discrete segments of the language. Spelling is one example; punctuation, mechanics, and certain aspects of grammar are others. By the time children reach the upper elementary grades, they should have mastery of these conventional aspects of language use. Evidence points to the achievement of this mastery in stages. Gunderson (1990) has pointed out, for example, that children go through stages of writing development that take them from the "pre-phonetic" through the "conventional or mature." Chow's (1986) study of children in whole language classes where children were encouraged to write daily in log books but were not instructed in the conventions of writing revealed five stages of development. In the first, the pre-phonetic stage, the children produced letters, numbers, and shapes resembling letters, apparently without understanding that there is a correspondence between the symbols and sounds or words. Next, in the semi-phonetic stage, they began to use letters symbolically, to stand for words or parts of words. Writers at the third stage of development, the phonetic stage, demonstrated their awareness that letters stand for sounds and that they know which letters stand for which sounds. Invented spellings were very common at this stage, but for the most part they are rule-governed inventions. That is, children used their knowledge of the relationship between letter and sound to create their own spellings. Many times, of course, these spellings will be the same as conventional spellings.

At the transitional stage, children began "to process words as visual units" (Gunderson, 1990, p. 129). Children at this stage typically continue to use invented spelling, but their writing will also contain conventional patterns as well as patterns that appear irregular. They might spell *through* "though," for instance, not because they do not hear the "r" sound or know how to write it but because they are now working from a visual memory of the word and that memory is sometimes faulty. The final stage of development identified by Chow found mature or conventional writers mostly in command of the conventions of writing. The mechanics of writing had become largely automatic, leaving these writers free to write longer and more complex pieces.

Many children will proceed through these stages, achieving mastery of the conventions without requiring any overt intervention at all; they will have learned them from their own reading and writing. Others will have asked the kinds of questions asked by the girl in Teacher Y's class and learned in that way. But some children need more help in passing from stage to stage. Teachers may need to search for or to foster actively those "teachable moments" during which such learning is possible.

Principle 5: A Second Language Is an Asset Some Children Bring to School.   Teachers all too commonly think about ESL children as having some kind of deficit or limitation on their ability to learn. Labels such as LEP (limited English proficiency) perpetuate this misconception. ESL children are deficient *only* if we persist in looking at what they do not have instead of what they do. What they *do* have is a well-established and fully functional first language on which to build a second language. When we think of children as missing something, our natural tendency is to provide it. In the case of ESL learners, what we want to provide is language. We may well be tempted to tell them about or to "teach" them language, and while this might not always be a bad idea, it can lead to some disastrous practices, especially with young children.

When we refuse to think of bilingual children as lacking something, however, and see them instead as having something very special when they come to school, then our response is not to try to correct or fill the deficit but to build on strength. We can do so with confidence. After all, we have seen in earlier chapters that the particular language the child learns at home is not as important to school success as the experience of having acquired a first language and the existence of literacy-related activities in the home. By seeing ESL children in this more positive light, it is easier to see that the same language-rich, language-integrated environment that helps native speakers to acquire literacy and to further their oral language learning will also help ESL students to add English to their home language.

Principle 6: Make Sure the Method of Evaluation Corresponds to What Happens in the Classroom.   Several years ago when I was doing a collaborative research project with a grade two teacher in Calgary, something occurred that underscored the importance of this principle. The teacher's class was what I considered at that time, and still consider for the most part, to be an ideal learning environment for grade two children. It was a whole language classroom, before the whole language concept had taken hold in Canada. Writing was a central component of her curriculum and there were no basal readers in the room. The children wrote every day and for much longer periods than the "experts" claimed children of this age were capable of. They liked to write and enjoyed sharing their writing with their teacher, with me on the days when I was there, and with all other visitors to their classroom. More than half the children in this class were ESL learners, and most of them beginners or near-beginners. Nevertheless, they participated fully in all activities of the class because the teacher made the adaptations that made their participation possible. In short, this teacher was doing a commendable job.

Just after Christmas, however, she experienced what she later called a "minor panic attack." She was reminded by one of the grade three teachers that the children would be taking a provincial examination in language in grade three. This test included a traditional spelling test. The grade two teacher began to worry that the children would not be able to pass such a test because she spent almost no time teaching spelling. When she talked her worry over with me, I pointed out that, in the first place, the pieces her children "published" had generally excellent spelling, and in the second, that the invented spellings they used showed them to be well aware of sound-symbol correspondence and, in some cases, to be in that transitional phase when their spelling shows that they are developing some awareness of what the word looks like in print. She wanted to believe I was right. She even *knew* I was right. Nonetheless, she worried.

Finally, after a few weeks, she decided to put her mind at rest by administering a standard spelling test. She selected the words by asking the grade three teacher about the words that had appeared on the previous year's examination and then deleting those she was sure the children wouldn't know and adding a few that she knew they had encountered. The results did nothing to abate her concern. The children did very poorly on the test, the only test they had taken that year. Many of the children expressed surprise at having to do such an activity; several expressed anxiety over the outcome. The teacher talked to me again. "I really wanted them to do well just to prove that my way is as good as the skills method. What's going to happen to them when they have to write the provincial test next year?" I asked her what she was going to do. "I just can't go back to that way. They're doing so well. You've seen their stories and you've seen how eager they are when they come to school every day."

"Yes," I replied. I *had* listened to them read their wonderful stories. I pulled one I had copied from my desk drawer and read it aloud to her. It was a Vietnamese child's account of her neighborhood and is reproduced in Figure 11.1.

"Do you want to give this up to teach spelling?"

"No, of course not, but will they be all right?"

We then talked for a long while about why the children did so poorly on the test and what she wanted to do about it. In this case, as she pointed out, the test was a completely alien experience. These children had never had a spelling test; they had, in fact, never had a formal spelling lesson. In giving them the test, she had asked them to do things with language that were unnatural and outside their experience of language inside or outside the classroom. It is small wonder that they did so poorly.

"What do the results mean?" I asked. After thinking for a few seconds, she replied that they only meant that the children were not very good at performing on this particular task. It said nothing about their development as spellers or even about how they would spell those words at this time *under normal circumstances*. The teacher shortly concluded that the results of the test were meaningless and should not influence her decision about how to proceed with the children who, by all reasonable standards, were progressing marvelously. She decided that if she had to, she could in a very short time teach them how to take such a test, but that she would neither change her curriculum nor, until that time, subject the children to further tests of this type. She decided to put her trust in the writing process approach and in her knowledge of language acquisition. She was right, of course, and the next year, after the grade three teacher had taken a little time to teach them how to take the test, the children performed well above the provincial average on all aspects of

Figure 11.1
Thuy's neighborhood

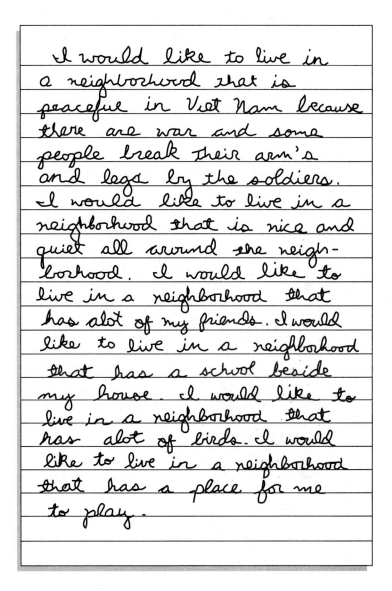

I would like to live in a neighborhood that is peaceful in Viet Nam because there are war and some people break their arm's and legs by the soldiers. I would like to live in a neighborhood that is nice and quiet all around the neighborhood. I would like to live in a neighborhood that has alot of my friends. I would like to live in a neighborhood that has a school beside my house. I would like to live in a neighborhood that has alot of birds. I would like to live in a neighborhood that has a place for me to play.

the language arts test. On the way to learning to write and loving to write, they had learned to spell as well.

The test in this example was a provincially mandated examination of the type that is coming back into vogue in many U.S. states and Canadian provinces. Some of these tests are constructed and scored in such a manner as to permit children to demonstrate their facility with language. Others are not; they consist of a series of unrelated questions requiring children to perform unnatural acts with language. If such tests cannot be avoided, then some time may have to be spent teaching children how to take the tests. What is more important is that the teacher work to convince the school and the public that results of such tests reveal very little either about what children have learned or how well they have been taught.

Unfortunately, teachers may have little control over government-decreed tests. But they do have control over the evaluation that occurs in their own classrooms and here it is especially important that the test match the task. As Serebrin observes of children's writing:

> We must not confuse the products of their efforts with the processes operating within particular contexts. This means that their efforts must not be evaluated by the yardstick of correct form—conventional spelling, punctuation, and sentence structure—but rather in terms of decision-making events within specific contexts. To see only their products would be to miss the significant 'language events'—language users bringing all they currently know to bear upon the task with which they are faced. (Serebrin, 1985, p. 53)

Evaluation is the part of the job that many teachers like least, yet most realize that it is a necessary part of the teaching and learning process. While a complete discussion of assessment in language education is beyond the scope of this chapter,[1] a few observations must be made not only about what is to be evaluated but by whom. Since language is social in nature and since most meaningful language activities in the classroom involve the learner and at least one other, and since we have accepted the principle that the test should reflect the task, it is also reasonable to involve the learner and possibly others in the task of evaluation. Children should be involved in making the decisions about how their learning will be evaluated, and peer evaluation may prove useful as well. Certainly, teachers should make sure that parents understand how their children's learning will be evaluated and why. They might also be invited to participate. But regardless of who is involved in the evaluation process, the paramount principle to remember is the one stated above: Children should not be evaluated in ways that are incompatible with the ways in which they have experienced learning.

About Diversity

The last three principles are intended to guide teachers as they attempt to reconcile the diverse views of parents, other educators, and the wider community in which they all live. But first a comment about why such a

---

[1]See Goodman, Goodman, and Hood (1989) for an excellent collection on evaluation within the whole language framework.

reconciliation is necessary. First, for obvious reasons it is desirable to create as much harmony as possible between children's homes and the school. If there is discord, then children are the ones who suffer. Most teachers realize, too, that their job is hard enough without having to deal with disgruntled parents. The second reason is that schools are funded by public money, and it is not in the interest of educators to have a large portion of the public dissatisfied with what they do. This is not to say that teachers should be governed by public opinion but only that they should take precautions, at the least, not to antagonize the public and, ideally, to involve them actively in education. This is our seventh principle.

Principle 7: Involve Parents and the Community.   The participation of parents in education is deemed so important today that Chapter 1 legislation in the United States requires that schools foster parental involvement activities. Involvement, under that legislation, means "helping parents understand the academic growth of their children" as well as getting them to participate in "actual reading and writing activities that support classroom learning" (Smith, 1991, p. 700). Parental participation is now deemed such a vital component of literacy education that the term *family literacy* no longer refers exclusively to the level of reading and writing attained by all family members, but to "families working together to promote mutual learning" (Nickse, 1989; cited in Smith, 1991, p. 700).

We saw in the last chapter that parents participate in their children's education to different degrees. It would be a mistake to assume, however, that those parents who are not active, that is, who do not come to meetings with teachers or PTA meetings or who do not respond to letters sent home, are disinterested in their children's welfare. A great many children are being brought up by single parents who must work, sometimes at more than one job, and shoulder the entire responsibility for their children's care. They may simply not have the time that other parents have to share actively in their children's school life.

Ideally, all parents would fall into the category Snyder calls "available parents." But since they do not, it is imperative that teachers find ingenious ways of enlisting their support if not their active participation. The benefits accrue to the teacher as well as to the children. Writing of the importance of involving parents in whole language programs, Snyder says,

> When parents accept a broadened view of literacy learning, they become increasingly involved in the educative process, as models, participants and audience. Their children, as excited and achieving learners, become powerful influences for continued parental support. (Snyder, 1990, p. 221)

Snyder implies that most parents participate without realizing it, when they talk with their children, listen to and with them, read with them. When teachers make the importance of these simple acts known to them, they can expect that many parents will seek to participate in other ways.

One way of involving parents is to keep them informed not only about their children's progress but about what kinds of activities are being planned for the class. If parents know ahead of time that the class is going to do a particular activity and that the activity is one about which they have some specialized knowledge, they may volunteer to assist in some way. It would not be inappropriate for a teacher to send home a book with a child with a note requesting the parent to read it aloud to the child, as long as the teacher knows that the parent is literate. If the parent is not, or if there is some doubt, then it is helpful to send home an audio tape with the book so that parent and child may share the experience of reading. If she knows that the family does not speak English, a teacher might send a child home with a book in his native language with a request that the parent and child read it together. Giving children assignments that require them to interview or talk to their parents about specific topics is also a good way of involving parents in their children's language education.

We have already seen that parents are part of a larger community, and this community is a major stakeholder in language education. Partnership between the larger community and schools is essential because full participation in the community means that one needs to be able to read and to express oneself effectively orally and in writing, and these are prominent functions of schools. It is thus imperative that we extend our thinking beyond parents when we think about community participation in language education. Although it may take some effort on the teachers' behalf to engage the community in the life of the school, it is well worth the effort. There are a number of roles community members might play which directly affect language education. Some of the more commonly used techniques are listed in Table 11.2.

Principle 8: Don't Be Dogmatic. Teachers are professionals and, as such, we may be tempted to think of ourselves as having the answers or, at least, of knowing better than the lay community how children should be taught. Of course, to some degree, this is true, otherwise all those years of specialized education would not be necessary and we could hire teachers through the local employment agency much as we hire waiters, pizza delivery drivers, and janitors. But even though we *do* have specialized education and, most of us, fairly strong opinions about education, it would be a mistake to allow ourselves to become inflexible, to insist that our way is the best and only way. For one thing, from a purely practical perspective, to do so would essentially close the door on much of the community participation for which I have been arguing. For another, we would be forgetting the first principle above. A specific example illustrates the danger.

In recent years, the tendency has been to view whole language as providing the *only* way to organize the elementary school curriculum. At least, some supporters of the approach hold such a strong view. Although it is easy to understand why they would hold such an opinion, it is also easy to see how such dogmatism can backfire. I was recently conducting a two day materials-development workshop for ESL teachers who came together at the university to write and assemble ESL materials for their classes. In the district in which most of the teachers work, the Board of Education has made a firm and public commitment to whole language. While they have not mandated whole language for ESL classes, most of the teachers teach both ESL and English-speaking children and are thus familiar with the tenets of whole language. Familiar! Their devotion to whole language was so extreme that they dismissed from consideration any materials that even smacked of "skills." In doing so, they denied learners the benefit of materials that were comprehensible and meaningful *to them* and denied themselves some important tools for managing classrooms in which students' English ability is heterogeneous.

Table 11.2
Nine ways to involve the public in language education

1. Invite community members to the school to share their expertise or interest with students.
2. Encourage visitors to read a favorite book or tell a favorite story.
3. Encourage repeat visits from guests the students find especially interesting.
4. Ask community members to correspond with students on areas of mutual interest.
5. Encourage community members to become volunteer tutors in the school. Senior citizens are an especially valuable resource.
6. Invite businesses to "sponsor" a class in the school. Their sponsorship may involve having their employees volunteer in the class, buying books or computer software for the class, or sponsoring or helping organize field trips.
7. Have students interview business and professional people about their reading habits, that is, what they read and why.
8. Have students interview community members for the school or class newspaper.
9. Ask businesses to display children's stories or artwork in their establishments thus providing a real "audience" for the students' work.

By taking such a strong stance, these teachers also called into question the competence of the few ESL teachers who had learned from experience that many learners need explanation and practice with certain grammar points or with spelling or with certain idioms. Finally, they risked offending (and thus losing the cooperation of) the parents of the ESL children in their classes. Many of these families have come from countries with educational systems that differ greatly from those of the United States and Canada, and their children have succeeded within those systems. They have developed certain expectations about learning, and while it is not incumbent on schools to live up to all those expectations, it *is* incumbent on them to take into account the previous experience the learner has of language *and* of learning. Being dogmatic jeopardizes professional harmony and community participation in education.

A corollary of this principle is *be willing to compromise*. Compromise can usually be reached on any issue without abandoning those aspects of a belief that one holds dearest. Besides, it is necessary. Most people are wary of large-scale change but will fairly readily accept small-scale change. Thus, if teachers want to alter radically the approach to language teaching in a school but are meeting with community resistance, they should consider taking small steps. It probably will take no longer to accomplish their goals since, in this way, they are more likely to have the cooperation of parents and the larger community.

Principle 9: Be Professional.   Mary Ashworth (1985) has pointed out that if teachers want to be taken seriously and to be treated like professionals, then they must *act* like professionals. With regard to establishing collaborative relationships with the community, however, certain aspects of professionalism are particularly important. One is that we become and stay informed about the community; the school's relationship with the community is a symbiotic one, and we cannot expect the community to be interested in the school if we show no interest in the community. Another aspect of professionalism, which Ashworth highlights, improves the credibility of both the individual teacher and the profession: Teachers should engage in classroom research to support your beliefs about instruction (and possibly to modify them) and, if possible, write articles describing this research (1985, p. 111). Writing these articles for the lay audience and publishing them in the local press will enhance the school's profile and reputation as well as the teacher's. One teacher I know used to write an open letter to the local newspaper every week or two in which she described her own struggles with evaluation. She openly shared with the public why she felt she needed to alter the way in which children's language development was assessed and her attempts to find solutions. After a few weeks, others in the community started to write to the newspaper to make suggestions or to praise her for the thoughtful way in which she tackled what was for them a critical issue.

CONCLUSION

These principles do not constitute an exhaustive list of *dos and don'ts* about teaching nor even about how to reconcile the numerous views about language teaching held by individuals and groups who might be termed stakeholders in the educational process. They are instead guidelines, things to remember that might make the task a little easier. Unfortunately, following these principles will not ensure success but they will improve the chances. Following them will also allow us to proceed in the knowledge that we are not compromising the interests of the principal shareholders—the children.

Chapter Twelve

Language For *All* Our Children

In the last chapter, I extracted several key ideas from earlier chapters in the book and suggested nine principles for synthesizing them in actual classroom practice. No methods or techniques were suggested, for that is not the purpose of this book, but it was suggested that the principles could be adopted in a number of ways, all of which would lead to meaningful classroom experiences for children. That chapter served to synthesize several chapters of analysis—analysis of language, of language learning in monolingual, bilingual, and special needs children, analysis of the relationship between language and learning and how that relationship is exemplified in the home and in the school, and analysis of other influences on the decisions teachers make with regard to language.

No more analysis is needed, and the synthesis is largely done, too. So in this chapter, I am exercising my prerogative as an author to weave the various threads together in a more personal way. During the two years I spent writing, I formulated a number of different endings for the book. Usually, the chapter I had just completed would bias me toward a particular finish. But once the time came to write it, I was stymied. I thought I had said it all in Chapter 11, but I still had the last chapter listed on the table of contents, and a few pages permitted me by my editor. And besides, what writer has ever said all she has to say?

One day in midsummer I was sitting before my computer screen writing and then rapidly deleting ideas for these pages when a young man who had been in my student-teaching seminar the previous year stopped by my office to visit. Mark had just been hired by a school district in Ontario and had come to share his news and to thank me for a letter of reference. We got to talking about a number of matters educational, and in the course of our conversation he mentioned the name of the school that he had attended in Prince Edward Island. He had talked about the school before, but on this day, I turned on the tape recorder.

He left my office after about an hour of talk, but other university responsibilities kept me from playing back the tape for several days. When I did, I finally knew what I wanted this chapter to be. Because so much of this book has been based on the lives of real people and has been told as stories are told—children's stories and teachers' stories—I decided to continue in that vein. In this final story, I am going to take the reader with me to visit a school. I had thought from the time that I began the book that I would conclude with a particular school, specifically the one in which Mary Kennedy teaches in Calgary, Alberta. But I moved from there some time ago, and besides, I had already told a number of teachers' and children's stories from that school earlier in the book. So, although I hadn't planned to "visit" the school in Prince Edward Island, the chance meeting with a former student teacher has led me across the Northumberland Strait. In interviewing Mark, I discovered that the school embodies most of the principles set forth in the last chapter, not that I want to belabor that point here.

Instead, we will pay our visit with a young man who is now a beginning teacher but who, twenty years ago, was a student at the Glen Duncan School. After learning about the school through his recollections, I doubt that I will be able to resist entirely my analytic predilection, and will draw from his account some of the characteristics that made this school so memorable and so obviously effective.

THE GLEN DUNCAN SCHOOL

Nestled among the lush green rolling hills of Prince Edward Island, in the country that was home to Lucy Maud Montgomery's *Ann of Green Gables,* is a neighborhood school that children still walk to each day except in the worst days of winter. It would be presumptuous to claim that it is a model school, for there are many possible models on which to base an ideal school, but in its faculty, curriculum, and practice, it represents much that is ideal. I first learned of the school when I met some of its alumni, young people in their twenties studying to be teachers at Saint Mary's University in Halifax. Some ten or fifteen years after leaving the Glen Duncan Elementary School, which is not its real name but what we shall call it, these neophyte teachers recalled it fondly and told stories about their education that made it sound like a truly progressive place.

Several things struck me as noteworthy. First, it was unusual that so many of the students I encountered had attended this school. Saint Mary's admits only forty students to the Bachelor of Education degree each year, and these are selected from between 600 and 800 applicants from across Canada. For more than one student to have attended the same elementary school is rare; three or four suggests that the university's selection process is somehow biased in their favor. Second, I have found only infrequently that university students recall their primary education at all; usually, they speak of their high school years, evaluating their experiences with what they read and see of education. But the four students I met in my first year at Saint Mary's all spoke well of their years at Glen Duncan. The account that follows is based on the memories of the young man who happened into my office on a summer day. Mark, who was a gold medalist in biology at another university before coming to do his teacher education at Saint Mary's, talked to me about his years at Glen Duncan.

A Student's Recollection

M: I didn't know until I started my Early School Experience [a period of observation in schools that students complete prior to beginning their student teaching] that there was anything different about Glen Duncan. But after I'd visited a few classes, I remember thinking 'Wow. Times sure have changed.' But when I got to talking with some of the others [students in the teacher education program] who had gone to other schools, they said that things seemed pretty much the same to them as always.
T: So what was different about Glen Duncan?
M: Well, in retrospect, I have to say that most of what I knew before I went to university I learned there.
T: That's a pretty tall claim. You learned nothing in high school?
M: Well, I'm sure I did. But what I mean is that at Glen Duncan I, we all, learned to learn. It's funny. I remember learning but I don't remember being taught much.
T: Can you explain that?
M: I'm not sure I can. The teachers were always there to help and to make suggestions if we needed them, but, except for one, I can't remember them standing up in front of the room talking to us, telling us about things. I remember that we used to read a lot. Most teachers would read to us at some time in the day, even when we got into the upper grades,

and we always loved that. And we had silent reading periods as well when we could read anything we wanted. We wrote a lot, too. Stories, plays, newspaper articles, letters. Every day, we had to write but it wasn't a chore or anything. I really liked to write. When it was my turn to be editor of the class newsletter, I didn't like the job much. I preferred writing stories to deciding what would go into the paper and editing other people's work.

T: You had a newsletter?

M: Yes, every class had one. There were articles about what the class had been doing, what they were planning to do, that kind of thing. I remember writing the obituary for the class gerbil as well as a lot of birth announcements the year we had a rabbit for a science project.

T: What did you do with the newsletter?

M: It went home to our parents, of course, but it also went to local businesses and to the local newspaper.

T: Tell me about some of your other writing.

M: I wrote a Christmas play in grade five. A musical, believe it or not.

T: Was it staged?

M: No, not that one. I tried but I couldn't get enough of my classmates interested. One girl got hers produced, though. I think that was in grade six. She wrote the play and several of us helped write revisions and worked on the dialogue. I wrote two songs for it.

T: Was it a success?

M: Well, it didn't make it to Broadway, if that's what you're asking. But it enjoyed a three-night run in Charlottetown and was written up in the local paper. Or maybe it was just the school paper, but it was a big deal to me at the time.

T: Can you tell me anything more specific about your years at Glen Duncan? How about a typical day?

M: I don't think there was any such thing as a typical day. I remember walking to school most days and wondering what we'd be doing that day. I actually looked forward to it.

T: What might you have been doing one day in, say, grade three or four?

M: Well, after the morning routine—

T: What was the morning routine?

M: We sang "O Canada" and then had the morning news report. We had to predict one item that would be in the newspaper when it arrived later in the day. That meant that we had had to hear or see the news in the morning or talked to someone else about what was going on. We'd dictate the headlines to Mrs. Marchand—she was my grade three teacher—and she'd write them on a flip chart and leave them until later when the newspapers came. We'd get four or five copies in the class and we'd divide them up and comb the paper for stories to go with our headlines.

T: What happened after the morning routine?

M: Well, we'd usually settle down to our writing. We kept these large note-books, and we could write about anything we chose but there were also certain writing assignments we had to do each week.

T: The teacher gave you topics to write about?

M: No, not exactly. She gave us tasks. One week I might have to write a letter for the class inviting someone famous to visit.

T: Did you send the letter?

M: Oh, yes, definitely. That's one of the things that I remembered when we were talking in the methods class about whole language and authentic language. Even then, most of the writing assignments were real. I already mentioned the school paper, but sometimes she would ask some of us to write a piece for the local newspaper—to collaborate on an article. Sometimes our required writing was related to other things we were studying. I remember one of my assignments was the description of one of my classmate's entries in the Science Fair. That was for the local paper.

T: Why not your own?

M: Because I already knew about my own. I guess she figured that if I wrote about someone else's I'd have to learn about it.

T: What would happen after writing time?

M: That would sometimes go on for the entire morning. Other times, though, we would work on math or science until lunch time.

T: What do you remember about math and science?

M: That it was fun, then. We used to do a lot of experiments, but before we did them, we had the most interesting discussions. She would encourage us to ask all kinds of questions and then think of all kinds of ways of finding the answers. She'd ask us 'What do you think will happen if. . . ?' or 'What will it mean if. . . ?' questions.

T: Such as?

M: Well, when we were on our way to 'discovering' Archimedes's principle—and, you know, we really thought we *had* discovered it?—we had designed an experiment on water displacement using a marble, a baseball, a softball, and a twelve-pound bowling ball. We thought we had it all worked out and then she asked, 'What will happen if the bowling ball is the same diameter but weighs only four pounds?' The discussion on that was pretty animated but going nowhere until she asked 'Suppose the ball is made of Styrofoam?'

T: You have very clear memories about that.

M: Yes, probably because I went on into science and I've even borrowed that technique from her. But I remember the talk about science to be the most interesting thing about it. The same was true about social studies.

T: Oh, right, the newspaper.

M: Yes, the newspaper seemed to be the starting place for all our social studies lessons. The end of the Vietnam War was in the news then and we spent a lot of time trying to understand what had happened and why. We learned about other wars and talked a lot about beliefs and trade and all the reasons that countries get into wars. We learned about negotiation and compromise in our discussions based on those news stories.

T: Were there any children who didn't speak English when you were at Glen Duncan?

M: Yes, but only a few. There was a French-speaking girl who came in grade two and stayed until grade four and a boy who came in grade three.

T: What do you remember about them?

M: Well, there were no ESL classes. But there weren't many ESL kids either. I remember that the teacher would assign a each new kid a 'buddy' every week, and that buddy would help them to understand what was going on in class and on the playground. I don't remember much more except that eventually, they learned English. The girl went on to university, too. She was a biology major, like me.

T: Do you remember learning to read?

M: Not really. I remember that our grade one teacher read to us a lot. Oh yeah, and she'd have us tell her stories, and she'd write them on a big piece of paper and we'd read them out loud.

T: Language experience?

M: Is that what it's called? But if you're asking whether I remember being taught what sound a "b" makes, no, I don't. I guess I must have been, 'cause I learned to read at some point and I always liked it.

T: Were all your classes and teachers like the ones you've described?

M: With one exception, yes. There was a grade five teacher who came to the school the year I was in grade six. She was my brother's teacher and she was very rigid compared to the other teachers in the school. She gave a lot of tests and seatwork and I don't think anyone was very happy. She left after only one year.

T: In the years since you left Glen Duncan, have you thought about why that one school attracted so many fine teachers?

M: Actually, until I started my teacher education program, I hadn't thought about it at all. I thought *all* teachers were like the ones at Glen Duncan. But now I realize that they aren't, and thinking about it, I'd have to say that it was the principal who probably made the difference.

T: How so?

M: He was really special. He didn't just stay in his office the way I see some of these guys doing now. He spent a lot of time in the classrooms working with the kids. He knew all the kids in the school and their parents, too. I think the parents all liked him. He was really good at getting them involved in the school.

T: How did he go about that?

M: Well, the school couldn't afford a full-time librarian and so he wrote to the parents.

T: Asking for volunteers?

M: Yes. I remember because my mother was thinking about working there. He wrote a long letter explaining why the library was so important to the life of the school and why he had to make the hard decision to eliminate the librarian's position. His idea was to turn the library into a community resource. He got enough volunteers—qualified ones, too— that the library could stay open three nights a week.

T: Was there material in an elementary school library to interest adults?

M: There was when he finished lobbying all the local businesses. He held an annual library fund-raising drive and managed to get enough contributions to keep a good collection. Parents and former students also donated a lot of books and magazines. It was an odd assortment, for sure, but it was an interesting place to spend time.

T: It sounds like all of Glen Duncan might fit that description.

M: Yes. I learned to read and to write and to think and to learn there. I'd really like to go back there to teach one day. If they'll have me.

Mark attended the Glen Duncan school from 1971 until 1977. His recollections of his years there raise a number of intriguing questions. The first and most obvious is whether the school *was* special or was it typical of most others of its time. We can say with a fair degree of certainty that the Glen Duncan school would be considered special today even if measured against the strictest criteria of excellence in language teaching. That it was special nearly twenty years ago cannot be doubted. The second question is why. To anyone reading the chapters that preceded this one, the answers should be obvious. Nevertheless, it is appropriate as a conclusion to the book to summarize them.

Accounting for Success

Mark's account was by no means exhaustive, but it provided a window not only on the personal experience of one child, but on the curriculum, the teachers, and the principal that contributed to the school's effectiveness. While there are doubtless many reasons for its success, five stand out from reading his recollection:

1. Children participated daily in authentic tasks involving authentic language.
2. They used both reading and writing as a means of discovery, as a way of learning.
3. Subject areas were integrated so that language played a central role across the curriculum.
4. ESL students were not segregated but participated fully in the life and activities of the class.
5. Education was a joint-venture enterprise whose success depended on the partnership of teachers, principal, and community.

It seems obvious to me that these are axioms that could guide any elementary school. This is true, I believe, not because they are profound statements of educational philosophy nor even particularly insightful statements about the nature of human learning. They are basically just common sense *if* we take to heart the truths about children's language and learning that we explored in the previous chapters. Let us consider the five axioms individually.

Authentic Tasks Involving Authentic Language.   This participation began with the morning routine. In asking children to predict the stories and the headlines in the afternoon paper, the teacher was engaging the children in genuine talk in which they used language for a number of functions. The primary function was *forecasting and reasoning*. In this activity, it is likely that language such as the following would be common:

> There was a bad hurricane in Florida that killed some people. That will *have* to be in the news.

In talk such as this and in other instances in which children speculated about the probability that various events would make the afternoon news and talked about causes and effects and discussed the reasons, they were using language for forecasting and reasoning. This daily routine would also provide opportunities for children to engage in the *informing* function of language in telling each other about the newscasts they had already heard. In the simple act of constructing headlines for their predicted stories, the children would have learned a great deal about the message-carrying properties of language—that some words carry more meaning than others, which can be left out—and about ambiguity that resulted when they left out too much information or the wrong information.

Later in the day, when the newspapers came, the purposeful language continued. Children read the paper, searching for stories to match their predicted headlines and then talked about the stories they read. It is not difficult to imagine the language and the functions involved:

"Hey, look at this. Here's the story about the hurricane."
(Controlling; informing)

"Where do you think they'd put a story about the school play?"
(Informing using the subfunction of requesting information)

"I don't think it's here. That's strange. I guess they thought the story about the whale was more important." (Forecasting and reasoning; projecting)

"Look! There's a story about the zoo on page six but I can't find anything about the aquarium. Why do you think that is?" (Controlling; informing; reasoning)

As in much classroom talk, there were undoubtedly many opportunities for children to use the social language required for maintaining relationships with teacher and peers. An important point to remember was that the talk that engendered so many functional possibilities was not contrived but purposeful.

The authenticity of language use continued in the routine of morning writing. Children must be given the freedom to write about whatever they want and in whatever form. That is the nature of much true writing, after all. Except for journalists who may be assigned particular stories from time to time, most writers have a great deal of freedom in deciding what and how they will write. Children were thus encouraged to write whatever they wanted, and in doing so they likely employed all five functions of language although it is likely that some were more heavily used than others. The social and projecting functions, for example, would be rather more heavily used in personal letters with the informing and forecasting and reasoning functions used more in letters attending to classroom business.

It is also necessary to their development as writers that children experience a variety of different writing formats. The teachers at Glen Duncan assigned tasks to provide that variety. Notice, however, that the tasks Mark remembered were legitimate writing tasks of the type that all of us might have to do in real life. They were not just realistic; they were real. This is an important distinction, I believe, because even very young children understand the difference between "pretend" and real activities.

Like adults, they will care more about the letters they write to the president of the United States, the prime minister of Canada, or to Santa Claus if they have a reasonable expectation that they will be read. The more they care, the more they will learn. They will ask questions about the form their letters should take, about the way to state a thought more clearly, or the exact word they need to express a particular idea. In asking these questions and getting them answered, they engage in even more purposeful talk.

Reading and Writing as a Means of Discovery and Learning.   Reading and writing were not segregated as separate and independent subjects in the curriculum of Glen Duncan. Rather, they formed an integral and essential component of all classroom learning. We saw in the newspaper exercise one example of purposeful reading. Mark's account does not specifically mention others, but it is perhaps interesting that he cannot recall a reading period or "learning to read" as a separate activity. He remembers his grade one teacher using a language experience technique, apparently with success since he became a successful reader. Later, in his account of the principal's support of the school library, he conveys a school atmosphere in which reading is a vitally important but a natural part of school life.

Mark's recollection of one of his required writing tasks is telling. In being assigned to write an article about a classmate's science project rather than his own, he was forced to learn something that he might not otherwise have learned except superficially. In writing as a journalist about a scientific experiment for an audience who knew nothing of it, Mark had to understand it in far more detail than he might have had he been interested only in his role of classmate. Notice, too, that the emphasis on reading and writing did not come at the expense of oral language. Mark's account of his day is of one rich in talk. Talk about current events, about war and negotiation and compromise, talk about science, hypothesizing and predicting the results of experiments, talk to get the newsletter produced, to write and stage plays—this was the talk of his school years and always it was connected to reading and writing and to the real world in which he lived. Here are many excellent examples of language and learning authentically supporting one another.

Integrated Subject Areas.   Language across the curriculum was a popular educational notion of the late 1970s and early 1980s, but long before that there were elementary teachers for whom this was standard practice. Obviously, this was the case for the teachers at Glen Duncan. We have already seen how language was linked to social studies. Reading the newspaper was the starting point for lively class discussions about current events and their causes. It is easy to imagine how much more vital these classes must have seemed than the all-too-typical history or social studies class of the open-your-book-to-page-ten variety. Children in these classes put language to a great many authentic uses and learned about the world around them at the same time. Skeptics about the unifying capacity of language in integrating the subjects of the curriculum might argue that language and social studies are naturally compatible in ways that language and math or science are not. The teachers at Glen Duncan demonstrated the falsity of this argument.

Mark's memory of the excitement engendered by his science classes was of the *talk* they fostered. It is probably not an exaggeration to say that children learned to reason scientifically through the questions and answers raised in their discussion of scientific experiments. The hypothesizing they did before the experiment provided excellent *use*, not *practice*, of forecasting and reasoning language. Without this talk, most of the children would never have achieved the reasoning. As we saw in Chapter 8, children's language and cognitive growth go hand in hand. This is as true of the kind of reasoning required in science as it is of memory or conceptual development, other aspects of cognitive growth.

The generalizations Mark and the others had to reach as a result of their experimentation, for instance in their "discovery" of Archimedes's principle, were examples of informing language. The forecasting and reasoning and the informing functions are fairly typical "school functions," that is, purposes to which language is more typically put in schools, but the ways in which these functions were embodied were interesting, authentic, and memorable. It is also reasonable to assume that in the talk that surrounded the experiments the children carried out as well as in the talk in which the teacher engaged them, there was also much use of the less formal functions of language, the social and the projecting.

In Mark's case, the interdependence of language and science had a noteworthy result. Out of the talk in which science was embedded (or perhaps it was the other way around) grew the love of science that led to his later career choice.

ESL Students Not Segregated.   A few years ago, an elementary teacher explained to me that the ESL children in her class were always "involved" in the activities of the class. When I asked how they were involved, she answered, "Oh, in lots of ways. I read and they listen. And they always sit and listen while other children share the stories they've written." While I had no doubt that the children derived some benefit from such "involvement," I could not help but think of the distinction Joan Kirner made between participation and involvement:

> It was Farmer Brown's birthday. The hen and the pig, who loved her dearly, were discussing what to buy for a birthday present.
>
> They found it a difficult task to think of a present for one whose material needs were few. Suddenly the hen hit on an idea, "I know," she said, "we can take her home-grown, home-made fresh bacon and eggs for breakfast. She'd love that. If we made it ourselves, she'd know we really cared.
>
> The pig thought about the hen's idea for a minute, then firmly snorted in reply, "No way am I going to give her bacon and eggs for breakfast."
>
> "Why not,' said the hen, disappointed.
>
> 'Simple,' snorted the pig. 'You'd be involved but I'd be participating.'
> (cited in Potter, 1989, p. 32)

At the Glen Duncan School, the evidence points to the ESL children's participating rather than simply being involved. Although Mark could not speak from their perspective, what he did tell us of the school and of ESL learners in the school suggests that they played active roles. It is difficult to imagine that teachers who were so caring in their fostering and nurturing of language learning in the English-speaking children would forsake all their principles in providing for ESL learners. What Mark's recollection does tell us is encouraging. ESL children were not segregated but stayed in the same classroom as the English speakers. It is hard to imagine that they did not derive considerable benefit from the rich environment Mark described.

Indeed, teachers who have insisted on their ESL children's remaining in the classroom rather than being segregated have made a number of helpful suggestions for ESL children that would be useful for mainstream students as well. Writing of the Fair Oaks School in Redwood, California, Lois Bridges Bird stresses the importance *and the effectiveness* of authentic language. The mostly Spanish-speaking children at Fair Oaks write real memos requesting that the furniture be repaired, they write letters in protest of government policies in Central America, and they even broadcast a half-hour radio program to the community every Friday morning. Teachers provide support and guidance but also encourage the importance of self-reflection in the learning process. The freedom, support, and respect that their language program provides gives the students at Fair Oaks a sense of belief "in themselves as capable, creative learners, knowing what they need and how to get it" (Bird, 1991a, p. 92).

Freedom does not mean that the children are not taught. But as one of their teachers, Roberta Lee, points out, they learn by doing. In producing their radio show, the children at Fair Oaks have to write letters of invitation to potential guests (including the Queen of England!) as well as thank you letters to people who appear; they have to write the scripts for the show and learn to conduct interviews on the show. Obviously, there must be some instruction as to the form these letters, scripts, and interviews should take, but it is directed toward a real purpose that the children understand (Bird, 1991b, p. 93). Precisely because it is an authentic radio show, the language learning that it fosters will be linked to a number of subjects. Social studies is an obvious one but one can also envision a "science" or "environment" spot as well as music, drama, and literature. It is an ideal learning situation. Moreover, it is one that is ideal for both first- and second-language learners.

A Joint Venture Enterprise.   If such a partnership is to work, there should be no "silent" partners, although it is reasonable to assume that one might speak with a louder voice than the other. At Glen Duncan, it appears that the principal was a "senior partner." The fact that Mark remembered him well led in part to that conclusion. These days, it is not unusual for elementary children not to know the principal at all or to know her or him only as a remote figure who does paperwork, meets with parents, and perhaps dispenses discipline. For a child to remember a principal as an active member of the school, someone who spent a lot of time in the classroom and devoted her or his energies to improving the library, speaks well of that principal.

The Glen Duncan principal's way of getting parents to solve the library problem was effective because the solution brought benefits not only to the school but to the community as well. There were the indirect benefits of securing and channeling the parents' interest in the school, but there were also direct benefits as well. The small community gained a stationary library where previously it had only the mobile branch from the nearby city. The library and the school became a community center where it was quite natural for parents and others in the community to find out about the life of the school. Of course, I am not suggesting that any of this made up for the loss of the librarian, for the librarian is a central figure in helping to establish a relationship between children and print. But when the principal could not save the librarian's position, he turned a potential disaster into an advantage for the school and for the community. Moreover, the incident demonstrated his understanding that the library's collection of print, visual, and audio materials was crucial to the school's functions.

Shortly after my interview with Mark, I telephoned the school to find out whether the principal was still there. It was a long shot that he would be, after nearly twenty years, but he was. So were some of the teachers who had been there when Mark attended. I went to Prince Edward Island to visit the school, and my visit confirmed that the school probably had been as unique twenty years ago as Mark had indicated, since it is still a very special place to be.

LANGUAGE FOR *ALL* OUR CHILDREN

No matter what the backgrounds of the children who populate our classes, certain truths are unavoidable. The first is that in the life of the child and in the life of the school, *language is special.* It is the "subject" children know best when they begin school and it is the one that will largely determine their success in all the other subjects they encounter. This is true not only because teachers rely so heavily on language but because language is uniquely linked with cognitive processing. The second is that language does not require much teaching; most of it children will learn if they are given the opportunity to do so. For second-language learners the opportunities may have to be more numerous and more attention may have to be paid to meaning in the language they hear and see, but the process is natural enough if we do not impede it with overemphasis on structure and form. Third, no one cultural group has an exclusive claim on language or any aspect of it. Pronunciation, word choice, grammar, function, and even purposes of literacy have many acceptable variations within and between cultures. While there is no doubt that language has structure, neither is there any doubt that whatever form the child brings to school is a correct form. There is a great danger of placing "correctness" judgments on children's language. We may later wish to talk about standard forms of writing, always within genuine contexts, but to evaluate children's language is to evaluate them. Respecting children's language is remembering that the particular variety individual children bring to school is as much a part of their identity as the teacher's language is to her.

And now I have come full circle. The only task remaining is to make a statement of belief. More precisely, it is to state how belief is shaped, how our best knowledge about language, about language acquisition, about children's learning, and about the complex interrelationship among the three influence teaching practice. Throughout the book, I have implied, suggested, and even stated outright how I believe this knowledge should inform us as teachers. But I will make the statement succinctly here: The experiences of language and learning that children have in classrooms must be in harmony with the experiences they have had outside. Not *identical to,* for there is no point in reproducing past experience; not *reflective of,* for we would not be helping children to grow if we did not push them beyond their prior ways of learning and knowing. Being *in harmony with* means that the school experiences we help to shape resonate with those already in children's minds. We take what children know of language and learning as the first note and add in school at the second and third intervals to create a consonant, harmonious chord. Thus the child who has not learned to read at home but who has learned that her father reads to find out who won the baseball game, what's going on in the world, and for entertainment begins school and learns *how* to read for some of the same purposes (the first interval) and for additional purposes of her own (the second interval). Children learn to talk as part of becoming socialized to the family and community. That is the first note of the chord. That experience continues in school and further socializing talk and other functions of talk are imposed on it to create a harmonious whole language for all children.

For *ALL* children. . . . If we do it right, this is a concert of language in which all children participate. ESL children, children with special needs, all children who come to school expecting to learn will learn. The key to helping all children is to remember that that first note, the child's previous experience of language and learning in the home, may differ from child to child. It is very easy to assume that the experience of the white middle class child defines the experience of all children when, of course, this is not true. Just as there is no universal pattern of child-rearing, there is no single description of the complex interaction between language and socialization across different cultures. To assume that there is leads almost without fail to some kind of a "deficit" hypothesis—there is something wrong with certain children that must be corrected before they can be taught, or to continue the musical analogy, we cannot create a chord starting with this note; let's change it. Let's make sure that all our chords are C major.

Musicians know, of course, that this is nonsense. We can create beautiful harmonies beginning with any note, but of course, we cannot if we impose the *wrong* second and third notes on it. This is what happens too often in school: We impose the second and third notes of the chord without listening first to the note that is the child's first note. If we fail to understand, for example, that Chipewyan parents do not expect their children to talk before they are five years old because they believe that it takes a lifetime to learn their language and that effective learning requires long periods of observation, we run the risk of taking the children's silence as evidence of language delay or as a void that must be filled. If we assume that children who come from nonliterate homes do not know about stories, we may well be assuming the wrong starting note for there are homes in North America in which the tradition of the story is strongly maintained through oral retelling. Language for all our children must respect all their experiences, and since we cannot know in advance what the nature of those experiences might be, we must develop increased sensitivity to and better methods for discovering what their experience is. It goes without saying that we must respect it.

Bibliography

Aaron, I. E., Chall, J. S., Durkin, D., Goodman, K., & Strickland, D. (1990a, January). The past, present, and future of literacy education: Comments from a panel of distinguished educators, Part I. *The Reading Teacher*, pp. 302–311.

Aaron, I. E., Chall, J. S., Durkin, D., Goodman, K., & Strickland, D. (1990b, February). The past, present, and future of literacy education: Comments from a panel of distinguished educators, Part II. *The Reading Teacher*, pp. 302–311.

Abudarham, S. (1980). The problems of assessing the linguistic potential of children with dual language systems and their implications for the formulation of a differential diagnosis. In F. M. Jones (Ed.), *Language disability in children*. MTP Press Ltd.

Allen, P., Swain, M., & Harley, B. (1988). Analytic and experiential aspects of core French and immersion classrooms. *Bulletin of the Canadian Association of Applied Linguistics, 10*, 59–68.

Anderson, A. B., & Stokes, S. J. (1984). Social and institutional influences on the development and practice of literacy. In H. Goelman, A. Oberg, & F. Smith (Eds.), *Awakening to literacy* (pp. 24–37). Portsmouth, NH: Heinemann Educational Books.

Applebee, A. N., Langer, J. S., & Mullis, I. V. S. (1987). *Learning to be literate in America*. Princeton, NJ: Educational Testing Service.

Ashworth, M. (1985). *Beyond methodology, second language teaching and the community*. Cambridge: Cambridge University Press.

Ashworth, M. (1988). *Blessed with bilingual brains*. Vancouver, BC: Pacific Educational Press.

Asselin, M., Pelland, N., & Shapiro, J. (1991). *Storyworlds, linking minds and imagination through literature*. Markham, Ontario: Pippin Publishing.

Atkinson, R. C., & Shiffrin, R. M. (1968). Human memory: A proposed system and its control processes. In K. W. Spence & J. T. Spence (Eds.), *Advances in child development and behavior*. New York: Academic Press.

Atkinson-King, K. (1973). Children's acquisition of phonological stress contrasts. (UCLA Working Papers in Phonetics 25). Los Angeles: University of California at Los Angeles.

Baker, L., & Brown, A. L. (1984). Metacognitive skills and reading. In P. D. Pearson (Ed.), *Handbook of reading research, Part 2*. New York: Longman.

Baker, N., & Nelson, K. (1985). Recasting and related conversational techniques for triggering syntactic advances by young children. *First Language, 5,* 3–22.

Barik, H. C., & Swain, M. (1974). English-French bilingual education in the early grades: The Elgin study. *The Modern Language Journal, 58,* 392–403.

Barik, H. C., & Swain, M. (1975). Three-year evaluation of a large scale early grade French immersion program: The Ottawa study. *Language Learning, 25,* 1–30.

Barik, H. C., Swain, M., & Guadino, V. (1976). A Canadian experiment in bilingual education in the senior grades: The Peel study through grade two. *International Review of Applied Psychology, 25,* 99–113.

Barke, E. M., & Parry-Williams, D. E. (1938). A further study of the comparative intelligence of children in certain bilingual and monoglot schools in south Wales. *British Journal of Educational Psychology, 8,* 63.

Barnes, S., Gutfreund, M., Satterly, D., & Wells, G. (1983). Characteristics of adult speech which predict children's language development. *Journal of Child Language, 10,* 65–84.

Basser, L. S. (1962). Hemiplegia of early onset and the faculty of speech with special reference to the effects of hemispherectomy. *Brain, 85,* 427–460.

Bates, E. (1976). *Language and context: Studies in the acquisition of pragmatics*. New York: Academic Press.

Bates, E., Benigni, L., Bretherton, I., Camaioni, L., & Volterra, V. (1979). *The emergence of symbols: Cognition and communication in infancy*. New York: Academic Press.

Bates, E., & MacWhinney, B. (1987). Competition, variation, and language learning. In B. MacWhinney (Ed.) *Mechanisms of language acquisition*. Hillsdale, NJ: Lawrence Erlbaum.

Bates, E., & Snyder, L. (1985). The cognitive hypothesis in language development. In I. Uzgiris & J. M. Hunt (Eds.), *Research with scales of psychological development in infancy*. Champaign-Urbana: University of Illinois Press.

Beardsmore, H. B., & Kohls, J. (1988). Immediate pertinence in the acquisition of multilingual proficiency: The European schools. *Canadian Modern Language Review, 44,* 680–701.

Beatty, R. (1983). Windyfoggery and bureaucratese. *International Review of Applied Linguistics, 62,* 53–66.

Benton, R. (1964). *Research into the English language difficulties of Maori school children, 1963–1964*. Wellington, New Zealand: Maori Education Foundation.

Bereiter, C., & Scardamalia, M. (1982). From conversation to composition: The role of instruction in a developmental process. In Glaser, R. (Ed.), *Advances in instructional psychology*. Hillsdale, NJ: Lawrence Erlbaum.

Berger, J. (1991, January 5). Fernandez proposes placing warranties on graduates in '92. *New York Times*, p. 1.

Berko, J. (1958). The child's learning of English morphology. *Word, 14,* 150–177.

Berko, J., & Brown, R. (1960). Psycholinguistic research methods. In Paul H. Mussen (Ed.), *Handbook of research methods in child development* (pp. 517–557). New York: John Wiley & Sons.

Berns, M. (1990). Why language teaching needs the sociolinguist. *Canadian Modern Language Review, 46,* 339–353.

Bever, T. G. (1972). Perceptions, thoughts and language. In J. B. Carroll & R. O. Freedle (Eds.), *Language, comprehension and the acquisition of knowledge*. Washington, DC: John Wiley & Sons.

Beveridge, M. (Ed.) (1982). *Children thinking through language*. London: Edward Arnold.

Beveridge, M., & Brierley, C. (1982). Classroom constructs: An interpretive approach to young children's language. In M. Beveridge (Ed.), *Children thinking through language*. London: Edward Arnold.

Bialystok, E. (1987). Words as things: Development of word concept by bilingual children. *Studies in Second Language Acquisition, 9,* 133–140.

Bird, L. (1991a). Joyful literacy at Fair Oaks school. In K. S. Goodman, L. B. Bird, & Y. M. Goodman (Eds.), *The whole language catalog* (pp. 92–93). Santa Rosa, CA: American School Publishers (Macmillan).

Bird, L. (1991b). Classroom demonstrations. In K. S. Goodman, L. B. Bird, & Y. M. Goodman (Eds.), *The whole language catalog* (p. 93). Santa Rosa, CA: American School Publishers (Macmillan).

Bissex, G. L. (1984). The child as teacher. In H. Goelman, A. Oberg, & F. Smith (Eds.), *Awakening to literacy* (pp. 87–101). Portsmouth, NH: Heinemann Educational Books.

Blakeslee, T. R. (1980). *The right brain*. New York: Berkley.

Block, E. (1986). The comprehension strategies of second language learners. *TESOL Quarterly, 2,* 463–491.

Block, E., & Kessel, F. (1980). Determinants of the acquisition order of grammatical morphemes: A reanalysis and reinterpretation. *Journal of Child Language, 7,* 181–189.

Bloom, L. (1973). *One word at a time: The use of single-word utterances before syntax*. The Hague: Mouton.

Bloom, L., & Lahey, M. (1978). *Language development and language disorders.* New York: John Wiley & Sons.

Bloom, L., Lahey, M., Hood, L., Lifter, K., & Fiess, K. (1980). Complex sentences; acquisition of syntactic connectives and the semantic relations they encode. *Journal of Child Language, 7,* 235–261.

Bloomfield, L. (1933). *Language.* New York: Holt, Rinehart, & Winston.

Bohannon, J., & Stanowicz, L. (1988). The issue of negative evidence: Adult responses to children's language errors. *Developmental Psychology, 24*(5), 684–689.

Bohannon, J. N., & Warren-Leubecker, A. W. (1989). Theoretical approaches to language acquisition. In J. B. Gleason (Ed.), *The development of language* (2nd ed.). Columbus, OH: Merrill, an imprint of Macmillan Publishing Company.

Bolinger, D. (1980). *Language, the loaded weapon: The use and abuse of language today.* London: Longman.

Bowen, J. D., Madsen, H., & Hilferty, A. (1985). *TESOL techniques and procedures.* Rowley, MA: Newbury House.

Bowerman, M. (1981). The child's expression of meaning: expanding relationships among lexicon, syntax, and morphology. In H. Winitz (Ed.), *Native language and foreign language acquisition.* New York: The New York Academy of Sciences.

Bowlby, J. (1960). Grief and mourning in infancy and early childhood. *Psychoanalytic Study of the Child, 15,* 9–52.

Braine, M. D. S. (1963). The ontogeny of English phrase structures: The first phase. *Language, 39,* 1–13.

Braine, M. D. S. (1971a). On two types of models of internalization of grammars. In D. I. Slobin (Ed.), *The ontogenesis of grammar.* New York: Academic Press.

Braine, M. D. S. (1971b). The acquisition of language in infant and child. In C. E. Reed (Ed.), *The learning of language.* Englewood Cliffs, NJ: Prentice-Hall.

Braine, M. D. S. (1974). On what might constitute a learnable phonology. *Language, 50,* 270–299.

Braine, M. D. S. (1976). Children's first word combinations. *Monographs of the Society for Research in Child Development, 41* (Serial No. 164).

Brannon, J. (1968). Linguistic word classes in the spoken language of normal, hard-of-hearing and deaf children. *Journal of Speech and Hearing Research, 11,* 279–287.

Brent Palmer, C. (1979). A sociolinguistic assessment of the notion 'immigrant' semi-lingualism from a social conflict perspective. *Working Papers on Bilingualism, 17,* 137–180.

Britsch, S. (1989). The contribution of the preschool to a native American community. *Language Arts, 66*(1), 29–43.

Britton, J. (1967). *Talking and writing.* London: Methuen & Company, Ltd.

Britton, J. (1970). *Language and learning.* Harmondsworth, UK: Penguin.

Brown, H. D. (1980). *Principles of language learning and teaching.* Englewood Cliffs, NJ: Prentice-Hall.

Brown, R. (1973). *A first language.* Cambridge, MA: Harvard University Press.

Bruck, M., Lambert, W., & Tucker, G. R. (1975). *Assessing functional bilingualism within a bilingual program: The St. Lambert project at grade eight.* Paper presented at TESOL Convention.

Bruner, J. (1973). Organization of early skilled action. *Child Development, 44,* 1–11.

Bruner, J. S. (1983). *Child's talk.* New York: Norton Press.

Bruner, J. S. (1984). Language, mind, and reading. In H. Goelman, A. Oberg, & F. Smith (Eds.), *Awakening to literacy* (pp. 193–200). Portsmouth, NH: Heinemann Educational Books.

Bruner, J. S. (1986). *Actual minds, possible worlds.* Cambridge, MA: Harvard University Press.

Burns, G. E., & Olson, C. P. (1989). Planning and professionalizing other FSL programs. *Canadian Modern Language Review, 45,* 502–516.

Burt, M. K., Dulay, H. C., & Hernandez-Chavez, E. (1975). *Bilingual syntax measure.* New York: Harcourt Brace Jovanovitch.

Cairns, H. S., & Hsu, J. R. (1978). Who, why, when and how: a developmental study. *Journal of Child Language, 5,* 477–88.

Calkins, L. M. (1983). *Lessons from a child: On the teaching and learning of writing.* Portsmouth, NH: Heinemann Educational Books.

Calkins, L. M. (1985). Learning to think through writing. In A. Jaggar & M. T. Smith-Burke (Eds.), *Observing the language learner.* Champaign-Urbana, IL: NCTE.

Caplan, David (1987). *Neurolinguistics and linguistic aphasiology.* Cambridge, U.K.: Cambridge University Press.

Carmichael, L., Hogan, H. P., & Walter, A. A. (1932). An experimental study of the effect of language on visually perceived form. *Journal of Experimental Psychology, 15,* 73–86.

Carrell, P. (1983a). Background knowledge in second language comprehension. *Language, Learning, and Communication. 35,* 183–200.

Carrow, Sister M. A. (1957). Linguistic functioning of bilingual and monolingual children. *Journal of Speech and Hearing Disorders, 22,* p. 371.

Carter, C. (Ed.). (1982). *Non-native and nonstandard dialect students.* Champaign-Urbana, IL: NCTE.

Case, R. (1980). *Intellectual development in infancy: A neo-Piagetian interpretation.* Paper presented at the International Conference for Infant Studies, New Haven, CT.

Cazden, C. (1968). The acquisition of noun and verb inflections. *Child Development, 39*, 433–448.

Cazden, C. (1987). English for academic purposes: the student-talk register. *English Education, 19*,(1), 31–44.

Celis, W. (1990, November 22). Growing number of parents are opting to teach children at home. *New York Times*, p. 1.

Chafe, W. (1982). Integration and involvement in speaking, writing, and oral literature. In D. Tannen (Ed.), *Spoken and written language.* Norwood, NJ: Ablex.

Cheshire, J. (1982). Dialect features and linguistic conflict in schools. *Educational Review, 34*, 53–67.

Chomsky, N. (1965). *Aspects of the theory of syntax.* Cambridge, MA: The MIT Press.

Chomsky, C. (1969). *The acquisition of syntax in children from 5 to 10.* Cambridge, MA: The MIT Press.

Chomsky, N. (1975). *Reflections on language.* New York: Pantheon.

Chomsky, N. (1980). *Rules and explanations.* New York: Columbia University Press.

Chow, M. (1986). Measuring the growth of writing in the kindergarten and grade one years: How are the ESL children doing? *TESL Canada Journal, 4*, 35–47.

Clark, E. V. (1977). Strategies and the mapping problem in first language acquisition. In J. Macnamara (Ed.), *Language learning and thought.* New York: Academic Press.

Clark, M. M. (1984). Literacy at home and at school: Insights from a study of young fluent readers. In H. Goelman, A. Oberg, & F. Smith (Eds.), *Awakening to literacy.* Portsmouth, NH: Heinemann Educational Books.

Clarke, M. A., & Silberstein, S. (1979). Toward a realization of psycholinguistic principles in the ESL reading class. In R. Mackay, B. Barkman, & R. R. Jordan (Eds.), *Reading in a second language: hypotheses, organization, and practice.* Rowley, MA: Newbury House.

Clay, M. M. (1973). Reading: *The patterning of complex behavior.* Auckland, NZ: Heinemann Educational Books.

Clyde, J. (1990). A natural curriculum. In H. Mills & J. A. Clyde (Eds.), *Portraits of whole language classrooms* (chap. 2). Portsmouth, NH: Heinemann Educational Books.

Clyne, M. (1985). Development of writing skills in young second language learners. *International Review of Applied Linguistics, 67–68*, 9–24.

Coady, J. (1979). A psycholinguistic model of the ESL reader. In R. Mackay, B. Barkman, & R. R. Jordan (Eds.), *Reading in a second language: hypotheses, organization, and practice.* Rowley, MA: Newbury House.

Commins, N. L. (1989). Language and affect: Bilingual students at home and at school. *Language Arts, 66*(1), 29–43.

Connors, K., Menard, N., & Singh, R. (1978). Testing linguistic and functional competence in immersion programs. In M. Paradis (Ed.), *Aspects of bilingualism*. Columbia, SC: Hornbeam.

Cook, V. J. (1985). Universal grammar and second language learning. *Journal of Applied Linguistics, 6,* 2–18.

Corrigan, R. (1978). Language development as related to stage six object permanence development. *Journal of Child Language, 5,* 173–190.

Cotton, E. G. (1978). Noun-pronoun pleonasms: The role of age and situation. *Journal of Child Language, 5,* 489–499.

Crystal, D. (1976). *Child language, learning and linguistics*. London: Edward Arnold.

Crystal, D. (1987). *The Cambridge encyclopedia of language*. Cambridge: Cambridge University Press.

Cummins, J. (1978). Educational implications of mother tongue maintenance in minority language groups. *The Canadian Modern Language Review, 34,* 3.

Cummins, J. (1979a). Linguistic interdependence and the educational development of bilingual children. *Review of Educational Research, 49,* 222–251.

Cummins, J. (1979b). Cognitive academic language proficiency, linguistic interdependence, the optimum age question and some other matters. *Working Papers on Bilingualism, 19,* 197–205.

Cummins, J. (1980). The cross-lingual dimensions of language proficiency: Implications for bilingual education and the optimal age issue. *TESOL Quarterly, 14,* 25–60.

Cummins, J. (1984). Wanted: A theoretical framework for relating language proficiency to academic achievement among bilingual students. In C. Rivera (Ed.), *Language proficiency and academic achievement*. Clevedon, UK: Multilingual Matters.

Cummins, J. (1988). From multicultural to antiracist education: An analysis of programmes and policies in Ontario. In T. Skutnabb-Kangas & J. Cummins (Eds.), *Minority education: from shame to struggle*. Clevedon, UK: Multilingual Matters.

Curtiss, S. (1977). *Genie: A psycholinguistic study of a modern-day "wild child."* New York: Academic Press.

Curtiss, S. (1981). Dissociations between language and cognition: Cases and implications. *Journal of Autism and Developmental Disorders, 11,* 15–30.

Curtiss, S., & Yamada, J. (1978). *Language = cognition*. Paper presented at the Third Annual Boston University Conference on Language Development, Boston, MA.

Curtiss, S., Yamada, J., & Fromkin, V. (1979). How independent is language? On the question of formal parallels between action and grammar. *UCLA Working Papers in Cognitive Linguistics, 1,* 131–157.

Cuvo, A. J. (1975). Developmental differences in rehearsal and free recall. *Journal of Experimental Child Psychology, 19,* 65–78.

Dale, P. S. (1976). *Language development: Structure and function* (2nd ed.). New York: Holt, Rinehart, & Winston.

Dalrymple, K. S. (1989). 'Well, what about his skills?' Evaluation of whole language in the middle school. In K.S. Goodman, Y. M. Goodman, & W. J. Hood (Eds.), *The whole language evaluation book* (chap. 10). Portsmouth, NH: Heinemann Education Books.

Danesi, M. (1988a). Neurological bimodality and theories of language teaching. *Studies in Second Language Acquisition, 10,* 13–31.

Danesi, M. (1988b). Neurobiological differentiation of primary and secondary language acquisition. *Studies in Second Language Acquisition, 10,* 303–337.

d'Anglejan, A. (1978). Language learning in and out of classrooms. In Richards, J. C. (Ed.), *Understanding second and foreign language learning.* Rowley, MA: Newbury House.

Davies, A. (1977). *Language and learning in early childhood.* London: Heinemann Educational Books.

Davies, A., Criper, C., & Howatt, A. P. R. (Eds.) (1984). *Interlanguage.* Edinburgh: Edinburgh University Press.

Davis, K. (1975). Severe social isolation. In S. Rogers (Ed.), *Children and language.* London: Oxford University Press.

Davis, P. S. (1991, April). Parents writing with students. *English Journal,* 62–64.

De Keyser, R. M. (1986). Individual differences in first language acquisition and some educational implications. *International Review of Applied Linguistics, 73,* 1–26.

deHirsch, K., Jansky, J., & Langford, W. (1966). *Predicting reading failure.* New York: Harper & Row.

Demetras, M., Post, K., & Snow, C. (1986). Feedback to first language learners: The role of repetitions and clarification questions. *Journal of Child Language, 13,* 275–292.

Derwing, B. L. (1977). Is the child really a 'little linguist'? In J. Macnamara (Ed.), *Language learning and thought.* New York: Academic Press.

Derwing, B. L., & Baker, W. J. (1977). The psychological basis for morphological rules. In J. Macnamara (Ed.), *Language learning and thought.* New York: Academic Press.

deVilliers, J. G., & deVilliers, P. A. (1973). A cross-sectional study of the acquisition of grammatical morphemes in child speech. *Journal of Psycholinguistic Research, 2,* 267–278.

Dickinson, D., Wolf, M., & Stotsky, S. (1989). Words move: The interwoven development of oral and written language. In J. B. Gleason (Ed.), *The develop-

ment of language (2nd ed.). Columbus, OH: Merrill, an imprint of Macmillan Publishing Company.

Dillon, D. (1980). Teaching about language itself. In G. S. Pinnell (Ed.), *Discovering language with children.* Champaign-Urbana, IL: NCTE.

Dillon, D. (1989). Editorial. *Language Arts, 66*(1), 7-9.

Donaldson, M. (1978). *Children's minds.* Glasgow: Fontana/Collins.

Donaldson, M. (1984). Speech and writing and modes of learning. In H. Goelman, A. Oberg, & F. Smith (Eds.), *Awakening to literacy.* Portsmouth, NH: Heinemann Educational Books.

Dulay, H., & Burt. M. K. (1974). Natural sequences in child second language acquisition. *Language Learning, 24,* 37–53.

Dulay, H., Burt, M. K., & S. D. Krashen (1982). *Language two.* New York: Oxford University Press.

Dunn, L., & Dunn, L. (1981). *Peabody Picture Vocabulary Test-Revised (PPVT-R).* Circle Pines, MN: American Guidance Service.

Durkin, D. (1966). *Children who read early.* New York: Teachers College Press.

Eagan, R., & Cashion, M. (1988). Second year report of a longitudinal study of spontaneous reading in English by students in early French immersion classes. *Canadian Modern Language Review, 33,* 523–535.

Edelsky, C. (1982). Writing in a bilingual program: The relation of L1 and L2 texts. *TESOL Quarterly, 6,* 211–228.

Edelsky, C. (1986). *Writing in a bilingual program: Habia una vez.* Norwood, NJ: Ablex.

Edelsky, C., Altwerger, B., Barkin, F., Flores, B., Hudelson, S., & Jilbert, K. (1983). Semilingualism and language deficit. *Applied Linguistics, 4*(1), 1–22.

Eilers, R. E., Gavin, W. J., & Wilson, W. R. (1979). Linguistic experience and phonemic perception in infancy: A crosslinguistic study. *Child Development, 50,* 14–18.

Eimas, P. D., Siqueland, E. R., Jusczyk, P., & Vigorito, J. (1971). Speech perception in infants. *Science, 171,* 303–306.

Elliot, A. J. (1981). *Child language.* Cambridge: Cambridge University Press.

Ellis, R. (1985). *Understanding second language acquisition.* Oxford: Oxford University Press.

Engel, W. von R. (1965). Del bilinguismo infantile. *Archivio Glottologico Italiano, 50,* 175–180.

Engel, W. von R. (1966). Linguaggio attivo e linguaggio passivo. *Orientamenti Pedagogici, 13,* 893–894.

Erikson, E. H. (1959). Identity and the life cycle: Selected papers. *Psychological Issues, 1,* 1–171.

Ervin-Tripp, S. (1981). Social process in first- and second-language learning. In H. Winitz (Ed.), *Native language and foreign language acquisition*. New York: The New York Academy of Sciences.

Fagan, W. T., & Hayden, H. M. (1988). Writing processes in French and English of fifth grade French immersion students. *Canadian Modern Language Review, 44*, 653–668.

Fanselow, J. (1987). *Breaking rules: Generating and exploring alternatives in language teaching*. White Plains, NY: Longman.

Ferguson, C., & Farwell, C. (1975). Words and sounds in early language acquisition: English initial consonants in the first 50 words. *Language, 51*, 431–491.

Ferguson, C., & Garnica, O. (1975). Theories of phonological development. In E. Lenneberg & E. Lenneberg (Eds.), *Foundations of language development*. UNESCO.

Ferguson, C., & Slobin, D. (Eds.). (1973). *Studies of child language development*. New York: Holt, Rinehart, & Winston.

Ferreiro, E. (1984). The underlying logic of literacy development. In H. Goelman, A. Oberg, & F. Smith (Eds.), *Awakening to literacy*. Portsmouth, NH: Heinemann Educational Books.

Ferreiro, E., & Teberosky, A. (Translated by Karen Goodman Castro) (1982). *Literacy before schooling*. Portsmouth, NH: Heineman Educational Books.

Field, T., Woodson, R., Greenberg, R., & Cohen, D. (1982). Discrimination and imitation of facial expressions by neonates. *Science, 218*, 179–181.

Finn, C. E., Jr. (1991, May 27). Accounting for results. *National Review*, pp. 38–41, 61.

Fisher, C. J., & Terry, C. A. (1990). *Children's language and the language arts*. Boston: Allyn & Bacon.

Fishman, J., Cooper, R. L., & Ma, R. (1975). *Bilingualism in the barrio: Language science monographs*, (Vol. 7). Bloomington, IN: Indiana University Press.

Fletcher, P., & Garman, M. (Eds.). (1979). *Language acquisition*. Cambridge: Cambridge University Press.

Flower, L., & Hayes, J. R. (1981). A cognitive process theory of writing. *College Composition and Communication, 32*, 365–387.

Foley, K. S., Harley, B., & d'Anglejan, A. (1988). Research in core French: A bibliographic review. *Canadian Modern Language Review, 44*, 593–618.

Forrest, D. L., & Walker, T. G. (1979, March). Cognitive and metacognitive aspects of reading. Paper presented at the meeting of the Society for Research in Child Development, San Francisco, CA.

Foster, J. C. (1991, February). The role of accountability in Kentucky's education reform act of 1990. *Educational Leadership*, pp. 34–36.

Froese, V. (Ed.). (1990). *Whole-language practice and theory*. Scarborough, Ontario: Prentice-Hall Canada, Inc.

Gagne, R. M. (1965). *The conditions of learning.* New York: Holt, Rinehart, & Winston.

Galloway, L. (1981). Bilingualism: Neuropsychological considerations. *Journal of Research and Development in Education, 15,* 12–28.

Gardner, B. T., & Gardner, R. A. (1975). Evidence for sentence constituents in the early utterances of child and chimpanzee. *Journal of Experimental Psychology, 104,* 244–62.

Garnica, O. K. (1973). The development of phonemic speech perception. In T. E. Moore (Ed.), *Cognitive development and the acquisition of language.* New York: Academic Press.

Garnica, O. K., & Herbert, R. K. (1979). Some phonological errors in second language learning: Interference doesn't tell it all. *International Journal of Psycholinguistics, 6,* 5–19.

Gary, J. O. (1975). Delayed oral practice in initial stages of second language learning. In M. Burt & H. Dulay (Eds.), *New directions in second language learning, teaching, and bilingual education* (pp. 89–95). Washington, DC: TESOL.

Gass, S. (1984). A review of interlanguage syntax: Language transfer and language universals. *Language Learning, 34,* 115–132.

Genesee, F. (1983). Bilingual education of majority-language children: The immersion experiments in review. *Applied Psycholinguistics, 4,* 1–46.

Genesee, F., & Lambert, W. E. (1983). Trilingual education for majority-language children. *Child Development, 54,* 105–114.

Genesee, F., Tucker, G. R., & Lambert, W. E. (1976). Communication skills of bilingual children. *Child Development 46,* 1010–1014.

Gibson, E. J., & Levin, H. (1975). *The psychology of reading.* Cambridge, MA: The MIT Press.

Giles, H., Bourhis, R., & Taylor, D. (1977). Toward a theory of language in ethnic group relations. In H. Giles (Ed.), *Language ethnicity and intergroup relations.* New York: Academic Press.

Giles, H., & Byrne, J. (1982). An intergroup approach to second language acquisition. *Journal of Multilingual and Multicultural Development, 3,* 17–40.

Gleason, J. B. (Ed.). (1989). *The development of language,* (2nd ed.). Columbus, OH: Merrill, an imprint of Macmillan Publishing Company.

Gleitman, L., & Wanner, E. (1982). Language accquisition: The state of the state of the art. In E. Wanner & L. Gleitman (Eds.), *Language acquisition: The state of the art.* Cambridge: Cambridge University Press.

Glucksberg, S., & Danks, J. H. (1975). *Experimental psycholinguistics: An introduction.* New York: John Wiley & Sons.

Godby, C. J., Wallace, R., & Jolley, C. (1982). *Language files: Materials for an introduction to language.* Reynoldsburg, OH: Advocate Publishing Group.

Goelman, H., Oberg, A., & Smith, F. (Eds.). (1984). *Awakening to literacy.* Portsmouth, N.H.: Heinemann Educational Books.

Goldberg, E., & Costa, L. D. (1981). Hemisphere differences in the acquisition and use of descriptive systems. *Brain and Language, 14,* 144–173.

Golinkoff, R. (1983). The preverbal negotiation of failed messages: Insights into the transition period. In R. Golinkoff (Ed.), *The transition from preverbal to verbal communication.* Hillsdale, NJ: Lawrence Erlbaum.

Goodman, G. (1989). Worlds within worlds: Reflections on an encounter with parents. *Language Arts, 66*(1), 14–20.

Goodman, K. S. (1967). Reading: A psycholinguistic guessing game. *Journal of the Reading Specialist, 32,* 34–41.

Goodman, K. S., Bird, L. B., & Goodman, Y. M. (1991). *The whole language catalog.* Santa Rosa, CA: American School Publishers (Macmillan).

Goodman, K. S., Goodman, Y. M., & Hood, W. J. (Eds.). (1989). *The whole language evaluation book.* Portsmouth, NH: Heinemann Educational Books.

Goodman, Y. (1984). The development of initial literacy. In H. Goelman, A. Oberg, & F. Smith (Eds.), *Awakening to literacy.* Portsmouth, NH: Heinemann Educational Books.

Goodman, Y. M. (1986). Children coming to know literacy. In W. H. Teale & E. Sulzby (Eds.), *Emergent literacy: Writing and reading.* Norwood, NJ: Ablex.

Grabo, R. P. (1931). A study of the comparative vocabularies of junior high school pupils from English and Italian speaking homes. (Bulletin No. 13). Washington, DC: U.S. Office of Education.

Graham, A. (1975). The making of a nonsexist dictionary. In B. Thorne & N. Henley (Eds.), *Language and sex: Difference and dominance.* Rowley, MA: Newbury House.

Graham, L., & House, A. S. (1971). Phonological oppositions in children: A perceptual study. *Journal of the Acoustical Society of America, 49,* 559–569.

Graves, D. (1977). *Balance the basics: Let them write.* New York: The Ford Foundation.

Graves, D. (1983). *Writing teachers and children at work.* Portsmouth, NH: Heinemann Educational Books.

Greenberg, J. H. (1966). *Language universals: With special reference to feature hierarchies.* The Hague: Mouton.

Gregg, K. R. (1984). Krashen's monitor and Occam's razor. *Applied Linguistics, 5,* 79–100.

Grunwell, P. (1982). *Clinical phonology.* London: Croom Helm.

Gunderson, L. (1990). Reading and language development. In V. Froese (Ed.). (1990). *Whole-language practice and theory.* Scarborough, Ontario: Prentice-Hall Canada, Inc.

Gunderson, L. (1991). *ESL literacy instruction, a guidebook to theory and practice.* Englewood Cliffs, NJ: Prentice Hall Regents.

Halliday, M. A. K. (1975). *Learning how to mean.* London: Edward Arnold.

Halliday, M. A. K. (1976). *System and function in language.* London: Oxford University Press.

Halliday, M. A. K. (1978). *Language as a social semiotic: The social interpretation of language and meaning.* Baltimore: University Park Press.

Halliday, M. A. K. (1985). It's a fixed word order language is English. *International Review of Applied Linguistics, 67–68,* 91–116.

Hammermeister, F. (1972). Reading achievement in deaf adults. *American Annals of the Deaf, 116,* 25–28.

Hansen, Jane. (1983). First grade writers who pursue reading. In P. L. Stock (Ed.), *Forum: Essays on theory and practice in the teaching of writing* (pp. 155–162). Upper Montclair, NJ: Boynton-Cook.

Harding, C. G., & Golinkoff, R. M. (1979). The origins of intentional vocalizations in prelinguistic infants. *Child Development, 50,* 338–340.

Harlin, R., Lipa, S. E., & Lonberger, R. (1991). *The whole language journey.* Markham, Ontario: Pippin Publishing Company. Harste, J. C., Woodward, V. A., & Burke, C. (1984). *Language stories and literacy lessons.* Portsmouth, NH: Heinemann Educational Books.

Hatch, E. (Ed.) (1978a). *Second language acquisition.* Rowley, MA: Newbury House.

Hatch, E. (1978b). Acquisition of syntax in a second language. In J. Richards (Ed.), *Understanding second and foreign language learning: Issues and approaches.* Rowley, MA: Newbury House.

Hatch, E. (1978c). Discourse analysis and second language acquistion. In E. Hatch (Ed.), *Second language acquisition.* Rowley, MA: Newbury House.

Hatch, E. (1978d). Discourse analysis, speech acts and second language acquisition. In W. Ritchie (Ed.), *Second language acquisition research.* New York: Academic Press.

Hatch, E. M. (1983). *Psycholinguistics.* Rowley, MA: Newbury House.

Haugen, E. (1956). *Bilingualism in the Americas.* University of Alabama Press.

Hayes, C. W., Ornstein, J., & Gage, W. W. (1987). *The ABC's of languages and linguistics.* Lincolnwood, IL: The National Textbook Company.

Heath, S. B. (1978). *Teacher talk: Language in the classroom.* Washington, DC: Center for Applied Linguistics.

Heath, S. B. (1983). *Ways with words: Language, life, and work in communities and classrooms.* Cambridge: Cambridge University Press.

Heath, S. B. (1986). Separating 'things of imagination' from life: Learning to read and write. In W. H. Teale & E. Sulzby (Eds.), *Emergent literacy: Writing and reading.* Norwood, NJ: Ablex.

Heath, S. B., & Thomas, C. (1984). The achievement of preschool literacy for mother and child. In H. Goelman, A. Oberg, & F. Smith (Eds.), *Awakening to literacy*. Portsmouth, NH: Heinemann Educational Books.

Heatherington, M. E. (1980). *How language works*. Cambridge, MA: Winthrop Publishers.

Hersov, L. A., Berger, M., & Nicol, A. R. (Eds.) (1980). *Language and language disorders in childhood*. Oxford: Pergamon Press.

Hickman, J., & Kimberley, K. (Eds.). (1988). *Teachers, language and learning*. London: Routledge.

Hills, E. C. (1914). The speech of a child two years of age. *Dialect Notes, 4,* 84–100.

Hirsh-Pasek, K., Treiman, R., & Schneiderman, M. (1984). Brown and Hanlon revisited: Mothers' sensitivity to ungrammatical forms. *Journal of Child Language, 11,* 81–88.

Hoff-Ginsberg, E. (1986). Function and structure in maternal speech: Their relation to the child's development of syntax. *Developmental Psychology, 22,* 155–163.

Holt, J. (1967). *How children learn*. New York: Merloyd Lawrence (Dell).

Holt, J. (1983). *How children learn* (revised ed.). New York: Merloyd Lawrence (Dell).

Holt, J. (1989). *Learning all the time*. Reading, MA: Addison-Wesley.

Horgan, D. (1978). The development of the full passive. *Journal of Child Language, 5,* 65–80.

Hurtado, A., & Rodriguez, R. (1989). Language as a social problem: The repression of Spanish in south Texas. *Journal of Multilingual and Multicultural Development, 10*(5), 401–419.

Hutchings, M. (1986). What teachers are demonstrating. In J. Newman (Ed.), *Whole language theory in use*. Portsmouth, NH: Heinemann Educational Books.

Ingram, D. (1974). Phonological rules in young children. *Journal of Child Language, 1,* 49–64.

Ingram, D. (1976). *Phonological disability in children*. New York: Elsevier.

Ingram, D. (1979). Phonological patterns in the speech of young children. In P. Fletcher & M. Garman (Eds.), *Language acquisition*. Cambridge: Cambridge University Press.

Ingram, D. (1989). *First language acquisition, method, description and explanation*. Cambridge: Cambridge University Press.

Itoh, H., & Hatch, E. (1978) Second language acquisition: A case study. In E. Hatch (Ed.), *Second language acquisition*. Rowley, MA: Newbury House.

Jacob, E. (1984). Learning literacy through play: Puerto Rican kindergarten children. In H. Goelman, A. Oberg, & F. Smith (Eds.), *Awakening to literacy*. Portsmouth, NH: Heinemann Educational Books.

Jagger, A. (1980). Allowing for language differences. In G. S. Pinnell (Ed.), *Discovering language with children*. Champaign-Urbana, IL: NCTE.

Jago, C. (1989). Whose book is it anyway? *Language Arts, 66,* 1, 29–43.

Jakobson, R. (1941). *Kindersprache, Aphasie und allgemeine Lautesetze.* Uppsala: Almquist und Wiksell.

Jakobson, R., & Halle, M. (1956). *Fundamentals of language.* The Hague: Mouton.

Jakobson, R. (Translated by A. Keiler). (1968). *Child language, aphasia, and phonological universals.* The Hague: Mouton.

Johnson, D. (1990, November 4). Indian rootlessness. *New York Times,* sec. 4A, p. 27.

Just, M. A., & Carpenter, P. A. (1987). *The psychology of reading and language comprehension.* Newton, MA: Allyn & Bacon.

Kavanagh, J. F., & Mattingly, I. G. (1972). *Language by ear and by eye.* Cambridge, MA: The MIT Press.

Kellerman, E. (1979). Transfer and non-transfer: where we are now. *Studies in Second Language Acquisition, 2,* 37–57.

Kellerman, E. (1984). The empirical evidence for the influence of the L1 interlanguage. In A. Davies, C. Criper, & A. P. R. Howatt (Eds.), *Interlanguage.* Edinburgh: Edinburgh University Press.

Kerr, A. (1984). Language and the education of immigrants' children in Sweden. In C. Kennedy (Ed.), *Language planning and language education.* London: George Allen and Unwin.

Kessler, C. (1971). *The acquisition of syntax in bilingual children.* Washington, DC: Georgetown University Press.

Khubchandani, L. M. (1978). Multilingual education in India. In B. Spolsky & R. L. Cooper (Eds.), *Case studies in bilingual education.* Rowley, MA: Newbury House.

Kinsbourne, M. (1981). Neuropsychological aspects of bilingualism. In H. Winitz (Ed.), *Native language and foreign language acquisition.* New York: The New York Academy of Sciences.

Kiparsky, P., & Menn, L. (1977). On the acquisition of phonology. In J. Macnamara (Ed.), *Language learning and thought.* New York: Academic Press.

Kornfeld, J. (1971). Theoretical issues in child phonology. *PCLS,* Seventh Regional Meeting, 454–468.

Kossan, N. (1981). Developmental differences in concept acquisition strategies. *Child Development, 52,* 290–298.

Krashen, S. D. (1973). Lateralization, language learning, and the critical period: Some new evidence. *Language Learning, 23,* 63–74.

Krashen, S. D. (1977a). The monitor model for second language performance. In M. Burt, H. Dulay, & M. Finocchiaro (Eds.), *Viewpoints on English as a second language.* New York: Regents.

Krashen, S. D. (1977b). Some issues relating to the monitor model. In H. Brown, C. Yorio, & R. Crymes (Eds.), *On TESOL '77.* Washington, DC: TESOL.

Krashen, S. D. (1978). Individual variation in the use of the monitor. In W. Ritchie (Ed.), *Second language acquisition research.* New York: Academic Press.

Krashen, S. D. (1979). A response to McLaughlin, 'The monitor model: some methodological considerations.' *Language Learning, 29,* 151–167.

Krashen, S. D. (1981). *Second language acquisition and second language learning.* Oxford: Pergamon Press.

Krashen, S. D. (1982). *Principles and practices of second language acquisition.* Oxford: Pergamon Press.

Krashen, S. D. (1985). *The input hypothesis: issues and implications.* London: Longman.

Kuschner, D. (1989). From the personal world of childhood to the public world of school. *Language Arts, 66,* 1, 44–49.

Labov, W. (1972). *Sociolinguistic patterns.* Philadelphia: University of Pennsylvania Press.

Labov, W. (1982). Objectivity and commitment in linguistic science; the case of the Black English trial in Ann Arbor. *Language in Society, 11,* 165–201.

Lalonde, R. N., Lee, P. A., & Gardner, R. C. (1987). The common view of the good language learner: An investigation of teachers' beliefs. *Canadian Modern Language Review, 44,* 16–34.

Lamendella, J. (1977). General principles of neurofunctional organization and their manifestations in primary and non-primary acquisition. *Language Learning, 27,* 155–196.

Lamendella, J. (1979). The neurofunctional basis of pattern practice. *TESOL Quarterly, 13,* 5–19.

Lanauze, M., & Snow, C. (1989). The relation between first- and second-language writing skills: Evidence from Puerto Rican elementary school children in bilingual programs. *Linguistics and Education, 1,* 323–339.

Language Files (4th ed.) (1988). Columbus, OH: The Ohio State University Department of Linguistics.

Larsen-Freeman, D. (1983). Second language accquisition: Getting the whole picture. In K. M. Bailey, M. H. Long, & S. Peck (Eds.), *Second language acquisition studies.* Rowley, MA: Newbury House.

Larsen-Freeman, D., & Long, M. (1991). *An introduction to second language acquisition research.* New York: Longman.

Lasky, R. E., Syrdal-Lasky, A., & Klein, R. E. (1975). VOT discrimination by four to six and a half month old infants from Spanish environments. *Journal of Experimental Child Psychology, 20,* 215–225.

Leichter, H. J. (1984). Families as environments for literacy. In H. Goelman, A. Oberg, & F. Smith (Eds.), *Awakening to literacy.* Portsmouth, NH: Heinemann Educational Books.

Lenneberg, E. (1967). *Biological foundations of language.* New York: John Wiley & Sons.

Leopold, W. F. (1939). *Speech development of a bilingual child: A linguist's record* (Vol. 1). Evanston, IL: Northwestern University Press.

Leopold, W. F. (1947). *Vocabulary growth in the first two years* (Vol. 2). Evanston, IL: Northwestern University Press.

Leopold, W. F. (1948). Semantic learning in infant language. *Word, 4,* 173–180.

Leopold, W. F. (1949a). *Sound learning in the first two years* (Vol. 3). Evanston, IL: Northwestern University Press.

Leopold, W. F. (1949b). *Grammar and general problems in the first two years* (Vol. 4). Evanston, IL: Northwestern University Press.

Leung, C. (1989). The multilingual classroom: The case for minority pupils. *Journal of Multilingual and Multicultural Development, 10*(6), 461–472.

Levelt, W. J. M. (1978). Skill theory and language teaching. *Studies in Second Language Acquisition, 1,* 53–70.

Lewis, M., & Rosenblum, L. A. (Eds.). (1977). *Interaction, conversation, and the development of language.* New York: John Wiley & Sons.

Lieven, E. V. M. (1982). Context, process and progress in young children's speech. In M. Beveridge (Ed.), *Children thinking through language.* London: Edward Arnold.

Limber, J. (1973). The genesis of complex sentences. In T. E. Moore (Ed.), *Cognitive development and the acquisition of language.* New York: Academic Press.

Lindfors, J. W. (1987). *Children's language and learning.* Englewood Cliffs, NJ: Prentice-Hall.

Loban, W. D. (1963). *The language of elementary school children.* Champaign-Urbana, IL: National Council of Teachers of English.

Lorenz, K. (1971). *Studies in animal behavior.* Cambridge, MA: Harvard University Press.

Luria, A. R., & Yudovich, F. I. (1971). *Speech and the development of mental processes in the child.* London: Staples Press.

Lynwander, L. (1990, October 7). Pupils get financial incentives. *New York Times,* sec. 12, p. 6.

MacGinitie, W. H. (1991, March). Reading instruction: Plus ca change... *Educational Leadership,* pp. 55–58.

Mackay, R., Barkman, B., & Jordan, R. R. (Eds.) (1979). *Reading in a second language: Hypotheses, organization, and practice.* Rowley, MA: Newbury House.

Macken, M. A. (1979). Developmental reorganization of phonology: A hierarchy of basic units of acquisition. *Lingua, 49,* 11–49.

Macken, M. A., & Barton, D. (1980). The acquisition of the voicing contrast in English: A study of voice onset time in word-initial stop consonants. *Journal of Child Language, 7,* 41–75.

Macnamara, J. (1966). *Bilingualism in primary education.* Edinburgh: Edinburgh University Press.

Macnamara, J. (Ed.). (1977). *Language learning and thought.* New York: Academic Press.

Macnamara, J. (1977). On the relation between language learning and thought. In J. Macnamara (Ed.), *Language learning and thought.* New York: Academic Press.

MacWhinney, B. (Ed.) (1987). *Mechanisms of language acquisition.* Hillsdale, NJ: Lawrence Erlbaum.

MacWhinney, B. (1987). The competition model. In B. MacWhinney (Ed.), *Mechanisms of language acquisition.* Hillsdale, NJ: Lawrence Erlbaum.

Maguire, M. H. (1989). Teaching English and French as first languages: Are changes necessary? *Bulletin of the Canadian Association of Applied Linguistics, 11,* 29–50.

Major, D. (1974). *The acquisition of modal auxiliaries in the language of children.* The Hague: Mouton.

Malsheen, B. (1980). Two hypotheses for phonetic clarification in the speech of mothers to children. In G. Yeni-Komshian, J. F. Kavanagh, & C. A. Ferguson (Eds.), *Child phonology, Perception* (Vol. 2). New York: Academic Press.

Maratsos, M., Gudeman, R., Poldi, G., & DeHart, G. (1987). A study in novel word learning: The productivity of the causative. In B. MacWhinney (Ed.), *Mechanisms of language acquisition.* Hillsdale, NJ: Lawrence Erlbaum.

Markman, E. M. (1979). Realizing that you don't understand: Elementary school children's awareness of inconsistencies. *Child Development, 50,* 543–655.

Marler, P. (1970). A comparative approach to vocal learning: Song development in white-crowned sparrows. *Journal of Comparative and Physiological Psychology, 71*(2, Pt. 2), 1–25.

Marler, P. (1977). Sensory templates, vocal perception, and development: A comparative view. In M. Lewis & L. A. Rosenblum (Eds.), *Interaction, conversation, and the development of language.* New York: John Wiley & Sons.

Martin-Jones, M. (1986). Review of Bilingualism or not: The education of minorities. *Journal of Multilingual and Multicultural Development, 7*(4), 319–324.

Martin-Jones, M., & Romaine, S. (1986). Semilingualism: A half-baked theory of communicative competence. *Applied Linguistics, 7*(1), 26–38.

Mattes, L. J., & Omark, D. R. (1984). *Speech and language assessment for the bilingual handicapped.* San Diego: College-Hill Press.

McCutchen, D., & Perfetti, C. A. (1982). Coherence and connectedness in the development of discourse production. *Text, 2,* 113–139.

McGill, J. (1988). In the history classroom. In J. Hickman & K. Kimberley (Eds.), *Teachers, language and learning.* London: Routledge.

McLaughlin, B. (1978). *Second language acquisition in childhood.* Hillsdale, NJ: Lawrence Erlbaum.

McLaughlin, B. (1981). Differences and similarities between first- and second-language learning. In H. Winitz (Ed.), *Native language and foreign language acquisition.* New York: The New York Academy of Sciences.

McLaughlin, B. (1984). *Second-language acquisition in childhood: Preschool children* (Vol. 1) (2nd ed.). Hillsdale, NJ: Lawrence Erlbaum.

McLaughlin, B. (1985). *Second-language acquisition in childhood: School-age children* (Vol. 2) (2nd ed.). Hillsdale, NJ: Lawrence Erlbaum.

McLaughlin, B. (1987). *Theories of second language acquisition.* London: Edward Arnold.

McLaughlin, B., Rossman, T., & McLeod, B. (1983). Second-language learning: An information-processing perspective. *Language Learning, 33,* 135–158.

McLeod, B., & McLaughlin, B. (1986). Restructuring or automaticity? Reading in a second language. *Language Learning, 36,* 109–123.

McNeill, D. (1966) Developmental psycholinguistics. In F. Smith & G. Miller (Eds.), *The genesis of language: A psycholinguistic approach.* Cambridge, MA: The MIT Press.

Menn, L. (1971). Phonotactic rules in beginning speech. *Lingua, 26,* 251–255.

Menn, L. (1976). *Pattern, control, and contrast in beginning speech: A case study in the acquisition of word form and function.* Unpublished doctoral dissertation, University of Illinois.

Menn, L. (1983). Development of articulatory, phonetic, and phonological capabilities. In B. Butterworth (Ed.), *Language production* (Vol. 2). London: Academic Press.

Menn, L. (1989). Phonological development: Learning sounds and sound patterns. In J. B. Gleason (Ed.), *The development of language,* (2nd ed.). Columbus, OH: Merrill, an imprint of Macmillan Publishing Company.

Menyuk, P. (1969). *Sentences children use.* Cambridge, MA: The MIT Press.

Menyuk, P. (1971). *The acquisition and development of language.* Englewood Cliffs, NJ: Prentice-Hall.

Mills, H., & Clyde, J. A. (Eds.) (1990). *Portraits of whole language classrooms.* Portsmouth, NH: Heinemann Educational Books.

Milon, J. P. (1975). Dialect in the TESOL program: If you never you better. In M. Burt & H. Dulay (Eds.). *New directions in second language learning, teaching, and bilingual education.* Washington, DC: TESOL.

Mitchell, C. A. (1989). Linguistic and cultural aspects of second language acquisition: Investigating literature/literacy as an environmental factor. *Canadian Modern Language Review, 46,* 73–82.

Mollica, Anthony (1989). The immersion experience. *Canadian Modern Language Review, 45,* 434.

Moore, T. E. (Ed.). (1973). *Cognitive development and the acquisition of language.* New York: Academic Press.

Morrow, L. M. (1989). *Literacy development in the early years: Helping children read and write.* Englewood Cliffs, NJ: Prentice-Hall.

Moskowitz, A. (1973). On the status of vowel shift in English. In T. E. Moore (Ed.), *Cognitive development and the acquisition of language.* New York: Academic Press.

Moskowitz, B. A. (1980). Idioms in phonology acquisition and phonological change. *Journal of Phonetics, 8,* 69–83.

Murrell, M. (1966). Language acquisition in a trilingual environment: Notes from a case study. *Studia Linguistica, 20,* 9–35.

Myers, D. T. (1964). *Understanding language.* Upper Montclair, NJ: Boynton-Cook.

Nakazina, S. A. (1962). A comparative study of the speech developments of Japanese and American English in childhood (1): A comparison of the developments of voices at the prelinguistic period. *Studia Phonologica, 2,* 27–46.

Nelson, K. (1973). Structure and strategy in learning to talk. *Monographs of the Society for Child Development, 38,* 149.

Nelson, K. (1977). The conceptual basis for naming. In J. Macnamara (Ed.), *Language learning and thought.* New York: Academic Press.

Netton, J. E., & Spain, W. H. (1989). Student-teacher interaction patterns in the French immersion classroom: Implications for levels of achievement in French language proficiency. *Canadian Modern Language Review, 45*(3), 485–501.

Newman, J. (Ed.) (1985a). *Whole language theory in use.* Portsmouth, NH: Heineman Educational Books.

Newman, J. (1985b). Using children's books to teach reading. In J. Newman (Ed.), *Whole language theory in use* (chap. 4). Portsmouth, NH: Heineman Educational Books.

Newman, J. (1985c). What about reading? In J. Newman (Ed.), *Whole language theory in use* (chap. 9). Portsmouth, NH: Heineman Educational Books.

Newport, E. (1976). Motherese: The speech of mothers to young children. In N. Castellan, D. Pisoni, & G. Potts (Eds.), *Cognitive theory* (Vol. 2). Hillsdale, NJ: Lawrence Erlbaum.

Nickse, R. S. (1989). *The noises of literacy: An overview of intergenerational and family literacy programs* (ERIC Document Reproduction Service No. ED 308 415). Washington, DC: Office of Educational Research and Improvement.

O'Connor, N. M., & Rotatori, A. F. (1987). Culturally diverse special education students. In A. Rotatori, M. M. Banbury, & R. A. Fox (Eds.), *Issues in special education.* Mayfield Publishing.

Oksaar, E. (1970). Zum Spracherwerb des Kindes in zweisprachiger Umgebung. *Folia Linguistica, 4,* 330–358.

Olson, D. R. (1977). The contexts of language acquisition. *Language learning and thought.* New York: Academic Press.

Olson, D. R. (1984). "See! Jumping!" Some oral language antecedents of literacy. In H. Goelman, A. Oberg, & F. Smith (Eds.), *Awakening to literacy.* Portsmouth, NH: Heinemann Educational Books.

O'Malley, J. M., Chamot, A. U., & Walker, C. (1987). Some applications of cognitive theory to second language acquisition. *Studies in Second Language Acquisition, 9,* 287–306.

Omark, D. R., & Erickson, J. G. (Eds.). (1983). *The bilingual exceptional child.* San Diego: College-Hill Press.

O'Neill, C. (1989). Dialogue and drama: The transformation of events, ideas, and teachers. *Language Arts, 66*(2), 147–159. Page, M. M. (1966). We dropped FLES. *Modern Language Journal, 50,* 139–141.

Paradis, M. (Ed.). (1978). *Aspects of bilingualism.* Columbia, SC: Hornbeam.

Peal, E., & Lambert, W. (1962). The relation of bilingualism to intelligence. *Psychological Monographs, LXXVI, 27,* 1–23.

Pease, D. M., Gleason, J. B., and Pan, B. A. (1989). Gaining meaning: Semantic development. In J. B. Gleason (Ed.), *The development of language,* (2nd ed.). Columbus, OH: Merrill, an imprint of Macmillan Publishing Company.

Penfield, W., & Roberts, L. (1959). *Speech and brain mechanisms.* Princeton: Princeton University Press.

Penner, P. G., & McConnell, R. E. (1980). *Learning language.* Toronto, Ontario: Gage Publishing Ltd.

Penner, S. (1987). Parental responses to grammatical and ungrammatical child utterances. *Child Development, 58,* 376–384.

Perera, K. (1984). *Children's writing and reading: Analysing classroom language.* Oxford: Basil Blackwell.

Perfetti, C. A. (1984). *Reading ability.* New York: Oxford University Press.

Pflaum, S. W. (1986). *The development of language and literacy in young children.* Columbus, OH: Merrill, an imprint of Macmillan Publishing Company.

Phinney, M. (1981) Children's interpretation of negation in complex sentences. In S. L. Tavakolian (Ed.), *Language acquisition and linguistic theory.* Cambridge, MA: The MIT Press.

Piaget, J. (1955). *The language and thought of the child.* Cleveland: World Publishing Company.

Piaget, J. (1962). *Play, dreams and imitation in childhood.* New York: Norton.

Piaget, J., & Inhelder, B. (1969). *The psychology of the child.* New York: Basic Books.

Pinker, S. (1984). *Language, learnability and language development.* Cambridge, MA.: Harvard University Press.

Pinnell, G. S. (Ed.). (1980). *Discovering language with children.* Champaign-Urbana, IL: NCTE.

Piper, T. (1983). Phonics for ESL learners. *Reading- Canada-Lecture, 2,* 56–62.

Piper, T. (1984a). Phonological processes in the ESL learner. *TESL Canada Journal, 1,* 71–80.

Piper, T. (1984b). Observations on the second language acquisition of the English sound system. *The Canadian Modern Language Review, 40,* 542–551.

Piper, T. (1984c). Successive approximation in second language acquisiiton. *Canadian Journal of Linguistics, 29,* 2.

Piper, T. (1986a). A tale of two learners. *Canadian Children, 11*(1), 41–60.

Piper, T. (1986b). The role of prior linguistic experience on second language acquisition. *Reading-Canada-Lecture, 4,* 68–81.

Piper, T. (1986c). Learning about language learning. *Language Arts, 65,* 466–471.

Piper, T. (1987). On the difference between L1 and L2 acquisition of phonology. *Canadian Journal of Linguistics, 32,* 245–259.

Piper, T., & McEachern, W. R. (1988). Content bias in cloze as a general language indicator. *English Quarterly, 1,* 41–48.

Porter, J. (1977). A cross-sectional study of morpheme acquisition in first language learners. *Language Learning, 27*(1), 47–62.

Potter, G. (1989). Parent participation in language arts programs. *Language Arts, 66*(1), 29–43.

Power, D., & Quigley, S. (1973). Deaf children's acquisition of the passive voice. *Journal of Speech and Hearing Research, 25*(16), 5–11.

Premack, A. J. (1976). *Why chimps can read.* New York: Harper & Row.

Premack, D., & Premack, A. J. (1983). *The mind of an ape.* New York: Norton.

Pyles, T., & Algeo, J. (1970). *English: An introduction to language.* New York: Harcourt, Brace & World, Inc.

Quigley, S., Montanelli, D., & Wilbur, R. B. (1974). Some aspects of the verb system in the language of deaf students. *Journal of Speech and Hearing Research, 19,* 536–550.

Quigley, S., Montanelli, D., & Wilbur, R. B. (1976). Some aspects of the verb system in the language of deaf students. *Journal of Speech and Hearing Research, 19,* 536–550.

Quigley, S., Smith, N., & Wilbur, R. B. (1974). Comprehension of relativized sentences by deaf students. *Journal of Speech and Hearing Research, 17,* 325–341.

Quigley, S., Wilbur, R. B., & Montanelli, D. (1974). Question formation in the language of deaf students. *Journal of Speech and Hearing Research, 17,* 699–713.

Quigley, S., Wilbur, R. B., & Montanelli, D. (1976). Complement structures in the language of deaf students. *Journal of Speech and Hearing Research, 19,* 448–457.

Rasinski, T. V., & Fredericks, A. D. (1988, December). What do parents think about reading in the schools. *The Reading Teacher,* pp. 262–263.

Ratner, N. B. (1989) Atypical language development. In J. B. Gleason (Ed.), *The development of language,* (2nd ed.). Columbus, OH: Merrill, an imprint of Macmillan Publishing Company.

Reich, P. A. (1986). *Language development.* Englewood Cliffs, NJ: Prentice-Hall.

Resnick, D. P., & Resnick, L. B. (1985). Standards, curriculum, and performance: a historical and comparative perspective. *Educational Researcher, 14*(4), 5–21.

Richards, J. (Ed.). (1978). *Understanding second and foreign language learning: Issues and approaches.* Rowley, MA: Newbury House.

Richards, J., Platt, J., & Weber, H. (1985). *Longman dictionary of applied linguistics.* London: Longman.

Richards, J. C., & Rodgers, T. S. (1986). *Approaches and methods in language teaching.* Cambridge: Cambridge University Press.

Ridley, L. (1990a, May). Enacting change in elementary school programs: Implementing a whole language perspective. *The Reading Teacher,* pp. 640–646.

Ridley, L. (1990b). Whole language in the ESL classroom. In H. Mills & J. A. Clyde (Eds.), *Portraits of whole language classrooms* (chap. 11). Portsmouth, NH: Heinemann Educational Books.

Rigg, P., & Allen, V. G. (Eds.) (1989). *When they don't all speak English.* Champaign-Urbana, IL: NCTE.

Ritchie, W. (Ed.). (1978). *Second language acquisition research.* New York: Academic Press.

Roeper, T., Lapointe, S., Bing, J., & Tavakolian, S. (1981). A lexical approach to language acquisition. In S. L. Tavakolian (Ed.), *Language acquisition and linguistic theory.* Cambridge, MA: The MIT Press.

Rogers, S. (Ed.) (1975). *Children and language.* London: Oxford University Press.

Roller, C. (1989). Classroom interaction patterns: Reflections of a stratified society. *Language Arts, 66*(5), 492–500.

Romney, J. C., Romney, D. M., & Braun, C. (1989). The effects of reading aloud in French to immersion children on second language acquisition. *Canadian Modern Language Review, 45,* 530–538.

Rondal, J. A. (1980). Fathers' and mothers' speech in early language development. *Journal of Child Language, 7,* 353–369.

Ronjat, J. (1913). *Le developpement du langage observe chez un enfant bilingue.* Paris: Champion.

Rosch, E., Mervis, C. B., Gray, W. D., Johnson, D. M., & Boyes-Braem, P. (1976). Basic objects in natural categories. *Cognitive Psychology, 8,* 382–439.

Ruke-Dravina, V. (1965). The process of acquisition of apical /r/ and uvular /r/ in the speech of children. *Linguistics, 17,* 56–68.

Ruke-Dravina, V. (1967). *Mehrsprachigkeit im Vorschulalter.* Lund: Gleerup.

Saer, D. J. (1922). An enquiry into the effects of bilingualism upon the intelligence of young children. *Journal of Experimental Pedagogy, 6.*

Sachs, Jacqueline (1989). Communication development in infancy. In J. B. Gleason (Ed.), *The development of language,* (2nd ed.). Columbus, OH: Merrill, an imprint of Macmillan Publishing Company.

Saville-Troike, M. (1980). Discovering what children know about language. In G. S. Pinnell (Ed.), *Discovering language with children.* Champaign-Urbana, IL: NCTE.

Schacter, F. F., Kirshner, K., Klips, B., Friedrickes, M., & Sanders, K. (1974). Everyday preschool interpersonal speech usage: methodological development and sociolinguistic studies. In *Monographs of the Society for Research and Child Development.* Chicago: University of Chicago.

Schickedanz, J. D., York, M. E., Stewart, I. S., & White, D. (1990). *Strategies for teaching young children* (3rd ed.). Englewood Cliffs, NJ: Prentice-Hall.

Schieffelin, B. B., & Cochran-Smith, M. (1984). Learning to read culturally: Literacy before schooling. In H. Goelman, A. Oberg, & F. Smith (Eds.), *Awakening to literacy.* Portsmouth, NH: Heinemann Educational Books.

Schieffelin, B. B., & Ochs, E. (1983). A cultural perspective on the transition from prelinguistic to linguistic communication. In R. Golinkoff (Ed.), *The transition from preverbal to verbal communication.* Hillsdale, NJ: Lawrence Erlbaum.

Schumann, J. (1978a). *The pidginization process: A model for second language acquisition.* Rowley, MA: Newbury House.

Schumann, J. (1978b). Social and psychological factors in second language acquisition. In J. Richards (Ed.), *Understanding second and foreign language learning: Issues and approaches.* Rowley, MA: Newbury House.

Schumann, J. (1978c). The acculturation model for second language acquisition. In R. Gingras (Ed.), *Second language acquisition and foreign language teaching.* Arlington, VA: Center for Applied Linguistics.

Schumann, J. (1981a). Discussion of 'Two perspectives on pidginization as second language acquisition.' In R. Anderson (Ed.) (1981). New dimensions in second language acquisition research. Rowley, MA: Newbury House.

Schumann, J. (1981b). Reaction to Gilbert's discussion of Andersen's paper. In R. Andersen (Ed.) (1981). New dimensions in second language acquisition research. Rowley, MA: Newbury House.

Schumann, J. (1982). Simplification, transfer and relexification as aspects of pidginization and early second language acquisition. *Language Learning, 32,* 337–366.

Scollon, R., & Scollon, S. (1981). *Narrative, literacy and face in interethnic communication.* Norwood, NJ: Ablex.

Scovel, T. (1982). Questions concerning the application of neurolinguistic research to second language learning/teaching. *TESOL Quarterly, 16,* 323–331.

Scoville, R. (1983). Development of the intention to communicate: The eye of the beholder. In L. Feagans, C. Garvey, & R. Golinkoff (Eds.), *The origins and growth of communication.* Norwood, NJ: Ablex.

Segalowitz, N. (1986). Skilled reading in the second language. In J. Vaid (Ed.), *Language processing in bilinguals: psycholinguistic and neuropsychological perspectives.* Hillsdale, NJ: Lawrence Erlbaum.

Selinker, L. (1972). Interlangauge. *International Review of Applied Linguistics, X,* 209–230.

Selinker, L., & Lamendella, J. (1976). Two perspectives on fossilization in interlanguage learning. *Interlanguage Studies Bulletin, 3,* 144–191.

Selinker, L., Swain, M., & Dumas, G. (1975). The interlanguage hypothesis extended to children. *Language Learning, 25,* 139–191.

Serebrin, W. (1985). Andrew and Molly, Writers and context in concert. In J. Newman (Ed.), *Whole language theory in use.* Portsmouth, NH: Heinemann Educational Books.

Shacter, F. F., Kirshner, K., Klips, B., Friedrickes, M., & Sanders, K. (1974). Everyday preschool interpersonal speech usage: Methodological development and sociolinguistic studies. In *Monographs of the Society for Research and Child Development.* Chicago: University of Chicago Press.

Shafer, R. E., Staab, C., & Smith, K. (1983). *Language functions and school success.* Glenview, IL: Scott, Foresman & Company.

Shapiro, J. (1990). Research perspectives on whole language. In V. Froese (Ed.). (1990). *Whole-language practice and theory* (pp. 268–305). Scarborough, Ontario: Prentice-Hall Canada, Inc.

Shvachkin, N. (1973). The development of phonemic speech perception in early childhood. In C. A. Ferguson & D. I. Slobin (Eds.), *Studies of child language development.* New York: Holt, Rinehart, & Winston.

Siegler, R. S. (1986). *Children's thinking* (1st ed.). Englewood Cliffs, NJ: Prentice Hall.

Siegler, R. S. (1991). *Children's thinking* (2nd ed.). Englewood Cliffs, NJ: Prentice Hall.

Sinclair, H. (1977). The cognitive basis of the comprehension and production of relational terminology. *Journal of Experimental Child Psychology, 24,* 40–52.

Skinner, B. F. (1957). *Verbal Behavior.* Englewood Cliffs, NJ: Prentice-Hall.

Skuktnabb-Kangas, T. (1984). *Bilingualism or not: the education of minorities.* Clevedon, UK: Multilingual Matters.

Slobin, D. (1966). Comments on developmental psycholinguistics. In F. Smith & G. Miller (Eds.), *The genesis of language: A psycholinguistic approach.* Cambridge, MA: The MIT Press.

Slobin, D. (1971). *Psycholinguistics.* Glenview, IL: Scott, Foresman & Company.

Slobin, D. (1973). Cognitive prerequisites for the acquisition of grammar. In C. A. Ferguson & D. I. Slobin (Eds.), *Studies of child language development.* New York: Holt, Rinehart, & Winston.

Slobin, D. (1979). *Psycholinguistics* (2nd ed.). Glenview, IL: Scott, Foresman & Company.

Slobin, D. (1982). Universal and particular in the acquisition of language. In E. Wanner & L. Gleitman (Eds.), *Language acquisition: The state of the art.* Cambridge: Cambridge University Press.

Slobin, D. (Ed.) (1985). *The cross-linguistic study of language acquisition: The data* (Vol. 1). Hillsdale, NJ: Lawrence Erlbaum.

Smith, C. (1991). Family literacy: The most important literacy. *The Reading Teacher, 44*(9), 700–701.

Smith, E. B., Goodman, K. S., & Meredith, R. (1976). *Language and thinking in school* (2nd ed.). New York: Holt, Rinehart, & Winston.

Smith, F. (1975). *Comprehension and learning: A conceptual framework for teachers.* New York: Holt, Rinehart, & Winston.

Smith, F. (1983). *Essays into literacy.* Portsmouth, NH: Heinemann Educational Books.

Smith, F. (1984). The creative achievement of literacy. In H. Goelman, A. Oberg, & F. Smith (Eds.), *Awakening to literacy.* Portsmouth, NH: Heinemann Educational Books.

Smith, F. (1985). *Reading without nonsense* (2nd ed.). New York: Teachers College Press.

Smith, F. (1988). *Joining the literacy club: Further essays into education.* Portsmouth, NH: Heinemann Educational Books.

Smith, F., & Miller, G. (Eds.) (1966). *The genesis of language: A psycholinguistic approach.* Cambridge, MA: The MIT Press.

Smith, M. E. (1933). A study of the speech of bilingual children in Hawaii. *Psychological Bulletin, 30.*

Smith, M. E. (1935). A study of the speech of eight bilingual children of the same family. *Child Development, 6,* 19–25.

Smith, N. V. (1973). *The acquisition of phonology: A case study.* London: Cambridge University Press.

Snow, C. (1972). Mother's speech to children learning language. *Child Development, 43,* 549–565.

Snow, C. (1979). The role of social interaction in language acquisition. In W. A. Collins (Ed.), *Minnesota symposia on child psychology* (Vol. 12). Hillsdale, NJ: Lawrence Erlbaum.

Snow, C., & Ninio, A. (1986). The contracts of literacy: What children learn from learning to read books. In W. H. Teale & E. Sulzby (Eds.), *Emergent literacy: Writing and reading.* Norwood, NJ: Ablex.

Snyder, G. (1990). Parents, teachers, children and whole-language. In V. Froese (Ed.). (1990). *Whole-language practice and theory.* Scarborough, Ontario: Prentice-Hall Canada, Inc.

Soudek, L. I. (1981). Two languages in one brain: recent work in neurolinguistics and its implications for second-language learning. *English Language Teaching Journal, 35,* 219–224.

Spolsky, B. (1978). *Educational linguistics.* Rowley, MA: Newbury House.

Spolsky, B. (1985). Formulating a theory of second language learning. *Studies in Second Language Acquisition, 7,* 269–288.

Spolsky, B., & Cooper, R. L. (Eds.). (1978). *Case studies in bilingual education.* Rowley, MA: Newbury House.

Staab, C. (1990). Talk in whole-language classrooms. In V. Froese (Ed.). (1990). *Whole-language practice and theory* (chap. 2). Scarborough, Ontario: Prentice-Hall Canada, Inc.

Staab, C. (1991). Teachers' practices with regard to oral language. *Alberta Journal of Educational Research, 37*(1), 31–48.

Stampe, D. (1979). *A dissertation on natural phonology,* J. E. Hankamer (Ed.). New York: Garland Publishing Company.

Steiner-Khamsi, G. (1990). Community languages and anti-racist education: The open battlefield. *Educational Studies, 16*(1), 33–47).

Stephens, D., Huntsman, R., O'Neill, K., Story, J., Watson, V., & Toomes, J. (1990). We call it good teaching. In H. Mills & J. A. Clyde (Eds.), *Portraits of whole language classrooms* (chap. 15). Portsmouth, NH: Heinemann Educational Books.

Stern, D., Beebe, B., Jaffe, J., & Bennett, S. (1977). The infant's stimulus world during social interaction: A study of caregiver behaviors with particular reference to repetition and timing. In H. Schaffer (Ed.), *Studies in mother-infant interaction.* New York: Academic Press.

Stevick, E. W. (1990). *Humanism in language teaching.* Oxford: Oxford University Press.

Strickland, D. S., & Morrow, L. M. (Eds.). (1989). *Emerging literacy: Young children learn to read and write.* Newark, DE: The International Reading Association.

Strickland, R. G. (1962). The language of elementary school children: Its relationship to the language of reading textbooks and the quality of reading of selected children. *Bulletin of the School of Education, 38,* 4. Bloomington: University of Indiana.

Stringer, D., Bruce, D., & Oates, J. (1973). *Generative linguistics: An introduction to the work of Noam Chomsky; Language acquisition: Language and cognition.* Milton Keynes, UK: The Open University Press.

Stubbs, M. (1986). *Educational linguistics.* Oxford: Basil Blackwell.

Sullivan, M. W., Rovee-Collier, C. K., & Tynes, D. M. (1979). A conditioning analysis of infant long-term memory. *Child Development, 50,* 152–162.

Swain, M. (1974). French immersion programs across Canada: Research findings. *Canadian Modern Language Review, 31,* 117–129.

Swain, M. (1976). Bibliography: Research on immersion education for the majority child. *Canadian Modern Language Review, 32,* 592–596.

Swain, M. (1978). French immersion: Early, late or partial? *The Canadian Modern Language Review, 34,* 557–585.

Swain, M. (1979). Bilingual education: Research and its implications. In C. Yorio, K. Perkins, and J. Schachter (Eds.). *On TESOL 1979: The learner in focus.* Washington, DC: TESOL.

Swain, M., Barik, H., & Nwanunobi, E. (1973). *Bilingual education project: Evaluation of Elgin County Board of Education partial immersion program for grades one, two and three.* Unpublished Paper. Toronto: Ontario Institute for Studies in Education.

Swain, M., & Lapkin, S. (1982). *Evaluating bilingual education: A Canadian case study.* Clevedon, UK: Multilingual Matters.

Tabouret-Keller, A. (1962). L'acquisition du langage parle chez un petit enfant en milieu bilingue. *Problemes de Psycholinguistique, 8,* 205–219

Tager-Flusberg, H. (1989). Putting words together: morphology and syntax in the preschool years. In J. B. Gleason (Ed.), *The development of language,* (2nd ed.). Columbus, OH: Merrill, an imprint of Macmillan Publishing Company.

Tardif, C., & Weber, S. (1987). French immersion research: A call for new perspectives. *Canadian Modern Language Review, 44,* 67–78.

Tarone, E. (1982). Systematicity and attention in interlanguage. *Language Learning, 30,* 417–431.

Tavakolian, S. L. (Ed.). (1981). *Language acquisition and linguistic theory.* Cambridge, MA: The MIT Press.

Teale, W. H. (1986). Home background and young children's literacy development. In W. H. Teale & E. Sulzby (Eds.), *Emergent literacy: Writing and reading.* Norwood, NJ: Ablex. Teale, W. H., & Sulzby, E. (Eds.). (1986). *Emergent literacy: Writing and reading.* Norwood, NJ: Ablex.

Teitelbaum, H., & Hiller, R. J. (1977). The legal perspective. In *Bilingual education: Current perspectives (Law), 3,* 1–64.

Temple, C., & Gillet, J. W. (1989). *Language arts: Learning processes and teaching practices.* Glenview, IL: Scott, Foresman, & Company.

Templin, M. C. (1957). *Certain language skills in children: Their development and interrelationships* (Institute of Child Welfare Monograph 26). Minneapolis, MN: The University of Minnesota Press.

Terrace, H. S. (1980). *Nim: A chimpanzee who learned sign language.* New York: Knopf.

Tierney, R. J. (1983). Writer-reader transactions: Defining the dimensions of negotiation. In P. L. Stock (Ed.), *Forum: Essays on theory and practice in the teaching of writing* (pp. 147–151). Upper Montclair, NJ: Boynton-Cook.

Tierney, R. J., & Pearson, P. D. (1984). Toward a composing model of reading. In J. M. Jensen (Ed.), *Composing and comprehending.* Champaign-Urbana, IL: NCRE/ERIC.

Titone, R., & Danesi, M. (1985). *Applied psycholinguistics: An introduction to the psychology of language learning and teaching.* Toronto: University of Toronto Press.

Tittle, C. E. (1973). Women and educational testing. *Phi Delta Kappan, 55*(2), 118–119.

Torrey, J. W. (1973). Learning to read without a teacher: A case study. In F. Smith (Ed.), *Psycholinguistics and reading.* New York: Holt, Rinehart, & Winston.

Totten, G. O. (1960). Bringing up children bilingually. *American Scandinavian Review, 48,* 42–50.

Tough, J. (1977). *The development of meaning.* London: George Allen & Unwin.

Tough, J. (1979). *Talk for teaching and learning.* London: Ward Lock Educational.

Toukomaa, P., & Skutnabb-Kangas, T. (1977). *The intensive teaching of the mother tongue to migrant children of pre-school age and children in the lower level of comprehensive school.* Helsinki: The Finnish National Commission for UNESCO.

Trybus, R., & Karchmer, M. (1977). School achievement scores of hearing impaired children: National data on achievement status and growth patterns. *American Annals of the Deaf, 122,* 62–69.

Tucker, G. R., & Gray, T. C. (1980). The pursuit of equal opportunity. *Language and Society, 2,* 5–8.

Tulving, E. (1983). *Elements of episodic memory.* New York: Oxford University Press.

Vaid, J. (Ed.) (1986). *Language processing in bilinguals: Psycholinguistic and neuropsychological perspectives.* Hillsdale, NJ: Lawrence Erlbaum.

Valian, V., Winzemer, J., & Erreich, A. (1981). A 'little linguist' model of syntax learning. In S. L. Tavakolian (Ed.), *Language acquisition and linguistic theory.* Cambridge, MA: The MIT Press.

Van Buren, P. (1975). Semantics and language teaching. In J. P. B. Allen & S. P. Corder (Eds.), *The Edinburgh course in applied linguistics: Papers in applied linguistics* (Vol. 2). London: Oxford University Press.

Van Lawick-Goodall, J. (1971). *In the shadow of man.* Boston: Houghton Mifflin.

Velten, H. V. (1943). The growth of phonetic and lexical pattern in infant language. *Language, 19,* 281–292.

Vihman, M. M., & McLaughlin, B. (1982). Bilingualism and second-language acquisition in preschool children. In C. J. Brainerd & M. Pressley (Eds.), *Progress in cognitive development research: Verbal processes in children.* Berlin: Springer Verlag.

Vocolo, J. M. (1967). The effect of foreign language study in the elementary school upon achievement in the same language in high school. *Modern Language Journal, 51,* 463–469.

von Raffler Engel, W. (1973). The development from sound to phoneme in child language. In C. A. Ferguson & D. Slobin (Eds.), *Studies of child language development.* New York: Holt, Rinehart, & Winston.

Voss, M. M. (1988). "Make way for applesauce": The literate world of a three year old. *Language Arts, 65*(3), 272–278.

Vygotsky, L. S. (1962). *Thought and language.* Cambridge, MA: The MIT Press.

Walkerdine, V. (1982). From context to text: a psychosemiotic approach to abstract thought. In M. Beveridge (Ed.), *Children thinking through language.* London: Edward Arnold.

Warren-Leubecker, A. W., & Bohannon, J. N. (1989). Pragmatics: Language in social contexts. In J. B. Gleason (Ed.), *The development of language,* (2nd ed.). Columbus, OH: Merrill, an imprint of Macmillan Publishing Company.

Waterhouse, L. H. (1986). Problems in facing the nature/nurture question in child language acquisition. *Language Sciences, 8*(2), 153–168.

Wells, A. S. (1992, January 6). In the market for a public school? *New York Times,* sec. 4A, p. 6.

Wells, G. (1986). *The meaning makers: Children learning language and using language to learn.* Portsmouth, NH: Heinemann Educational Books.

Wexler, K. (1982). A principle theory for language acquisition. In E. Wanner & L. Gleitman (Eds.), *Language acquisition: The state of the art.* Cambridge: Cambridge University Press.

Whitaker, H. A., Bub, D., & Leventer, S. (1981). Neurolinguistic aspects of language acquisition and bilingualism. In H. Winitz (Ed.), *Native language and foreign language acquisition.* New York: The New York Academy of Sciences.

White, R. W. (1960). Competence and the psychosexual stages of development. In M. Jones (Ed.), *Nebraska symposium on motivation* (pp. 97–141). Lincoln: University of Nebraska Press.

Whitehurst, G., & Vasta, R. (1975). Is language acquired through imitation? *Journal of Psycholinguistic Research, 4,* 37–59.

Whorf, B. L. (1975). The organization of reality. In Rogers, S. (Ed.), *Children and language.* London: Oxford University Press.

Wiggins, G. (1991, February). Standards, not standardization: Evoking quality student work. *Educational Leadership,* pp. 18–25.

Wilbur, R. B., Montanelli, D., & Quigley, S., (1976). Pronominalization in the language of deaf students. *Journal of Speech and Hearing Research, 19,* 120–140.

Wilkerson, I. (1990, November 4). Blacks look to basics. *New York Times,* sec. 4A, p. 26.

Winitz, H. (Ed.). (1981). *Native language and foreign language acquisition.* New York: The New York Academy of Sciences.

Winter, M., & Rouse, J. (1990, February). Fostering intergenerational literacy: The Missouri parents as teachers program. *The Reading Teacher,* pp. 382–386.

Wiss, C. (1989). Early French immersion programs may not be suitable for every child. *Canadian Modern Language Review, 45,* 517–529.

Wode, H. (1980). Operating principles and 'universals' in L1, L2 and FLT. In Nehls, D. (Ed.), *Studies in language acquisition.* Heidelberg: Julius Groos.

Wootten, J., Merkin, S., Hood, L., & Bloom, L. (1979, March). *Wh-questions: Linguistic evidence to explain the sequence of acquisition.* Paper presented at the biennial meeting of the Society for Research in Child Development, San Francisco.

Wright, T. (1987). *Roles of teachers and learners.* Oxford: Oxford University Press.

Yamada, J. (1981, August). On the independence of language and cognition: evidence from a hyperlinguistic retarded adolescent. Paper presented at the International Congress of Child Language, University of British Columbia, Vancouver.

Yardley, A. (1973). *Young children thinking.* London: Evans Brothers Ltd.

Yule, G. (1985). *The study of language.* Cambridge: Cambridge University Press.

Zareba, A. (1953). Jezyk polski w szwecji. *Jezyk Polski, 33,* 29–31, 98–111.

Zutell, J. (1980). Learning language at home and at school. In G. S. Pinnell (Ed.), *Discovering language with children.* Champaign-Urbana, IL: NCTE.

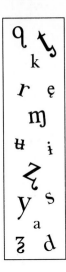

Author Index

Subject Index